KU-607-190

CONTENTS

Part Two - The Human Contribution

The Restless Biosphere:

An Introduction to the Chemistry of Gaia

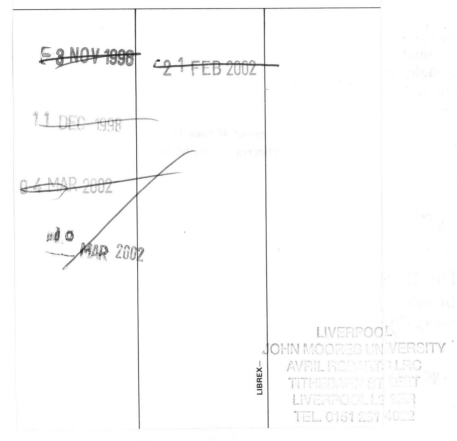

(204) 453 7429
fax (204) 453 6598

Wuerz Publishing Ltd
Winnipeg, Canada

The Restless Biosphere:
An Introduction to the Chemistry of Gaia
Eaton, Donald R

ISBN 0-920063-44-6

Printed in the United States of America

Part Three - Far From Equilibrium

Preface

This book provides the basis for a one semester course in chemistry. It is specifically intended for the liberal arts student. It is based on the premise that such students require a text specifically oriented to their needs, rather than a modified version of the type of book written for science students. The course for which it was written is open to students in all Faculties at McMaster University except Science and Engineering. It has a prerequisite of one high school chemistry course, rather than the two required of students in the Faculty of Science. Some familiarity with the language and elementary concepts of chemistry is all that is really required.

The author has taught chemistry at all university levels, and is aware of at least some of the problems inherent in designing a course of this nature. A major stumbling block is the wide range of interests, abilities and levels of motivation found in a group of students drawn from different years and diverse disciplines. The standard solution to this problem is to aim the course at the middle 70% of the class, which leaves the bottom 15% stranded and the top 15% bored. In this course an attempt has been made to include material at three different levels and to evaluate each level independently. The students are given a choice of level with the foreknowledge that if they choose the lowest level of effort their maximum grade will be C, for the middle choice it will be B, and for the top level A. This approach to evaluation means that it is no longer necessary to reach all the students all the time.

The course objective is to concentrate on those areas of chemistry most relevant to the education of a well informed person who is not a scientist. In the author's opinion this is the chemistry of the biosphere, and the modifications of this chemistry induced by human activities. This theme is developed systematically in the book's ten chapters. It is intended that the material in these ten chapters be covered in approximately thirty lectures. In general, a description of the chemical components of the biosphere, both inanimate and living, the various cycles which contribute to the dynamics of the interactions between the different parts, the products of the chemical industry, and environmental effects such as acid rain, provide the material required to successfully complete the course at the lowest level. This material is used as a basis to develop the fundamental ideas of modern chemistry. An understanding of these ideas represents the second level of the course. Chapter 8 includes material on non-equilibrium thermodynamics not usually contained in an elementary text, but essential to the understanding of the chemistry of complex living systems.

In addition to the ten chapters, the book includes a prologue, five interludes and an epilogue. The material in these sections is of more general interest; it is intended to constitute a link between the chemical content of the course and a range of other disciplines. The topics are only loosely connected to the adjacent chapters and provide material for four or five lectures or tutorials. The choice of these topics is obviously quite personal, and a different instructor could easily replace them by a completely different set of lectures, representing one's own inclinations in this area. This part of the course is intended to stimulate the interests of the A level students and to suggest topics for an essay assignment.

Mathematics, or the lack of it, is a recurrent problem in teaching lower-level science classes. In the present case this problem has been avoided by using no mathematics beyond simple arithmetic. (A small exception has been made in using logarithms to discuss pH and acid rain). In cases where mathematical equations would normally be used, they can be replaced by computer simulations projected directly from a microcomputer, or saved on videotape. Gas laws, chemical equilibria, activation energies, chaos and oscillating chemical reactions lend themselves to readily understood visual simulations, without introducing detailed mathematical calculations. The author subscribes to the heretical view that the initial approach to chemistry should be qualitative and non-mathematical. Chemistry is also an experimental science and most lectures can be enlivened by suitable demonstrations. Suggestions are included at the end of each chapter.

It is only the availability of microcomputers which has made practical the approach adopted. In our own case at McMaster University, hardware donated by IBM Canada Ltd as part of a Cooperative Project with McMaster U has provided much of the necessary infrastructure. The author wishes to express his thanks to IBM Canada Ltd, for this support and to the McMaster Centre for Instructional Development for a grant to help with the development of the testing data base.

Chemistry as a Liberal Arts Subject

Introduction

An introduction to a book should provide a perspective. How does the subject matter fit into the discipline involved? How does the subject matter relate to that of other courses taken by the student? In the present case these are broad questions. Why should a student in Humanities or Social Science take a course in science? If she should, why a course in chemistry? If in chemistry, why should it be based on the biosphere? (What is the biosphere anyway?)

The North American academic scene was recently surveyed by Allan Bloom in his book *The Closing of the American Mind*. The prognosis was pessimistic. The old concept of a liberal education is dead and the universities have been reduced to training schools for the professions. Each of the academic disciplines was reviewed, and many found wanting. The sciences fared better than most.

"Natural science is doing just fine. Living alone, but happily, running along like a well wound clock, successful and useful as ever". (Bloom, p 356)

To someone observing science from the inside, things perhaps do not appear to be running quite as smoothly as is suggested by this description. The most disturbing phrase though, is "living alone". Science has made a major contribution to intellectual development in the twentieth century, but does not seem to have succeeded in becoming part of the mainstream of intellectual life. It is reputed to be difficult to approach, riddled with mathematics, and generally inaccessible to all but the true devotee. The days when natural philosophy was part of general education are said to be past and gone. Bloom indeed concludes that a genuine liberal education can only be attained by a return to the study of the classic "great books".

All this may perhaps be true, but we should not surrender too easily; the excitement of science need not be confined to high profile research at the frontiers of knowledge. There has been a spate of well-written popular books on science published in the last five years, in which the problems of presenting complex material to the general reader in a comprehensible manner have been faced and conquered. The science departments have perhaps been a little slow in extending this progress to undergraduate teaching. There are indeed college courses offered such as "Physics for Poets" but they are few in number, and science is still not seen as an essential part of general education. The usual criticism is that the offerings to non-science students are either too watered down or too theoretical, with no relationship to everyday life, or are confused with technology (how does a personal computer work?) It has to be acknowledged that many chemistry faculty members see a freshman course as merely the first small step in an eight or ten year campaign leading to a PhD. It doesn't have to be so.

Defining a "liberal education" is difficult. There are three broad requirements for any course which aspires to be included in such a curriculum:

a) There should be relevance and applicability to modern life and culture.
b) It should have generality and accessibility.
c) It should have intellectual challenge.

Science can certainly provide the intellectual challenge. Some parts of science are frankly esoteric and of very limited general interest; others are inaccessible to all but a few, with an extensive prerequisite background in mathematics or some other discipline; still others can be made comprehensible and are intellectually challenging, but really do not have much relevance to any of the major problems of life. The same of course is true of some areas of philosophy and other non-science subjects. Having eliminated this much science, what is left? Certainly a great deal of "mainline" physics, chemistry, and biology; these are the core subjects which seek answers to questions first asked by the Greek philosophers. Physics has a reputation, not entirely unwarranted, for conceptual difficulty; modern biology is very complex. The subject is still at a stage where new discoveries tend to make matters more complicated, rather than simpler. This is not to say that either physics or biology is unsuitable for a liberal arts course. They just offer a little more challenge to the instructor. Chemistry is not a difficult subject if the material is chosen judiciously, and provides much material which is suitable for a liberal arts course.

The Place of Chemistry in the Hierarchy of Science

Science can be divided and subdivided into a myriad of disciplines and sub-disciplines. Some are clearly more closely related than others. In some cases it is difficult to determine where one subdiscipline ends and another begins. In other cases two different parts of science may seem to be completely independent. There is though, a commonly used ordering - mathematics, theoretical physics, experimental physics, chemistry, biochemistry, biology, physiology, psychology - proceeding from mathematical to descriptive, or from "hard" to "soft". In general the "higher" level science is "explained" in terms of the "lower" level science. Thus chemistry is explained in terms of the ideas about atomic structure developed by physicists, and the observations of biochemistry and biology are interpreted using chemical concepts. This process is known as reductionism. Quarks are the most basic entities and are combined to give protons and neutrons; these particles, plus electrons, combine to give atoms; atoms combine to make molecules of great complexity such as the nucleic acids. We can proceed from there to chromosomes, to living cells, to livers and hearts, to complete animals and finally, some would have us believe, to the mind itself. In principle, according to this philosophy, the whole of science could be logically taught by starting with the appropriate mathematics and working through to psychology by way of chemistry. Aside from the impracticability of such a project, there is also a suspicion that there may be some properties of a complex system which cannot be deduced from the sum of its simple parts. This attitude, which emphasizes the necessity of looking at a system in its entirety, is known as holism and is the other side of the coin to reductionism. It may well be that quarks are entirely an invention of the human mind, in which case using quarks to explain the mind involves a very circular argument. The holistic approach has become more fashionable in recent years with the realization that some things, such as weather systems and probably brains, cannot be completely analyzed and unambiguously predicted from the properties of their components.

If we are not to start at the beginning with quarks, where should we start? We do not need to know about quarks to understand chemistry. It is sufficient to take protons, neutrons and electrons as the "fundamental " particles. Heinz Pagels in his recent book *The Dreams of Reason* has stated this in the form that physics and chemistry are "causally decoupled". He states that "causal decoupling between the levels of the world implies that to understand the material basis of certain rules I must go to the next level down; but the rules can be applied with confidence without any reference to the more basic level". It is this feature of science which leads to the classification into the hierarchy of sciences listed above. In general each science is causally decoupled from the next one below it and from the one above it, in the hard-to-soft sequence of sciences. Thus Mendel developed genetics without understanding how genes are constructed from DNA molecules, and we can discuss psychological concepts without understanding the details of the chemistry involved in firing a neuron in the brain. We can therefore start wherever we like in the scheme; chemistry is as good a starting point as any, and in fact better than most. All science, in the final analysis, is based on observation. Some observations are made rather directly as, for example, the observation that a balloon full of hydrogen and oxygen produces a loud noise when ignited with a candle. Others, such as the "observation" of a very short-lived strange particle in high energy physics, depend on inference from very indirect experiments. A balloon of hydrogen and a candle are on the human scale of size and energy and the result of the experiment can be appreciated directly; a strange particle is much smaller and more energetic than anything that we can experience and its detection is not something that impinges on our primary senses. Chemistry is constructed on a human scale and is therefore a good starting point for working downwards to the mysteries of physics or upwards to the complexities of biology.

Why the Biosphere?

Chemistry is a large subject and some parts are closer to the human experience than others. Some are more difficult to understand than others and some, if we take our measure of importance as "influence on our daily lives", more important than others. It would be desirable to keep an introductory course in chemistry for non-scientists as simple as possible, as non-mathematical as possible, and as relevant as possible to the "real" problems of life. Fortunately most of chemistry can be causally decoupled from mathematics, and the advent of microcomputers, (particularly computer graphics) has given us a tool for illustrating the consequences of mathematical laws without becoming too involved in the causes behind them. We desire, according to the first criterion for a liberal arts course suggested above, relevance and applicability to modern life and culture. This requirement leads almost inevitably to the chemistry of the biosphere, since this is where we live and this is where chemistry and life interact most strongly.

This book is divided into three parts: the first, entitled Simple Molecules, will introduce the handful of molecules, oxygen, water, salt and a few others, which constitute the major part of our surroundings, and will use them to illustrate the basic concepts of chemistry. Man has added a great many molecules not found in Nature:

the second part of the book, Man's Contributions, will examine both the positive and negative aspects of our chemical "improvements" on what Nature has to offer. Balancing the books to determine whether a chemical product contributes a net gain or a net loss to human welfare involves much more than chemistry: economics, politics, sociology, and medicine are some of the major determining factors. However, it is usually not possible for a rational person to reach a sensible conclusion on a contentious issue involving chemicals, unless there is some basic understanding of the underlying chemistry. Major decisions on these issues are inevitably, and rightfully, made by non-scientists, but a strong case can be made that all educated people should have sufficient chemical background to participate meaningfully in this decision-making. The third part of the book, entitled Far from Equilibrium, asks the question: What makes the chemistry of life different from reactions taking place in a test tube? (A more difficult area, but well worth the effort required to understand some of the newer ideas which represent the most active part of chemical research at the present time.) The unifying theme for these three parts is provided by the model of the biosphere developed by J. E. Lovelock and named in honor of the Greek goddess, Gaia. This is where we will start in Chapter 1 and it is also where we will finish in Chapter 10. At the beginning of the book the components of Gaia will be taken apart in a reductionist manner. At the end they will hopefully be successfully reassembled, to give a more holistic appreciation of the chemistry of Man and of his environment.

Finally, in addition to this prologue and an epilogue, a number of "Interludes" have been inserted at appropriate places in the book. Chemistry may be causally decoupled from other disciplines, but this does not mean that it is isolated from other intellectual activities. It has its obvious interfaces with its neighbors such as physics and biology. It relates to the history and philosophy of science as a whole. It also contributes to medicine, to paleontology and to geology. As befits a discipline which has given rise to a major industry, it is involved in economics and its bedfellow politics. Echoes of chemistry can even be found in literature. The interfaces with some of these diverse subjects will be explored in these diversions from the chemical content of Chapters 1-10. These interjections provide an opportunity to stand back a little distance from the details of the topic under development and try to see how chemistry fits into the broader spectrum of academic disciplines.

Further Reading

Allan Bloom, *The Closing of the American Mind*, Simon and Schuster (1987). Touchstone (Paperback) (1988). A survey of the North American intellectual scene.

Heinz Pagels, *The Dreams of Reason*, Simon and Schuster (1988). Discusses, at a readable level, the philosophy of the modern "sciences of complexity" and particularly the impact of computers.

Douglas R. Hofstadter, *Godel, Escher, Bach*, Vintage Books (1980). A formidable, but fascinating, book discussing, among many other topics, reductionism and holism in modern science.

Part I: Simple Molecules

CHAPTER 1

The Nature and Composition of the Biosphere

Introduction

It has become fashionable to make the point that the advent of space travel, which has allowed us to view our home planet in its entirety, has provided a new perspective on humanity's place in the universe. It is certainly true that the view of earth from outer space is striking and of great beauty. The colors of the sea and clouds are accentuated by the contrast with the darkness of the surrounding space. What we see, of course, is only the surface of the earth, but this is the unique part of the planet - the **biosphere**, which contains and supports life. Viewed from the surface, the tendency is to emphasize the individual components, the air and the sea and the land, the mountains and the streams, the flora and the fauna. Viewed from outside, we appreciate it as a whole. The whole may well have characteristics not readily apparent in the parts. The view from space emphasizes the unity of our environment.

■ What is the biosphere?

The term biosphere, although its use can be traced back to the nineteenth century, has only achieved recent popularity. It has been simply defined by J. E. Lovelock in his recent book *The Ages of Gaia*, as "that part of the earth where living things normally exist". In common usage this definition is extended to include living things themselves. This usage will be followed in the present book, since a major theme is the linkage between the living and the inanimate parts of nature. We shall also include the upper reaches of the atmosphere, even though this is a place inimical to life, since what happens there has a significant influence on life at the surface. Similarly the oil and minerals, recovered by man from depths beyond the normal range of life, also play their part in the overall economy of the biosphere. Even with these extensions the biosphere is small even by terrestrial standards. It is a layer at most thirty or forty kilometers thick, on a globe some thirty thousand kilometers in circumference; a very thin skin on a rather large onion. This then is the arena. It provides the stage for impressive displays of nature's power, such as volcanos and hurricanes, and for the even more impressive dramas played out by the multitudinous living entities which have evolved as the biosphere has developed. The basic rules of performance in this arena are to a large extent the rules of chemistry. The functioning of the rules, and Life's existence under the rules, is the major theme of this book.

The Scales of Chemistry

Having settled on the biosphere as our subject for chemical study, we need to answer a few preliminary questions about it and the chemistry which occurs within it. How big is it compared to other objects? What is its temperature and how much energy is involved in the changes we will discuss? What is the time scale involved in these chemical changes? What is the chemical constitution of the biosphere? This is also a convenient place to introduce the scientific notation used for dealing with very large and very small numbers.

■ *Powers of ten and scientific notation...*

Physical science is based on measurement, and accuracy is usually considered a virtue in making measurements; there are times though, when excessive accuracy confuses rather than enlightens. It is often more important to have an idea of the general scale of things than to know the exact dimensions. J. B. S. Haldane wrote an illuminating essay, *On Being the Right Size*, in which he pointed out that the life styles of different animals were largely determined by their sizes. For example, as far as a human is concerned, it doesn't really matter whether we are 1.8 or 2.0m tall, but it does matter that we are not 0.2 or 20m tall. The numbers 0.2, 2.0 and 20 differ by powers of ten (or orders of magnitude). A book by Philip and Phylis Morrison, entitled *Powers of Ten*, demonstrates the concept of an order of magnitude in a very dramatic fashion using illustrations of views covering progressively different areas. A square of 1m size accommodates most of a man's body. Stepping back to view a square of 10 m x 10m gives a picture of a beach with several human figures. A 1000m, or 1km, square includes a significant part of a city. A 1000km view includes a substantial part of a continent and a 10,000km square, most of the earth. Figure 1.1 summarizes the scale of some of the objects found in the universe.

This figure also serves as a reminder of the scientific notation for dealing with very large and very small numbers. 10^{10} is ten multiplied by itself ten times, ten thousand million, a very large number. It is much more convenient to write it in this manner than as 10,000,000,000. The superscripted number simply tells us how many zeros follow the 1. 10^{-10} is 1 divided by 10^{10} and is a very small number. We shall have cause to use this system regularly throughout this book. 10^{0}m, or 1m, is the size of man. (Perhaps not quite the size, but certainly the general scale. He may be a little taller and —hopefully— not quite so wide, but the order of magnitude is correct.)

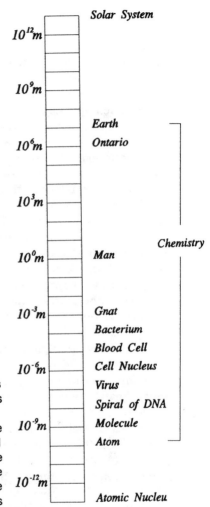

Fig. 1.1: The Size of Things. We measure size in meters (m), approximately 40 inches. The size of the universe is approximately 10^{26}m and the size of an atomic nucleus 10^{-13}m. Quarks, leptons and other subatomic particles are even smaller. Chemistry is only concerned with a restricted set of objects, varying from an atom at 10^{-10}m to the size of the biosphere at 10^7m. Some of the steps in this range are shown in the figure - note that each step increases the size by a factor of 10. The size of a human being, 10^0m is almost in the middle of this range.

10^{25} m is the scale of the universe, which is some ten thousand times bigger than the scale of a galaxy at 10^{21}m, and very much bigger than the scale of the solar system at 10^{13} m. 10^{-16}m is the scale of quarks, the smallest entity about which modern physics has any reasonably certain knowledge. Theoreticians can speculate about happenings on scales down to 10^{-32}m, but speculation is at present all it is. Chemists are content with a much narrower span. 10^{-10}m (0.0000000001m) is the size of an atom, the currency common to all chemical reactions, and as small as we want to go. 10^7m is the size of the earth and its accompanying biosphere, and as large as we need to go. A person can visualize the size of the earth, since she can readily visit most places on its surface, but the sizes of stars and galaxies cannot fully be comprehended. Anything that we can see directly, or with the help of a microscope, is also within the realm of comprehensibility. With the latest advances in microscopy this pushes us down to about 10^{-8}m, the size of a large protein molecule. There is still a gap of two or three orders of magnitude down to the size of a small atom but imagination, and a modest amount of indirect experimentation, can fill this gap reasonably well. (Quarks are beyond the imagination of the average person.) Chemistry is therefore basically a science which is built on a human scale. The most important parts of the subject can be seen and demonstrated in the lecture room. Water is wet, steel is hard, hydrogen and oxygen explode when ignited - all concepts which can be directly demonstrated with simple apparatus.

■ *The absolute scale of temperature starts at -273°C ...*

Scales can be constructed for variables other than distance: we will look at two other variables, energy and time, as they relate to the biosphere. There are various scales for measuring energy but that of temperature is perhaps the closest to direct experience. Increasing temperature corresponds to increasing energy: if energy is removed from a body it becomes colder. A visit to Northern Canada in mid-winter provides a lower limit to the temperatures normally experienced. A visit to a steel mill provides a vivid impression of the heat given off by molten steel. Scientists prefer to measure temperature on the so-called absolute scale. One degree on this scale is just the same as one degree on the more common celsius scale, which is defined by the conditions that 0° C is the freezing point of water and 100 °C the boiling point of water. On the absolute scale the units of temperature are Kelvins (K) and are the same as °C, but 0K = -273 °C. To convert from °C to K we simply add 273. On this scale the difference in temperature between Arctic air and molten steel is approximately one order of magnitude; from 200K (-73°C, a little chilly even for Canada) to 2000K for molten steel. This range covers chemistry very nicely; few molecules are stable above 2000K and few chemical reactions occur at any significant rate below 200K. Our body temperature is conveniently at the midpoint of the range. The physicists need a much wider scale; nuclear fusion involves temperatures of 10^8K and cosmology and the Big Bang demand even higher energies. There are also very interesting effects, involving superconductivity and other cooperative phenomena, occurring at 10^{-2}K which approaches the lowest practically attainable temperature. Figure 1.2 presents a scale of energies and illustrates the narrow range of chemical importance. Chemistry again is a subject corresponding closely to the human scale. This should not be surprising since, after all, biological systems rely on chemical reactions to keep the organism running.

Time is a tricky concept. The human brain can be surprisingly precise in judging whether two events are simultaneous, showing an appreciation of very short time intervals. A nerve impulse take around 10ms (10 milliseconds or 10^{-2}s), to reach the brain from a distant part of the body. 1ms, or 10^{-3}s, is a time interval which can be directly appreciated and detected by the brain. A human lifetime is of the order 10^8s and the age of the universe 10^{20}s. The lifetimes of subatomic particles are often in the nanosecond (10^{-9}s) or picosecond (10^{-12}s) ranges. The time scale of interest to chemists is again very similar to that within our direct experience. A reaction which occurs within 1ms is fast.

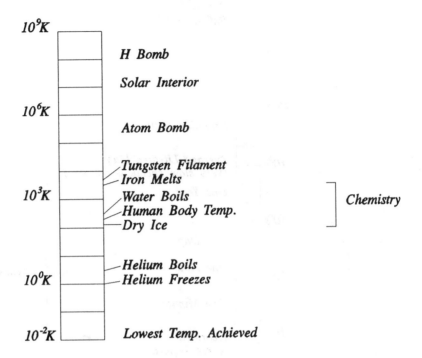

Fig. 1.2: Temperature and Energy. We measure temperature in degrees Kelvin (K). Temperature is a meaasure of energy. Temperatures reach 10^9K in a Hydrogen bomb explosion, and much more in the centers of large stars and in the "Big Bang" at the formation of the universe. Low temperature physicists have achieved temperatures as low as $10^{-2}K$. In chemistry we are only concerned with a narrow range of temperatures from 10^2K to 10^3K.

Some reactions involving very weak bonds are faster, down to microseconds (10^{-6}s), but on this short timescale the distinction between chemical and physical events becomes blurred. Some chemistry occurs on a geological timescale, but again it is usually physical processes such as diffusion which determine the rate of reaction. Different timescales are illustrated in Figure 1.3 and the coincidence of chemical and human times is apparent. Again this coincidence is not surprising; nerve impulses are propagated by rapid chemical reactions and aging is the slow, but inevitable, consequence of chemical changes in the body. Once again though, the chemical scale is approximately the human scale.

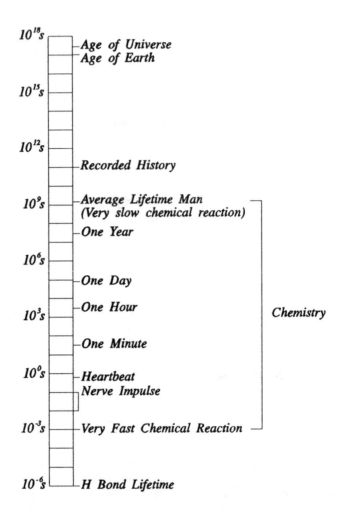

Fig. 1.3: Time Scales. The unit of time is the second (s), a tick on your watch. The age of the universe approaches 10^{18}s and the lifetimes of subatomic particles are often less than 10^{-12}s. A fast chemical reaction is over in 10^{-3}s and a human lifetime is approximately 10^9s. These limits represent the time range of chemistry, and a day is approximately halfway between them.

The Raw Materials

The building blocks of the biosphere are the **chemical elements which combine to give a much larger number of chemical compounds**. All substances are constructed from these basic building blocks. Table 1.1 gives the relative abundances in the earth's crust of the twenty most common elements.

Table 1.1: The Top Twenty Elements

ELEMENT	ATOMIC NUMBER	ABUNDANCE %	OCCURRENCE
1. Oxygen	8	49.4	Rocks, water, air.
2. Silicon	14	25.8	Granite, sand.
3. Aluminum	13	7.5	Rocks, clay.
4. Iron	26	4.7	Oxides, granite.
5. Calcium	20	3.4	Chalk, limestone.
6. Sodium	11	2.6	Salt, rocks.
7. Potassium	19	2.4	Potash, rocks.
8. Magnesium	12	1.9	Granite.
9. Hydrogen	1	0.9	Water.
10. Titanium	22	0.6	
11. Chlorine	17	0.2	Salt.
12. Phosphorus	15	0.12	
13. Manganese	25	0.10	
14. Carbon	6	0.08	Limestone,organic.
15. Sulfur	16	0.06	Volcanoes.
16. Barium	56	0.05	
17. Chromium	24	0.03	
18. Nitrogen	7	0.03	Atmosphere.
19. Rubidium	37	0.03	
20. Strontium	38	0.03	

■ *The most common elements...*
■ *Elements, compounds and substances...*

These data reflect the composition of the atmosphere, the hydrosphere (the sea) and the lithosphere (the uppermost layer of the land). The earth's core is mainly iron and the mantle, which surrounds the core, contains mostly iron, calcium, magnesium, silicon and oxygen. The core and the mantle are not part of the biosphere. The abundances in Table 1.1 are dominated by the composition of the lithosphere and do not reflect the importance of the elements in the biosphere. However, all of the important elements in the biosphere are included in the top twenty. Oxygen is the most abundant element in Table 1.1; most of it is combined with the next three elements, silicon, aluminum and iron in the earth's crust. If the measurement were based on atom percent rather than mass percent, hydrogen would be the third most abundant element at 15.4%. Most of this is combined with oxygen in water. The top ten elements provide 99.2% of the total mass. Most of the biologically important elements, carbon, phosphorus, nitrogen, and sulfur, are in the second group of ten and are therefore of intermediate scarcity. Some of the rare elements, often called trace elements, are also essential to life. The various elements can combine together to give **compounds**; there are hundreds of thousands of compounds known to chemists and each compound corresponds to a different substance. A large number of substances occur naturally in the earth's crust. Fortunately only a handful of simple substances are important components of the non-living part of the biosphere. It is the chemistry of these substances, and their distribution in the different parts of the biosphere, which will be emphasized in the first part of this book. We start with an overview of the chemical composition of the different parts of the biosphere.

The Air, the Sea and the Land

■ *Photochemical reactions are brought about by light...*

The earth's atmosphere is conventionally divided into several regions. The lowest 10-15km comprise the **troposphere**. The temperature in the troposphere falls with increasing altitude at a rate of about 1°C per 100m. The top of the troposphere, the height of a jet at cruising altitude, is a chilly -50°C. The summit of Mt. Everest is approaching this altitude and is a notably hostile environment. The **stratosphere** lies above the troposphere and is a region in which the temperature rises with altitude, reaching a maximum of +80°C. This rise in temperature is caused by the heat evolved from photochemical reactions brought about by sunlight. The **photochemistry** (chemistry brought about by light) which occurs in the stratosphere has a significant effect on conditions at the surface, and will be the subject of subsequent discussion. Above the stratosphere, at heights greater than 50km, the density of the gases is too low to support active photochemistry, as there just aren't enough molecules around to react, and the temperature again falls. This region contains the **ionosphere**, an electrically charged layer responsible for the Northern Lights and the reflection of radio waves. About 75% of the mass of the atmosphere is in the troposphere and almost all the rest in the stratosphere. Table 1.2 lists the components of the atmosphere.

Table 1.2: The Composition of the Atmosphere

Constituent	Formula	Concentration(ppm)
Nitrogen	N_2	780,840.00
Oxygen	O_2	209,460.00
Water vapor	H_2O	10,000 (very variable)
Argon	Ar	9,340.00
Carbon dioxide	CO_2	322.00
Neon	Ne	18.18
Helium	He	5.22
Methane	CH_4	1.50
Krypton	Kr	1.11
Hydrogen	H_2	0.50
Nitrous oxide	N_2O	0.27
Carbon monoxide	CO	0.19
Xenon	Xe	0.09
Ozone	O_3	0.02
Ammonia	NH_3	0.004

A more convenient concentration for low concentrations: 1% = 10,000ppm

■ *Carbon dioxide - low abundance, high importance...*

Two gases, oxygen and nitrogen, make up 99% of the total in dry air. The third most abundant gas, water vapor, is so variable in its concentration that it would be deceptive to rank it. On a warm day with a humidity approaching 100%, it will comprise some 3% of the air. On a cold day with low humidity the percentage will be very small. Argon, the next most abundant gas, is chemically inert and plays no significant role in the biosphere. There is then a large drop in abundance to carbon dioxide at 0.0314% or 314 parts per million. The abundance of carbon dioxide may be low, but its importance is high. It supports plant life by photosynthesis, and its role as a "greenhouse" gas means that it plays an important part in controlling the earth's temperature. Of the remaining gases on the list, methane and nitrous oxide are photochemically important and will be encountered later. Ozone (an allotrope, or form, of oxygen) does not occur naturally in the troposphere. It is exceedingly poisonous and its production in photochemical smog is highly undesirable. It does occur naturally in the stratosphere and serves an important role in screening out unwanted ultra-violet radiation.

■ *Cations positive, Anions negative...*

The total mass of the oceans is 250 times that of the atmosphere. The major constituent is water, but there are also substantial amounts of dissolved salts. Typically the salt concentration is around 3.4%. A very characteristic and important property of water is that dissolved salts are dissociated into positive and negative particles known as ions. Thus common salt, sodium chloride (NaCl), is present as sodium (Na^+) and chloride (Cl^-) ions. The concentrations of the individual ions rather than those of the salts should therefore be stated, since salts formed by all possible combinations of the positive and negative ions are equally valid descriptions of the composition. The particular salt which crystallizes out from the mixture is the one which happens to be least soluble under the conditions of the experiment. The concentrations of the most abundant ions in sea water are given in Table 1.3.

Table 1.3: The Composition of Sea Water

Ion	Formula	Concentration(ppm).
Chloride	Cl^-	18,980
Sodium	Na^+	10,561
Sulfate	SO_4^{2-}	2,649
Magnesium	Mg^{2+}	1,272
Calcium	Ca^{2+}	400
Potassium	K^+	380
Bicarbonate	HCO_3^-	142
Bromide	Br^-	65

The major **cations** (positive) are sodium and magnesium and the most abundant **anions** (negative), chloride and sulfate. (Within each pair, the former ion is about ten times as abundant as the latter.)

■ *Soil and humic material...*

Chemical reactions in the solid state proceed much more slowly than those in solution or in the gas phase. The land is therefore a site of stability, rather than of change. **Sand**, **soil** and **rock** are its major constituents. Sand is silicon dioxide, a relatively unreactive substance although it is a raw material for the production of glass. Soil is a mixture of inorganic material, such as sand or clay (an aluminum silicate) and organic material resulting from the decay of plants. The latter material is called humic material or humic acid. Surprisingly, its true chemical composition is still far from established, but its value in promoting the growth of new plants is very clear. (Trying to grow vegetables in straight sand or clay is a sure route to frustration.) Soil represents a path for recycling valuable organic material from one generation of plant life to the next. The difficulty in chemical characterization arises because it is a complex mixture of **polymeric** (large molecules constructed from many small molecules) materials which varies from sample to sample, and tends to decompose under the conditions used for most forms of analysis. Rocks come in several chemical forms: some, such as limestone, which is calcium carbonate, were formed from the shells of marine organisms: a second type are the granites which are essentially silicates of magnesium and calcium with various admixtures of other metal ions. Metal ores, such as iron oxides or lead sulfides, exist as relatively small fractions of the earth's crust, but have considerable economic importance.

These are the basic building blocks of the biosphere. However, the biosphere is not a static entity. There is a continuous flux of material passing between the atmosphere and the sea, the land and the sea, the atmosphere and the land, and between living and inanimate matter. The sun provides energy to drive these changes, and this energy is transformed into a multitude of forms. Evolution changes the nature of living things and modifies their interactions with the rest of the biosphere. More recently the industrial and agricultural activities of man have become large enough to become significant on a planet-wide scale. The biosphere is indeed restless and its dynamic characteristics are its most important property. We will now consider how some of the interactions between the substances described above make life possible.

Relationships between Components of the Biosphere

Oxygen and Nitrogen

The two major components of the atmosphere, nitrogen and oxygen, differ considerably in their chemical reactivity. Nitrogen is generally inert and reacts, if at all, only with great difficulty. Oxygen, at reasonably high temperatures, is one of the most reactive substances known and combines readily with almost everything. If there were no oxygen, life as we know it certainly would not exist, since it is essential for respiration and the maintenance of the body's metabolism. If the atmosphere were 100% oxygen we would also be in trouble. (Below 12% oxygen it would not be possible to light a fire; above 25%, a forest fire once started would burn until all possible fuel was exhausted, no matter how damp the undergrowth.) In these circumstances all organic matter would be inherently unstable.

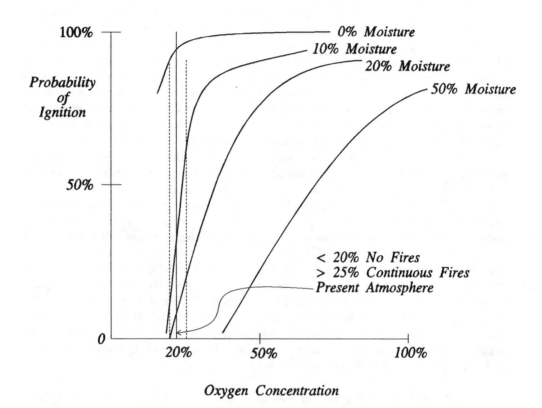

Fig. 1.4: Forest Fires and the Concentration of Oxygen. Oxygen is required for fires to burn, and how easily they burn also depends on the moisture content of the air. This diagram shows how the probability of a forest fire depends on the oxygen and moisture contents of the air. Below 20% oxygen fires would not burn. Above 25%, except in very moist conditions, they would burn continuously.

■ *21% oxygen is just right for life...*

The present level of 21% oxygen makes life possible for oxygen-breathing animals without too much danger from uncontrolled combustion. The narrow range of tolerable oxygen levels is illustrated in Figure 1.4.

Water and Salt

■ *The importance of biological membranes...*

As noted above, the sea contains some 3.4% salt. Human blood is also salty, but less so than the sea, with a salt concentration of 0.8%. It has been suggested that this demonstrates an oceanic origin for life, and that the fact that the ocean is now more salty results from the gradual accumulation of salts in the sea by leaching from the land. However, since the rate of addition of salts to the sea would lead, over the known time span of evolution, to a much higher concentration than is presently observed, there must be some mechanism for removing salt from the ocean. The probable means of removal involves isolation of salt lagoons associated with the formation of reefs by marine organisms, evaporation to give solid salts, and burial of the resulting salt beds by geologic processes. Such underground deposits are now mined to obtain brine. Ions are also directly removed from sea water by small marine life forms, which construct sea shells from calcium carbonate or silica.

All life forms depend on the existence of biological membranes to preserve the integrity of the cells. Such membranes are formed from a particular type of molecules, which are partly ionic, and interact with each other and with water so as to stick together and make a semipermeable barrier. (I.e., some substances, required by the organism, are allowed entry but others are excluded.) The glue fails if the concentration of ions is too high since the biomolecules and water then stick to the ions rather than to other biomolecules. The critical concentration of ions is around 6%. Above this, life does not flourish, as is shown by the Dead Sea in Palestine. If there was no mechanism for salt removal, the oceans would have died long ago. There is also a lower limit to acceptable salinity. The membranes need some permeability to ions to allow the cell to function properly. If there are no salts present the membrane is altogether too stable to allow the passage of stable substances. For many millions of years the sea has been maintained at a level of salinity compatible with the operation of biological membranes.

Liquid Water and Water Vapor

■ *Water is a unique substance...*
■ *Rain contains dissolved gases...*

Although most of earth's water is in the sea, significant quantities are found in the atmosphere as water vapor, and on land as lakes and streams. Exchange of water between these reservoirs is crucial to the maintenance of the biosphere. It contributes to the temperature control of the planet, and it makes available a vital raw material needed by all living organisms. For chemical reasons which will be discussed later, water has a number of unique properties. Its melting point and boiling point are abnormally high and it requires a large amount of energy to raise its temperature, or to be changed from a solid to a liquid, or from a liquid to a gas. Sunlight provides energy to the sea and vaporizes water. The energy used in this process does not raise the temperature of the sea, which therefore remains cooler than might have been expected, and cools the land in summer. Conversely, the condensation of water vapor gives out heat and thus provides a reservoir of heat to warm the land in winter. The annual fluctuations of temperature are in this way minimized. Heating of air close to the surface of the earth reduces its density and causes it to rise. Moist hot air rises, but the temperature of the troposphere decreases with height, leading to the condensation of water vapor and the formation of clouds. Clouds do not rise into the stratosphere because there the temperature increases with height and any water which reaches this region would re-evaporate. Clouds reflect a portion of the incident sunlight and contribute to the cooling of the earth. A combination of the pressure differences (caused by non-uniform heating of the surface) and the earth's rotation, gives rise to winds which transport the water vapor to other sites. The water can be returned to earth as rain or snow. This water cycle is illustrated in Figure 1.5.

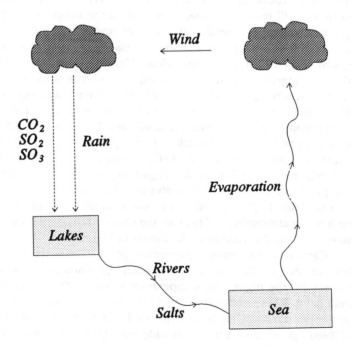

Fig. 1.5: The Water Cycle. Water circulates continuously between the land, the sea and the atmosphere, and transports dissolved solids and gases during this cycle.

Evaporation from the sea, followed by condensation of the water vapor as rain, results in the removal of salt from water and renders it fit for biological usage. After such use it is returned to the air or the land by respiration or excretion. Although salt is removed, other substances remain dissolved in rain water. Most important is carbon dioxide which makes the water slightly acid. This has an important influence on the weathering of rocks. It has been suggested that the very small amounts of ammonia in the atmosphere suffice to restrict the acidity of rainwater. Man-made acid rain poses a threat to this control system. The water is returned to the sea via the freshwater system of lakes and rivers; in the process it transports soluble salts to the sea.

Carbon Dioxide and Metal Carbonates

■ *The weathering of rocks...*

Most of the earth's carbon is stored as **carbonates** of calcium and magnesium ($CaCO_3$ and $MgCO_3$), such as limestone and dolomite, in the earth's crust; only a small fraction is contained in living structures. Carbon is made available to living things in the form of atmospheric carbon dioxide (CO_2). Geological processes cycle carbon between the rocks (carbonates) and the atmosphere (carbon dioxide); acid groundwater will react with limestone and similar rocks to give more soluble carbon compounds. There is a similar, but slower, reaction with silicate rocks. Carbonates and silicates, removed from the rocks by this weathering process, are transported to the sea by route of the rivers and lakes. Here they can become the raw material for the shells of marine organisms. During this process some of the carbon dioxide is liberated, and is returned to the atmosphere, making it available again to plants. Silica travels a similar route and is incorporated in the shells of diatoms. The calcium carbonate from shells becomes the chalk and limestone found in the earth's crust. There is a second geological method of returning the carbon to the atmosphere. In the course of time, carbonates and silicates from dead sea organisms are buried to a great depth, react together at the high temperatures encountered, and the carbon dioxide produced returns to the atmosphere via volcanic activity. A long-term balance is thus maintained - plants remove carbon from the atmosphere, geological processes return it to the atmosphere. This balance has been maintained for many millennia and is summarized in the carbon cycle shown in Figure 1.6.

Carbon dioxide in the atmosphere plays an important role in the temperature control of the earth. It is a so-called "greenhouse" gas and the higher its concentration, the higher the temperature of the earth. This topic will be discussed in detail later. These geological processes provide for long-term temperature control of the temperature. It has been suggested that society's activities in burning carbon based fuels, producing carbon dioxide, are interfering with nature's temperature control mechanisms.

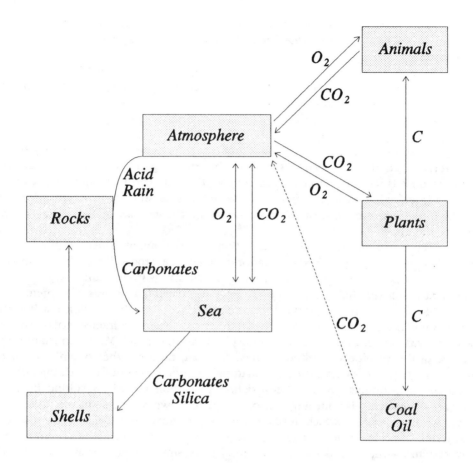

Fig. 1.6: The Carbon Cycle. Living things circulate carbon by photosynthesis and respiration. Geochemical processes contribute to the cycle by storing carbon as rocks (limestone) and as coal.

Carbon Dioxide and Oxygen

■ *Plants take in carbon dioxide and produce oxygen...*
■ *Animals take in oxygen and produce carbon dioxide...*

The carbon cycle is in part biologically driven. Plants remove carbon dioxide from the atmosphere by the process of photosynthesis. This process is driven by solar energy. It effectively uses the hydrogen from water to combine with the carbon dioxide, and returns the water's oxygen to the atmosphere. It also leads to the formation of organic compounds, most notably carbohydrates. These, in turn, serve as food for animals, which may in turn be eaten by other animals. Combustion of organic material provides the energy source for animals. Combustion requires oxygen which is taken from the atmosphere. The products of combustion are carbon dioxide and water, which are returned to the environment. Thus a steady-state is maintained.

Removal of tropical forests reduces photosynthesis and interferes with this cycle; this provides another cause for concern that humans are affecting their environment in a negative way.

Since this process tends to maintain a constant carbon dioxide concentration in the atmosphere, it acts to regulate the temperature of the biosphere. More carbon dioxide leads to more plant growth, which removes carbon dioxide and adds oxygen to the atmosphere. The water cycle is the short-term regulating mechanism for the climate, and the geological processes discussed above the long-term mechanism. The biological carbon cycle contributes a medium-term component. The absolute amount of material circulated is much less than in the case of geological activities, but the response time is shorter. Over long periods of time the earth's temperature has not remained perfectly constant. There have been ice ages and warm periods. We will consider temperature control in more detail in the course of discussion of the greenhouse effect.

There are other minor contributions to the maintenance of the carbon dioxide/oxygen balance. If water vapor reaches the stratosphere the ultraviolet radiation it encounters there will decompose it to hydrogen and oxygen. The hydrogen, being very light, escapes to outer space, leaving a surplus of oxygen. This process is probably not important at present, since very little water reaches the stratosphere, but may have played a part in times past when the intensity of ultraviolet radiation was greater in determining atmospheric composition. More important is the burying of the products of photosynthesis as coal, oil and other organic deposits. Since in the course of synthesizing this material, oxygen was added to the atmosphere, burial of the products prevents re-oxidation to carbon dioxide, resulting in a net addition of oxygen. By burning carbon-based fuels we are negating this effect. A corresponding process which leads to the net removal of oxygen occurs in the weathering of rocks. Iron changes to rust by reaction with oxygen, thus removing it from the atmosphere, and there are a number of similar reactions involved in the weathering of rocks.

Nitrogen, Sulfur and Iodine Cycles

■ *All elements needed by living organisms must be recycled...*

Any element used in living systems must be recycled. We have only a limited quantity of anything, and if substances were not recycled, the raw material would have been used up long ago. Fortunately elements and chemical substances are efficiently recycled. The soil and its humic material provide the most direct recycling process; dead vegetable material is largely decomposed by bacteria, which use carbohydrates and similar compounds as fuel for their metabolism. Carbon dioxide and water revert to the environment, and some nitrogen is returned to the atmosphere as nitrogen gas. In this form it cannot be used by living organisms. Fortunately other bacteria, found in the root nodules of certain plants, can react with nitrogen gas and restore it to a form useful to life. This process is now largely supplemented by the use of artificial fertilizers. In the absence of air, bacteria will convert carbon-containing material to methane (natural gas); this again is cycled through the atmosphere and photochemically oxidized to water and carbon dioxide. Much material remains in the soil to provide a source of essential compounds for the next generation of plants.

There is however a limit to this direct reclamation process. If the plant is to obtain a nutrient from the soil the nutrient must be soluble in water. If it is soluble, some will be lost to running water and eventually to the ocean. Mechanisms are needed to return this material to the land. The chemistry of some of these processes is now known: for example, sulfur reaches the sea as sulfate ions and certain algae and seaweeds can change sulfate ions to the volatile compound dimethyl sulfide. The process is analogous to the removal of mercury by algae as methylmercury compounds, which can be a serious source of pollution. Dimethyl sulfide escapes to the atmosphere, where it can react with oxygen and be returned to the earth as soluble sulfates. Iodine, another element important in trace amounts, has a similar cycle. Iodides are soluble and revert to the sea. The volatile methyl iodide, produced biologically, is returned to the atmosphere and eventually to the soil as iodide ions. Nitrogen and sulfur cycles are shown in Figure 1.7.

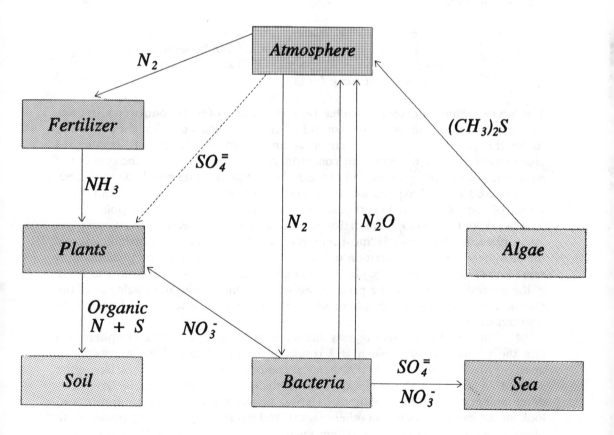

Fig. 1.7: Nitrogen and Sulfur Cycles. All the elements vital to life must be recycled. This diagram illustrates some of the routes taken by nitrogen and by sulfur.

Cooperative Chemistry

■ *The Gaia hypothesis...*

The above examples have illustrated some of the ways in which inanimate matter and living organisms combine to control and maintain the composition of the biosphere. It appears to be very much a cooperative project. The detailed mechanisms are, in each case, chemical. It could be coincidental that things just happen to fit together as well as they do. However this situation has prevailed over many millions of years, during which the chemical composition and temperature of the biosphere have remained favorable for the continued propagation of life. J.E.Lovelock noted these fortunate coincidences, and some ten years ago published a book called *Gaia*. Gaia is the Greek name for the goddess of the earth and of fertility and is a remarkably apt term for the theme of the book. In this book he put forward the "Gaia hypothesis" that

> "The earth's living matter, air, oceans and land
> surface form a complex system which can be seen as
> a single organism and which has the capacity to keep
> our planet a fit place for life."

This is a sweeping statement which has been the subject of some controversy. It gives a large role to living things in the control of matters which were thought previously to be the preserve of physical, chemical and geological forces. It emphasizes cooperation rather than Darwinian competition in nature. It extends the concept of what constitutes a living entity. All of these claims have been disputed. Nevertheless, it has proved a useful hypothesis. It has got people talking and thinking, and this is a sign of success for any hypothesis. It also provides both a starting point and a framework for the development of that part of chemistry most relevant to everyday life. "Most relevant", here, means 'most important to the operation and maintenance of the biosphere'. A full appreciation of Gaia involves a variety of subjects in addition to some knowledge of chemistry. In the Epilogue to this book we will return to some of the broader issues. For the present, we will be content with the catalogue of the chemical contents of the biosphere given above, and the brief list of interactions between them.

The Gaia hypothesis suggests that life is an integral part of the biosphere and that the whole complex system is a result of the presence of life. A reasonable question to ask is: What would the chemical composition of the earth look like in the absence of life? The above question was actually the starting point in Lovelock's development of the Gaia hypothesis. He was involved in designing experiments to look for the existence of life on other planets, and suggested that a comparison of the planetary atmospheres of Mars and Venus with that of the earth, would be informative. This comparison is made in Table 1.4.

Table 1.4: Planetary Atmospheres[*]

Planet	Pressure(Atmos)	Temperature(°C)	N_2	O_2	Ar	CO_2
Earth	1	13	78%	21%	1%	0.08%
Venus	90	477	1.9%	trace	0.1%	98%
Mars	0.0064	-53	2.7%	0.13%	2%	95%
Equilibrium on Earth	60	290	1.9%	trace	0.1%	98%

[*] Data from *Gaia* by J. E. Lovelock

The important difference is that on the other planets the atmosphere has reached **chemical equilibrium** with the material forming the rest of the planet. Calculations can be carried out to give the atmospheric composition on earth under this condition. The results of such calculations are also given in Table 1.4. There is no oxygen, very little nitrogen and a great deal of carbon dioxide, leading to conditions of high temperature and pressure very similar to those on Venus. Life, as we know it, would not be possible under such an atmosphere. There are in fact good arguments suggesting that any form of life would be impossible under such conditions. These arguments hinge on the nature of chemical equilibrium and the conditions under which chemical reactions will proceed. They will be pursued in subsequent chapters.

Further reading

J. E. Lovelock, *Gaia - A New Look at Life on Earth*, Oxford University Press (1979).

J. E. Lovelock, *The Ages of Gaia*, W. H. Norton (1988).

W. S. Broecker, *How to Build a Habitable Planet*, Eldigio Press (1985).

R. A. Berner and A. C. Lasaga, "Modelling the Geochemical Carbon Cycle", *Scientific American*, p74 (March, 1989).

J. B. S. Haldane, *On Being the Right Size*, Oxford University Press (1985). A selection of essays by a distinguished biologist.

Philip Morrison and Phylis Morrison, *Powers of Ten*, Scientific American Books (1982). A survey of the scale of things.

CHAPTER 2

The Chemistry of Oxygen

Introduction

The Chinese have named chemistry 'hua hsueh' -- "the study of change". This accurately summarizes the science, as without change there is no chemistry. If there were intelligent beings on Mars, since the whole planet has reached equilibrium, there could never develop a science of chemistry, because there would never be the opportunity of studying a chemical reaction. The constituent of the biosphere which contributes most directly to the lack of equilibrium on Earth is oxygen; this gas is present in the earth's atmosphere, but is absent on Venus and Mars. Oxygen is therefore the natural starting point for a discussion of the chemistry of the biosphere.

Table 1.4 showed that the earth's atmosphere differs chemically from those of the other planets in that its component gases are not at "equilibrium". What is meant by equilibrium in this context? This is a question to which we will return in later chapters, but for the present a partial definition suffices. Examination of a typical chemical reaction, sodium carbonate plus hydrochloric acid is a suitable example, provides a clue. On mixing the two solutions there is a rapid evolution of gas, a sure indication that a chemical reaction is occurring. However the gas does not continue to evolve indefinitely; after a period of time the reaction slows down, and eventually stops. This is true of all chemical reactions. The time that it takes to go to completion may be quite short, as in the reaction demonstrated, or it may be thousands of years, as in some geochemical reactions; sooner or later though, the reaction will be finished. The system has then reached "chemical equilibrium".

Demonstration 2.1
The reaction of sodium carbonate with hydrochloric acid. When solutions of these two compounds are mixed a chemical reaction occurs, as is made evident by the evolution of gas. After a while the evolution of gas slows down and eventually appears to cease all together. The reaction is over and equilibrium has been attained.

■ *Oxygen is the atmospheric gas furthest from its equilibrium concentration...*

If all the possible reactions between the chemicals present have reached equilibrium, no further chemistry is possible.

Oxidation

The first man or woman to light a fire was the first chemist. Ever since that time humans have been fascinated by the process of combustion and for many centuries this was the focus of chemical investigation. Aristotle, the Greek philosopher, considered that everything was made from the four "elements" of earth, air, water and fire. This theory held for many centuries. The alchemists living in this period reasoned that since different materials only differed in the proportions of these elements, one material could be transmuted into another by suitable manipulations to change the balance between its elements. A major objective was to produce gold from less expensive starting materials. Most of their experiments involved burning and heating substances in a variety of furnaces and vessels. It was clear that these operations lead to the formation of products different from the starting materials. There seemed to be no particular limitations on the transformations produced by heating and burning and the alchemist's objectives were, in the light of contemporary knowledge, quite reasonable. We now associate fire and burning with the reaction of the combustible material with atmospheric oxygen; the process is known as oxidation.

Reactions of Oxygen

■ *Burning is oxidation...*

Oxygen is one of the chemically most reactive substances known. It is an **element**, defined as a substance which is composed of only one kind of atom. **Compounds** are constructed from more than one kind of atom. The reactions of oxygen with other elements and compounds lead to the formation of oxides. Thus typically, sulfur will burn slowly in air, with a blue flame, to give a pungent smelling gas. In pure oxygen the flame is much brighter, and the reaction clearly occurs more readily. This reaction is expressed by the chemical equation:

$$S + O_2 \rightarrow SO_2$$

The product is named sulfur dioxide. Reactions with other elements can be written similarly. With hydrogen the reaction proceeds so rapidly that an explosion results.

$$2H_2 + O_2 \rightarrow 2H_2O$$

The water produced is in the form of steam. Carbon (charcoal) behaves in a manner very similar to sulfur, giving carbon dioxide.

$$C + O_2 \rightarrow CO_2$$

This, however, is not the only oxide of carbon and if insufficient oxygen is present carbon monoxide will be formed.

$$2C + O_2 \rightarrow 2CO$$

Demonstration 2.2
Burning sulfur, carbon and phosphorus. All these three elements will burn in air. However they burn much more brightly in oxygen, showing that oxygen is the chemically active component of the air. The oxides formed can be dissolved in water. These solutions will be saved for a future test of their acidic or basic properties.

Nitrogen, the second major component of the atmosphere, in contrast to oxygen is chemically non-reactive. It will form an oxide, the colorless gas nitric oxide, with difficulty at high temperature. In nature the necessary high temperatures are only achieved in lightning discharges.

$$N_2 + O_2 \rightarrow 2NO$$

If this reaction occurred more readily, the oxygen in the earth's atmosphere would have been used up long ago. Nitric oxide will react easily with more oxygen to give the brown gas nitrogen dioxide.

$$2NO + O_2 \rightarrow 2NO_2$$

There is a third oxide of nitrogen, nitrous oxide N_2O, which can only be made by indirect means. Phosphorus, an element which is in some ways similar to nitrogen, reacts very readily with oxygen to give either phosphorus pentaoxide, P_2O_5, or phosphorus trioxide, P_2O_3, depending on the amount of oxygen available.

$$P_4 + 3O_2 \rightarrow 2P_2O_3$$

$$P_4 + 5O_2 \rightarrow 2P_2O_5$$

Many metals will also burn brightly in oxygen, although some react more vigorously than others. Thus lithium or magnesium both burn very easily, but iron reacts less readily and gold simply melts if it is heated in the flame in an attempt to ignite it.

$$2Li + O_2 \rightarrow Li_2O$$

$$3Fe + 2O_2 \rightarrow Fe$$

Demonstration 2.3
Burning lithium, magnesium and iron. These are metallic elements rather than the non-metals of the previous experiment. They also burn in air, and more brightly in oxygen. In this case the oxides produced are not uniformly soluble in water. In the case of lithium the solubility is quite good, in the case of magnesium quite small, and in the case of iron there is no solubility. Where there is some solubility the solutions will be saved for a future test of acidic or basic properties.

Not only elements react with oxygen: octane, for example, is a component of gasoline and will burn readily, to give carbon dioxide and steam. The equation is a little more complicated, but not basically different from those given above.

$$2C_8H_{18} + 25O_2 \rightarrow 16CO_2 + 18H_2O$$

The Atomic Theory

The reactions described by the above chemical equations serve to illustrate several of the fundamental laws of chemistry. These principles were discovered toward the end of the eighteenth century and the beginning of the nineteenth century, and have survived virtually unchanged until the present. The basic model is the "atomic theory", first put forward by John Dalton in 1803. There are three primary postulates in this theory:

1) All substances are composed of atoms. It is imagined that a quantity of the substance is taken and subjected to continuous division. The question is asked whether this process of division can continue indefinitely, to give smaller and smaller pieces of matter, or whether at some point we obtain the smallest possible piece which still retains the properties of the substance. Dalton considered the latter view to be true, and described this smallest quantity as an atom of the substance.

2) The atoms of one substance are all alike and in particular have the same weight. Atoms of other substances are different.

3) Chemical action consists of the union, separation and interchange of atoms. These processes are represented by the chemical equations we write. The atoms themselves are not changed during the reaction.

Modern chemists differ from Dalton in one detail: Dalton used the word "atom" for the smallest fragment of any substance; modern usage restricts the application to chemical elements, defined in the previous paragraph. Most substances are compounds, formed by the combination of two or more atoms, and the smallest fragment of a compound is now called a molecule. Molecules are therefore made up of atoms. Thus O and H are atoms of the elements oxygen and hydrogen respectively; O_2 and H_2O are molecules formed from these elements.

■ *The Law of the Conservation of Mass...*
■ *Balanced equations...*

This theory provides a ready explanation of the basic observations of quantitative chemistry. The Law of the Conservation of Mass states that mass is neither created nor destroyed in the course of a chemical reaction. At this point we note the difference between mass and weight; mass is a measure of the amount of material present in a body, weight measures the attraction of the body by the earth. Providing we remain on the surface of the earth, where the force of gravity is constant, mass is consistently measured by weight and this is the method used for determining mass. If we went to the moon, where the force of gravity is less, the mass of a body would be the same as on earth but its weight would be less. With the same muscles you could lift a much more massive body on the moon than on the earth. It is mass which is conserved, not weight. If atoms are the entities which possess mass, and if a chemical reaction merely rearranges the combinations of atoms to give different molecules, then mass must be conserved. This law is expressed in the chemical equations that we write, as exemplified by the oxidation reactions described in the previous section of this chapter. The number of each kind of atom must be the same on the left and right hand sides of a chemical equation. If they are the same, mass is conserved; if they are not the same, the equation has been incorrectly "balanced". This law stood unchallenged until the twentieth century. Einstein's demonstration of the equivalence of mass and energy leads to a small modification; in **nuclear** reactions significant amounts of mass can be created or destroyed and are replaced by an equivalent (large) amount of energy. Since we are only concerned, in the present context, with **chemical** reactions, for which the energies are relatively small, we may take the Law of the Conservation of Mass as absolute.

■ *Pure substances and mixtures...*

The second general law rationalized by the atomic theory is the law of the constant composition of matter. If a sample of carbon dioxide, obtained by burning charcoal, is analyzed it will be found to contain 27.3 g of carbon and 72.7 g of oxygen for every 100 g of carbon dioxide. A second sample, prepared on a different day by a different chemical reaction, perhaps by the reaction of sodium carbonate with hydrochloric acid, will be found to have exactly the same chemical composition. So will all other samples of carbon dioxide obtained from any source by any method. This property is now used to distinguish between **compounds** and **mixtures**. If we mix salt with sand, combinations in any proportions may be used. The two components can be recovered by dissolving the salt in water and leaving the sand behind. Similarly, if we mix salt with water, solutions of a variety of concentrations may be prepared. The salt can be recovered by evaporation. These are examples of mixtures. By contrast, if we prepare carbon dioxide it always has the same composition and cannot be readily decomposed to its components. This is a chemical compound. The distinction between mixtures and compounds was not at all clear to the early chemists before the advent of the atomic theory. This theory, in which identical molecules are formed by combining specific atoms, demands that a true compound must have a well defined and constant composition.

Finally, Dalton was aware of the Law of Multiple Proportions. This law states that if two elements form more than one compound, and the weight of one element is kept constant, the weights of the other element will be in simple, whole number, ratios. (We state this law in terms of weights since it is an experimental law, and this is the way the experiment is carried out. The law is true because weight measures mass.) This law can be illustrated by taking the case of the three oxides of nitrogen encountered above. Nitrous oxide has a composition of 63.6% nitrogen and 36.4% oxygen by weight; nitric oxide analyses at 46.7% nitrogen and 53.3% oxygen and nitrogen dioxide at 30.4% nitrogen and 69.6% oxygen. If instead of expressing these compositions as percentages, we ask what weight of oxygen will combine with 1g of nitrogen, a little arithmetic gives the answer of 0.57g, 1.14g and 2.29g for the three oxides of nitrogen. These weights are clearly in the ratios of 1:2:4.

	N-N-O	*N-O*	*O-N-O*
% Composition	*63.6% N*	*46.7% N*	*30.4% N*
	36.4% O	*53.3% O*	*69.6% O*
Wt of Oxygen that will combine with 1g of Nitrogen	*0.57 g*	*1.14 g*	*2.29 g*
Ratio	*1*	*2*	*4*

Fig. 2.1: The Law of Multiple Proportions. Nitrogen forms three oxides. The weights of oxygen combining with one g of nitrogen in these three oxides are in the simple ratio of 1:2:4.

The atomic theory provides a very simple explanation of such regularities. In the three compounds N_2O, NO and NO_2, the number of atoms of oxygen combining with one atom of nitrogen are 0.5, 1 and 2. Since all atoms of oxygen weigh the same, the weights of oxygen are therefore in the observed ratios of 1:2:4.

It should be noted that Dalton used the above three laws to argue for the validity of his atomic theory. Once the theory was accepted, further progress could be based on this model.

Atomic Masses, Molecular Masses and Molecular Formulae

Simple atomic theory suggests that the atoms of different elements differ only in their relative masses. Atomic masses and molecular masses are often called atomic weights and molecular weights but the use of "mass" is now preferred. Analytical data on simple compounds can be used to calculate these relative atomic masses, providing we know the formula of the molecule analyzed. Conversely, if we know the relative masses of the constituent atoms, we can easily calculate the molecular formula. If we know neither, some further information is required to break the impasse. Thus analytical data show that 1g of hydrogen combines with 8g of oxygen to form 9g of water. If the formula for water were HO the atomic mass of oxygen, relative to hydrogen, would be 8. If, to be contrary, the formula is H_2O then the atomic mass of oxygen would be 16. This, of course, does not exhaust the possibilities. The formula could be H_3O or HO_2 or any number of other possibilities. If, on the other hand, we know that the atomic mass of oxygen is 16 the analytical data fix the formula for water as H_2O. In the early nineteenth century there was, not surprisingly, some confusion about the correct values of atomic masses, and corresponding uncertainty about the correct formulae for molecules.

■ Boyle's Law and Charles' Law...

This confusion was dispelled mainly by studies on the reactions of gases. The physical properties of gases had been widely investigated; for example, Boyle had trapped air above mercury in a sealed tube and demonstrated that, at constant temperature, the volume of the gas varied inversely as the pressure. If the pressure, as measured by the height of the mercury column, was doubled, the volume was halved as is illustrated in Figure 2.2. This became known as Boyle's law. It was also found that at constant pressure the volume of a gas increased with increasing temperature; if the temperature were lowered the volume decreased. In principle, if the temperature were sufficiently reduced, the volume would become zero as shown in Figure 2.3; in practice, of course, the gas would liquefy before this happened. Charles' law, stating that at constant pressure volume is proportional to temperature, lead however to the idea of an absolute zero in temperature, at which point the volume of a "perfect" gas would become zero. Absolute zero was estimated to be -273 °C. It is now common practice to call this temperature 0° and to measure upward from there. This is the Kelvin scale of temperature. Thus 20 °C, a pleasant room temperature, would be 20 + 273 = 293 K.

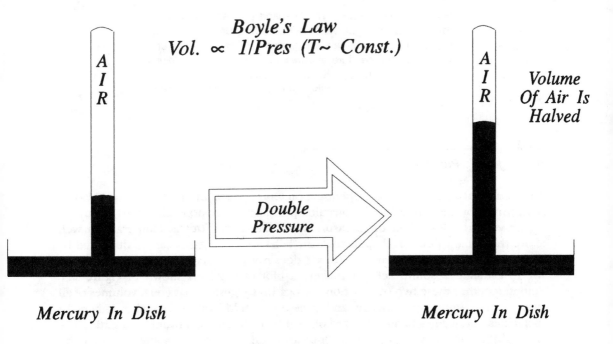

Fig. 2.2: Boyle's Law. Doubling the pressure of a gas halves its volume. Halving the pressure doubles its volume.

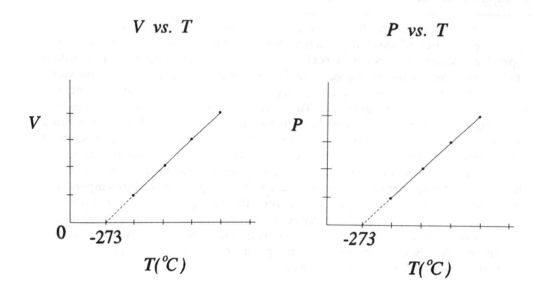

Fig. 2.3: Charles' Law. The left-hand diagram shows how the volume of a gas varies with temperature at constant pressure. The right-hand diagram show how the pressure varies with temperature at constant volume. The Absolute Zero of temperature (0 K, -273°C) can be estimated as the temperature at which either the volume or the pressure reaches zero.

■ *Avogadro's Principle...*

The volume of a gas, as well as depending on temperature and pressure, must also be determined by the number of molecules present; more molecules must occupy a bigger volume. Providing the measurements are carried out at temperatures well above the boiling point of the material, the behavior of all gases can be described by the same mathematical equation. Thus it does not particularly matter which gas we use to estimate absolute zero by making a plot of the kind shown in Figure 2.3. Putting together these two observations, Avogadro suggested that equal volumes of all gases at the same temperature and pressure would contain equal numbers of molecules. Molecules behave as hard billiard balls, bouncing around and hitting the sides of the containing vessel to produce a pressure; it doesn't matter whether the billiard balls are red or blue on this model. Similarly it doesn't matter whether our vessel is filled with hydrogen or with carbon dioxide, as equal numbers of molecules at the same temperature will produce the same number of collisions and the same pressure.

■ *Gay-Lussac's Law...*

One more piece of information is required to tie this knowledge of the properties of gases to chemical reactions. This is provided by Gay-Lussac's Law, which he discovered by studying a large number of reactions involving gases. Gay-Lussac's law states that in chemical reactions between gases, the ratios of the volumes of the reacting gases are small whole numbers. Thus it is found that in the reaction between hydrogen and chlorine, one volume of hydrogen will combine with one volume of chlorine, to give two volumes of hydrogen chloride. If equal volumes contain equal numbers of molecules, as required by Avogadro's principle, then one **molecule** of hydrogen must react with one **molecule** of chlorine, to give two **molecules** of hydrogen chloride. Thus we may write the chemical equation:

$$H_2 + Cl_2 \rightarrow 2HCl$$

This result immediately establishes that the elements hydrogen and chlorine have two atoms per molecule; if they were monatomic it would not be possible to form two molecules of hydrogen chloride from one atom of hydrogen and one atom of chlorine. In the reaction between hydrogen and oxygen, it is found that two volumes of hydrogen react with one volume of oxygen, to give two volumes of steam. This leads to the equation:

$$2H_2 + O_2 \rightarrow 2H_2O$$

■ *Avogadro's Number...*
■ *Moles...*

Using the analytical data that 1g of hydrogen combines with 8g of oxygen, this establishes that the atomic mass of oxygen is 16, based on an atomic mass of 1 for hydrogen. In similar manner a list of atomic masses of the different elements can be constructed. Once these are known, the analytical data for a given compound can be used to deduce its chemical formula. The molecular mass of a compound, also known as its formula mass, is simply obtained as the sum of the constituent atomic masses. For example, the formula for sulfuric acid is H_2SO_4, and its molecular mass is $(2 \times 1 + 32 + 4 \times 16) = 96$, since the atomic masses of hydrogen, sulfur and oxygen are 1, 32 and 16 respectively. This leads to a definition of **Avogadro's Number**: the molecular mass, expressed in grams, of any pure substance must contain the same number of molecules and this is Avogadro's number, 6.022×10^{23}. It is a very large number. A conception of its size is perhaps provided by the statistic that if we start with a particle of 1 micron dimension, the smallest object that can be viewed with an ordinary microscope, 10^{23} of these particles, if placed side by side would stretch for 10 light years, which is more than the distance to the nearest star. The molecular mass, in grams, of any substance is called a **mole** of that substance. Thus one mole of sulfuric acid weighs 96g. One mole of any substance contains Avogadro's number of molecules.

Chemists nowadays have a large variety of instrumental techniques for determining the molecular masses, the formulae and the **structures** of almost any compound, no matter how complex. A knowledge of the structure of a molecule involves knowing the order in which the atoms are joined together, the overall geometry of the molecule and, preferably, the distances between the constituent atoms and the angles which determine their relative orientations. Thus among the simple molecules which we have encountered thus far, carbon dioxide is a linear molecule, with the carbon atom between the two oxygens, nitrous oxide is again a linear molecule but one of the nitrogens is the central atom, and water is a bent molecule with the two hydrogens being attached to the central oxygen. The geometries of these and other molecules are illustrated in Figure 2.4. Modern techniques for determining

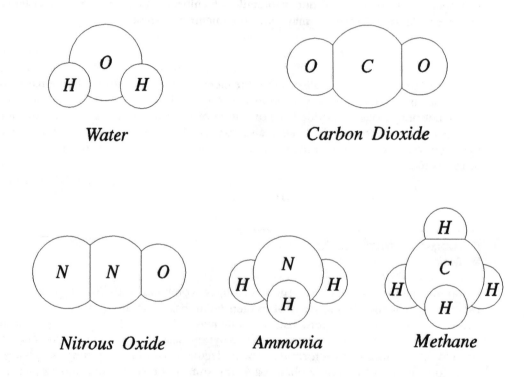

Water   *Carbon Dioxide*

Nitrous Oxide   *Ammonia*   *Methane*

Fig. 2.4: Molecular Models. Space-filling models can be used to show the geometry of molecules. Note that different atoms have different sizes - hydrogen is smaller than oxygen or nitrogen.

molecular structures, particularly those of large molecules, are often quite complex and not easily understood without knowing a great deal of physics theory. It is important to remember though, that the basic ideas regarding atoms and molecules are simple, and were established without recourse to sophisticated instrumentation. You don't have to know about X-Ray Diffraction or Nuclear Magnetic Resonance —two of the methods most widely used to establish molecular structures— in order to appreciate the structures of even very complicated molecules such as DNA or proteins.

The Chemistry of Oxides

■ *Acids, Bases and Salts...*

If combustion was the first chemical reaction discovered, oxides are the first reaction products. The products of oxidation are very different from the starting materials, and this observation suggested the next stage of chemical investigation. Elements can be broadly divided into metals and non-metals. Metals are characteristically lustrous and ductile, and have been for many centuries prized as materials for fabricating useful artifacts. Non-metals, on the other hand, vary very much; some, such as chlorine and nitrogen are gases, bromine is a liquid, and many, such as carbon and sulfur, are solids. All non-metals share the characteristic that their oxides react with water to give **acids**. The oxides of metals, on the other hand, react with water to give **bases**. Acids and bases react with each other to give **salts**. The chemistry summarized in the last three sentences is crucial to the maintenance of our biosphere.

Sodium (symbol Na) is a soft, low-melting, silver colored metal which is chemically very reactive. Its most important oxide, Na_2O, reacts vigorously with water to give sodium hydroxide, NaOH.

$$Na_2O + H_2O \rightarrow 2NaOH$$

Sodium hydroxide is a strong **base**. When dissolved in water, sodium hydroxide does not exist as NaOH molecules, but splits apart to give a positive sodium ion, Na^+, and a negative hydroxide ion, OH^-. **Ions** are simply atoms or molecules which bear electric charges. Sodium hydroxide is described as an ionic compound because of its facile dissociation to give two ions bearing opposite charges; it is a base because it gives hydroxide ions. Covalent compounds, an example of which is sugar, do not dissociate to ions when dissolved in water or other solvents. Calcium (symbol Ca) is a metal which is harder, higher melting, and rather less reactive than sodium. It forms an oxide, CaO, commonly called quicklime, which again reacts with water to give a base, slaked lime.

$$CaO + H_2O \rightarrow Ca(OH)_2$$

Calcium hydroxide does not dissociate to ions as readily as does sodium hydroxide. It is therefore a less prolific source of hydroxyl ions, and is described as a weaker base.

Other metals such as iron (Fe) and zinc (Zn) will burn to give oxides which are largely insoluble in water, therefore do not produce a solution containing very many hydroxide ions, and are classified as still weaker bases. In all of these cases the oxides lack the characteristics of the parent metals. They are mostly white or colored powders lacking any of the properties of ductility etc which make metals useful and desirable.

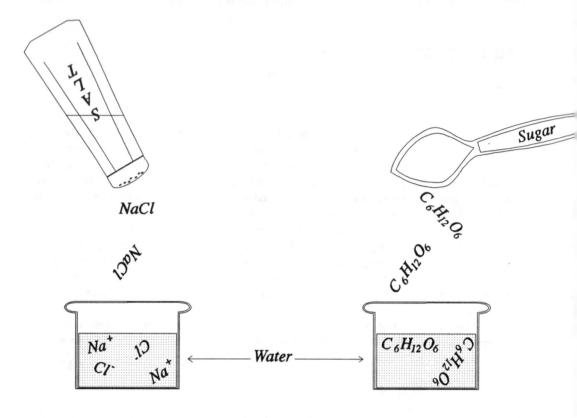

Fig. 2.5: Solubility in Water. Many substances dissolve in water but the resulting solutions may differ. Salt, NaCl, dissociates in solution to Na^+ ions and Cl^- ions. Glucose, $C_6H_{12}O_6$, exists in solution as undissociated molecules.

■ *Solutions of oxides in water...*

Burning sulfur, a yellow solid, gives, as we have seen, sulfur dioxide, a pungent smelling gas. Sulfur dioxide dissolves in water to give an **acid**, sulfurous acid:

$$SO_2 + H_2O \rightarrow H_2SO_3$$

Sulfurous acid is an acid because it dissociates and reacts with more water to give hydronium ions, H_3O^+.

$$H_2SO_3 + H_2O \rightleftharpoons H_3O^+ + HSO_3^-$$

■ Hydronium ions...

The hydronium ion is simply a combination of a hydrogen ion, H^+, with an additional molecule of water; it is very common to simply refer to it as a hydrogen ion, but this is strictly speaking incorrect, since the additional water molecule is always there. Nevertheless in many books you will find reference to "hydrogen ion concentrations" rather than to hydronium ion concentrations. Notice that a double arrow has been used in the above equation to indicate that the reaction does not proceed entirely to the right. This implies that sulfurous acid is not a particularly good source of hydronium ions. This is another way of saying that it is a relatively weak acid.

Demonstration 2.4
Acids and Bases. Indicators and pH meters can both be used to test for acids and bases. Litmus turns red in acids and blue in bases. Phenolphthalein is pink in bases and colorless in acids. Using these tests it is found that the solutions of the oxides of non-metals give acids, and those of metals bases. We can also use a pH meter to obtain this information. Low pH's correspond to acids and high pH's to bases.

■ Strong and weak acids and bases...

Sulfur dioxide is not the only oxide of sulfur. Under the right conditions it can be further oxidized to sulfur trioxide, SO_3. Sulfur trioxide dissolves in water to give sulfuric acid, a strong acid.

$$SO_3 + H_2O \rightarrow H_2SO_4$$

The fact that sulfuric acid is a strong acid means that it is, under most circumstances, completely dissociated to H_3O^+ and HSO_4^-, the bisulfate ion. In fact further dissociation, to give another hydronium ion and a sulfate ion SO_4^{2-}, can occur.

$$HSO_4^- + H_2O \rightarrow H_3O^+ + SO_4^{2-}$$

Sulfuric acid is referred to as a diprotic acid since it can provide two hydronium ions, and hence, as we shall see below, react with two equivalents of base. By an analogous argument, calcium hydroxide, $Ca(OH)_2$, which can provide two hydroxyl ions and hence react with two equivalents of acid, is a dibasic compound.

Demonstration 2.5
The Conductivities of Strong and Weak Acids. Strong and weak acids differ in the extent to which they dissociate to give ions. The greater the number of ions, the better the conduction of electricity by the solution. Acetic acid (vinegar) is a weak acid and hydrochloric acid a strong acid. Two solutions of the same concentration in both acids (0.1M) and a sample of pure (distilled) water can be tested for electrical conductivity by observing the brightness of a light bulb connected in the circuit containing the solution. In the case of hydrochloric acid the bulb glows brightly, acetic acid gives only a dim light, and distilled water no light at all.

Sulfuric acid, H_2SO_4, nitric acid, HNO_3, hydrochloric acid, HCl, and perchloric acid, $HClO_4$ are examples of strong acids. Sulfurous acid, H_2SO_3, carbonic acid, H_2CO_3, and acetic acid (vinegar) are examples of weak acids. Sodium hydroxide, NaOH, and potassium hydroxide, KOH, are strong bases. Ammonium hydroxide, NH_4OH, is a weak base.

An acid is thus defined as a source of positively charged hydronium ions and a base as a source of negatively charged hydroxide ions. If an acid and a base are brought together, these oppositely charged ions will combine to give water.

$$H_3O^+ \ + \ OH^- \ \rightarrow \ 2H_2O$$

This process is known as neutralization. Water consists almost entirely of undissociated H_2O molecules but also contains small, and equal, numbers of hydronium, H_3O^+, and hydroxide, OH^-, ions. If equal numbers of hydronium ions and hydroxide ions are mixed, the resulting solution will be neither acidic nor basic, but "neutral" as is water. However, all acids contain the hydronium ion plus another negative ion, (an anion) and all bases contain the hydroxide ion plus another positive ion (a cation). There is therefore always a second product in a neutralization reaction, obtained by combining the anion from the acid with the cation from the base. This product is known as a **salt**. Thus if hydrochloric acid is neutralized with the base sodium hydroxide, in addition to water, the salt, sodium chloride, is produced.

$$HCl \ + \ NaOH \ \rightarrow \ H_2O \ + \ NaCl$$

■ *The neutralization of acids by bases...*

Sodium chloride is the common salt used for flavoring food, but the term "salt" is used, in chemistry, to refer to any product of the neutralization of an acid by a base. Salts are usually completely ionized in water; sodium chloride is present as a mixture of Na^+ cations and Cl^- anions. It has been noted above that sulfuric acid is a "diprotic" acid and will react with two molecules of the "monobasic" sodium hydroxide, i.e.

$$H_2SO_4 \ + \ NaOH \ \rightarrow \ H_2O \ + \ NaHSO_4$$
$$NaHSO_4 \ + \ NaOH \ \rightarrow \ H_2O \ + \ Na_2SO_4$$

The initial salt produced, $NaHSO_4$, is named sodium hydrogensulfate and the final product is sodium sulfate.

From the point of view of the biosphere, carbon dioxide is a particularly important oxide. Although it is only present in the atmosphere at low concentration, it is crucial for plant growth. Compared to oxygen it is chemically unreactive, and can indeed be used to extinguish fires. The fire extinguisher provides a blanket of carbon dioxide which prevents the access of oxygen to the combustible material, and is itself completely non-reactive. Carbon dioxide condenses directly to a solid, known as dry ice, at -78 °C. In this form it is a useful refrigerating agent, and also suitable for producing fog and other special effects in theatrical performances. Carbon dioxide is only slightly soluble in water, giving the weak acid, carbonic acid.

$$CO_2 + H_2O \;\rightleftharpoons\; H_2CO_3$$

■ *Chemical properties of carbon dioxide...*

Carbonic acid is a dibasic acid and will therefore give two sets of salts, carbonates, e.g. Na_2CO_3, sodium carbonate, and $NaHCO_3$, sodium hydrogen carbonate, often called sodium bicarbonate. The salt calcium carbonate, $CaCO_3$, occurring naturally as chalk and limestone, is of particular importance in the biosphere. It is insoluble in water, is produced by marine organisms, and the resulting seashells provide a large reservoir of carbon which is not immediately available to plants.

Silicon dioxide, SiO_2, (often called silica) is another oxide which occurs commonly in the biosphere. Carbon and silicon belong to the same chemical family, and some resemblance between their oxides might have been anticipated. They are, in fact, quite different. Silicon dioxide occurs as sand or quartz and is a solid, in contrast to the gaseous carbon dioxide. The origins of this difference will be considered in the discussion of chemical bonding in Chapter 4. With water it forms the weak acid, silicic acid, and with bases a series of silicate salts. Many of the salts, particularly those involving aluminum, magnesium and iron, are important constituents of the rocks which form the earth's crust. Historically its most important property has been as the raw material for the manufacture of glass, one of the oldest known chemical processes. Sand itself can be melted to give a glassy substance, but this requires high temperatures; the melting point, and the ease of working with the material, can be reduced by adding sodium carbonate (soda ash) and/or calcium carbonate (limestone). When these compounds are heated with sand, carbon dioxide is lost and sodium or calcium silicates are formed.

$$SiO_2 + Na_2CO_3 \rightarrow Na_2SiO_3 + CO_2$$

■ *Glass...*

Ordinary glass is a mixture of silica with these metal silicates. It can be colored by adding small quantities of other metal oxides to the reaction mixture. Iron oxide (ferrous - FeO), which is often present as an impurity in the sand, gives a green color, and cobalt oxide (CoO) a blue color.

One more acidic oxide will be considered, phosphorus pentaoxide, P_2O_5. This is the product of burning phosphorus in excess air or oxygen. It has a great affinity for water, and is often used as a drying agent. It dissolves to give phosphoric acid, H_3PO_4, a triprotic acid.

$$P_2O_5 + 3H_2O \rightarrow 2H_3PO_4$$

Although phosphorus is not one of the most abundant constituents of the biosphere, phosphates play a key role in biochemistry. The property which determines this role is their ability to form short, chain-like molecules. An example is shown in the reaction below:

$$2HPO_4^{2-} \rightarrow \{O_3POPO_3\}^{4-} + H_2O$$

The chain can be extended to give three phosphorus atoms linked by oxygen atoms, and derivatives of these di- and tri-phosphates play a key role in plant and animal metabolism. None of the other oxides considered above can participate in this type of chemistry.

Metals from Oxides

The first metals known to man were the noble metals, gold and silver, which occur as free metals; they are soft and malleable, and can easily be fashioned into ornamental artifacts. Most other metals are not so readily obtained; they occur as compounds, known as **ores**, rather than as free metals, and chemical processing is required to liberate the metal. The most common ores are oxides and sulfides. Heating the sulfide in air usually leads to a metal oxide, e.g. in the case of lead (Pb):

$$2PbS + 3O_2 \rightarrow 2PbO + 2SO_2$$

■ *Reduction is the opposite of oxidation...*
■ *The extraction of metals...*

The problem becomes one of reclaiming the metal from its oxide. It will be recognized that this process is the opposite of that of oxidation considered above. To obtain a metal, or any other element, from its oxide, involves **reduction,** the converse of oxidation. The first metals to be obtained in this way were copper (Cu), tin (Sn) and lead (Pb). The reducing agent is charcoal, e.g.

$$CuO + C \rightarrow Cu + CO$$
$$2CO + O_2 \rightarrow 2CO_2$$

This process will occur by simply mixing the metal ore with charcoal and allowing the mixture to burn. The molten metal may be run off from the bottom of the furnace.

Demonstration 2.6
The Reduction of Copper Oxide. Copper oxide is a black powder and so is charcoal. When the two are heated together in a test tube shiny, red metallic copper is formed. Copper is one of the easiest metals to obtain which is why it has been used for many centuries. The product of the reduction of the copper oxide is carbon dioxide. This can be demonstrated by passing the gases evolved into lime water. The milky precipitate is a test for carbon dioxide.

The alloying of copper and tin, to make the superior bronze, goes back to at least 3000 BC. Bronze is hard enough to make an edged sword and tough enough to make a shield; this was the state of the art in weapons technology at the time of the Trojan war. It is speculated that bronze may have first been made accidentally by heating a mixed ore of Cu and Sn, but intentional alloying was certainly practised from a very early date. At a rather later time, perhaps around 1000 BC, furnaces were designed which produced sufficient heat to smelt the more difficult ores of iron. The Iron Age began and has been with us ever since. Some form of mechanical forced air draft is necessary to achieve a high enough temperature to smelt the ore. Nowadays the process is carried out in a blast furnace. Two reactions are involved. Coal or charcoal is burned to give carbon monoxide, followed by reduction of the iron oxide.

$$2C + O_2 \rightarrow 2CO$$
$$Fe_2O_3 + 3CO \rightarrow 2Fe + 3CO_2$$

Demonstration 2.7

The Reduction of Iron Oxide. Iron oxide is more difficult to reduce than copper oxide. Charcoal is not a strong enough reducing agent to reduce iron oxide in a laboratory demonstration, and the more powerful aluminum powder is used. The iron oxide and the aluminum are mixed in a crucible and the reaction started by adding sulfuric acid to a small quantity of sugar and potassium chlorate. This acts as a "detonator". Once started the reaction proceeds vigorously and shows why this mixture, known as thermite, was used in incendary bombs during the second world war. After allowing a period for cooling, the nature of the blob of iron metal remaining in the bottom of the crucible can be demonstrated by lifting it out with a magnet.

$$Fe_2O_3 + 2Al \rightarrow Al_2O_3 + 2Fe$$

In this reaction the iron has been reduced and the aluminum oxidized.

The above equations simplify the process by neglecting the impurities, mainly silica, which are always present in iron ore. To remove them, limestone is included in the furnace charge; this will give calcium oxide, which in turn reacts with the silica.

$$CaCO_3 \rightarrow CaO + CO_2$$
$$CaO + SiO_2 \rightarrow CaSiO_3$$

■ *Steelmaking...*

The calcium silicate produced is the "slag", which can be separated from the molten metal. The iron produced by a blast furnace contains a fair amount of carbon, since this is used in the reduction process, and a number of other impurities. To obtain steel the carbon content must be reduced to less than 1.5%. This is accomplished by blowing in oxygen and burning the excess carbon and other impurities. To make certain special kinds of steel, small quantities of other metals are added at this stage. Steel making requires still higher temperatures and it is now common practice to use pure oxygen, rather than air, for the oxidation step.

Not all metals can be reduced by carbon, even at these high temperatures; the most important metal in this category is aluminum (Al). Not until the nineteenth century was a viable process for obtaining aluminum metal from the readily available oxide, Al_2O_3, discovered. This is not a chemical process, but an electrochemical process, and its discovery had to await the availability of electric power in large quantities. The usual ore is bauxite, a mixture of aluminum and iron oxides. The aluminum oxide can be separated from the iron oxide by dissolving in caustic soda, adding carbon dioxide to reprecipitate aluminum hydroxide, and recovering aluminum oxide by heating.

$$Al_2O_3 + 2NaOH + 3H_2O + Fe_2O_3 \rightarrow 2Na^+ + 2Al(OH)_4^- + Fe_2O_3$$
$$Al(OH)_4^- + CO_2 \rightarrow Al(OH)_3 + HCO_3^-$$
$$2Al(OH)_3 \rightarrow Al_2O_3 + 3H_2O$$

■ *Manufacturing aluminum...*

The purified aluminum oxide is dissolved in the mineral cryolite (Na_3AlF_6), to give a relatively low-melting mixture (less than 1000C). This molten mixture is then electrolysed to produce metallic aluminum. The essentials of this process are that Al^{3+} ions migrate to the negatively charged electrode, where they each acquire three electrons to become a neutral aluminum atom.

$$Al^{3+} + 3e \rightarrow Al$$

In this process electrons are provided directly as the reducing agent rather than a chemical, such as the carbon used in the reduction of iron oxide.

INTERLUDE

Paradigms and Paradoxes

Just the place for a Snark, the Bellman cried,
As he landed his crew with care,
Supporting each man on the top of the tide,
By a finger entwined in his hair.
Just the place for a Snark, I have said it twice,
That alone should encourage the crew.
Just the place for a Snark, I have said it thrice,
And what I tell you three times is true.
(Lewis Carroll, **The Hunting of the Snark**)

Introduction

Truth in science is as elusive as truth elsewhere. Some sixty or seventy years ago, E. J. Holmyard, writing on the history of chemistry, described the situation as follows.

> "Scientific truth is a matter of convenience. So long as a theory knits together facts which are otherwise disconnected, has corollaries which are susceptible to experimental proof or disproof, and is not incompatible with any well-authenticated observation, it is scientifically true. Whether scientific truth will ever approach absolute truth is a question which there is no immediate necessity for scientists to discuss, but, bearing in mind the fate of theories of the past, he would be a brave man who asserted that those of today are likely to escape the general doom."

Nowadays we tend to take ourselves more seriously and to downplay the fragility of scientific truth. It is often associated with "scientific proof", a phrase familiar to viewers of television commercials for a variety of non-prescription drugs. It becomes involved, in many peoples minds, with solemn figures in clean white lab coats performing mysterious operations in surroundings filled with flashing lights and exotic glassware; this is clearly misleading - in real life the lab coats are never clean. A characteristic of scientific truth is that it changes with time, a process euphemistically called progress. What is scientifically true yesterday may not be scientifically true today, and today's version quite probably won't be believed tomorrow. In spite of these shortcomings, scientific truth is still highly regarded by many non-scientists and it is worth asking why this is so, and to what extent it is justified.

There have been times when it has been claimed that physics, the quintessential science, had reached its final form and progress would cease; this was the case at the end of the nineteenth century. Apart from a few loose ends, such as the black body radiation problem, everything had presumably been satisfactorily explained. There is a story, probably apocryphal, that the Head of the Physics Department at Harvard at this time was advising students to avoid physics, since there would be no problems left for them to investigate by the time they graduated. This period was immediately followed by the appearance of relativity and quantum theory, which ushered in one of the most productive eras in the whole history of science. Similar pronouncements have been heard recently, suggesting that once a few small problems associated with Grand Unified Theories (GUT's) and quantum gravity have been disposed of (this is expected to happen any day now), physics will end. Most scientists, particularly those in disciplines other than physics, are sceptical.   In chemistry the number of new compounds available for discovery certainly shows no signs of ending, but one can argue that the proliferation of experimental facts is perhaps not always accompanied by a corresponding yield of new chemical ideas and concepts. Lord Rutherford, a hard-core physicist, relegated the type of research which leads primarily to data acquisition to the category of stamp collecting. If science is ever reduced to the collection of additional facts - all consistent with existing theories - then we will indeed be able to expound definitive scientific truth. It seems safer, at present, to assume that this will not happen and that we will continue to operate from a base constructed on shifting sands.

There are two approaches which may ameliorate this uncertain prospect. We can look to the philosophy of science to find the core of unchanging truth in the eye of the hurricane of scientific progress. Alternatively we can look to the history of science to see what has changed, and what has stayed constant, in the flux of past ideas. Perhaps this will guide us in our present predicament. The problem with the philosophers is that they are, if anything, even more confused than the scientists; the historians at least have some reasonably solid "facts" to work with. We will therefore take the historical route. If science is perpetually changing, there are two broad ways for change to occur: change can be evolutionary or it can be revolutionary. If it is evolutionary then the problem is simpler, since what we will believe tomorrow will only be sightly modified from what we believe today. If it is revolutionary, what we believe tomorrow may bear little resemblance to what we believe today. Current thinking favors the revolutionary model. Thus Cohen has extensively documented the changes in science and shown that many of them fit the concept of revolutionary change.   Kuhn, in a much quoted book entitled *The Structure of Scientific Revolutions*, has followed the process in some detail. He introduced the idea that a revolution in science was accompanied by a change of "paradigm".

The concept of a paradigm is broader than that of a theory. It is a way of looking at a subject, and when this overall outlook changes, the experimental facts, as well as the theories change. This is usually because different questions are asked, which elicit a whole new body of experimental data. Kuhn suggested that most of the time, most scientific research is involved in filling in the details of an accepted paradigm, and that only occasionally does someone produce an idea or an experimental finding which is sufficiently original to change a paradigm. This model has limited popularity with active scientists since it places most of them in Rutherford's category of stamp collectors, concentrating on minor problems, the solutions of which serve to reinforce the current paradigm. Although not all scientific revolutions can be forced into the same mold, Kuhn's viewpoint certainly has merit in many cases. Typically a paradigm is stretched as far as it can be to accommodate new experimental data; there comes a point when further expansion bursts the bubble. Frequently, the development of a paradox, within the framework of the accepted paradigm, is the pin that bursts the bubble. Poundstone has discussed the nature of paradoxes in his book **The Labyrinths of Reason** and has produced the definition -

> "A paradox starts with a set of reasonable premises. From these premises it deduces a conclusion which undermines the premises."

If the premises form the basis of a current paradigm, the situation is clearly uncomfortable for the practitioners of that particular branch of science, and something has to give. There is typically a period of dispute and uncertainty until a new paradigm becomes established. Often though, the senior scientists committed to the old paradigm will go to great lengths, involving much convoluted logic, to preserve the status quo. At times such as this, several competing versions of the scientific truth are likely to be current.

We will look at three case histories to see how scientific truth has changed as a function of time. The Chemical Revolution occurred at the end of the eighteenth century and was brought to fruition at the beginning of the nineteenth century. It marked the final end of alchemy and the start of modern chemistry. The discovery of the double helix structure of DNA took place in the 1950's. It was the result of a very elegant piece of chemical research, which had an enormous effect on the development of biology. It caused very little controversy because it fitted well into the contemporary paradigms of both chemistry and biology. Quantum theory originated in the 1900's and has been bubbling and boiling ever since. It provides the underlying explanations for all of chemistry, as well as of many other branches of science. It is causally decoupled from chemistry, but is too important for chemists to ignore. In some respects it differs from 19th century physics in much the same way that 19th century chemistry differed from the mid-18th century version; it may therefore be compared to the Chemical Revolution. It still contains a number of paradoxes which are a source of discomfort to philosophically inclined physicists.

The Phlogiston Theory

Throughout the late middle ages Aristotle was the overwhelming influence on science, and indeed on all other forms of intellectual activity. Aristotle was a realist; he did not have much time for anything which he could not observe, classify and assign a cause to. His contribution to chemical theory was to classify all materials as mixtures of the four elements fire, air, earth and water, modified by the four qualities moist, dry, hot and cold. This was the starting point from which the alchemists, initially Arab scholars, constructed their art. To this starting material they added a large number of sound chemical observations and garnished the mixture with various appeals to magic, astrology and the greediness of sponsors anxious to benefit from the transmutation of gold or to acquire the philosophers' stone. Alchemy retained respectability well after the development of "real" physics. Newton devoted considerable time to the subject during a period when he was also developing the classical theory of celestial mechanics. The phlogiston theory marks a transition between alchemy and scientific chemistry. It has been described as the first theory of modern chemistry, but it could also be regarded as the last gasp of Aristotelian natural philosophy.

The theory of phlogiston was based on common sense; it set out to codify the observations which a conscientious alchemist would make in the course of his professional activities. It is obvious to anybody watching a fire burn, that something is given off, and is escaping up the chimney. It is sensible to conclude that all things that burn do so by a common mechanism. Therefore, what is given off is common to all things that burn, and was called phlogiston. This proposal was first made by Becher in 1669 and the theory was elaborated by Stahl in a book published in 1702. It was the accepted theory from then until nearly the end of the 18th century. The idea was derived from the earlier alchemists who regarded combustion as a process of decomposition and considered sulfur to be the volatile component. Since sulfur is clearly not involved in all burning processes, a more generalized substance, phlogiston, seemed called for. Phlogiston is not fire itself, but is the material of fire, which is contained in all combustible substances and is given up on burning. Burning a metal gives a calx (in modern terminology a metal oxide) plus phlogiston. Charcoal is rich in phlogiston so that heating a calx with charcoal provides phlogiston to the calx and converts it back to the metal. Noble metals, such as gold, hold their phlogiston strongly and therefore will not burn or react. Cavendish produced hydrogen gas by reacting zinc with acid. He also found that zinc calx (zinc oxide) gave the same material with acid as did zinc, but no gas was evolved; since the calx is the metal less phlogiston, the hydrogen evolved must be "nearly pure phlogiston". Priestley obtained oxygen by heating mercury calx (mercuric oxide); since the calx had acquired phlogiston to form the metal, the product, oxygen, must be "dephlogistonated air". The whole system was perfectly self-consistent and was wholeheartedly supported by Cavendish, Priestley, Scheele and all the other major chemists of the eighteenth century.

There was only one small snag. When a metal or a non-metal was burnt the weight of the calx was greater than that of the initial metal. This was known from experiments of Jean Rey in 1630 and more extensive investigations by Robert Boyle in the 1660's. This observation implies either that mass is not conserved or that phlogiston has negative mass. Both of these alternatives were acceptable to 18th century phlogistonists. Their paradigm did not include the conservation of mass, and in any case Aristotle had pointed out that massive things fall, and since fire rises it must have "levity" rather than weight.

The Chemical Revolution - The Retreat of Common Sense

In the opinion of Cohen "the chemical revolution has a primary place among revolutions in science". It occurred at a time in history when the American and French political revolutions were taking place, and intellectually the time was ripe for the overthrow of existing doctrines. Lavoisier, its chief architect, was politically active and was indeed executed at the guillotine. Lavoisier's fundamental contribution was to change the emphasis of chemistry from observation to measurement. The building blocks for chemical theories ceased to be chemicals and their reactions, and became measurements on chemicals and their reactions. Qualitative observations, carefully and reproducibly made, are the basis of common sense; quantitative measurements lead to abstract science. Chemistry was thus set on a path pioneered by physics a hundred years earlier. It was transformed from a "soft" science to a "hard" science.

Lavoisier's instrument of change was the chemical balance. He confirmed the observations of his predecessors that burning materials increased their weight. More importantly, he also measured the changes in the air during combustion. He found that if a large lump of phosphorus was burned in a closed vessel, combustion ceased when 1/5 of the air was consumed. On letting more air into the vessel, further burning was possible. He weighed the closed vessel in which tin was burnt before and after burning and showed that there had been no overall change in weight. He was able to show that the gain in weight of the solid (the calx) had been balanced by the loss in weight of the gas. Lavoisier was visited by Priestley in 1774 who described his discovery of "dephlogistonated air". Lavoisier identified this gas as the active fraction in air which led to combustion, and named it oxygen or "acid producer" since, on burning non-metals such as phosphorus or sulfur, acids were produced. He demonstrated that this same fraction of air was necessary to maintain life in animals and correctly identified the equivalence of combustion and respiration. Thus whereas the phlogiston theorists wrote:

$$element \rightarrow calx + phlogiston$$

Lavoisier expressed the combustion process as:

$$element + oxygen \rightarrow oxide$$

This reformulation provided a new approach to defining elements and Lavoisier's table of elements, shown in Table IN1.1, is similar to a part of the present-day Periodic Table.

Table IN1.1: Lavoisier's Elements

Gases	Non-metals	Metals	Earths
Light	Sulfur	Antimony, Mercury	Lime (CaO)
Caloric	Phosphorus	Silver, Molybdena	Barytes(BaO)
Oxygen	Carbone	Arsenic, Nickel	Magnesia(MgO)
Azote(N)	Muriatic radi-	Bismuth, Gold	Argill(Al_2O_3)
	cal (Cl)	Cobalt, Platina	Silex(SiO_2)
Hydrogen	Fluoric radi-	Tin, Tungsten	
	cal (F)	Iron, Zinc	
	Boracic radi-	Manganese	
	cal (B)		

Lavoisier himself realized that the earths such as lime (CaO), barytes (BaO) and magnesia (MgO) were probably the oxides of as yet undiscovered metals. He really erred only in including light and caloric (heat), which we now recognize as forms of energy rather than of matter.

Lavoisier's greatest contribution, though, was in formulating the Law of the Conservation of Mass, which was the direct consequence of his emphasis on quantitative measurement. Once this principle was accepted, the fact that substances gained weight when phlogiston was lost became a paradox. The paradox was resolved by Lavoisier's theory of oxidation, and this therefore became the basis for a new paradigm of chemistry.   Older chemists, such as Priestley, remained faithful to phlogiston until the end of their lives. The new approach proved immediately fruitful; the laws of the constant composition of compounds and of multiple proportions followed from the application of Lavoisier's emphasis on quantitative gravimetric (weighing) experiments.   These in turn gave birth within thirty years to Dalton's atomic theory, and modern chemistry was truly launched. Gravimetric measurements have been supplemented by measurements of heat capacities, of spectra, of the diffraction of X-rays and of a host of other properties, but henceforth measurement reigned supreme.

The Double Helix - Paradigms Preserved

A short paper was published in the journal *Nature* in April 1953, entitled "Molecular Structure of Nucleic Acids: A Structure for Deoxyribose Nucleic Acids". The authors were James D. Watson and Francis H. C. Crick. They, together with a third scientist, Maurice Wilkins, were awarded the Nobel prize for physiology or medicine in 1962, for the work on which the *Nature* paper of 1953 was based. (The only minor surprise in 1962 was that the prize was awarded in physiology rather than in chemistry; it was universally agreed that the findings were of sufficient importance to merit a Nobel prize, and it has indeed been very plausibly described as the greatest scientific discovery of the twentieth century.) It is of interest to compare the discovery of Watson and Crick with those Lavoisier made 180 years earlier, not from the point of view of assessing relative merit, which would clearly be impossible, but because they represent different types of discovery, and perhaps different types of scientific truth.

Watson and Crick used a standard chemical structure-determining technique, X-ray crystallography, and some well-accepted principles concerning atomic sizes and molecular geometries, to solve the problem of the structure of deoxyribonucleic acids (DNA). The importance lies in the fact that DNA isn't just any molecule - it is <u>THE</u> molecule which controls heredity in biology.   Their solution, the double helix structure, answered two important biological questions - chemically, how is genetic information coded and chemically, how is this information disseminated. DNA is a very high molecular weight polymer and consists of two polymeric chains entwined in a double spiral or helix. The two chains are held together by hydrogen bonds which are strong enough to make the combination stable, but can be readily broken by appropriate enzymes without the expenditure of a large amount of energy. There are four different kinds of units involved in the polymer. It is the ordering of these units in the chain which provides the coding mechanism by which genetic information is transmitted and the ability to separate into individual chains, each of which can form another double helix, which provides for the transmission of heritable characteristics. The details of how this works will be discussed in Chapter 9.

It is apparent, even to the non-specialist, that this model has great elegance, a quality much admired by scientists. It obeys all the rules determining chemical structure which chemists have built up since the time of Lavoisier; it provides a rationale for the rules of heredity discovered by biologists; if it had been suggested a hundred years earlier, it would have disturbed biologists who believed in the vitalist principle, that living things require something beyond physical science to give them their characteristic properties. The vitalists though, had been defeated many years ago and the current paradigm of biology was reductionist in outlook, holding that all the phenomena of life have a chemical basis. The double helix model therefore provided a vindication and justification of all that both chemists and biologists had been taught to believe. It is not surprising that it was received with universal acclaim.

This model was the starting point for the new subdiscipline of molecular biology, which rapidly achieved a very high profile in the scientific world. The history of the meteoric rise of this research has been told, in a very approachable form, by Horace F. Judson in his book *The Eighth Day of Creation*. The title of this book imparts something of the conviction shared by the molecular biologists, that they were discovering very significant truths. Francis Crick set the tone by naming an important feature of the theoretical development of the subject, The Central Dogma; this states that "DNA makes RNA makes protein", and defines the roles of the major chemical constituents of living cells. The use of the word "dogma" in a non-religious context is indicative of the great confidence the molecular biologists felt for the essential truth of their findings. This is in marked contrast to the uncertainties of physicists after the enunciation of quantum theory.

Quantum Theory - Common Sense Routed

As was noted earlier, at the end of the nineteenth century physics was left with only a few loose ends to tidy up. Unfortunately, pulling on these loose ends completely unravelled the well-knit fabric of the subject. The main culprit was quantum theory, which is simultaneously the most successful theory ever and the most controversial scientific theory ever. It was developed to account for a host of experimental observations, obtained at the beginning of the twentieth century, relating to atomic structure and radiation. The success of the theory lies in the fact that it is a mathematical theory, and solution of the appropriate equations gives answers which agree excellently with experimental measurements. It can be applied to a wide variety of problems, and it works every time. As far as chemistry is concerned, there seems to be no basic theoretical barrier preventing the calculation of the structures and reaction rates of all molecules and chemical reactions. There are a few practical difficulties, particularly in the calculation of reaction rates, but in principle it can be done. The problem lies in the fact that it is much easier to use the mathematics than it is to interpret it in terms of physical concepts. Most scientists are content to leave this latter aspect of the subject to the philosophers, but it is, as Arthur Fine reminds us in a recent book, *The Shaky Game*.

Quantum theory gives rise to paradoxes and at present neither scientists nor philosophers can resolve these paradoxes in a manner that satisfies everybody. Electrons sometimes behave as particles, and sometimes behave as waves, and the two sets of properties are contradictory; one aspect of their behavior is used to account for the results of some experiments, but the other aspect must be used to account for the results of other experiments. What happens to one electron appears to influence the results of an experiment on a distant electron when there is no possible means of communication between the electrons. The peculiarities are not confined to electrons but infect all small particles and have their complement in the properties of quantized energy. Logic would dictate that we should abandon the theory, but it is a very successful theory and we don't have anything better to replace it with. There are two ways of proceeding, which were staked out in the early days of the theory in debates between the two great scientists Niels Bohr and Albert Einstein. Bohr said, in effect, that we have to accept the paradoxes because that is the way nature is. We can make measurements on a well defined system and we can predict the results of these measurements. The measurements are the ultimate coinage of science - there is no point in looking beyond to something which has a reality independent of the measurements we make. Einstein never accepted this limitation and devised many tests to try and demonstrate the existence of some ultimate reality which is there whether we observe the system or not. Einstein was unsuccessful and the Bohr view was upheld in every suggested test. More recently, scientists have proposed ever more subtle tests, but all have failed to establish a reality behind the measurements. The current paradigm is therefore the Copenhagen interpretation of quantum mechanics due to Bohr: only measurements have meaning. Effectively common sense has been banished. Lavoisier introduced quantitative measurements to chemistry, but the measurements were still performed on real objects. Quantum theory has left the measurements but removed the real objects behind them, leaving, as it were, only the smile on the face of the Cheshire cat. The defeat of phlogiston has been completed.

Conclusion

In this Interlude we have considered three major advances in chemistry which have occured during the last 200 years. Each has had a major impact, not only on chemistry, but on science as a whole. They all qualify for the title of a "Scientific Revolution". Each of them has lead to new " scientific truths" which are accepted by virtually all practicing scientists. Scientific truth though is not a simple concept; the three examples have given rise to three different kinds of scientific truth.

Lavoisier's rejection of the phlogiston theory marked the beginning of chemistry as a modern science. Lavoisier's theory was not accepted by his own generation of chemists. Paradoxes such as the gain in weight of a substance when it lost phlogiston were eventually no longer accepted. Qualitative observations were henceforth replaced by quantitative measurements; Galileo and Newton had brought about this change in physics a century earlier. Henceforth the paradigm of these "hard" sciences was to be based on careful experimental measurements, generalized to give theories which could be used to predict the results of more experimental measurements. If the verifying experiments gave the expected results, the theory was provisionally classified as "true". This is the truth defined by Holmyard in the quotation at the beginning of this Interlude.

Watson and Crick's double helix model for DNA fits this paradigm but does not extend it. Biologists and chemists found it very satisfying to have a model which linked biological reproduction with molecular structure and embraced it with enthusiasm. Most had believed in the existence of such a linkage ever since they were students. The model was therefore almost immediately accepted as "true".

Quantum theory takes us a stage further. It is a very acceptable theory in the sense that it accurately predicts the results of a wide variety of experiments. It is an unsatisfactory theory in that it leads to paradoxes - electrons sometimes behave as waves and sometimes as particles. The theory is "true" in the scientific sense but does not provide us with any satisfactory picture of what is <u>really</u> happening at the atomic level. The present conventional view is that to ask what is <u>really</u> happening is not a fair scientific question. Einstein never accepted this limitation and some contempory physicists agree with Einstein.

      To most non-scientists scientific truth rests in the answer to such questions as "am I going to get skin cancer because of the increasing concentrations of CFC's in the upper atmosphere" or "will the level of the oceans rise because of the greenhouse effect". These statements may be either true or false, but the nature of the truth involved is quite different to the truths of the previous three paragraphs. No scientific theory can give an absolute answer to these questions and there is good reason to believe that no theory ever will be able to. For the same reasons it is doubtful whether weather forecasts will ever be reliable for more than three days in advance. Models based on scientific theories can indeed be usefully applied to these problems, but at best they will only provide statistical probabilities for certain types of occurence. The use and abuse of statistics to predict the consequences of environmental abuses will be considered in a later chapter.

      The resolution of paradoxes is still a major concern for scientists. Some, such as Zeno's Paradox, are the result of the improper application of mathematics. Others, such as Einstein's twin paradox, by which a twin returning from a distant space flight will be younger than his brother remaining at home, are only apparent paradoxes. It seems certain in this case that if the experiment could be carried out, the result predicted by relativity theory would be obtained. Where does this leave quantum theory? It seems to most people that the paradoxes of quantum theory represent a real limitation on the scope of science. What we observe is a product of the human mind, and is influenced by the limitations of the human mind. If this is the case, we may never resolve the paradoxes of particles and waves and of non-locality, and the belief that quantum theory is based on any form of reality becomes a matter of faith. As the Bellman maintained in the epigraph to the present interlude, in repetition lies truth.

Quantum theory is true,
Quantum theory is true,
Quantum theory is <u>really</u> true.
If we say it often enough we may come to believe it.

Further Reading

E. J. Holmyard, ***Chemistry to the Time of Dalton***, Oxford Univ. Press (1925).
J. R. Partington, ***A Short History of Chemistry***, MacMillan and Co (1939).
Ira D. Garrard, ***Invitation to Chemistry***, Doubleday (1969).
Some short books on the history of chemistry, particularly phlogiston theory and the chemical revolution.

I. Bernard Cohen, ***Revolution in Science***, Harvard Univ. Press. (1985). An extensive history of scientific revolutions.

Thomas S. Kuhn, *The Structure of Scientific Revolutions*, 2nd Ed, Univ. of Chicago Press (1970). The classic book on the theory of scientific revolutions.

Horace F. Judson, *The Eighth Day of Creation*, Simon and Schuster (1979). A complete historical account of the discovery of the genetic code and other recent developments in biology.

William Poundstone, *Labyrinths of Reason*, Doubleday (1988).

John Gribbin, *In Search of Schrodinger's Cat*, Bantam Books (1984).

Richard Feynman, *The Character of Physical Law*, M.I.T. Press (1967).

Arthur Fine, *The Shaky Game*, Univ. of Chicago Press (1986).

E. J. Holmyard, *Alchemy*, Dover Publications, (1990, first published 1957). A history of the subject.

CHAPTER 3

The Chemistry of Water

Introduction

Oxygen is the key chemical component of the atmosphere. Water plays the dominant chemical role on the surface of the earth. About 0.5% by weight of the earth is water. The majority of this water resides in the oceans, which contain some 2.7×10^{14} kg of the substance. About a tenth as much, 2×10^{13} kg, is locked up in deposits in the earth's crust; fresh water, in rivers and lakes, accounts for 8×10^{12} kg; the Polar Ice Caps provide about half as much, 4×10^{12} kg; relatively small amounts remain in the troposphere (3×10^9 kg) and stratosphere (5×10^5 kg). The latter amount represents a potential source of loss of water from the earth, since at this high altitude it can be decomposed by ultraviolet radiation into its component elements, hydrogen and oxygen, and the very light hydrogen is rapidly lost to outer space. As discussed in Chapter 1, there is a continuous circulation of water among the various reservoirs; this cycle is essential for the continuity of life on earth. Another commonly quoted statistic is that 80% of the human body is water.

The properties of water are very different from those of oxygen. In general the higher the molecular mass of a substance, the higher its melting point and boiling point; compounds with similar molecular masses usually have similar melting and boiling points. These trends can be conveniently illustrated with a set of compounds such as the hydrocarbons. Table 3.1 gives some data on the molecular weights, the melting points, and the boiling points of some simple substances. Oxygen is about where it would be expected relative to hydrocarbons of similar molecular mass.

Table 3.1: Melting and Boiling Points of Molecular Substances

Compound	Molecular Weight	B.P.°C	M.P.°C
H_2	2	-253	-259
CH_4	16	-162	-182
NH_3	17	-33	-78
H_2O	18	100	0
N_2	28	-196	-210
CO	28	-90	
C_2H_6	30	-89	-183
O_2	32	-183	-218
H_2S	34	-60	-86
HCl	36.5	-85	-114
F_2	38	-188	-220
CO_2	44	-79	
C_3H_8	44	-42	-188
C_4H_{10}	58	-0.5	-138
C_5H_{12}	72	36	-130
C_6H_{14}	84	69	-95
C_7H_{16}	100	98	-91

■ *The boiling point and melting point of water are both anomalously high...*

Most of the other simple liquid or gaseous substances we have encountered to this point have boiling points and melting points which increase smoothly with molecular mass. Table 3.1 indicates that ammonia, NH_3, is a little higher in boiling point than might have been anticipated. Water, though, is the major anomaly being substantially higher, both in its melting point, 0 °C, and in its boiling point, 100 °C. It is also anomalous in several other physical properties. Thus the density of the liquid is higher than that of the solid at the melting point. Ice therefore floats on water. Water also has a very high heat capacity - more heat is required to raise its temperature by a specified amount than is the case for most substances. These properties are crucial to the role that water plays in the biosphere. Thus aquatic life would be very difficult to maintain in the winter if, in line with the behavior of most substances, ice was more dense than water. The layer of ice formed on top of a pond or lake in cold weather effectively insulates the remaining water, leaving a liquid habitat for biota below. Only the smallest ponds freeze solid even in severe winter conditions. If, on the other hand, ice sank to the bottom, many lakes would freeze completely and aquatic life would not survive the winter. The high heat capacity of water means that lakes and seas act as effective heat reservoirs; heat is absorbed in the summer and only slowly lost in the winter. This property moderates the climate of neighboring land masses, making them much more suitable to support life. The business of chemistry is to explain observations such as these in terms of molecular structure. We need to account for the peculiar properties of water, and to explain why they differ from those of methane which has the same molecular mass. This we will do in Chapter 4.

Reactions of Water with Metals

Water is, on the whole, a less reactive substance than oxygen. Most things burn; most things do not react in any violent way with water. Water is, in fact, commonly used to extinguish fires. There are exceptions to this rule: adding a small pellet of the metal potassium (symbol K) to a beaker full of water illustrates such an exception.

Demonstration 3.1
Reactions of Water with Metals. Small quantities of the metals K, Na, Li, Ca, Zn, Fe and Cu are added to water containing an indicator which turns blue in basic solution. The first four metals react with decreasing vigor, evolving hydrogen. The reaction with K is sufficiently vigorous to spontaneously ignite the hydrogen, which burns with a lilac flame. Na reacts quite vigorously and the gas evolved can be ignited and burns with a yellow flame. Lithium and calcium react less vigorously and both cases the gas burns with a red flame. The remaining metals do not react. The color of the flames is determined by the presence of a few metal atoms in the flame. In each case the remaining aqueous solution is colored blue, indicating the presence of a base.

There is a vigorous reaction, hydrogen gas is evolved and sufficient heat is generated to ignite the gas, which burns with a violet flame. The color is due to potassium atoms in the vapor, which emit light of a characteristic purple hue.

$$2K + 2H_2O \rightarrow 2K^+ + 2OH^- + H_2$$

The product, potassium hydroxide (KOH), remains in solution and is written as potassium ion (K^+) and hydroxide ion (OH^-) in keeping with the earlier discussion that it is a strong base and therefore completely dissociated in solution.

It is instructive to repeat this experiment using other metals. A clear sequence of reactivities is apparent. Sodium reacts vigorously, but not usually sufficiently so to ignite the hydrogen evolved. It can be lit and burns with a bright yellow flame, a color characteristic of Na atoms.

$$2Na + 2H_2O \rightarrow 2Na^+ + 2OH^- + H_2$$

Lithium and calcium both react with water but with considerably less vigor than the previous cases. The resulting hydroxides have limited solubility in water.

$$2Li + 2H_2O \rightarrow 2LiOH + H_2$$
$$Ca + 2H_2O \rightarrow Ca(OH)_2 + H_2$$

■ *Metal hydroxides...*

We have written lithium and calcium hydroxides in an undissociated form to make the point that they mostly remain as solids, but it should be realized that the soluble fraction is considerably, if not completely, dissociated in water. The series of metal reactivities can be extended by investigating the reaction of water with zinc (Zn), iron (Fe) and copper (Cu). In these cases no evolution of hydrogen is observed.

It has been stated previously that water dissociates to a small extent to give hydrogen (or more correctly hydronium) and hydroxide ions. It is instructive to replace the water molecules by these ions in one of the above equations; the reaction with sodium illustrates the point.

$$2Na + 2H_2O \rightarrow 2Na^+ + 2OH^- + H_2$$
or
$$2Na + 2H^+ + 2OH^- \rightarrow 2Na^+ + 2OH^- + H_2$$
or
$$2Na + 2H_3O^+ + 2OH^- \rightarrow 2Na^+ + 2OH^- + H_2 + 2H_2O$$

With chemical equations, as with algebraic equations, it is permissible to cancel terms which appear on both sides of the equation, in this case OH^-.

$$2Na + 2H_3O^+ \rightarrow 2Na^+ + H_2 + 2H_2O$$

■ *Balancing charges...*

It should be noted that this latter equation remains balanced, both with regard to the number of atoms (the Law of Conservation of Mass), and with regard to the total charge; the left-hand side has two positive charges, the right-hand side also has two positive charges. It is perfectly permissible to write chemical equations involving single ions, such as Na^+, which are not paired with an ion of the opposite charge, providing the balance of charges is maintained. Examination of the equation for the sodium reaction in its last form suggests that the reaction is essentially between the metal and the hydronium ion. If the concentration of hydronium ions were increased, perhaps metals which are typically unreactive with water might be persuaded to react. Acids are the source of hydronium ions; let us therefore examine the reactions of the unreactive metals Zn, Fe and Cu with a dilute acid: hydrochloric acid is suitable.

Demonstration 3.2
Reactions of Metals with dilute hydrochloric acid. The metals unreactive in the last demonstration are added to dilute hydrochloric acid. Iron and zinc both react readily to give hydrogen. Copper remains unreactive.

■ *The reactions of metals with acids...*

In the cases of Fe and Zn vigorous evolution of hydrogen is observed, confirming the essential nature of this type of reaction as an interaction between metals and hydronium ions. In the case of Cu there is still no reaction. Cu is apparently even less reactive than Zn or Fe.

$$Zn + 2H_3O^+ \rightarrow Zn^{2+} + H_2 + 2H_2O$$
$$Fe + 2H_3O^+ \rightarrow Fe^{2+} + H_2 + 2H_2O$$

When the reaction of sodium with water was written in its original form, hydroxide ions appeared as one of the products. These ions have been "cancelled out" in the equations which focused on the positive ions. In Demonstration 3.1 it was observed that the solution resulting from the reaction of sodium with water is basic, and therefore contains an excess of hydroxide ions. Clearly, writing the equation in the ionic form misses part of the chemistry; the missing part lies in the dissociation of water.

$$2H_2O \rightleftharpoons H_3O^+ + OH^-$$

This equilibrium is present in all aqueous solutions. If hydronium ions are removed, as they are in this case by reaction with the metal, there will be an excess of hydroxide ions in the solution, which will be basic. This point will be developed in a more quantitative form later in the present chapter. In a similar vein, the reaction between hydrochloric acid and zinc is often written:

$$Zn + 2HCl \rightarrow ZnCl_2 + H_2$$

It will be recognized that this equation is obtained from the equation involving hydronium ions by adding two chloride ions to both the left-hand side and the right-hand side of the equation. The above chemical equations all describe essentially the same chemical reaction. The version of the equation involving the hydronium ion emphasizes the common features of the reaction, and makes it clear that all acids, in so far as they are simply sources of hydronium ions, behave in the same way with respect to their reactions with metals. Thus there is often no absolute "right" way to write a chemical equation; the version chosen often depends on the aspect of the chemistry which is to be emphasized.

Reactions of Water with Non-metals

The extent of the reactions of water with non-metals is much more limited than with metals. We will consider only two: the first illustrates a point of theoretical interest and the second, one of practical importance. Fluorine is a gaseous element, chemically similar to chlorine. If fluorine is bubbled through water a gas is evolved; this gas proves to be not hydrogen, as in the case of the reaction of water with metals, but <u>oxygen.</u>

$$2F_2 \ + \ 2H_2O \ \rightarrow \ 4HF \ + \ O_2$$

It is significant that fluorine, a non-metal, reacts with water to give oxygen, whereas metals react with water to give hydrogen. Just as not all metals react with water to give hydrogen, not all non-metals react to give oxygen. In fact fluorine is the <u>only</u> non-metal which behaves in this way. The reason for the unique behavior of fluorine in this reaction will be considered in Chapter 4.

■ *Producing hydrogen on an industrial scale...*

Carbon, in the form of graphite, does not react with liquid water. However, many reactions which do not occur at room temperature will take place at higher temperatures. In the present case, if steam at 1000 °C is passed over coke (an impure form of carbon) hydrogen is produced.

$$C \ + \ H_2O \ \rightarrow \ CO \ + \ H_2$$

This reaction was used for many years as a commercial method for producing hydrogen. The necessary high temperature can be obtained by reacting some of the carbon with air. The carbon monoxide produced can be reacted further with more steam to produce additional hydrogen.

$$CO \ + \ H_2O \ \rightarrow \ CO_2 \ + \ H_2$$

■ *Catalysts...*

Not surprisingly this second step is even more difficult to bring about than the first step. It requires a <u>catalyst;</u> catalysts are materials which increase the <u>rate</u> of a chemical reaction but do not influence the nature of the reaction. They are of great industrial importance and, in the form of enzymes, crucial to the chemistry of life. An alternate industrial process for making hydrogen is to pass steam over heated iron.

$$3Fe \ + \ 4H_2O \ \rightarrow \ Fe_3O_4 \ + \ 4H_2$$

This reaction provides a second example of the effect of increasing temperature on chemical reactivity since, as demonstrated earlier, water does not react (at any appreciable rate) with iron at room temperature. Neither of the above reactions is currently the major industrial source of hydrogen; instead it is usually produced from natural gas, mostly methane, by reaction with steam.

$$CH_4 + H_2O \rightarrow CO + 3H_2$$

The 3:1 mixture of hydrogen and carbon monoxide produced in this reaction is known as <u>synthesis gas</u> and is the starting point for the manufacture of a variety of industrial chemicals.

Water as a Solvent

■ *The solubility of salts...*

Perhaps the single most important property of water is its ability to dissolve a wide range of substances; it is described as a good solvent. In Chapter 1, the composition of the sea was described. Sea water contains relatively high concentrations of a variety of salts of which common salt, sodium chloride, is only the most abundant. All salts are ionic and dissociated in aqueous solution; not all salts though are highly soluble. Thus silver chloride, AgCl, although formally very similar to sodium chloride, is virtually insoluble in water. (If two solutions, one containing Ag^+ ions and one containing Cl^- ions, are mixed the insoluble silver chloride, AgCl, will be precipitated. A large number of other salts can be precipitated in a similar manner.)

Demonstration 3.3
Insoluble salts. Not all salts are soluble. If the ions which make up an insoluble salt are both present the compound will be precipitated. Thus sodium chloride (NaCl) and silver nitrate ($AgNO_3$) are both soluble but if the two solutions are mixed a white precipitate of insoluble silver chloride (AgCl) appears. In the same way barium sulfate ($BaSO_4$ white) can be precipitated from sodium sulfate and barium chloride mixtures, and yellow lead iodide (PbI_2) from sodium iodide and lead nitrate. The appearance of these precipitates often serves as a convenient qualitative test for different ions. Thus if we wished to test for the presence of sulfate ions in solution a solution of barium chloride would be added. The appearance of a white precipitate confirms sulfate.

■ *Solutions of salts conduct electricity...*

An important property of solutions of soluble salts such as sodium chloride is that they conduct electricity. As was pointed out above, salt exists in solution as Na^+ and Cl^- ions. If two electrodes, one connected to the positive terminal of a battery and the other to the negative terminal, are immersed in the solution Cl^- ions will be attracted to the positive electrode and Na^+ ions to the negative electrode. As a result, an electric current flows in the circuit. As well as the majority of Na^+ and Cl^-

ions present there are also a few H_3O^+ ions and OH^- ions resulting from the small amount of dissociation of water. Both Na^+ and H_3O^+ ions arrive at the cathode or negative electrode, and either can acquire an electron to make a neutral atom. The H_3O^+ ion acquires an electron much more readily than the Na^+ ion, and it is therefore hydrogen gas which appears at the cathode.

$$2H_3O^+ + 2e^- \rightarrow H_2 + 2H_2O$$

Similarly, at the anode, or positive electrode, either Cl^- or OH^- can be discharged and it is the latter which is preferred in dilute solutions of NaCl. This leads to the evolution of oxygen at the anode.

$$4OH^- \rightarrow 2H_2O + O_2 + 4e^-$$

Demonstration 3.4

Electrolysis of aqueous solutions. If electrolyses are carried out in an apparatus consisting of two connected burettes, each containing an electrode, the products can be examined individually and, if gases, the relative volumes produced measured. A light bulb incorporated in the circuit shows whether the solution conducts electricity. Pure water fails to conduct electricity as demonstrated in Chapter 2. A dilute solution of salt (NaCl) conducts electricity, as shown by the lighted bulb. Gas is produced at both electrodes. The gas formed at the negative electrode (cathode) is hydrogen and explodes when lit with a taper after air has been admitted to the tube. The gas formed at the positive electrode (anode) is oxygen and relights a glowing splint. There are two volumes of hydrogen formed for every volume of oxygen. When the solution of salt is replaced by one of copper sulfate ($CuSO_4$), oxygen is still evolved at the anode but no gas is produced at the cathode. Instead the electrode becomes coated with a shiny layer of copper metal. The Cu^{2+} ions are more easily discharged than the H^+ ions.

It should be noted that the transportation of 4 electrons from the cathode to the anode produces 2 molecules of hydrogen and one molecule of oxygen. If the amounts of gas produced during electrolysis are measured, it is observed that 2 volumes of hydrogen are produced for each volume of oxygen. This therefore provides a direct proof that the correct formula for water is H_2O. If the metal ion in solution is more willing to acquire an electron - meaning that it is more easily reduced - than H_3O^+, metal will be deposited at the cathode. This is the case for the Cu^{2+} ion, so that the electrolysis of $CuSO_4$ does not produce any hydrogen but deposits a layer of copper metal at the cathode.

■ *Oils and fats are not soluble in water...*

Water will also dissolve some non-ionic substances: sugar is an example. Equally important though, is the fact that many non-ionic materials are insoluble in water. Paraffin wax, oil and fats are examples of water-insoluble materials. Water is the reaction medium for nearly all biochemical reactions. It is therefore clearly important that the reactants be soluble in water. On the other hand some compounds - such as those comprising cell membranes and bones - must be insoluble if the integrity of the organism is to be maintained.

It has previously been stated that solutions are mixtures, since they do not have a constant composition, as demanded by the definition of a "compound". This statement needs closer examination when applied to aqueous solutions. Solid sodium chloride is made up of positively charged sodium ions, Na^+, and negatively charged chloride ions, Cl^-. Positive charges attract negative charges, and if these ions are to be pulled apart, as they are during the process of solution, the loss of the electrostatic energy of attraction must be balanced by some corresponding gain. The source of gain lies in the interaction of both the positive ions and the negative ions with solvent water molecules. The ions, in solution, are each associated with a sheath of water molecules; the process is known as solvation or, in the specific case of water, aquation. A salt will tend to be soluble in water if the gain in aquation energy is greater than the loss of electrostatic attraction energy in the solid, although this is not the only factor determining solubility. In a solution of sodium chloride, the sodium ions are each attached to a number of water molecules through the oxygen atoms of the water molecules.

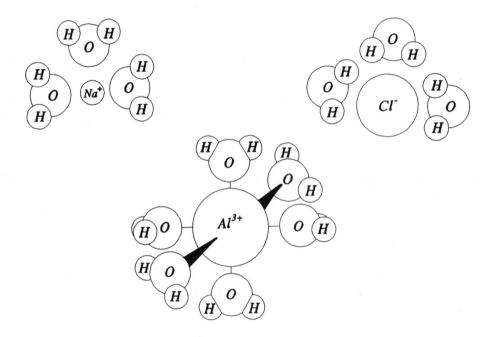

Fig. 3.1: The Solvation of Ions. Both anions and cations have molecules of water attached to them in aqueous solution. A monopositive cation such as Na^+ has a variable number of water molecules weakly bonded through the oxygen atoms. A chloride ion Cl^- has a similar sheath of solvent molecules, but they are attached through the hydrogen atoms. A small tripositive cation, such as Al^{3+}, forms a definite compound $Al(H_2O)_6^{3+}$ with strong Al-O bonds and a well-defined (octahedral) geometry.

■ *The solvation of ions in water...*

The chloride ions are similarly attached to the hydrogen atoms of water molecules. Figure 3.1 illustrates this equation. The line drawn between the sodium ion and the oxygen atom represents a chemical bond in just the same way as does the line drawn between oxygen and hydrogen in the water molecule; the same is true of the line drawn between hydrogen and Cl^-. The only difference is that the bonds involving the Na^+ and Cl^- ions are much weaker than the O-H bonds in water; as a result, they are being formed and broken very rapidly, so that there is a fluctuating number of bonds involving the ions over any period of time. If the bonds are stronger, as they are with the Al^{3+} ion, also illustrated in Figure 3.1, a specific compound is formed, in this case $Al(H_2O)_6^{3+}$ and this molecule exists as such in solution for a relatively long period of time. It may also exist in the solid state in association with an appropriate negative ion. Thus the solution of an ionic compound in water is a chemical process - breaking bonds in the solid and forming bonds in the solution - just as the burning of carbon or sulfur in oxygen is a chemical process. The only differences are that the bonds formed are relatively weak, and the resulting hydrated ions remain mixed with a large and variable excess of solvent water. The <u>hydrated ions</u> are true compounds, even though the bonds holding them together are weak. These hydrated ions can form a <u>mixture</u> of variable composition with the excess water present. Solutions of sodium chloride can be very concentrated or very dilute, but they all contain hydrated sodium and chloride ions. All biological processes take place in aqueous solution, and it is particularly important to recognize that water is a reactant in these processes, not just an inert solvent. The same considerations apply to solvents other than water, but the solvation energies are usually still smaller and can often be neglected.

Thermochemistry

■ *Exothermic and endothermic reactions...*

In the discussion thus far we have neglected one important aspect of chemical reactions. When the original chemist lit the first fire, the interest was not in the products of the chemical reaction but in the heat that was evolved during this reaction. All chemical reactions lead to either the evolution of heat or the absorption of heat. The study of this aspect of reactions is known as **thermochemistry**. Reactions which evolve heat are said to be **exothermic** and those which absorb heat **endothermic**. Heat changes are characteristic of chemical reactions; for instance, mixing sand and salt, which does not lead to chemical reaction, does not change the temperature of the constituents. Dissolving salts in water, which by the above discussion <u>is</u> a chemical process, does.

Demonstration 3.5
Heats of Solution and of Reaction. When salts dissolve in water heat can be either given out or absorbed. In the first case the reaction is exothermic and a thermometer placed in the solution shows a rise in temperature. In the second case it is endothermic and the thermometer shows a fall in temperature. The solution of lithium chloride (LiCl) provides an example of an exothermic reaction. Dissolving ammonium nitrate, on the other hand, is endothermic and the cooling effect is sufficient to form ice and freeze the beaker to a block of wood. The solution of sodium chloride (NaCl) is only very slightly endothermic and a small or zero change in temperature is recorded.

■ *Enthalpy changes...*

If the reaction is carried out in a **calorimeter** the amount of heat absorbed or heat evolved can be measured. In principle this is a very simple experiment; the heat evolved or absorbed is used to heat or cool a known weight of water. If we double the quantity of reactants, twice as much heat will be absorbed or evolved. It is therefore necessary to specify the amount of reactant. Conventionally the heat change for the reaction of one mole of reactant is specified. This quantity is known as the **enthalpy change** of the reaction. Every substance has a certain heat content (enthalpy) which is given the symbol H. During a chemical reaction one set of substances is replaced by another set of substances with different enthalpies (heat contents). The change in enthalpy appears as heat evolved or heat absorbed and is given the symbol ΔH. It is measured in units of energy. Nowadays the accepted units are joules (J), or kilojoules (kJ - 1kJ = 1000J) and the enthalpy change (ΔH) associated with a given chemical reaction is given at the end of the chemical equation. An example is:

$$H_2(g) \; + \; 1/2 O_2(g) \; \rightarrow \; H_2O(l) \qquad \Delta H = -286kJ$$

This equation tells us that one mole of hydrogen gas reacts with half a mole of oxygen gas to give one mole of liquid water with the evolution of 286kJ of heat. Several points should be noted. Firstly, it is necessary in thermochemical equations to specify the physical states of the reactants and products as gases(g), liquids(l) or solids(s). The enthalpy change will be different if the physical state of a reactant or product is changed, e.g.

$$H_2(g) \; + \; 1/2 O_2(g) \; \rightarrow \; H_2O(g) \qquad \Delta H = -242kJ$$

■ *Signs of enthalpy changes...*

In this case, the difference between 286kJ in the first equation and 242kJ in the second equation, represents the heat needed to change 1 mole of water from a liquid to a gas (steam). This is the heat of vaporization of water. Secondly, the convention is that if a reaction is exothermic, the enthalpy change is negative, and if it is endothermic the enthalpy change is positive. In an exothermic reaction the heat content of the products is less than that of the reactants, hence the negative sign for the change in enthalpy. The missing heat content appears as heat evolved. In an endothermic reaction, the heat content of the reacting substances increases and heat must be provided. The reaction between hydrogen and oxygen is clearly exothermic - a large amount of heat is evolved when hydrogen is burnt in air. A further implicit assumption is that the reaction is carried out at a constant gas pressure so that energy used to compress the gas, or energy obtained during the expansion of the gas, is zero.

Over the past one hundred years chemists have measured the enthalpy changes for a vast number of chemical reactions. When these data are examined, a number of regularities are found. A simple example, involving the reactions of carbon and oxygen, illustrates the point.

$$C(graphite) + O_2(g) \rightarrow CO_2(g) \quad \Delta H = -393.5kJ$$
$$C(graphite) + 1/2O_2(g) \rightarrow CO(g) \quad \Delta H = -110.5kJ$$
$$CO(g) + 1/2O_2(g) \rightarrow CO_2(g) \quad \Delta H = -283.0kJ$$

■ *Hess' Law...*

The first reaction produces carbon dioxide from graphite and oxygen in a single step. (Note that it is necessary to specify that the carbon is in the form of graphite because there is another solid form of carbon - diamond - and the results would not be quite the same if this form were used). The second and third reactions produce carbon dioxide in two steps. The regularity is that the enthalpy change does not depend on whether one step or two steps are involved - -393.5kJ = -(110.5kJ + 283.0kJ). This is an example of Hess' Law which states that the change of enthalpy for a chemical reaction is independent of the reaction path; Hess's law is illustrated diagrammatically in Figure 3.2.

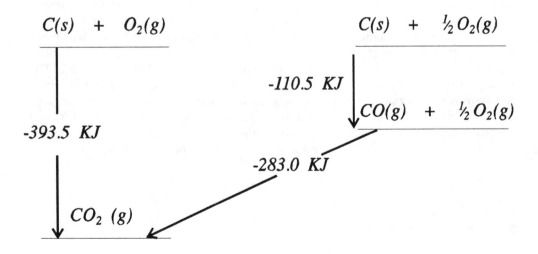

Fig. 3.2: Hess' Law. No matter whether carbon dioxide is formed directly from the elements or indirectly from carbon monoxide, the total amount of heat evolved is the same.

A more complex example is provided by the heat of combustion of glucose.

$$C_6H_{12}O_6(s) + 6O_2(g) \rightarrow 6CO_2(g) + 6H_2O(l) \quad \Delta H = -2816kJ$$

Glucose is a major source of energy for life. The reaction paths which lead from unreacted glucose to the final oxidation products, carbon dioxide and water, are varied and very complicated. The energy available from the oxidation of glucose is not all liberated in the form of heat, but as much as possible is used, a small amount at a time, to drive other chemical reactions and synthesize molecules of biochemical importance. However complex these pathways though, we can be sure that the overall energy available will be 2816kJ per mole of glucose reacted, no more and no less.

■ *The First Law of thermodynamics...*

Hess' Law is a special case of a much more general principle - the Law of the Conservation of Energy; this is also known as the First Law of thermodynamics. Energy can be neither created nor destroyed; it can only be changed from one form to another. In exothermic chemical reactions the chemical energy, in the form of chemical bonds, is partly converted to heat. This law exactly parallels the law of the conservation of mass introduced in Chapter 2. An external combustion engine can take heat from a hot source and transform some of this heat into useful work. A book on a desk has potential energy by virtue of its height above the floor. If it falls, the potential energy becomes kinetic energy; when it hits the floor the kinetic energy is replaced by heat energy. Work is necessary to replace the potential energy by lifting the book back to its place on the desk. In a chemical reaction some of the chemical energy can be transformed to heat if the reaction is exothermic. If on the other hand the reaction is endothermic, heat is transformed to chemical energy. In the course of all these transformations the total of energy of all kinds remains constant.

The First Law of thermodynamics allows all of the calorimetric data which has been collected on a range of chemical reactions to be expressed in a compact form; this is accomplished by defining an **enthalpy of formation** for each compound. The enthalpy (or heat) of formation is simply the enthalpy change of a reaction in which the compound is formed from its elements in their standard states. It is designated ΔH^0. The standard state of an element is the usual form of the element at 25 °C and atmospheric pressure. By definition, the enthalpy of formation of all elements in their standard states is zero. Consider the formation of methane from its elements.

$$C(graphite) + 2H_2(g) \rightarrow CH_4(g) \quad \Delta H^0 = ?$$

■ *Enthalpies of formation...*

ΔH^0 cannot be measured directly since this reaction just does not occur under convenient conditions of temperature and pressure. The required value can however be obtained by applying the First Law of thermodynamics in the form of Hess' Law. It is experimentally easy to measure the heats of combustion of all the reactants and products involved in the formation of methane.

$$C(graphite) + O_2(g) \rightarrow CO_2(g) \qquad \Delta H = -393.5kJ \ (1)$$
$$H_2(g) + 1/2O_2(g) \rightarrow H_2O(l) \qquad \Delta H = -285.9kJ \ (2)$$
$$CH_4(g) + 2O_2(g) \rightarrow CO_2(g) + 2H_2O(l) \quad \Delta H = -890.4kJ \ (3)$$

Since methane is formed from one mole of carbon and two moles of hydrogen, adding together Eq.1 and 2 x Eq.2 and subtracting Eq.3 gives the equation for the formation of methane, i.e., Equations 1, 2 and 3 suffice to form methane in an indirect manner. Hess' Law tells us that the enthalpy change obtained indirectly must be identical to that of the direct reaction. The enthalpy of formation of methane is therefore 393.5 - 2 x 285.9 + 890.4 = -74.9kJ.

■ *Calculating enthalpies of reaction...*

The enthalpies of formation of most common molecules have been obtained in a manner similar to the example of methane given above, and have been tabulated. There is a simple rule which allows these data to be used to obtain the enthalpy change in any reaction: the required enthalpy change is given by the sum of the enthalpies of formation of the products less the sum of the enthalpies of formation of the reactants. This rule can be easily verified by writing down the appropriate equations for the formation of both the reactants and products, adding them together, and obtaining the required chemical equation. An example illustrates the method: ammonia will react, under the right conditions, with chlorine to give nitrogen and hydrogen chloride.

$$2NH_3(g) + 3Cl_2(g) \rightarrow N_2(g) + 6HCl(g)$$

The enthalpies of formation of ammonia and hydrogen chloride are -46.2 and -92.3kJ respectively. The enthalpies of formation of chlorine and nitrogen are both zero since they are elements in their standard states. The required enthalpy of reaction is therefore (-6 x 92.3 + 2 x 46.2) = -461.4kJ/mol. It is thus predicted that this reaction will be highly exothermic.

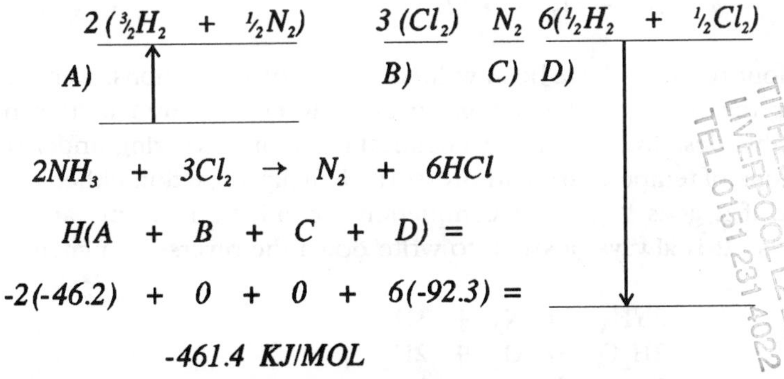

$$2\,(^3/_2H_2 \; + \; ^1/_2N_2) \qquad 3\,(Cl_2) \quad N_2 \; 6(^1/_2H_2 \; + \; ^1/_2Cl_2)$$

A) B) C) D)

$$2NH_3 \; + \; 3Cl_2 \rightarrow N_2 \; + \; 6HCl$$

$$H(A \; + \; B \; + \; C \; + \; D) =$$

$$-2(-46.2) \; + \; 0 \; + \; 0 \; + \; 6(-92.3) =$$

$$-461.4 \; KJ/MOL$$

Fig. 3.3: Enthalpy Changes from Enthalpies of Formation. The diagrams A,B,C and D show the enthalpies of formation of the reactants and products. The enthalpy change for the reaction can be obtained by summing the enthalpies of formation.

Chemical Equilibria, the Dissociation of Water and pH

At the beginning of Chapter 2 we introduced a simple criterion for chemical equilibrium; no further chemical reaction occurs when equilibrium has been reached. Another way of stating this, is that spontaneous chemical reaction can only occur when the reactants are not at chemical equilibrium. It is appropriate at this point to consider chemical equilibria in a little more detail, with a view to developing some predictive power regarding which chemical reactions will occur spontaneously, and those which will not. Note the use of the word "spontaneously" in this context; if we are prepared to provide energy, in a suitable form, to drive a reaction, it is possible to achieve chemical results not otherwise attainable. This occurs in living systems. We will return to this theme later but will initially consider equilibrium in isolated systems (i.e., no continuous energy input).

■ *Hydrides...*

Some reactions leading to the production of hydrogen from water were considered above. It is appropriate to use some of the reactions of hydrogen to illustrate chemical equilibria. The simplest reactions of hydrogen are with elements to form hydrides. Such reactions can occur with metals, but are relatively unusual; an example is that with lithium.

$$H_2 + 2Li \rightarrow 2LiH$$

Lithium hydride is a solid, salt-like material which exists as Li^+ and H- ions. More typical are the reactions with non-metals; that with oxygen to give water has already been encountered. Hydrides are also readily formed with non-metals such as nitrogen, chlorine and iodine.

$$3H_2 + N_2 \rightarrow 2NH_3$$
$$H_2 + Cl_2 \rightarrow 2HCl$$
$$H_2 + I_2 \rightarrow 2HI$$

These four reactions have been written as "one way" reactions, using a single arrow $\rightarrow$, as have the majority of reactions previously encountered in this book. This is a reasonable description of many chemical reactions occurring under readily accessible conditions of temperature and pressure. Usually a reaction either goes or it does not go, and if it goes it goes to completion, i.e. all the reactants are transformed into products. It is always possible to write down the reverse of a chemical reaction, e.g.

$$2NH_3 \rightarrow N_2 + 3H_2$$
$$2H_2O \rightarrow O_2 + 2H_2$$
$$2HI \rightarrow I_2 + H_2$$

Clearly if a reaction goes to completion in one direction, it will not go at all in the other direction and vice versa. The second reaction listed above provides an example of this type. The third reaction though, between hydrogen and iodine, provides an example of a reaction which will occur to a significant extent in either direction; at equilibrium therefore, appreciable quantities of hydrogen, iodine and hydrogen iodide are all present. It is usual to write the equation for such a reaction with a double arrow to show that it can go either way.

$$H_2 + I_2 \rightleftharpoons 2HI$$

■ *Equilibrium constants...*

Now, a chemical reaction at equilibrium is not really static. The true situation is that the rate at which any of the reactants is produced is exactly equal to the rate at which it is lost by reaction; there is therefore no net change in its concentration. A rather simple picture along these lines leads to the definition of an **equilibrium constant**. Consider a gas containing a mixture of hydrogen, iodine and hydrogen iodide molecules at equilibrium. All these molecules will be in rapid motion and there will be frequent collisions between molecules. The simplest way of obtaining hydrogen iodide from hydrogen and iodine is to imagine a collision between the hydrogen and iodine molecules, and the emergence from this collision of two molecules of hydrogen iodide. (This is not the only possible mechanism for the reaction, but it suffices for the argument developed below.) When a hydrogen molecule collides with an iodine molecule, there is a possibility (though not a certainty) that chemical reaction will occur. The number of molecules of hydrogen iodide formed in this manner is therefore proportional to the number of collisions between hydrogen and iodine molecules. The number of such collisions is in turn proportional to the product of the concentrations of hydrogen and iodine molecules. The more molecules of a given type are present, the greater the probability that one of them will take part in a collision. It is usual to represent concentrations, in this case in units of moles per litre of gas, by placing the chemical symbol in square brackets. The concentration of hydrogen is represented by $[H_2]$ and that of iodine by $[I_2]$. We may therefore write that the rate of reaction between hydrogen and iodine is given by the equation:

$$Rate = k_1[H_2][I_2]$$

k_1 is a proportionality constant, the rate constant, which is determined by the efficiency of collisions between hydrogen and iodine molecules in producing chemical reaction. By a similar argument, the rate of the reaction between two hydrogen iodide molecules - to give hydrogen and iodine - is determined by the number of collisions involving two hydrogen iodide molecules which is proportional to $[HI]^2$, i.e.,

$$Rate = k^{-1}[HI]^2$$

At equilibrium, since there is no net change in the concentrations of any of the reactants, the forward rate and the backward rate must be the same, i.e.

$$k_1[H_2][I_2] = k_{-1}[HI]^2$$

Therefore $$\frac{[HI]^2}{[H_2][I_2]} = \frac{k_1}{k_{-1}} = K$$

K is called the equilibrium constant. For the reaction under discussion, at a temperature of 425 °C, K has a value of 54.5. If we know the concentration of any two of the reactants and we know K, the concentration of the third reactant is easily calculated. At equilibrium, in this reaction, there are significant concentrations of all the reactants.

The above considerations apply to <u>any</u> reaction. An equilibrium constant can always be written as the product of the concentrations of the products divided by the concentrations of the reactants. Thus in the case of the reaction producing ammonia:

$$N_2 + 3H_2 \rightleftharpoons 2NH_3$$

$$K = \frac{[NH_3]^2}{[N_2][H_2]^3}$$

For many reactions, the value of K is either very small or very large. If it is very large, at equilibrium there is very little of the reactants remaining, and the reaction has virtually gone to completion. This is the case for the reaction of hydrogen with chlorine. If K is very small, at equilibrium very little of the product has been formed, and the reaction effectively has not occurred. This was the case for the reaction of copper metal with water. For a large number of reactions, "reversibility" can be ignored since the reaction is either complete or fails to begin. For some reactions though, at equilibrium, significant concentrations of both reactants and products are present.

There are situations, when even very small equilibrium constants become important. A case in point is the dissociation of water to hydronium and hydroxide ions which was introduced earlier in this chapter. The reaction is:

$$2H_2O \rightleftharpoons H_3O^+ + OH^-$$

■ *The dissociation of water...*

An equilibrium constant can be defined as:

$$K = \frac{[H_3O^+][OH^-]}{[H_2O]^2}$$

In this case the equilibrium constant is very small. Since we are also concerned with aqueous solutions, the concentration of water molecules is always very large, and does not change significantly when the other concentrations are changed. Since it is constant, the term involving water can be omitted, and the equation written:

$$K = [H_3O^+][OH^-]$$

Defined in this way, K has a numerical value of 10^{-14} at 25 °C.

■ *pH...*

We introduced the concept of acids and bases in Chapter 2. Acids are sources of hydronium ions; bases are sources of hydroxide ions. Strong acids are prolific hydronium ion sources and weak acids provide only a few hydronium ions. Strong and weak bases similarly provide more or less hydroxide ions. The above definition of the dissociation constant for water, K, allows us to put our ideas on acids and bases on a quantitative basis. To do this we need to define the **pH** of a solution.

In a neutral solution, the number of hydronium and hydroxide ions are equal. They must both be at a concentration of 10^{-7}M, since $10^{-7} \times 10^{-7} = 10^{-14}$. (Footnote 1) 10^{-7}M is a very low concentration - a 1M solution of hydronium ions is defined as the concentration of a solution containing the molecular mass of hydronium ions in 1 litre, which is 19g of ions per litre; a 10^{-7}M solution corresponds to about a millionth of a gram per litre, a quantity much too small to weigh. This is the quantity of hydronium ions present in a gram mole (18g) of pure water. It is convenient to introduce a different scale to describe hydronium ion concentration. A concentration of 10^{-7}M in hydronium ions corresponds to a pH of 7; the recipe is to take the exponent of the concentration and change the sign. This is the pH of a neutral solution; a 0.1M solution of a strong acid contains is 0.1M in hydronium ions, i.e. 10^{-1}M and therefore has a pH of 1; a 0.1M solution of a strong base has a hydroxide ion concentration of 0.1M or 10^{-1}M. Since the product of the hydronium and hydroxide ion concentrations is 10^{-14}, the hydronium ion concentration must be 10^{-13}M, giving a pH of 13. A pH of 2.5 corresponds to a solution between 1/100 (pH 2) and 1/1000 (pH 3) molar in hydronium ions.

pH

1	*0.1M HCl*
2	
3	*Vinegar*
4	*Acid Rain*
5	
6	*Normal Rain*
7	*Distilled Water*
8	
9	*Sea Water*
10	
11	
12	*Ammonia*
13	*0.1M NaOH*
14	*Drano*

Fig. 3.4: pH's of Some Common Substances.

---

[1] Multiplication of two numbers involves the <u>addition</u> of the exponents rather than their multiplication. A hundred (10^2) multiplied by a thousand (10^3) is a hundred thousand (10^5) <u>not</u> a million (10^6).

The pH scale is a logarithmic scale; each change of one unit corresponds to a factor of ten in the hydronium ion concentration. Thus it is important to remember that in discussions of acid rain a change from pH 5 to pH 4 represents a tenfold increase in acidity. In the example introduced in Chapter 1, a change of six powers of ten, corresponding to the change from a neutral solution to a dilute acid, takes the viewer from a partial view of a human body at 1m, to continental view at 1000km, a change of scale which is easily comprehended as being very large.

Hydrolytic Reactions

Our discussion of the chemistry of water would be incomplete without some mention of hydrolysis. This term includes a variety of reactions involving water, acids or bases. They all have the common feature that a bond, X-Y, is broken with H adding to one atom, to give X-H, and OH adding to the other atom, to give Y-O-H. The reactive species are usually H^+ (or H_3O^+) or OH· so it is not surprising that such reactions usually go best in either acidic or basic solution. A simple example is provided by adding water to silicon tetrachloride. A vigorous reaction results, with the evolution of clouds of hydrogen chloride and the precipitation of gelatinous silicic acid. The Si-Cl bonds are the site of attack, with the Cl acquiring a hydrogen atom and the Si, hydroxyl groups.

$$SiCl_4 + 4H_2O \rightarrow 4HCl + Si(OH)_4$$

■ *The hydrolysis of organic compounds...*

It is of interest to try the same reaction with carbon tetrachloride; the two liquids are immiscible and even vigorous shaking gives no apparent reaction.

Demonstration 3.6

A highly exothermic reaction. The decomposition of ammonium dichromate is a highly exothermic reaction and can be demonstrated by constructing a "volcano" containing the substance. The reaction can be started with a little sugar and sulfuric acid. Once the reaction has been started it proceeds spontaneously, giving off showers of sparks with the appearance of a miniature volcano. **Warning** - this is a very vigorous reaction and should be carried out on an asbestos sheet well separated from students and from any flammable material.

$$(NH_4)_2Cr_2O_7(s) \rightarrow N_2(g) + 4H_2O(g) + Cr_2O_3(s)$$

In the light of the discussion above, one would be tempted to infer that the equilibrium constant for the reaction with silicon tetrachloride is large, and that for the reaction with carbon tetrachloride, is small. This conclusion would be wrong; both of these reactions have large equilibrium constants. The reaction with carbon tetrachloride is very slow, whereas that with silicon tetrachloride is fast. There is a reaction mechanism for the hydrolysis of silicon tetrachloride which is not available for carbon tetrachloride. The origin of this mechanism will be discussed in the next chapter.

It is of great practical importance that the hydrolysis of many compounds involving C-X bonds is very slow in neutral, or near neutral, solutions. (If this were not so, many of the biochemicals in the human body would react rapidly with the surrounding water and we would be unable to maintain a stable body.) Many common organic groups such as amide, ester, and ether linkages, are susceptible to hydrolysis according to the following general equations.

$$-CONHC- + H_2O \rightarrow -COOH + H_2NC-$$
amide　　　　　　　→　　acid　　amine

$$-COOC- + H_2O \rightarrow -COOH + HOC-$$
ester　　　　　　　→　　acid　　alcohol

$$-COC- + H_2O \rightarrow -COH + HOC-$$
ether　　　　　　　→　　alcohol　alcohol

Figure 3.5 gives the structures of some typical molecules involving these linkages.

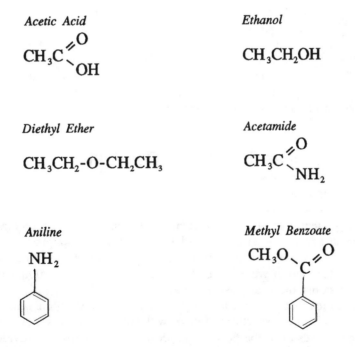

Fig. 3.5: The Structures of some Organic Compounds involved in Hydrolysis Reactions.

■ *Biopolymers are large molecules occurring in living organisms formed by joining together many small molecules...*

The equilibrium constants for these reactions are all large so that at equilibrium the compounds are almost completely hydrolyzed but, in the absence of catalysts, the hydrolysis reactions proceed only very slowly. Proteins and enzymes are polymers in which the subunit amino acids are linked by amide bonds. A living organism must produce protein by the reaction:

$$\text{acid} + \text{amine} \rightarrow \text{amide} + \text{water}$$

which is the opposite of the first of the hydrolysis reactions above. To synthesize protein, chemical energy must be provided to drive the reaction uphill. This would be of no avail though, if the resulting proteins were immediately hydrolyzed. (Fortunately they aren't.) Similar considerations apply to many other biopolymers such as the polysaccharides which are based on ether linkages. However not all carbon - based hydrolyses are slow, as is illustrated by the reactions of water with acid chlorides and acid anhydrides.

$$\begin{array}{ccc}
\text{-COCl} + H_2O & \rightarrow & \text{-COOH} + \text{HCl} \\
\text{acid chloride} & \rightarrow & \text{acid}
\end{array}$$

$$\begin{array}{ccc}
\text{-COOOC-} + H_2O \rightarrow & \text{-COOH} + & \text{HOOC-} \\
\text{acid anhydride} \quad\rightarrow & \text{acid} & \text{acid}
\end{array}$$

Not surprisingly, acid anhydride links are absent from important biopolymers.

This discussion indicates that the chemistry we encounter depends on **both** the position of equilibrium and the rate at which equilibrium is attained. This is particularly important for biochemical reactions.

What Determines Equilibrium Constants?

■ *The Second Law of thermodynamics...*

It is clearly important to chemists to be able to predict which chemical reactions will occur spontaneously and which will not. More precisely, we would like to be able to calculate the equilibrium constant for any chemical reaction. To obtain a complete description we also need to know the rates of reaction, but knowing the equilibrium constants is at least half-way.

The idea that certain changes occur spontaneously while others do not, is not restricted to chemical reactions; books will fall from a desk but do not normally levitate themselves from the floor to the desk. Energy must be provided in the latter case to overcome the downward pull of gravity. The metaphor of "driving a reaction uphill" was used above to suggest a similar situation in chemical reactions. Heat will flow spontaneously from a hot source to a cold source, but not in the reverse direction. This latter statement is one way of expressing the Second Law of thermodynamics, which also determines which chemical reactions will occur spontaneously. A large equilibrium constant results in a reaction which will proceed spontaneously from left to right - A is transformed to B in the reaction,

$$A \rightleftharpoons B$$

A small equilibrium constant leads to a reaction which goes from right to left - A is the predominant species at equilibrium.

■ *Free energy...*

The idea that a spontaneous reaction is going "downhill" suggests that spontaneity may be associated with the change in enthalpy of the reaction. If the reaction is exothermic, the heat content (enthalpy) is decreased, just as the potential energy of the book decreases when it is transferred to a lower level on the floor. The stronger and more stable the chemical bonds of a substance, the further down it is in a chemical well, just as a book on the floor is closer to the center of the earth, and hence further down in the gravitational well. If this were the full story, endothermic reactions would never occur; this is contrary to experience. It is however only half the story; a spontaneous reaction is always associated with a decrease in **free energy**. In a spontaneous reaction free energy always decreases and reaches its minimum when the reaction mixture has reached equilibrium. A large negative change in free energy during a reaction leads to a large equilibrium constant, and the reaction will proceed spontaneously.

■ *Entropy...*

The question is, therefore: What determines the change in free energy of a chemical reaction? As implied above, one of the factors is the change in enthalpy. If a chemical reaction leads to the formation of stronger chemical bonds, the products will have a lower enthalpy than the reactants, and this favors a large equilibrium constant, leading to a spontaneous reaction. There must though be another factor involved. This second factor is the change in **entropy**. The free energy change is determined by the combination of the change in enthalpy during the reaction and the change in entropy. The obvious question is: What is entropy? A complete answer to this question would involve a full chapter's discussion and, for the present, we will be content with a very qualitative indication.

The idea of entropy can be approached by considering a very simple reaction - dissolving salt (NaCl) in water. The enthalpy change arises from the loss of electrostatic attraction energy between the positive and negative ions in the solid, compared to the gain in energy produced by solvation of the ions in solution. The reaction, as we have seen, is just slightly endothermic, so these two effects almost cancel. The other difference is that the structure of a sodium chloride crystal is very ordered, whereas the ions in solution are jumbled up with no specific geometric relation to each other. There are many more ways of achieving a disordered arrangement of the ions than of making an ordered crystal in which each positive ion is surrounded by negative ions and each negative ion surrounded by positive ions. If each arrangement is equally probable, the more random the arrangement, the more favored the reaction leading to this arrangement. An increase in entropy is associated with a decrease in order and leads to a decrease in free energy. Thus our understanding of entropy is that it reflects the tendency of systems to spontaneously seek the most disordered state available. Living systems are very ordered entities and hence cannot be at chemical equilibrium. This topic will be developed in more detail in the third part of this book.

CHAPTER 4

Atoms and Molecules

Introduction

Dalton's atoms were structureless and featureless. Their only required property was that atoms of the same element were identical and atoms of different elements were different. Some elements are more different than others; the two elements sodium and potassium are both metals and possess quite similar chemical and physical properties; they are clearly very different from the non-metals carbon and chlorine. Bromine and iodine, on the other hand, show similarities to chlorine. All of these observations suggest that atoms have an internal structure and that the similarities and differences should be explained by this structure. Clues to the nature of the internal structure of atoms appeared in the nineteenth century, but the real understanding of atomic structure was not achieved until the twentieth century. A complete mathematical description of atomic and molecular structure is now possible. In this chapter the structure of atoms, and the manner in which they are assembled to give molecules, will be described in a qualitative manner.

The Periodic Table

During the first half of the nineteenth century, the number of known elements increased sharply. Various attempts were made to classify these elements, to account for the properties of the known elements and predict new elements. A successful solution to this problem was proposed by the Russian chemist Mendeleev in 1869; his scheme is known as the Periodic Table and has remained virtually unchanged until the present day. An up-to-date version of the Periodic Table is provided at the end of this book. Based on the observed regularities in chemical properties, Mendeleev predicted the existence of three new elements. This prediction was fulfilled with the discovery of gallium (1874), scandium (1879) and germanium (1885). The only additions since that time have been the addition of the noble gases, the completion of the series of lanthanide elements, and the discovery of short-lived radioactive elements of high atomic mass.

■ *Periods and groups...*

The Periodic Table was constructed by listing the elements in order of increasing atomic mass; when this is done, it is observed that there is a characteristic repetition of chemical properties at regular intervals. Elements in the same column in the table belong to the same **group** and usually have similar chemical properties; elements in the same row belong to the same **period**. Later periods contain more elements than earlier periods. Thus the first period has just two elements - hydrogen and helium. The next two periods have eight elements each; they are often called the first and second short periods. They are followed by two periods each containing eighteen elements - the first and second long periods. A third long period parallels the first two, but has an additional fourteen elements, the lanthanides, inserted in the middle to give a total of thirty-two elements. The final period is incomplete; the heaviest elements become progressively less stable due to radioactive decay. The modern Periodic Table contains some 103 elements. Elements beyond 103 exist only for very short periods of time and are not usually included in the table.

Virtually all of the chemistry discussed in the present book involves elements in the earlier part of the Periodic Table. Hydrogen is the first element; carbon, nitrogen and oxygen are found in the first short period; sodium, phosphorus, sulfur and chlorine occur in the second short period, as do aluminum and silicon, the major elements of the lithosphere. These elements account for most of the chemistry of Gaia. If we add potassium, calcium, iron, copper and zinc from the first long period, the list, for all intents and purposes, is complete. This is not to say that "trace" elements do not play their part in Gaia. In fact they often serve important, though specialized, roles; examples of such usage will be encountered later in this book. For the time being though, the discussion will be confined to the two short periods and the first long period of the table.

■ *Metals and non-metals...*

The groups are numbered I to VIII from left to right in the Periodic Table. In the long period, ten "transition" metals are inserted between groups II and III, to increase the number of elements in a long period to eighteen. Metals occur on the left-hand side of the table, non-metals occur on the right-hand side; on going from left to right there is a steady transition from metallic to non-metallic properties. Group I contains the alkali metals, lithium (Li), sodium (Na) and potassium (K); they typically form salts such as lithium chloride (LiCl), sodium chloride (NaCl) and potassium chloride (KCl). The alkaline earth metals, beryllium (Be), magnesium (Mg) and calcium (Ca) are placed in group II; the metals are less reactive than their alkali counterparts, as was demonstrated in Chapter 3 by their reaction with water. The alkaline earths form salts such as $BeCl_2$, $MgCl_2$ and $CaCl_2$. As has been noted earlier, salts are dissociated to ions in aqueous solution. Since the alkaline earths each combine with two Cl^- ions, the metal ions must bear a positive charge of two, in contrast to the positive charge of one on the alkali ions. Thus potassium gives K^+ ions but the neighboring calcium gives Ca^{2+} ions. An equivalent statement is that potassium has a **valency** of one and calcium a valency of two. The concept of valency can be equally well applied to compounds which do not dissociate into ions. Thus in group III boron forms BCl_3 and in group IV carbon forms CCl_4. These are both non-ionic compounds - CCl_4 does not dissociate into C^{4+} and $4Cl^-$ - but the valencies of boron and carbon are three and four respectively, based on the number of chlorine atoms combining with a single atom of boron or carbon. A common valency is the chemically most significant property of elements in the same group of the Periodic Table; it was this property which lead Mendeleev to propose his system of classification. The valency of an element extends to its compounds with all elements, not just with chlorine. Thus the valencies of carbon, nitrogen, oxygen and fluorine may be deduced from the formulae of the hydrides, CH_4, NH_3, H_2O and HF as four, three, two and one respectively. Similarly the earlier elements form the oxides Li_2O,

BeO, B_2O_3 and CO_2. Since the valency of oxygen is two, this series leads to valencies of one, two, three and four for these elements, consistent with the deductions based on chlorine compounds. It should however be noted that some elements can show more than one valency; thus phosphorus forms both PCl_3 and PCl_5, indicating valencies of three or five. A theory of atomic structure should be able to account for both the consistencies and the variations in valency. In group III, boron (B) is a non-metal but aluminum (Al), in the second short period, is a metal. The element below aluminum in the first long period (gallium, Ga) is also a metal. In group IV both carbon and silicon are non-metals, but the corresponding element in the first long period, germanium (Ge), shows metallic properties. The heavy line in the Periodic Table marks the transition from metals to non-metals. The transition elements, which are inserted between groups II and III, are all metals; they show a characteristic feature of wide variability in valencies. Group VII, the halogens, fluorine (F), chlorine (Cl) and bromine (Br), show the most pronounced non-metallic properties; they consistently form anions, e.g. Cl^-, rather than cations such as Na^+. The final group, VIII, comprises the noble gases such as helium (He), neon (Ne) and argon (Ar). It used to be said that the noble gases formed no compounds, and therefore had no chemistry. More recently a few compounds of the heavier noble gases, particularly xenon (Xe), have been synthesized but their outstanding characteristic is nonetheless chemical inertness.

Electrons, Protons and Neutrons

■ *The atomic nature of electricity...*

It was originally postulated that atoms were the smallest conceivable particles; the discovery of still smaller entities destroyed this view and lead to the investigation of atomic structure. The first hint of subatomic structure was provided by Faraday's studies of electrolysis; the electrolysis of aqueous solutions to give hydrogen and oxygen or to deposit copper, has been described previously. Faraday found that a constant quantity of electricity lead to the production of a constant quantity of chemical product: one Faraday of electricity produces one mole of hydrogen atoms (or a half mole of hydrogen molecules), a half mole of copper, or a quarter mole of oxygen molecules in the electrolytic reactions described in Chapter 3. This suggested that electricity, like matter, must have an atomic nature and be associated on a one to one basis, with the atoms of matter. The atom of electricity was discovered later in the nineteenth century during studies of cathode rays in an early precursor of present-day television tubes. It was named the electron and proved to have a mass approximately 1/1800 that of a hydrogen atom and a negative charge. Avogadro's number of electrons, 6.02×10^{23}, comprises one Faraday of electric charge.

If electrons are one of the constituents of matter there must also be positive particles, since matter in bulk is electrically neutral. A variety of such particles was indeed discovered in the positive rays from electric discharges in gases; such discharges are now familiar in the form of fluorescent lights. The least massive, discovered in discharges in hydrogen gas, were named protons. The mass of a proton is very close to the mass of a hydrogen atom and the charge is equal, but opposite, to that of an electron. A third particle is needed to complete the picture at this level of sophistication; the neutron has a mass very similar to that of a proton, but it has no electric charge. The properties of these sub-atomic particles are summarized in Table 4.1.

Table 4.1: Properties of Subatomic Particles

Particle	Rel Mass	Abs Mass(g)	Charge
Proton	1.0000	1.6726×10^{-24}	+1
Neutron	1.0014	1.6749×10^{-24}	0
Electron	0.000545	9.1094×10^{-28}	-1

■ *The atomic nucleus...*

One other piece of information suffices to complete a model of atomic structure. In 1911 Rutherford bombarded metal foil samples with positively charged particles. Most of the particles passed through the foil with very little change of direction; a few were deflected through large angles. Rutherford explained this result by postulating that a metal atom in the foil has a small positively charged nucleus which is responsible for the large angle scattering. It was supposed that this nucleus was composed of protons and neutrons and contributed nearly all the mass of the atom. Electrical neutrality was obtained by having an appropriate number of electrons orbiting the central nucleus. The dimensions of the nucleus are only about 1/10,000 those of the atom, accounting for the small number of nuclear collisions. Nearly all of the atom consists of "empty space". The small size of the nucleus compared to the atom was noted in Figure 1.1 of Chapter 1.

Atomic Number and Isotopes

■ *Why atomic masses are not integral...*

A coherent picture of the structure of the Periodic Table can now be constructed. Different elements differ in the number of protons in their nuclei; hydrogen has one, helium two, lithium three and so on until the last naturally occurring element, uranium (U), which has 92. A neutral atom must have an equal number of electrons orbiting the central nucleus; the number of protons, or of electrons, is the **atomic number** of the element and determines its position in the Periodic Table. The existence of neutrons differentiates between atomic number and atomic mass; thus hydrogen, with atomic mass one, has one proton and no neutrons in its nucleus. Helium, atomic number two, has an atomic mass of four; its nucleus therefore contains two protons and two neutrons; fluorine, with atomic number 9 and atomic mass 19, must have 9 protons and 10 neutrons. Note that atomic masses, since they are multiples of the mass of a hydrogen atom, should be exact whole numbers. An examination of the Periodic Table, which gives the atomic mass of each element, shows that they are not. There are two reasons for this: one accounts for some small differences, and the other for the major discrepancies. The precise atomic masses of hydrogen and helium are in a ratio a little less than four; this difference represents the nuclear binding energy of helium. Energy and mass are equivalent, and if energy is gained in forming the stable helium nucleus, mass must be lost. The amount of mass lost is not very large, but it is the loss of this small amount of mass during the fusion of hydrogen nuclei to helium nuclei, which powers the sun and provides the driving force behind the story of Gaia.

The major discrepancies from non-integral atomic weights arise from the existence of **isotopes**. If two separate atoms contain the same number of protons and electrons they are chemically identical; but this rule says nothing about the number of neutrons in the two atoms. Two atoms containing the same numbers of protons, but different numbers of neutrons, are said to be isotopic; isotopes have nearly identical chemical properties. Some elements occur naturally as mixtures of isotopes. Thus chlorine is made up of two isotopes; one has 17 protons and 18 neutrons for a total mass of 35 units; the other has 17 protons and 20 neutrons for a total mass of 37 units. The constancy of the 17 protons in chlorine ensures that the two have the same chemical properties. In nature they occur in a constant mixture of 75.77% ^{35}Cl and 24.23% ^{37}Cl; as a result, the average atomic mass, which is what is measured in chemical experiments, is 35.453 which is not a whole number. Although isotopes lead to only very small chemical differences, they have great importance in nuclear reactions and we shall encounter them again in discussions of nuclear power.

The above considerations show that the periodic table should have been constructed using atomic numbers, rather than atomic masses. The existence of isotopes means that the order of atomic numbers is not necessarily the same as that of atomic masses. There is one case where atomic number and atomic mass are in reverse order: argon, atomic number 18, has atomic mass 39.95; potassium, atomic number 19, has atomic mass of 39.10. Based on atomic numbers, argon is in group VIII with helium and neon, and potassium in group I with lithium and sodium; based on atomic masses the assignments would be switched. The first choice is clearly correct. It is fortunate that this type of reversal is unusual, otherwise Mendeleev would have found the construction of the Periodic Table much more challenging.

Atomic Radii and Ionization Energies

Many physical properties of the elements, in addition to their chemical properties, show periodic behavior; these physical properties cast even more light on the structures of atoms. Two such properties are considered in the present section. Ions in solution have already been encountered in the discussion of acids, bases and salts; a typical example is Na^+. They can also be formed in the gas phase, where they are not solvated. A simple equation for the formation of the sodium ion can be written.

$$Na(g) \rightarrow Na^+(g) + e^- \qquad \Delta H = +496kJ$$

■ *The formation of ions...*

In this equation e^- represents an electron. The enthalpy change in this reaction is known as the ionization energy of sodium. Strictly speaking it is the first ionization energy, since a further reaction:

$$Na^+(g) \rightarrow Na^{2+}(g) + e^- \qquad \Delta H = +4563kJ$$

can be written to define a second ionization energy. Notice that the reactions refer to atoms and ions in the gas phase. As has been discussed previously, ions in solution are extensively solvated, and the enthalpy changes in aqueous solution would be quite different. Note also that ionization energies are positive - energy must be provided to remove an electron from a sodium atom - hence the reaction is endothermic. The second equation tells us that almost ten times as much energy is needed to remove the second electron as to remove the first. Part of this large increase is due to the fact that a negatively charged electron is being pulled away from a positively charged sodium ion; work must be done to overcome the electrostatic attraction between the two particles. However, by itself this factor is insufficient to account for the very large difference between the first and second ionization energies.

Figure 4.1 shows a graph of the first ionization energies for the first 20 elements;

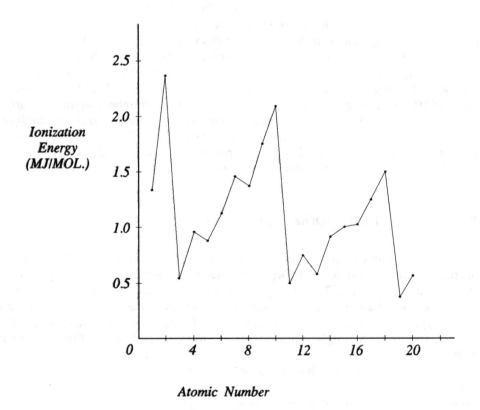

Fig. 4.1: Ionization Energies. The first ionization energies of the first twenty elements vary periodically.

■ Periodic properties...

Atomic radii provide a second periodic physical property. Some care is necessary in defining an atomic radius; for this purpose a diatomic molecule is viewed as two, touching, spherical atoms. The interatomic separation in a molecule of chlorine, Cl_2, can be measured; it has a value of 198pm, where a picometer (pm) is 10^{-9}m. The atomic radius of chlorine is half this distance, 99pm; the atomic radius of hydrogen, obtained in a similar manner, is 37pm; that of oxygen can be obtained from the O-H bond length of water by subtracting 37pm for the radius of hydrogen. In this way a table of radii can be built up. (It is difficult to obtain radii for the noble gases since they form very few compounds.) Figure 4.2 shows a plot of such radii for the first 20 elements, omitting the noble gases.

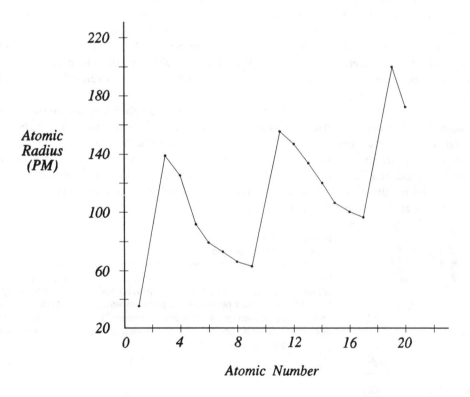

Fig. 4.2: Covalent Radii. The sizes (covalent radii) of the first twenty elements vary in a similar manner to the ionization energies.

Periodic behavior is again observed; the alkali metals have the largest atoms in a period; atomic radii decrease until the halogen is reached and then take a large jump to the next alkali metal. Within a group, the radii increase with increasing atomic number. The similarities between Figures 4.1 and 4.2 are obvious.

Electron Shells

■ *Building atoms...*

The key to understanding the periodic properties of atoms was provided by the discovery that the electrons orbiting around an atomic nucleus can only possess certain well defined energies. (The situation is quite different from that of planets revolving around a central sun. There is no rule of nature which says that planets can only be found at certain distances from the sun, and hence must have only certain potential energies; in principle a planet can orbit at any distance from the sun.) The permissible energies and orbits of electrons in atoms are specified by a set of **quantum numbers**; four such numbers are required. A second rule says that no two electrons can have all four quantum numbers the same. The latter rule is known as the Pauli principle. Every time a proton is added to the nucleus of an atom, an additional electron is required outside the nucleus. Electrons are added as economically as possible; higher energy slots are not used until the lower ones have been filled. The atoms that comprise the Periodic Table can therefore be built up in a systematic manner. The number of electrons and the energy levels filled, determine the chemistry of an element.

The statements made in the previous paragraph were all derived from **quantum theory**. This theory was originally developed to account for a number of what were at that time —the early part of the twentieth century— "anomalous" observations in spectroscopy and atomic physics. For example, different elements, when excited in a flame or electric discharge, emit light of characteristic wavelengths; thus sodium salts all impart a characteristic yellow color to a flame, potassium salts a lilac color and barium salts a green color. These are atomic spectra.

Demonstration 4.1
Flame tests for metal ions.
A property of atoms and ions is that they emit light of characteristic wavelengths when heated or excited in an electric discharge. An example is provided by the color of the discharge in a neon lamp. This property can be readily illustrated by dipping a platinum wire into solutions of different metal salts and then holding the wire in a flame. Lithium and strontium give red colors, barium, copper and boron various shades of green, sodium yellow and potassium a pale lilac.

■ *Quantum theory...*

Classical physics was unable to account for these different colors. Quantum theory allowed the emission wavelengths to be calculated precisely. More refined versions of the original theory have since taken over most of modern physics and a large part of chemistry and biology. We shall be content to take statements such as "no two electrons can have all four quantum numbers the same" as revealed truth. (In doing this, we are not really adopting a very different approach to that found in much more sophisticated and mathematically oriented textbooks.) Quantum theory provides the rules for calculating, with great accuracy, the values of many measurable quantities. To ask what, if anything, is behind the rules may not even be a permissible question. The statement of the Pauli principle, given above, can be paraphrased to say that the only measurable properties of an electron associated with a positively charged nucleus, are the values of four quantum numbers; if therefore, two electrons have all four quantum numbers the same, they are, by definition, the same electron. Sir Cyril Hinshelwood, in a learned footnote (in Latin) in his book *The Structure of Physical Chemistry*, pointed out that this logical argument had been suggested some time earlier by St. Thomas Aquinas, in a discussion of angels. It was concluded that "since angels have neither form nor matter, no two can be alike". The idea is certainly remarkably similar to that behind the Pauli principle.

■ *Energy levels...*

The original version of the quantum theory envisaged the electrons circulating about the nucleus, following trajectories similar to planetary orbits. Modern versions have abandoned this picture and the electrons are now said to occupy **orbitals**, which have some of the geometric properties of the original orbits, but which are much less specific. It is not possible to say that an electron is at a certain position at a certain time, as it is for planets, but only that it is more likely to be found in one place than in another. The energy levels available to electrons in atoms are not evenly spaced; the first two electrons can be accommodated at a low energy but the third requires a much higher energy. The first two elements are hydrogen and helium and the two electrons required complete the first electron **shell**. The much higher energy of the third electron is reflected in the lower first ionization energy of lithium. Electrons placed in a higher energy **orbital** require less energy for their removal. This third electron, first utilized in lithium, marks the start of the second electron shell. Again the second electron in the shell is added fairly economically to give beryllium. In this case though, the third electron requires only a modest amount of additional energy. The same is true of the next five electrons and the second shell is completed with the addition of a total of eight electrons. This brings us to neon, the second of the noble gases. The overall increase in ionization energy on progressing along the period is caused by the increasing positive charge on the nucleus. The greater the positive charge on the nucleus, the greater its attraction for a negatively charged electron, and the more ionization energy required to remove such an electron. After completing this second shell, the third shell starts with sodium. Again, this first electron in the shell is very easy to remove, leading to a low ionization energy. Thus the ion Na^+ is easily formed and plays a prominent part in the chemistry of sodium. However the removal of a second electron from sodium to give Na^{2+} would necessitate taking one from the previous filled shell. This requires a great deal of energy, and so Na^{2+} plays no part in the chemistry of sodium. The next element, Mg, has two easily removable electrons and so Mg^{2+} is the ion of choice in magnesium chemistry. The third shell again requires eight electrons and is completed at the noble gas argon. Filling the fourth shell is a little different. It starts off in much the same way with an alkali metal, K, and an alkaline earth, Ca. There is then a pause, corresponding to the filling of a set of ten orbitals (or strictly speaking, five orbitals each containing two electrons) which had previously been left empty because of their high energy, before the earlier pattern of elements is resumed. Filling this shell corresponds to the first long period of the table, and is completed with another noble gas, krypton.

■ *Orbital levels...*

The electron shells described above are closely related to the four quantum numbers required by theory. The principal quantum number, n, determines the number of the shell. There are subsidiary quantum numbers which can assume values leading to the accommodation of 2, 2 + 6, 2 + 6 + 10, 2 + 6 + 10 + 14, electrons for principal quantum numbers of 1, 2, 3 and 4 respectively. The orbitals holding the electrons in the sub-shells containing 2, 6, 10 and 14 electrons respectively, are labelled s, p, d and f. The principal quantum number determines the size of the orbital but the s, p, d and f orbitals have different shapes; the shapes of various orbitals are illustrated in Figure 4.3.

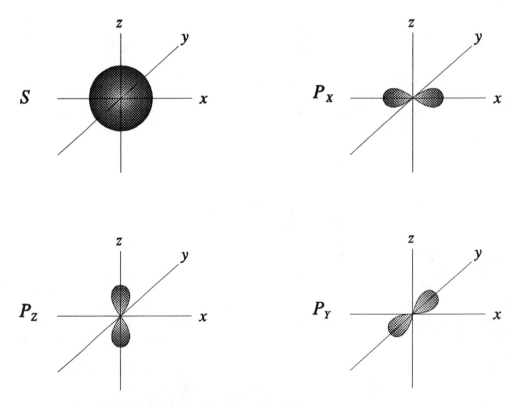

Fig. 4.3: The Shapes of Orbitals. There is only one s orbital for each principal quantum number. It is shaped like a sphere. There are three p orbitals, each having lobes pointing along the X, the Y or the Z axes.

The first shell corresponds to the filling of orbitals with principal quantum number 1 (1s) and the second shell to those with principal quantum number 2 (2s and 2p). The third shell fills only the first two subsets with n = 3 (3s and 3p). The third subset (3d), containing 10 electrons, is deferred until the n = 4 levels have been started. The building up of the heavier elements proceeds in a similar way with the filling of more and more subsets being deferred.

■ *The sizes of atoms...*

A final remark in this section deals with the periodic variation of atomic radii. The size of atoms is determined by how far the electron orbitals extend around the positively charged nucleus. If an atom is strongly bonded to another atom it will appear to be quite small; if it is not bonded, or weakly bonded, it will be large. If it is present as a positive ion it will be smaller than as a neutral atom; but a negative ion is always larger than the same atom with no charge. Care must be taken to compare only radii of atoms in similar bonding situations. The data plotted in Figure 4.2 have been selected according to this limitation. The regular variation with atomic number results from the shell structure of the electrons. While a shell is in the process of being filled, the increasing positive charge of the nucleus contracts the electron shell, and leads to a diminution in atomic radius. As soon as the shell is filled, the radius is determined by the radius of the next electron shell and a large increase is observed; hence the maximum radii occur with the alkali metals.

Ionic, Covalent and Polar Bonds

■ *Sharing electrons...*

This shell model for atomic structure can be readily extended to provide a simple model for molecular structure. Maximum stability is associated with filled shells, corresponding to noble gas, or octet, electron configurations; this can be achieved by forming molecules. The simplest case occurs when one atom has one electron more than a noble gas configuration, and the other has one electron less. An electron is transferred from the former to the latter, e.g. sodium and fluorine form the ionic compound Na^+F^-; both atoms in this way achieve the desired configuration. Extension to divalent metal compounds such as $MgCl_2$ is obvious. However, the successive ionization energies of metals become larger and larger, and ions with increasing multiple positive charges are rarer and rarer; Al^{3+} is one of the few tripositive ions. Similarly, most single atom anions are mononegative; O^{2-} exists in crystals, but not in solution, and there are very few other examples. Thus there are limitations to the number of compounds formed by ionic bonding. An alternative approach is provided by covalent bonding, in which the atoms achieve an octet, the preferred arrangement for short periods, by sharing electrons, rather than by transferring them. Fluorine atoms each have seven electrons in addition to the two which make up the helium noble gas shell. If two such atoms share a pair of electrons, each can achieve a count of eight to reach the neon configuration; the shared electrons are included in the count of each atom. The sharing of a pair of electrons constitutes a single, covalent bond. In contrast to ionic bonding, covalent bonding occurs best between identical atoms; if the electrons are to be shared and both atoms are the same, they will each get an equal share. For complete transfer of an electron to form an ionic bond, the atoms must be as far removed as possible in the periodic table. In a covalent bond the electrons are preferentially situated between the atoms and are attracted to both positively charged nuclei. Quantum theory calculations show that this leads to a net gain in energy. The increased attractions more than make up for the additional repulsions between the positive nuclei and between the negative electrons in the bond. Thus both ionic and covalent bonding rely on electrostatic attractions to hold the molecule or the crystal together. Quantum theory does not introduce any new force to explain chemical bonds; it simply provides the correct recipe for calculating the electrostatic interactions between charged particles.

■ *Double and triple bonds...*

This simple picture of bonding can be extended. An oxygen atom has six electrons over and above the two of helium; these electrons are often described as valence electrons. Two oxygen atoms have twelve valence electrons, and if each is to achieve a total count of eight, four must be shared; this constitutes a double bond. The energy gained by forming a double bond is greater than that gained by forming a single bond, but not twice as great; two single bonds are usually worth more than one double bond. Nitrogen atoms have five valence electrons and must share six —three from each atom— to form a triple bond, to reach the neon configuration. The triple bond in the N_2 molecule has very high stability, much more so than the double bond in O_2, and this is reflected in the greater chemical reactivity of oxygen compared with nitrogen described in Chapter 2. A different kind of situation occurs in the bonding between different atoms. A good example is provided by hydrogen chloride, HCl. Hydrogen has one valence electron and chlorine has seven. They could form an ionic compound by transferring the electron from hydrogen to chlorine to give H^+Cl^-. Alternatively they could share an electron pair and form a covalent bond. Hydrogen would attain the helium configuration instead of having an empty 1s orbital, and chlorine would still possess the argon configuration. The two alternatives are not mutually exclusive; the sharing of the electron pair can be unequal, so that the electrons are located closer to the chlorine atom than to the hydrogen atom. This is what happens and the result is known as a polar bond. All bonds between different atoms are polar to some extent. Only when the atoms are very different does the electron transfer become complete and an ionic compound result.

Dipole Moments and Electronegativity

■ *An electrophilic reagent looks for negative charge...*
■ *A nucleophilic reagent looks for positive charge...*

The polarity of chemical bonds is important in determining chemical reactivity. An electron-poor reactant (known as an **electrophile**), will preferentially react at an electron-rich site and an electron-rich reactant (a **nucleophile**), at a site with excess positive charge. This is simply a question of unlike charges attracting each other.

Some form of prediction concerning the polarity of bonds is clearly desirable. Experimentally, the distribution of charge within bonds can be deduced from the measurement of **dipole moments**; the dipole moment of a bond is the product of the atomic separation (the bond length) and the amount of charge transferred. A completely ionic bond corresponds to the complete transfer of one electron. The dipole moment for such a situation can be readily calculated. Comparison of the experimental value with this calculation provides a measure of the polarity of a bond; thus the bond in hydrogen chloride is found by this means to be 17% ionic. The bond in hydrogen fluoride is more ionic than that of hydrogen chloride, and that in hydrogen bromide less ionic. Data on dipole moments and other information can be used to construct a table of the relative affinities of different elements for electrons, which are known as **electronegativities**. Some electronegativity values are given in Table 4.2.

Table 4.2: Relative Electronegativities of Some Elements

H 2.2						
Li 1.0	Be 1.6	B 2.0	C 2.6	N 3.0	O 3.4	F 4.0
Na 0.9	Mg 1.3	Al 1.6	Si 1.9	P 2.2	S 2.6	Cl 3.2
K 0.8	Ca 1.0					Br 3.0

■ *Electronegativities...*

The absolute values of numbers assigned as electronegativities are not significant. The trend though is meaningful; the higher the electronegativity, the greater the tendency for an atom to be the negative end of a polar bond. The greater the difference in electronegativities of the two atoms, the closer the bond to ionic; the smaller the difference the more it resembles a pure covalent bond. On this scale, fluorine and oxygen are the most electronegative elements and sodium and potassium the least. A common feature in organic and biological molecules is the carbonyl group, $C=O$. The electronegativity of carbon is 2.6 and that of oxygen 3.4. The bond is therefore polar, with an enhanced positive charge on the carbon and an enhanced negative charge on the oxygen. A nucleophilic reagent, such as the hydroxyl ion OH^-, will therefore attack the carbon end of the bond; an electrophilic reagent, such as the hydronium ion H_3O^+, will tend to bond to the oxygen atom through the more electropositive H.

The Shapes of Molecules

Molecules have characteristic and well defined shapes. In the case of very complex molecules, such as proteins and nucleic acids, the shape is often very complicated and tied directly to the biochemical function of the molecule. In the case of simple molecules, such as those formed between elements in the first and second short periods, the geometries can be more easily described and explained. Various molecules in this category will be discussed in the present section. The next section will consider the rationalization of these geometries by simple bonding theories.

■ *Simple molecular geometries...*

Diatomic molecules are of necessity linear. In the first short period, multiple bonds are common, and many diatomic molecules are formed - N_2, O_2, F_2, CO, NO, HF. There are two possibilities for triatomic molecules, linear and bent; carbon dioxide, CO_2 and nitrous oxide, N_2O, are good examples of linear molecules and water, H_2O, is a prime example of a bent molecule. There are also two possibilities for tetratomic molecules - a planar triangular structure and a pyramidal structure; boron trifluoride, BF_3, is an example of the former, and ammonia, NH_3, of the latter. In these earlier periods all molecules of the type XY_4 are tetrahedral in geometry; methane, CH_4, and silicon tetrachloride, $SiCl_4$, are examples. (The alternative, square planar compounds, occurs only in transition metal chemistry.) In the second short period there is a much reduced tendency to form multiple bonds. To form an effective multiple bond it is necessary to squash the atoms close together; the second row elements are larger than those of the first row, and resist this process. They often adopt a different strategy to attain an octet configuration; thus phosphorus, instead of forming P_2 with a triple bond, exists as P_4 with the four atoms at the corners of a tetrahedron. Each phosphorus forms three single bonds to the other three atoms, rather than one triple bond to a second atom. Similarly sulfur exists as S_8 molecules in which the eight atoms form a puckered ring; each sulfur atom forms two single bonds rather than the double bond of O_2. In the second short period higher coordination numbers are possible. Examples are phosphorus pentachloride, which has trigonal bipyramidal structure, and silicon hexafluoride which is octahedral. The geometries of a number of these molecules are illustrated in Figure 4.4.

Lewis Structures and Molecular Geometry

Two bonding rules have been encountered thus far: bonds are formed by pairs of electrons and each atom prefers to accumulate an octet of eight electrons. Structures written according to these rules are often called Lewis dot structures, in honor of the originator of this formalism, and to recognize the fact that we usually represent the electrons by dots. Electrons not used up in bonds are still written in pairs and these are appropriately known as non-bonding, unshared or "lone" pairs. In Figure 4.5 Lewis dot structures are shown for a selection of the molecules which have been encountered previously.

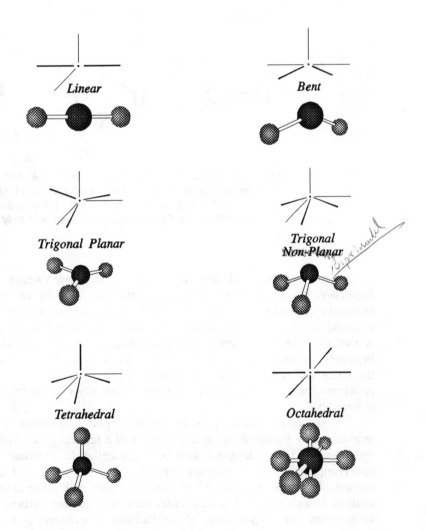

Fig. 4.4: Molecular Geometries. Some typical shapes of small molecules.

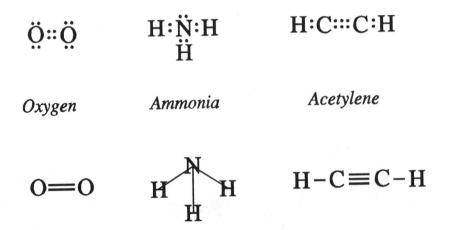

Fig. 4.5: Lewis Dot Structures. A single bond is represented by an electron pair (:) or a dash (N-H). A double bond is represented by four dots (::) or a double dash (O=O). Lone pairs (:) are associated with only one atom.

An extension of this theory is provided by Valence Shell Electron Pair Repulsion Theory (VSEPR). The additional feature is the recognition that negative charged electrons repel each other, and hence the electron pairs will keep as far apart as possible. This factor determines the geometries of molecules. A further refinement is that the repulsion between non-bonding pairs will be rather larger than that between bonding pairs, since the former are associated with a single atom, whereas the latter are partly delocalized to a more distant second atom. These very simple concepts lead to remarkably accurate predictions regarding the geometries of molecules.

An octet is made up of four electron pairs; repulsion between these pairs is minimized by having them at the corners of a tetrahedron. The preference for this configuration can be demonstrated by tying together four sausage shaped balloons and observing the geometry assumed. Unless otherwise constrained, they will point to the corners of a tetrahedron in order to interfere with each other as little as possible. The analogy is with tetrahedral molecules such as methane, carbon tetrachloride or the ammonium ion. A variation of the balloon experiment, is to replace one of the "bonding" balloons by a fatter balloon representing a non-bonding pair. The result is a pyramidal molecule, exemplified by ammonia or by the hydronium ion. The model correctly predicts that the angle between the N-H bonds will be rather less than a tetrahedral angle because the bulkier lone pair forces the hydrogens closer together. Two bonding pairs and two lone pairs lead to a bent molecule such as water with an H-O-H angle between 90° and 109.5°, the tetrahedral angle. The two lone pairs of water reduce the angle more (to 104.5°) than does the single lone pair of ammonia (which has an angle of 107.5°).

Demonstration 4.2

Illustration of molecular geometries using balloons.

The common geometries assumed by simple molecules can be illustrated by balloons representing electron pairs. The balloons, like the electron pairs, will assume the geometry which keeps them furthest apart. Four balloons automatically take up a tetrahedral configuration, five a trigonal bipyramid and six an octahedron. Lone pairs can be represented by slightly fatter balloons. A tetrahedron containing one lone pair, exemplified by the NH_3 molecule, has a slightly small bond angel than one with no lone pairs (e.g. CH_4) and one with two lone pairs (e.g.H_2O) has a still smaller angle.

■ *Planar and linear molecules...*

This model will also accommodate molecules containing multiple bonds. If an atom is involved in double bonding, four of its eight electrons are located in this bond; this leaves two more bonding or non-bonding pairs. These three sets of electrons —four in the double bond and two each in the single bonds or lone pairs— can best avoid each other by assuming a triangular planar configuration. A molecule such as ethylene, $CH_2{=}CH_2$, is therefore planar with angles of 120° between the bonds. Many organic molecules contain carbonyl groups, $C{=}O$, which are also planar; the carbon has a double bond and two bonding pairs and the oxygen a double bond and two unshared pairs. If a triple bond is involved, there are only two sets of electrons and these are best kept apart in a linear arrangement, with a 180° angle between the three atoms. Acetylene, C_2H_2, and hydrogen cyanide, HCN, are examples of this type of bonding. Linearity also occurs for the central atom of a molecule such as carbon dioxide, CO_2, which has two groups of four valence electrons. Lewis dot diagrams for these molecules are shown in Figure 4.5. These simple geometric rules, when applied to a large number of atoms joined together in a polymer, can account for the very complicated architecture of the large molecules involved in biological systems. Tetrahedral carbons and planar carbonyl groups, appropriately combined, can give molecules of almost any desired shape. An example of a model of such a complex shape is shown in Figure 4.6.

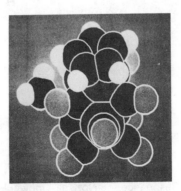

Fig. 4.6: Shapes of Large Molecules. A large molecule can have a very complex shape. This molecule has three cobalt atoms (two partly visible) with a carbon completing a tetrahedron; this carbon is linked through a COO-group to a ring of six carbons substituted with white hydrogens and black carbons which is visible at the top. The remainder of the molecule is comprised of two CO groups attached to each of the cobalt atoms.

■ *Why is silicon tetrachloride more reactive than carbon tetrachloride?*

The octet rule applies to most compounds formed from elements in the first two short periods. There are some exceptions; in some cases there are just not enough electrons to achieve octet configurations. This is the case for early elements such as boron, as illustrated by a compound such as BF_3. The boron has three bonding pairs which best avoid each other by adopting a planar arrangement. It should be noted that such molecules have a strong tendency to acquire an octet configuration; in this case it can be accomplished by adding a fluoride ion to give the BF_4^- ion, which is of course tetrahedral. In the second short period, expansion beyond the normal octet is permitted; thus compounds such as PCl_5 and SF_6 can be made. PCl_5 has five electron pairs surrounding the central phosphorus, which can be best accommodated in a trigonal bypyramidal arrangement. The six electron pairs of SF_6 adopt an octahedral geometry. Both of these structures are illustrated in Figure 4.4. The second short period is associated with the filling of the 3s and 3p electron orbitals. The filling of the 3d orbitals is postponed until the first long period. However these orbitals, although higher in energy, are present in second short period atoms and can be used to form compounds involving an expansion of the octet. This cannot happen in the first short period, so a compound such as NCl_5 is non-existent. The presence of the 3d orbitals can also be manifested in changes in chemical reactivity; the greatly increased susceptibility of $SiCl_4$ to hydrolysis compared with CCl_4 has already been mentioned. The 3d orbitals of silicon allow the formation of molecules with five groups attached to the silicon. Such molecules are not very stable, but a hydrolysing OH^- ion can form at least a temporary attachment to the silicon atom. This is all that is needed to provide a facile mechanism for hydrolysis.

There are some molecules for which a single Lewis dot structure cannot be drawn without violating the octet rule; an example is provided by sulfur dioxide, SO_2. This molecule has a total of 18 valence electrons and there are two arrangements, either of which can provide each atom with its complement of eight electrons. These Lewis dot structures are shown in Figure 4.7.

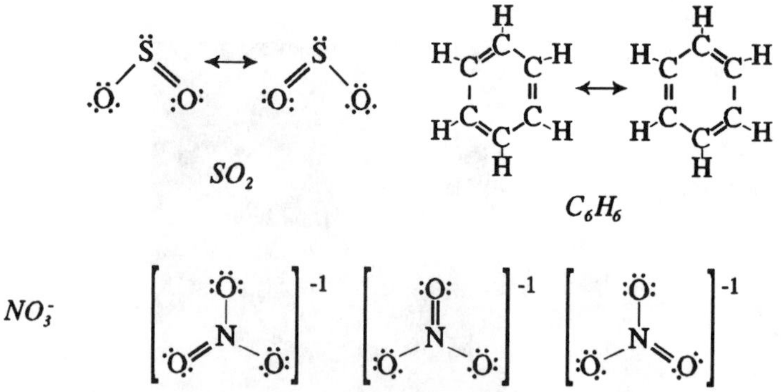

SO₂

C₆H₆

NO₃⁻

Fig. 4.7: Resonance. Not all molecules can be satisfactorily represented by a single Lewis dot structure. This diagram shows several examples of molecules and ions which can be equally well represented by two or three Lewis dot structures. The true structure is an average of these different electron arrangements.

■ *Resonance...*

The essential difference between the two structures is that one has a double bond between the sulfur and the left-hand oxygen, and the other has a double bond between the sulfur and the right-hand oxygen. Common sense says that the two structures must be equally probable, but it is still a valid question to ask whether a sulfur dioxide molecule will have one short (double) S-O bond and one long (single) S-O bond, or two equal S-O bonds of intermediate length. The latter alternative is correct. In the case of SO_2 it is also possible to draw allowable structures with more than eight electrons. There are a large number of similar cases, of which two are illustrated in Figure 4.7. The nitrate ion, NO_3^-, has three equivalent structures and the benzene molecule, C_6H_6, has two. In each case all of the bond lengths in question are equal. The individual Lewis dot structures are called **resonance** structures; the presence of resonance leads to a lowering of the energy of the molecule relative to that expected for one of the Lewis structures, and hence to additional stability. This is particularly important for molecules derived from benzene, and gives rise to a whole branch of organic chemistry devoted to the study of **aromatic** molecules.

The Hydrogen Bond

Molecules are held together by chemical bonds. There are also forces between molecules, known as intermolecular forces; they arise from electrostatic interactions, as does chemical bonding, but in a less direct way. It is these forces which cause a gas to condense to a liquid, and a liquid to crystallize as a solid. Generally intermolecular forces increase with the size of the molecule, since they are additive for each atom. For this reason large molecules usually exist at room temperature as solids, whereas small molecules form liquids or gases. If the solid has an ionic structure, such as sodium chloride, Na^+Cl^-, the forces holding the crystal together are strong, and the crystal has a high melting point. For covalent molecules the intermolecular forces are weak and the melting point is low. If the binding energy due to the intermolecular forces is small and comparable to the thermal energy of the molecules, as it usually is, the influence of intermolecular forces on the chemistry is negligible.

■ *Hydrogen bonds are not usually symmetric...*

There is however one form of weak interaction which is of great chemical importance, namely the **hydrogen bond**. A hydrogen bond occurs when a single hydrogen atom interacts with two electronegative atoms; in the large majority of cases the other atoms are nitrogen, oxygen or fluorine. All of these atoms have lone pairs of electrons which can interact with a hydrogen attached to another electronegative atom; they are also small enough to allow close approach of such a hydrogen atom. The hydrogen will be the positive end of a polar bond, and hence will be attracted to the non-bonding electrons on the second atom. Such a bond is usually written in the form O-H...O, which emphasizes the fact that the hydrogen is not symmetrically placed between the two oxygens. One of the few symmetric hydrogen bonds is that formed by a hydrogen placed between two fluorines; this is also the only hydrogen bond which has a strength comparable to that of a normal covalent bond. Most hydrogen bonds have only about one tenth the strength of normal covalent bonds, but this still makes them about ten times as strong as the intermolecular forces discussed in the previous paragraph. They are therefore not readily broken by the thermal jostling of neighboring molecules and play a very important part in determining the structures of substances such as proteins. They are, though, still weak bonds and their breaking does not represent a formidable barrier to desirable chemical reactions.

■ *The structure of ice...*

The unusual properties of water result from hydrogen bonding. Each water molecule has two hydrogen atoms and two lone pairs of electrons. Each hydrogen atom in a collection of water molecules, can therefore be associated with the lone pair from another molecule to form the maximum possible number of hydrogen bonds. This leads to a very open structure for ice, with each oxygen atom being surrounded tetrahedrally by four hydrogen atoms, two close in and two further away as shown in Figure 4.8.

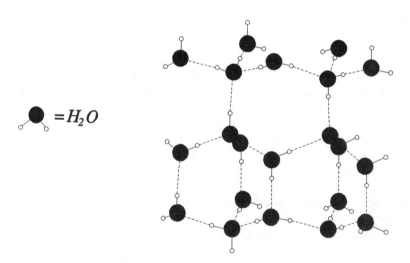

Fig. 4.8: The Structure of Ice. The structure of ice is determined by hydrogen bonding. Each oxygen atom (the large black circles) is surrounded tetrahedrally by four other oxygens. A hydrogen atom is situated between each pair of oxygens, but closer to one oxygen than the other. The short O-H distance is a covalent bond and the long O-H distance a hydrogen bond.

■ *Water plays a central role in biological chemistry...*

The open structure of ice results in its low density. When ice melts, some but not all of the hydrogen bonds are broken, allowing rather closer packing of the water molecules; this accounts for the higher density of water at the melting point of ice. Breaking of hydrogen bonds continues as the water is heated and the energy required gives rise to the high specific heat of water; water at room temperature still possesses an extensive hydrogen bonded-structure, which can be modified by the presence of other molecules. Hydrogen bonding is also largely responsible for the solvent properties of water. Such bonds are readily formed with the oxygen atoms of an anion such as SO_4^{2-}. They can also be formed with the hydroxyl groups of substances such as sugars, and the presence of such groups is usually a prerequisite for aqueous solubility. Where hydrogen bonding is not possible, there is usually no solubility. No other molecule is as well suited as water to form hydrogen bonds, and this is a particularly important aspect of the role of water in biological systems. Ammonia, for example, has three hydrogens for each lone pair and clearly cannot form as extensive a hydrogen bonding network as water; its melting and boiling points are correspondingly higher. Hydrogen sulfide offers the same geometric possibilities as water, but the sulfur has a much lower electronegativity and therefore does not readily form hydrogen bonds.

Trace Elements

"Curiouser and curiouser" said Alice.
*(Lewis Carroll, **Alice in Wonderland**)*

Introduction

The chemistry covered in the present book can, for the most part, be described as mainstream chemistry. The components of the biosphere are, almost by definition, the chemicals with which we have the closest contact, and close contact breeds careful study. Of the 100 plus elements in the Periodic Table, no more than a couple of dozen are of major importance in our everyday life. This leaves a large number in the shade of obscurity. Fortunately there are many chemists - enough to study both the obvious and the less obvious areas of the subject. Sometimes the lesser known byways of chemistry provide information at least as interesting as that found in the mainstream. In the present interlude three cases in which rare, or trace, elements have proved to have unusual or unexpected properties or uses will be described.

Selenium and Your Health

Selenium is a non-metallic (or semimetallic) element which is found below sulfur in the Periodic Table; it is quite rare, and by and large shows no surprising chemical properties. One might have anticipated that it would be poisonous since sulfur plays a major biochemical role, and selenium is sufficiently close to it in chemical properties, that it would be expected to take the place of sulfur in some biologically active compounds. It is on the other hand sufficiently different from sulfur that the resulting molecule will probably not perform its correct biological function. Arsenic, adjacent to selenium in the Periodic Table, has the same relationship to phosphorus and is indeed a notable poison.

Selenium begins our story in just this role. In 1900 the British government undertook a study of the purity of beer, an essential commodity in that country then as now, and was disturbed to find samples containing selenium, in addition to traces of arsenic. This occurred in the middle of the South African (Boer) war and the issue was debated in the House of Commons as a matter of some importance. *The London Times* of February the 16th, 1901 reported as follows.

"Boers and beer were the main topics of debate yesterday. Mr Chaplin was in possession of the House and lead off with the beer question. He knows all about the very newest scare which is the possible presence of selenium in glucose. Selenium is a rare element but it is just possible that traces of it may lurk in very unexpected places, just as gold

may be found in sea water, or copper in the feathers
of a parrot. Modern analysis is so refined that it
tends to prove the presence of a little of everything
almost everywhere, but common sense and universal
experience shows that the maxim *de minimis*[1] holds
in matters of health as well as in law. ..... No one
who knows the minuteness of the precautions taken
by the Inland Revenue in order to obtain the last
penny of duty, can doubt for a moment that the
absolute control of the materials used by brewers
could be obtained with ease were it sought with
equal zeal. .... In the meantime everybody concerned
will no doubt be particularly careful to at least
exclude arsenic and selenium."

Parliamentary debates on environmental matters have perhaps not changed a
great deal in the last ninety years.

Selenium next appears in a more benign role as an ingredient in anti-dandruff
shampoos and medicines; the material actually used is a buffered solution of selenium
sulfide. How the medicinal properties of this compound were discovered is unclear.
The proteins contained in hair are rich in sulfur, so it may be that the sulfur half of the
molecule encourages hair growth and the selenium half discourages the unwanted
dandruff. Whatever the true mechanism, it seems that the compound does indeed
work in the manner claimed.

Still more recently, it has been claimed that selenium makes a much more
positive contribution to human health. Its role is to enhance the effectiveness of the
immune system. The operation of the immune system, together with an account of
the effects of selenium, is described in a recent book by Robert S. Desowitz, entitled
The Thorn in the Starfish. The immune system is our chief protection against
chemicals, particularly proteins, which are introduced into the body from outside
sources. Such potential poisons are known as antigens, and the body produces
antibodies to neutralize them. Each antigen has its own specific antibody, and once
the organism has produced a given antibody it can produce more of these antibodies
very readily, if the same antigen is encountered again. This property provides the basis
for the vaccines used to immunize us against a variety of illnesses. If the production
of antibodies specific to the antigens associated with a certain disease can be induced,
the body retains its protection against this disease for an extended period of time. The
immune system is remarkably effective, but not perfect. Anything which will increase
the effectiveness of the immune system constitutes a very desirable medication;
conversely diseases such as AIDS which attack the immune system are particularly
deadly. It is usually better to improve the body's natural defenses than to introduce
drugs which do not normally occur in the living organism, since such drugs, although
they may indeed serve their purpose, almost always have undesirable side effects.

Desowitz describes some of the experiments that he has performed with mice.
He was attempting to immunize mice against a form of malaria without success - all
the mice died. There had been a report in the literature that selenium enhanced the

---

[1] *De minimis non curat lex* - "the law is not concerned with trivia." A common legal tag.

immune response of mice to some antigens, so he tried it to see whether it helped in the immunization process. The experiment was a success; he found that 2 parts per million of selenium in the mice's drinking water resulted in successful immunization, whereas the mice in a control sample with no selenium additive all died. The toxic properties of selenium resemble those of many other substances. It is an essential element at very low concentrations - 50 to 200 micrograms per day; this is a very minute amount and probably reflects the needs of a single selenium-requiring enzyme. This small amount is present in most normal diets but there are areas in China where selenium is lacking, and this results in a fatal degenerative disease. Yet at levels significantly in excess of the minimum requirement, selenium is toxic. The toxicity at high levels was recognized before the low level need was established, and was the cause of the beer scare of 1901. There is an intermediate level, just a little higher than the essential-element requirement, at which selenium appears to exert a very positive immunological effect. A variety of beneficial consequences have been reported; in mice both anti-inflammatory and anti-cancer effects have been described. There is some epidemiological evidence for similar benefits to humans; the incidence of cancer seems to be lower in areas where there is a high natural level of selenium than in low-level areas. A study in Finland suggested that a combination of selenium and vitamin E delayed the onset of the usual symptoms associated with aging. The study was performed on a group of patients in an old age home of average age 76.

A chemist would naturally like to ask: how does it work? Selenium, like sulfur, comes in two oxidation states, $+4$ giving selenites such as Na_2SeO_3, analogous to sulfites, and $+6$ giving selenates such as Na_2SeO_4, analogous to sulfates. Selenites are at the same time more beneficial and, at higher concentrations, more toxic than selenates. This suggests that the lower oxidation state is the active form. Sulfites and selenites are both reducing agents, since they can be oxidized to sulfates or selenates, but selenites are also oxidizing agents, giving elemental selenium in these circumstances. This difference in oxidation/reduction properties may be the key. Vitamin E, which is associated with selenium in its medical activity, is an anti-oxidant. It has been suggested that the site of selenium activity is the mitochondrion, the location of ATP production by oxidative phosphorylation. As will be discussed in Chapter 9, ATP is used in almost all the energy-requiring processes of the body, certainly including the manufacture of antibodies. Anything that enhances the ATP-producing process will be beneficial. It will also be noted in Chapter 9 that byproducts, such as superoxide, resulting from the incomplete reduction of molecular oxygen, are harmful and could, for example, destroy antibodies. Perhaps vitamin E and selenite can combine with just the right reducing power to destroy superoxides or other harmful oxidants very efficiently. At present we really do not know whether this type of explanation is basically correct or completely wrong. What is clear though, is that trace amounts of many substances can exert either detrimental of beneficial effects. Just because a substance is toxic in large doses, does not mean that it is also damaging in small doses; this fact is often neglected in considerations of pollution problems.

Yttrium and High Temperature Superconductivity

Selenium occurs towards the end of the first long period of the Periodic Table. If we proceed to the end of this period and then get started on the second long period, the third element brings us to yttrium. This is an element of considerable obscurity. Not only is it rare, but its chemistry is singularly uninteresting. (Selenium at least has several oxidation states and some interesting covalent chemistry in its elemental form.) Yttrium belongs to the same group as aluminum, has only one oxidation state, +3, is a very typical metal in its elemental state and forms predominantly simple ionic compounds. Nevertheless it has recently achieved a place in the limelight through its involvement in the story of high temperature superconductors.

Superconductivity was discovered by a Dutch physicist, Onnes, in 1911. He found that if mercury was cooled to 4 K, the temperature of liquid helium (the substance with the lowest known boiling point), it became a perfect conductor of electricity. Not just a very good conductor, but a perfect conductor; the electrical resistance becomes zero so that an electric current, once started in a closed loop, will continue indefinitely. At the time this was a very unexpected result. A number of other metals were found to exhibit similar properties and in due course the theorists were able to provide an explanation of the effect. A consequence of the theory, proposed by Bardeen, Cooper and Schrieffer (abbreviated BCS theory), was that superconductivity could only occur at low temperatures. This of course made the effect much less useful, since the difficulty and expense of cooling materials with liquid helium for most purposes more than offset the advantage of zero resistance. Over the years new superconductors were discovered, and the critical temperature - the temperature at which the material first becomes superconducting - was gradually raised. Up until very recently the record was 23 K for an alloy of niobium and tin, and according to theory this was close to the highest attainable. There are some commercial uses for these superconducting materials, most notably in the construction of scientific and medical instruments requiring very large magnetic fields. A magnetic field is usually made by passing an electric current through a coil of wire and the bigger the current, the bigger the magnetic field. Superconductivity allows very large currents but there is a limitation even here. Just as there is a high temperature limit for superconductivity, there is also a magnetic field limit, so that the material loses its superconducting properties if placed in a magnetic field larger than this critical value. Generally the higher the critical temperature, the greater the magnetic field attainable.

All of the above has been well known for the last 30 years and since the prospects for new advances in the field looked very unpromising, only a few researchers maintained an interest. The small number remaining were convinced that a major advance would be _very_ important. The real prize would be a material which would be superconducting at liquid nitrogen temperature, 77 K. The price and ease of handling liquid nitrogen are very much more favorable than for liquid helium, and many new commercial possibilities would open up. Of course an even larger jackpot would be a room temperature superconductor, but this was felt to be out of the question. The situation changed dramatically in September, 1986. Two IBM researchers, Bednorz and Muller, working in Zurich Switzerland, had the idea of examining metal oxides rather than metals for superconducting properties. At first sight this does not look very promising, since most oxides are insulators and do not conduct electricity at all. There had been indications in the research literature that some oxides might have superconducting properties and Bednorz and Muller hit the right combination with a mixed oxide of barium, lanthanum and copper, which became a superconductor at 30 K. This represented a much bigger increase in critical temperature than had been seen since the very early days of superconductivity research. Bednorz and Muller were quite conservative, and did not announce their discovery prior to the publication of a complete paper in the respected German journal, *Zeitschrift fur Physik*. This paper appeared in September, 1986. At this point scientific caution fell by the wayside and the race to extend and exploit the discovery was pursued with no holds barred. The story, both scientific and sociological, has been told by Robert M. Hazen in his book *The Breakthrough*.

There was no shortage of researchers who realized the significance of Bednorz and Muller's findings. This was a new class of superconductors, the old BCS theory probably did not apply, and the sky was the potential limit for critical temperatures.

There is a grapevine for spreading early news of major scientific discoveries among senior researchers, who are therefore rarely caught by surprise by a publication. If the topic looks to be worthy of further investigation these senior researchers, usually have the wheels in motion before the new finding appears in print. In this case the grapevine failed to operate, and everybody started from ground zero on the date of publication, September the 16th. The first order of business was to repeat the experiments reported in the German publication, since there had been many previous reports of superconductivity which had proved in the long run to be incorrect. In a matter of a week or two, most of the serious investigators had convinced themselves that this one was for real. Hazen's book follows the fortunes of the group lead by Paul Chu at the University of Houston, which was perhaps the most productive of the US groups. This group had a great deal of experience in superconductivity research and was in particular equipped to measure the dependence of the critical temperature on pressure. They showed that the material reported by Bednorz and Muller was a mixture of two compounds, only one of which was superconducting. The critical temperature of this compound was shown to increase dramatically at high pressure; this suggested a direction for further research. If squashing the atoms together increased the critical temperature, why not try smaller atoms? The theorists were of the view that copper was an essential component, which suggested changing either the lanthanum or the barium. In collaboration with another group at the University of Alabama, they tried both possibilities. Examination of the Periodic Table shows that the element above barium, which will be chemically similar but smaller in size, is strontium, and that above lanthanum is yttrium. The strontium substitution was successful, giving a critical temperature of 39 K, but the really exciting result was with yttrium, with a critical temperature of 93 K. The liquid nitrogen superconductor had been achieved, and yttrium had been rescued from its place of obscurity in the Periodic Table.

By this time the new field had become very competitive. It was known that groups in the well-equipped Bell Labs and elsewhere were close behind the University of Houston researchers. Results were even appearing concurrently from the People's Republic of China. A great deal of scientific prestige was at stake, to say nothing of the very large sums of money which would accrue to the holder of any key patents in the area. It is in fact a classic example of the commercialization of university research, which will be discussed in a future Interlude. In this type of situation there is a conflict between two objectives; to obtain credit for a major new discovery it must be published as quickly as possible in the scientific literature, preferably in a prestigious journal; to maximize the commercial advantage it must be kept secret as long as possible, so that the inventor can establish the maximum lead on competitors and submit the broadest possible patent applications. In principle, a paper submitted to a journal is confidential material until it appears in print. In practice, it passes through the hands of editors and referees and secretarial staff and, regrettably, the scientific grapevine alluded to above is often aware of developments before the formal publication.   Chu and his collaborators submitted a paper describing the very important yttrium results to *Physical Review Letters*, considered the most prestigious publication in physics. A strange thing happened though: the original manuscript contained a number of misprints, in particular yttrium was never spelled out and the symbol for this element, Y, was replaced by Yb, the symbol for another element ytterbium, in some two dozen places. The formula for the key compound was also misprinted. These misprints were corrected at the very last minute as the paper went to press. The interesting observation is that a number of groups shortly thereafter did indeed report studies of the Yb compound which ironically is also a superconductor, although not with as high a critical temperature as the Y compound. These events were of course the source of much scientific gossip.

The discovery of this superconductor was only the start of the real race. To achieve real success it is necessary to know the structure of the active compound and why this structure leads to the observed effects. (These questions are likely to be answered in this order.) It was fairly quickly shown that the original preparation, with the formula $Y_{1.2}Ba_{0.8}CuO_4$, was actually a mixture of two compounds, with the formulae Y_2BaCuO_5 (green) and $YBa_2Cu_3O_{6.5}$ (black). The black compound was the superconductor and the race was to determine its structure. The structure was finally announced at a conference on March 18th, 1987. The intensity of the competition became apparent when no fewer than four different groups announced their solutions to the problem on the same day. The agreement between the groups was not exact, but very close, and the way was cleared for theorists to work with firm structural data.

High temperature superconductivity is still a very active area of research. Muller and Bednorz were awarded the Nobel prize in physics in 1987 for their original discovery in the field. It was one of the most rapid Nobel recognitions for a major discovery on record. The yttrium compound has since lost its record for the highest critical temperature; Chu has reported a 120 K oxide superconductor containing bismuth, strontium and copper. There have been other claims as high as 240 K. Japanese companies were reputed to have filed more than 2000 patent applications in this subject area by January, 1988. The technological problems are still substantial: oxide compounds cannot be drawn into wires and fabricated using the methods developed for metals; the compounds are difficult to make reproducibly and the superconducting properties are anisotropic, which means that the crystals have to be oriented in a certain direction to obtain superconductivity. They will also remain quite expensive to produce. It seems unlikely that large-scale applications to such areas as the transmission of power over long distances or magnetically-driven trains will develop very quickly. The initial applications are more likely to be on a smaller scale, in computers. Technological problems take time to solve, but are usually resolved eventually, so it would be surprising if high temperature superconductors have not found a marketable application by the end of the century.

Iridium and the Fall of the Dinosaurs

Selenium occurs in the first long period of the Periodic Table and yttrium in the second long period. We have to proceed to the third long period to find iridium. It is a transition metal, occurs in the sequence iridium, platinum, gold and is rarer than either of its better known neighbors. Compared to yttrium it has a rich chemistry. Iridium forms a whole series of organometallic compounds, many of which have interesting catalytic properties. There may be very little of the element present at a given location, but modern analysis has progressed even further since Mr. Chaplin complained in 1901 of the ability of chemical analysis to detect a little of everything everywhere. Techniques such as neutron activation analysis and atomic absorption now allow the measurement of concentrations at the parts per billion level, rather than at the parts per million level of earlier in the century. The data discussed below were obtained by neutron activation analysis, a technique in which the sample is bombarded with neutrons from a nuclear reactor and the radioactivity from the fission products measured. The measurement of such minute quantities of such a rare element can however lead to vast inferences involving biology, paleontology, geology and astronomy as the present story will tell. The situation is reminiscent of Mark Twain's observation "there is something fascinating about science, one gets such wholesome returns of conjectures out of such a trifling investment of fact." A popular account of recent events involving iridium has been provided by one of the participants in the development of the saga, David M. Raup, in his book *The Nemesis Affair*.

Geologists have appreciated for more than a century that the different strata of rocks are of different ages; the topic of dating such strata by means of radioactivity will be considered elsewhere in this book. Since the right radioactive minerals are not always present, geologists are always on the lookout for alternative techniques. The problem would be easier if one knew the rate of sedimentation, the rate at which the various layers were laid down. Walter Alvirez, a geologist, had an idea that he could perhaps calculate the rate of sedimentation from the concentration of meteoric dust. This could be monitored by measuring the iridium concentration, since iridium is more abundant in meteoric material than in the earth's crust. Since the earth is thought to have been formed from the material as meteors, the suggestion is that iridium and the other noble metals have become concentrated in the earth's core, leaving a shortage in the crust. If the rate of deposition of meteoritic dust were constant, and if other sources of iridium did not interfere, the method might work. Some of the iridium data he obtained in Italy, published in the journal *Nature* in 1980, and some later results from a site in Montana are shown in Figure IN2.1.

The really interesting result is the location of these increases in the geologic record. Geologists have traditionally classified the different strata of rocks according to the types of fossils they contain. The early investigators found that a given layer of rock would contain very similar fossils throughout, but the next layer down would have a different selection. It was assumed that layers containing the same types of fossils were contemporary and the fossils therefore allowed the ages of rocks at different sites to be compared. The periods corresponding to the boundaries between different strata were associated with the extinctions of various species. The iridium anomalies shown in Figure IN2.1 occur at the so called Cretaceous-Tertiary (commonly abbreviated CT) boundary. This is dated at some 65 million years ago, and corresponds to the extinction of a large number of species, the best known of which were the dinosaurs.

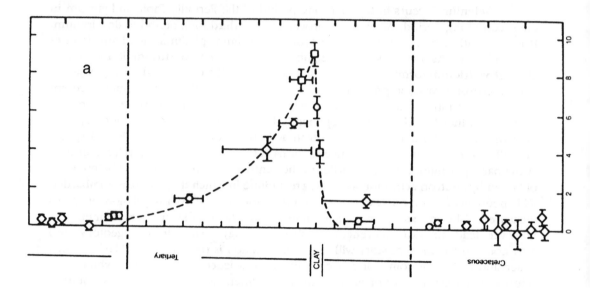

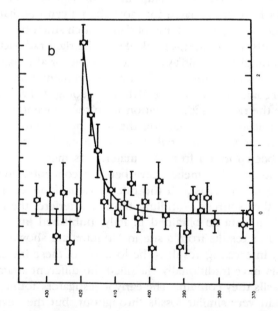

Figure IN2.1: Iridium Concentrations in Geologic Strata. Figure a is data obtained in Italy and Figure b data obtained in Montana. In Figure a the depth of the sample increases from left to right and in Figure b from right to left. In both cases the spike in iridium concentration occurs at the Cretaceous/Tertiary boundary. (Data from Raup - **The Nemesis Affair**).

The Tertiary period is the age of mammals; the Cretaceous was dominated by reptiles. Clearly this is an important turning point in our history. A point which has long been controversial is whether extinctions, such as that at the CT boundary, were sudden catastrophic events or whether they were more gradual occurrences. The orthodox view developed in the nineteenth century, known as uniformitarianism, favored the gradual outlook; geological change was considered a slow process with species waxing and waning in a continuous manner. This view was to some extent a reaction to biblical accounts of sudden floods and the like obliterating life overnight. Catastrophism, the alternative to uniformitarianism, has been revived by the measurement of trace amounts of iridium. By the end of 1983 the iridium anomaly at the CT boundary had been found at more than 50 sites spread throughout the world. Whatever had happened at this time was a world-wide phenomenon. If the origin of the iridium was meteoric, either an awful lot of small meteorites arrived at the same time, or one big one hit us. If it was a big one, could it have been responsible for the death of the dinosaurs and other species? This indeed is the suggested interpretation. The impact of a large meteor, perhaps several kilometers in diameter, would be equivalent (except for radioactivity) to the effect of a substantial number of atomic bombs. Computer modelling suggests that the vast amount of dust distributed in the atmosphere would restrict sunlight, kill plants and starve animals, hence the extinctions; the scenario is just that proposed for "nuclear winter" and the same computer programs have modelled both events.

The extinction at the CT interface is only one of a number of such events observed in the fossil record. An obvious question is whether there are similar iridium anomalies at other interfaces. The answer, though not yet definitive, is probably yes. In this case we are faced with a number of major meteoric impacts over the history of the earth. A scientist will obviously ask whether there is any temporal pattern to the impacts. Suitable computer analysis of all the available data will decide whether there is a statistically significant correlation, sufficient to claim a periodic regularity for the events. Again the results are ambiguous, and some researchers have claimed a 26-million-year periodicity and others a 30-million-year periodicity, but this was enough to fuel a further round in the story. Why should large meteoric impacts occur periodically in this way? This question allows the astronomers to enter the discussion; a series of communications published in the April 19th, 1984 issue of *Nature* produced two possible explanations. One suggests that the sun is oscillating through the galactic plane every 20 or 30 million years, and large numbers of meteors are encountered at some time in this cycle. Another proposed a small star, christened Nemesis, as a companion to the sun, and that this comet presumably periodically deflects comets from a postulated swarm into the path of the earth. A third theory, advanced later, postulates a new planet as the comet deflector. None of these ideas has achieved wide acceptance; an article in the journal *Science* in 1985 summarizes the contending theories and expresses scepticism about all of them.

This story demonstrates how one science builds on the results of others. The iridium results, which seem quite firm at least for the CT anomaly, are analytical chemistry. The meteoric interpretation has been challenged; some geologists suggest that volcanoes are a source of iridium and that there could have been a world-wide rash of volcanic eruptions 65 million years ago. The correlation of the extinction of the dinosaurs with the iridium anomaly is also not watertight. It could still have been a slow affair, dependent on a steady accumulation of unfavorable environmental factors, rather than on a sudden catastrophe. The current rate of species extinction is probably faster than at any time in the geological past, and does not involve meteorites. The paleontologists can argue this one. Nobody is quite sure how reliable the correlations are between the timings of different extinctions. The analysis of such correlations is a topic for study by statisticians and applied mathematicians. Finally, if we accept the recurring meteorite hypothesis as true, there is certainly no consensus that the astronomers have yet hit on the right explanation for regular meteorite bombardments of the Earth. Mark Twain's comments on science fit the story very well.

We began this interlude with a quotation from the *London Times* of 1901. A quotation from an editorial in the *New York Times* of April 2nd, 1985 is perhaps an apt conclusion.

> "During the close of the Cretaceous era some 65 million years ago, all dinosaurs disappeared from the earth. Paleontologists, the students of fossil life forms, have for decades debated inconclusively the reasons for that extinction, but five years ago their game was suddenly snatched away by two brash Berkeley scientists and a crowd of astronomers...... Terrestrial events, like volcanic activity or changes in climate or sea level, are the most immediate possible causes of mass extinctions. Astronomers should leave to astrologers the task of seeking the cause of earthly events in the stars."

Of course not all scientists will agree with this editorial, but differences of opinion are the stuff of science.

Further Reading

Robert S. Desowitz, *The Thorn in the Starfish*, W. W. Norton and Co. (1987). An entertaining account of recent developments in immunology with a very good discussion of AIDS.

Robert M. Hazen, *The Breakthrough*, Summit Books (1988). The story of the high temperature superconductor discoveries.

Bruce Schechter, *The Path of No Resistance*, Simon and Schuster (1989). Another account of the discovery of high temperature superconductivity.

David M. Raup, *The Nemesis Affair*, W. W. Norton and Co. (1986).

Richard A. Kerr, Periodic Extinctions and Impacts Challenged, *Science*, Vol. 227, p1451 (1985). The pros and cons of dinosaur extinctions.

Part II: Man's Contributions

CHAPTER 5

Photochemistry in the Atmosphere

Introduction

■ *Sunlight is only a small part of the electromagnetic spectrum...*

Previous chapters have discussed the chemistry of the major components of our biosphere. One important ingredient has so far been omitted - sunlight. It is the energy from the sun which makes the biosphere a dynamic, rather than a static, entity. It contributes very directly to life by the process of photosynthesis. Chemically, photosynthesis is a very complex process, and perhaps not the best starting point for a discussion of the sun's role in our affairs. We will therefore start with some much simpler photochemistry, involving oxygen and other atmospheric gases. This is also an appropriate stage to introduce the second major theme of the book - the effect of human chemical adventures and misadventures on our environment.

Sunlight is electromagnetic radiation; it was recognized as such by Clark Maxwell in the nineteenth century. It is however only one small part of the total electromagnetic spectrum. The radiowaves which carry our television, the radar which guides our aircraft, the microwaves which heat our meals, the emissions of heat lamps which warm us and the X-rays which locate our broken bones, are all electromagnetic radiation. They differ only in wavelength. Figure 5.1 presents an overview of the electromagnetic spectrum, starting with long wavelength radiation on the left-hand side of the diagram and progressing to short wavelength radiation on the right-hand side. It is convenient again to use a logarithmic scale, so that each interval corresponds to a decrease in wavelength by a factor of ten.

The radiation used in sound radio transmissions has a wavelength of hundreds of meters, that employed in television around one meter, and microwaves are around a centimeter in wavelength. Infra-red, or heat radiation, comes in at 10^{-4} to 10^{-5}m, and visible sunlight at 10^{-6} to 10^{-7}m. Ultraviolet light is of still shorter wavelength, around 10^{-8}m, and is followed by X-rays between 10^{-9} and 10^{-10}m and gamma rays, a component of radioactive emissions, down to 10^{-12}m. Still shorter wavelengths are found in cosmic rays originating in distant parts of the galaxy; sunlight comprises only a very narrow band of the total electromagnetic spectrum.

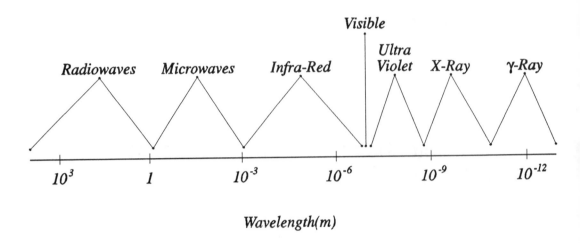

Wavelength(m)

Fig. 5.1: The Electromagnetic Spectrum. Wavelength (in meters) increase from right to left and energy from left to right. Each division represents an increase of 1000 in wavelength. Note that visible light is only a small part of the total electromagnetic spectrum.

It is, of course, not coincidental that our eyes are sensitive to radiation of just these wavelengths.

■ *Wavelength to energy conversion...* $10^3m = 1.2 \times 10^7 kJ$
$10^{-6}m = 120kJ$
$10^{-12}m = 1.2 \times 10^8 kJ$

Electromagnetic radiation is a form of energy. It was discovered in the twentieth century that energy comes in discrete packages, called quanta. The amount of energy in a package varies in a very simple way with the wavelength: the shorter the wavelength, the larger the quantum of energy. Figure 5.1 could therefore have been labelled in terms of energy, rather than of wavelength, with energy increasing from left to right on the diagram. We have encountered two units of energy previously, kilojoules and degrees of absolute temperature; for electromagnetic energy a third scale of inverse wavelength can be equally well specified. Electromagnetic energy can be converted to chemical energy, this is indeed the subject of photochemistry, and the kilojoule scale on Figure 5.1 will determine the effectiveness of radiation of a given wavelength in bringing about chemical reactions. The sun does not radiate equally at all wavelengths and the actual distribution of the sun's radiation is shown in Figure 5.2.

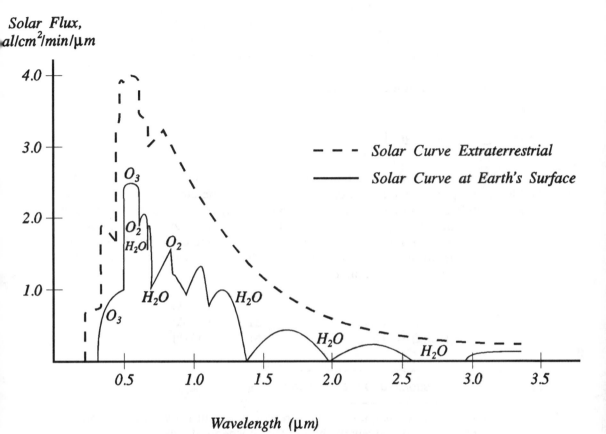

Fig. 5.2: Radiation from the Sun. Most of the radiation that reaches us from the sun falls in the visible part of the spectrum. Note that $1\mu m = 10^{-6}m$ and that blue light has a wavelength of $0.4\mu m$ and red light of $0.8\mu m$. There is some ultraviolet radiation at shorter wavelengths and some infrared at longer wavelengths. Less radiation reaches the surface than the top of the atmosphere. The gases absorbing at different wavelengths which cause this difference are noted on the diagram.

■ *Part of the solar radiation is absorbed by the atmosphere...*

The radiation that we receive from the sun is determined by three factors. The first is the temperature of the sun; the hotter a star, the more energy it has available, and the shorter the wavelength of the light it emits. Stars hotter than the sun appear blue, and stars cooler than the sun appear red for this reason. Some radiation, emitted from the sun's hot interior, is absorbed in the cooler layers of gas nearer the surface of the sun. This gives rise to some of the valleys apparent in Figure 5.2.

Analysis of these absorption lines in the spectrum of the sun and those of other stars, provides information on the chemical composition of the stars. Some radiation is also absorbed in our own atmosphere and fails to reach the surface of the earth. For this reason two curves are given in Figure 5.2, one corresponding to the radiation reaching the top of the atmosphere, and one corresponding to that experienced by life at lower altitudes. We are now in the position to ask what chemistry can be accomplished with the radiation that the sun has to offer.

Bond Energies and Free Radicals

The photochemical reactions of interest involve the breaking of chemical bonds, so the pertinent information in our analysis is the amount of energy which must be supplied to a molecule to break a bond. This type of information is available from thermochemical or spectroscopic measurements. For diatomic molecules there is an unambiguous definition of bond energy; it is simply the enthalpy of dissociation of the molecule to its component atoms. This can usually be measured by spectroscopic experiments. Some examples are:

$$H_2(g) \rightarrow 2H(g) \qquad \Delta H = +435kJ$$
$$Cl_2(g) \rightarrow 2Cl(g) \qquad \Delta H = +243kJ$$
$$HCl(g) \rightarrow H(g) + Cl(g) \qquad \Delta H = +431kJ$$

■ *Energy must be supplied to break a bond...*

Note that the enthalpies for these reactions are all positive, indicating that energy must be supplied to break the bond. Thermochemical measurements allow us to measure the enthalpy of the reaction:

$$H_2(g) + Cl_2(g) \rightarrow 2HCl(g) \quad \Delta H = -184kJ$$

This is an exothermic reaction, ΔH is negative, and the enthalpy change is, by definition, twice the enthalpy of formation of hydrogen chloride. We could also look at this reaction in a different way. What has been accomplished is to break the bond of a hydrogen molecule, to break the bond of a chlorine molecule, and to make two hydrogen - chlorine bonds. Breaking bonds costs energy, making bonds provides energy. Based on the bond energies given above, the enthalpy of the reaction should be (-2 x 431 + 435 + 243 = -184kJ), which agrees with the experimental value.

For molecules with more than two atoms, the situation is a little more complicated. Consider a triatomic molecule such as water; the dissociation of the molecule to its component atoms requires two steps, i.e.

$$H_2O(g) \rightarrow OH(g) + H(g) \qquad \Delta H = +501kJ$$
$$OH(g) \rightarrow O(g) + H(g) \qquad \Delta H = +425kJ$$

The notable feature is that the energy required to break the two bonds is not the same: breaking the first O-H bond makes it easier to break the second. Similarly in the case of methane, CH_4, there would be four successive bond-breaking steps, each requiring a different amount of energy. Adding together these individual bond energies and dividing by four gives a measure of the average energy required to break a C-H bond. We can experimentally determine this average bond energy if we know the heat of formation of methane, the bond energy of hydrogen and the heat of vaporization of carbon. The procedure is exactly the same as that used above to find the bond energy of hydrogen chloride. If we use this value for the enthalpy of a C-H bond and the enthalpy of formation of ethane, C_2H_6, a bond energy for the single C-C bond can be obtained. In this way a table of bond energies, such as those given in Table 5.1, can be constructed. It should be emphasized that the values are only approximate. Thus if the values were exact, we could calculate the enthalpy of combustion of ethyl alcohol, as expressed in the reaction:

$$C_2H_5OH(g) \ + \ 3O_2(g) \ \rightarrow \ 2CO_2(g) \ + \ 3H_2O(g)$$

by adding together the bond energies of all the bonds broken in the reaction, and subtracting the bond energies of all the bonds formed during the reaction. Using the values of Table 5.1 gives ΔH = -1031kJ which compares with an experimental value of -1236kJ. Not exact agreement, but close enough to make the calculation of bond energies useful.

Table 5.1: Bond Energies.

Bond	Energy kJ	Max Wave-length nm	Bond	Energy kJ	Max Wave-length nm
O=O	494	242	N=N	941	127
C-C	347	345	C-H	414	289
O-H	463	258	C-Cl	326	367
C-F	485	247	C=O	707	169
H-Cl	431	277	H-I	297	403
Cl-Cl	239	500	I-I	149	803

■ *Only energetic, i.e. short wavelength, light will break most bonds...*

If a chemical bond is to be broken an amount of energy at least equal to the bond energy must be provided; if more energy is provided, the excess can be carried away by the decomposition products as kinetic, or heat, energy. If the energy provided is insufficient the bond will not break. Since a bond energy can be equated with a wavelength of light, this means that to break a bond photochemically, light of a certain maximum wavelength must be used. (It is a <u>maximum</u> wavelength rather than a minimum wavelength, since energy increases with <u>decreasing</u> wavelength.) In Table 5.1, the approximate maximum wavelengths of light capable of breaking the various types of bond are indicated. In examining these numbers it should be remembered that blue light has a wavelength around 400nm, red light a wavelength around 800nm, and that these wavelengths represent the approximate limits of human vision. The ultraviolet light which reaches the earth's surface and causes sunburn, has a wavelength of around 350nm. The sun provides very little radiation at wavelengths shorter than 200nm, as is apparent from examination of Figure 5.2. The significant numbers are that nitrogen and carbon dioxide require light of 127nm and 169nm respectively to break their bonds, and are stable anywhere on earth, including the upper atmosphere. Oxygen and water require light of maximum wavelengths 242nm and 239nm respectively, and can therefore be decomposed by the light reaching the stratosphere but not by the light reaching the surface of the earth. Only a few bonds, such as the Cl-Cl bond in chlorine (492nm), can be broken by sunlight in the troposphere. This long wavelength for the absorption of light, is the reason that chlorine is a green colored gas. We may anticipate similar photochemical activity with other colored gases, such as the brown nitrogen dioxide.

■ *Free radicals are very reactive species...*

The significance of photochemical reactions lies not so much in the primary photolytic step as in the chemistry of the very reactive species which are produced by the photolysis. Thus if a molecule of water is photolytically decomposed it gives a hydrogen atom, H, and a hydroxyl radical, OH. In general the products of breaking bonds are **free radicals** which can undergo many subsequent reactions. It was pointed out in Chapter 4 that stable molecules and ions usually possess an octet of electrons, and attain this configuration by forming chemical bonds. A free radical does not have a octet configuration, and there is a considerable driving force to achieve such a stable structure by chemical reaction. Thus the oxygen of a hydroxyl radical has only seven electrons in its outer shell and will very readily react with almost any molecule containing hydrogen to make an additional O-H bond. In this way it becomes a very stable water molecule. However, in the process it usually produces another free radical which is itself very reactive. Thus hydroxyl reacts very readily with methane to give water and a methyl radical.

$$OH + CH_4 \rightarrow H_2O + CH_3$$

The methyl radical can in turn participate in a wide variety of further reactions. Free radical chemistry typically leads to <u>chain</u> reactions in which a single radical leads in succession to the reaction of a large number of other molecules. We will encounter examples of this type of reaction in the photochemistry discussed below, and also when we consider polymerization processes.

Ozone - The Natural Balance

It was deduced above that oxygen and water can be photolyzed in the stratosphere. Very little water reaches the stratosphere, since it mostly condenses as clouds at lower altitudes, and the low temperature of the upper troposphere keeps the amount of water, present as vapor, very small. Any that reaches the stratosphere is indeed photolyzed, decomposing in several steps to hydrogen and oxygen. Earth's gravity is insufficient to keep the light hydrogen in the atmosphere and it is lost to space. The story with oxygen is rather different. It is quite abundant in the stratosphere and is decomposed by the ultra-violet radiation to oxygen atoms. An oxygen atom can then react with another oxygen molecule to give the triatomic form of oxygen, **ozone**.

$$O_2 \rightarrow 2O \qquad\qquad \text{uv light} < 242nm$$
$$O_2(g) + O(g) + M(g) \rightarrow O_3(g) + M(g) \qquad \Delta H = -105kJ$$

■ *Ozone is produced in the stratosphere...*

In the second equation, M stands for any other gaseous molecule. Such a molecule is needed because the reaction is exothermic to the extent of 105kJ and if an ozone molecule was formed without the presence of a third body, it would be unable to dissipate the extra energy and would immediately fall apart again. With a third molecule present the energy can be safely removed in the form of kinetic energy associated with this additional molecule. It is the heat given off in this and similar chemical reactions which causes the temperature of the stratosphere to be greater than that of the troposphere. In the laboratory, ozone is usually made by passing an electric discharge through oxygen; as in the photochemical production, oxygen atoms are first produced and then react with more molecular oxygen. Ozone has a characteristic pungent smell and reacts readily with most organic molecules, as shown by its bleaching properties.

Demonstration 5.1
Preparation and Properties of Ozone. Ozone is prepared by passing an electric discharge through oxygen. The mechanism of this reaction is very similar to that of the natural production of ozone in the stratosphere. In this case the electric discharge, rather than ultra-violet radiation, provides the energy to dissociate an oxygen molecule, and the resulting oxygen atoms combine with more oxygen molecules to give ozone. Ozone has a characteristic odor and can be detected by this property around electrical equipment, and sometimes during thunderstorms. It is a very strong oxidizing agent, comparable to fluorine, and will oxidize virtually all organic molecules. This property can be demonstrated by bleaching colored cloth and decolorizing a solution containing an organic dye.

Ozone is not photochemically stable and strongly absorbs ultra-violet light, dissociating to an oxygen molecule and an oxygen atom.

$$O_3 \rightarrow O_2 + O \qquad\qquad \text{uv light}$$

This reaction can be accomplished by much less energetic radiation than is needed to split an oxygen molecule. Molecular oxygen removes most of the ultraviolet light between the wavelengths of 190 and 240 nm and ozone most of that between 230 and 290nm, plus part of the longer wavelength uv down to 350nm. The oxygen atom formed by the decomposition of ozone can recombine with another oxygen molecule to reform ozone. Oxygen atoms can also react with ozone molecules to destroy ozone.

$$O(g) + O_3(g) \rightarrow 2O_2(g) \qquad \Delta H = -390kJ$$

■ *Ozone protects us from ultraviolet radiation...*

This reaction is also exothermic and contributes to the heating of the stratosphere. A balance is established to give a steady state concentration of ozone, the rate of loss of ozone by the third and fourth equations of this section, is just balanced by its rate of formation by the first two equations so that the ozone concentration remains constant. The greater the height above the earth, the more ultraviolet radiation is available to form ozone, but less oxygen molecules are present to react; as a result the maximum ozone concentration is found at heights of 25-35km. The actual concentration is still quite low, some 20 or 30ppm (parts per million), but this is a thousand times greater than the concentration at sea level and suffices to remove nearly all of the short wavelength ultraviolet radiation. This removal of ultraviolet is fortunate for life at the surface. The reason is contained in the data of Figure 5.1. Short wavelength ultraviolet light is energetic enough to break almost any of the bonds listed. In particular it will break bonds in molecules of the human body. Even the relatively small amount of relatively low energy ultraviolet reaching us, suffices to cause sunburn; the damage to the cells of the skin is quite analogous to that caused by a burn from contact with a very hot object. Ultraviolet radiation is also thought to be a cause of skin cancer; the high incidence of skin cancer among the sun-loving Australians is cited as evidence for this contention. As will appear in the discussion in Chapter 7, cause and effect are not easy to establish for cancer and until we understand how the disease operates, its causes are likely to remain uncertain. According to the US Environmental Protection Agency, a 1% loss of the ozone layer would lead to an additional 10,000 to 20,000 cases of skin cancer in the USA. Skin cancer is presently responsible for 1% of cancer deaths in the USA. Ultraviolet radiation has also been said to lead to a loss in the efficiency of the body's immune system, an increase in the number of eye cataracts, and the likelihood of increased incidence of infections by herpes virus, hepatitis and infections of the skin caused by parasites. A 25% increase in uv leads to a 25% reduction in the yield of soybeans, and other plants are thought to be equally susceptible. The details of many of these effects seem quite speculative, but nevertheless there is clearly reasonable cause for concern regarding depletion of the ozone layer.

There are several natural processes which remove ozone from the stratosphere; the most important involve oxides of nitrogen. The key reactions are:

$$NO + O_3 \rightarrow NO_2 + O_2$$
$$NO_2 + O \rightarrow NO + O_2$$

■ *Nitric oxide destroys ozone...*

The first of these reactions destroys an ozone molecule and the second removes an oxygen atom, which otherwise could react to form an ozone molecule, and also regenerates NO to destroy more ozone. Nitrogen oxides are formed in the atmosphere by natural processes; denitrifying bacteria in the soil decompose nitrate, from decaying plants, to give either N_2 or N_2O. The former product simply completes the nitrogen cycle started by nitrogen-fixing bacteria. Nitrous oxide, N_2O, however escapes to the atmosphere and being relatively chemically unreactive, can reach the stratosphere where it reacts with oxygen atoms, from the photolysis of dioxygen, to give nitric oxide, NO.

$$N_2O + O \rightarrow 2NO$$

■ *There is a natural balance which results in a steady state concentration of ozone.*

Nitric oxide then participates in the above reactions, destroying ozone. Since this is a natural process, which has been going on for many millions of years, it is one of the factors which determines the level of ozone, and should not be a cause for concern. If though, human activities increase the concentrations of nitrogen oxides in the atmosphere, the chemistry outlined above provides an efficient mechanism for removing ozone.

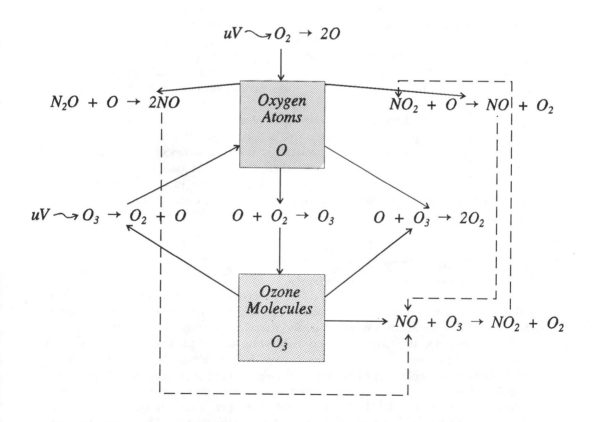

Fig. 5.3: Ozone in the Stratosphere. The formation and loss of ozone by natural causes.

Other natural mechanisms for ozone depletion are not currently considered important. It has been suggested that charged particles bombarding the earth as cosmic rays can lead to the formation of nitric oxide and destroy ozone. Again, in a steady state situation, this it not a cause for concern, but a large increase in cosmic ray activity could be a problem. This could happen because of astronomical occurrences, a nearby supernova for example, or because a reduction in the earth's magnetic field ceased to deflect charged particles to the magnetic poles. At one time it was suggested that the death of the dinosaurs resulted from such an event. Sunspots, lightning or high-flying aircraft (both giving NO) and various other possible mechanisms for ozone removal are similarly not now considered important.

Ozone - Disturbing the Balance

Several of man's activities have, or potentially could have, contributed to the depletion of the ozone layer. Anything which produces nitrogen oxides in the stratosphere will have this effect; the oxides of nitrogen NO and NO_2 are produced by internal combustion engines but generally react in the troposphere and thus do not reach the stratosphere. There is no large direct man-made source of nitrous oxide. However the extensive use of nitrogen fertilizers has considerably increased the amount of nitrate in the soil, providing sustenance for the denitrifying bacteria. It has been estimated that the use of such fertilizers has increased the nitrogen cycle by 50% and there is presumably a proportionate increase in N_2O production by the bacteria. An interesting statistic is that in the USA, 10% of all fertilizer is applied to golf courses. It may, therefore, be possible to make some savings on the nitrogen front without threatening food production. The very high temperatures produced by nuclear explosions could lead to the formation of large amounts of nitrogen oxides in the stratosphere and it has been estimated that a major nuclear war would destroy 65% of the ozone layer. (It would seem probable that the survivors of such a catastrophe would have more immediate concerns than the loss of ozone.) Perhaps more pertinent is the statistic that atmospheric nuclear testing in the 1960's destroyed between 2 and 4% of the ozone layer, although the ozone concentration may perhaps have recovered since that time.

■ *Ozone is destroyed by CFC's...*

The major threat to the ozone layer is now thought to arise from chlorofluorocarbons, commonly abbreviated as CFC's. These are synthetic chemicals, developed after the Second World War, and used for a variety of purposes. The most important uses are as refrigerants and as blowing agents to make plastic foams for cushions; other uses are as cleaning agents in the electronic industry, and as propellants in aerosol spray cans. It is convenient to use spray cans to deliver a large number of products including hair sprays, deodorants, paints and insecticides. It is estimated that, prior to 1974, about 5 to 6 billion spray cans had been produced in the world and that about half of them used CFC propellants. This usage has now been banned in many countries since it releases CFC's directly into the atmosphere. The boiling points, thermal properties and lack of toxicity of CFC's make them ideal chemicals for use in domestic refrigerators. In principle, these refrigerants should only be released under controlled conditions, so that the threat is less than in the case of spray can applications. Nevertheless there is a movement to ban even refrigeration usage.

The two main compounds are CCl_3F, known as Freon 11, and CCl_2F_2, known as Freon 12, although several other compounds in the same family are also used. They are very unreactive and non-toxic materials and were for many years held up as an ideal chemical product - useful but not dangerous. The problem is that they are too unreactive. James Lovelock, the author of *Gaia*, in the early 1970's designed a very sensitive detector to measure the very low concentrations of CFC's in the atmosphere, and was able to estimate the total amount of the materials in the whole atmosphere. This estimate agreed quite closely with the total amount which was calculated to have been released from spray cans to that date, suggesting the compounds are virtually indestructible. More recent research indicates that F11 lasts on the average for about 75 years in the atmosphere and F12 for about 110 years. There is no mechanism for destroying them in the troposphere; they therefore very slowly drift up to the stratosphere. Here they encounter ultraviolet radiation and can be photolyzed. Examination of Table 5.1 shows that the easiest bond to break is a C-Cl bond, which produces chlorine atoms. It is the chlorine atoms which cause the problems; once chlorine atoms are produced, the following chemical reactions will occur:

$$CF_2Cl_2 + uv \rightarrow CF_2Cl + Cl \qquad \text{(chlorine atom produced)}$$
$$Cl + O_3 \rightarrow ClO + O_2 \qquad (1)$$
$$ClO + O \rightarrow Cl + O_2 \qquad (2)$$
$$ClO + O_3 \rightarrow ClO_2 + O_2 \qquad (3)$$
$$ClO_2 + O \rightarrow ClO + O_2 \qquad (4)$$

■ *Destruction of ozone by CFC's is a chain reaction...*

Reactions (1) and (2) are analogous to the reactions with nitric oxide (NO) encountered previously. A chlorine atom destroys an ozone molecule in reaction (1) and then is regenerated in reaction (2). The situation is however worse than that of nitric oxide since a second cycle, involving the product of reaction (1) chlorine monoxide, ClO, also destroys ozone and regenerates ClO. It has been calculated that a single chlorine atom will destroy 100,000 molecules of ozone. Thus, even though the concentrations of CFC's in the stratosphere are minute, they can still cause a very real problem. Fortunately there are some reactions which remove chlorine atoms. Methane CH_4, for example, which is always present in the atmosphere since it is formed by the anaerobic decomposition of organic material, will react with chlorine atoms to give HCl.

$$CH_4 + Cl \rightarrow HCl + CH_3$$

It has been shown that the concentration of methane is increasing and this can help to offset the deleterious effects of CFC's in the stratosphere. There are in fact, an enormous number of photochemically driven reactions which can occur in the stratosphere and many may be important, even if the concentrations of the reactants are very small. For this reason calculations of ozone concentrations based on the models of the chemistry of the stratosphere developed by theoretical chemists have always been questioned.

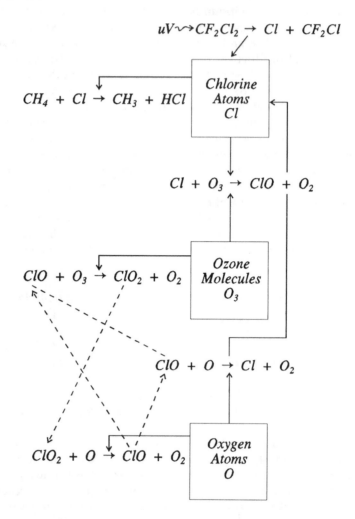

Fig. 5.4: Ozone and CFC's. Some of the reactions which lead to the destruction of ozone.

■ *The "hole in the sky"...*

While chemists were talking about mere 1 or 2% depletions of the ozone layer, in spite of arguments that these figures were significant, there tended to be a feeling that the problem was not urgent. More recently there have been some very well-publicized measurements of ozone concentrations in the polar regions of the earth showing depletions of 50% or more, and this has encouraged the politicians to take steps to ban the use of CFC's. The topic has been well discussed by John Gribbin in his book *The Hole in the Sky*. This "hole", meaning a considerable thinning of the ozone layer in the stratosphere, was first detected over Antarctica in the spring (southern hemisphere) of 1982, but was not widely recognized until 1984. It was examined in increasing detail in subsequent years, culminating in a major scientific investigation of the effect in spring 1987. This expedition not only confirmed the 30-50% depletions reported earlier but obtained data showing the depletion at some points as high as 97.5%. Even more importantly, the cause was unambiguously linked to CFC's by demonstrating parallel changes in ClO concentrations. The effects around the North pole are less spectacular and still the subject of some debate, but it seems fairly certain that real depletions were observed in 1987 and 1989. Even more recently, the Russians have reported ozone depletion over Northern Siberia.

It should be made clear that the ozone holes observed are seasonable and not permanent. Typically a "hole" appears in the spring and the ozone is regenerated later in the year. Since there is relatively little life or vegetation in the polar regions, the biological effects of ozone depletion cannot be experimentally investigated. Although the details are not completely known, the outline of what is happening in the stratosphere of the polar regions is now fairly clear. Very low temperatures lead to the formation of Polar Stratospheric Clouds, where conditions are such as to allow the condensation and trapping of a variety of photochemically reactive molecules such as CFC's. These molecules remain inert during the polar winter, but with the arrival of the sun, are readily photolyzed to give Cl atoms and ClO in large quantities. These species then destroy ozone according to the reactions described above. The extreme cold needed to form the stratospheric clouds required by this mechanisms, has been linked to climatic changes in prevailing air circulating patterns. Since ozone is responsible for warming the stratosphere, it has been speculated that the lack of ozone will result in more cooling, with a consequent deepening and spreading of the "hole" to non-polar regions. Even now it appears that the "hole" is not completely repaired before the next spring. Time alone will tell whether this scenario will prove accurate and if it does, whether the biological consequences will indeed be as disastrous outside the polar regions as forecast.

Photochemistry in the Troposphere - Air Pollution

If chemistry started when the first fire was lit, air pollution was invented at the same time. The atmosphere is large though, and provided the number of fires was small at any one place, the waste products of combustion could be dispersed without discomfort to the fire lighters. The recipe for too many fires too close together is to build large cities in cold climates. Metropolitan London was a prime example in the nineteenth century, particularly since coal, burnt in an open hearth, was the principal means of heating. Cold damp weather condenses water vapor to give fog, which combines with copious smoke from coal fires, gives suffocating smog. The extreme example of this process was reached in 1952 when 4,000 Londoners were estimated to have been killed during a particularly severe smog; the burning of coal in the city was subsequently banned and this particular environmental problem diminished in importance.

■ *Photochemical smog...*
■ *Ozone in the troposphere is a threat to health...*

There is however a second kind of smog which can be equally dangerous, namely photochemical smog. This is formed in sunny dry cities containing an excess of automobiles; Los Angeles and Mexico City are notorious examples. Temperature inversions, which occur when cool air gets trapped beneath a layer of hot air, can prevent the dispersion of the fumes from automobile exhausts. The main products from the combustion of gasoline are carbon dioxide and water, but there are a number of minor reaction products, some of which are photochemically active, and which cause the problem. Table 5.2 gives the active ingredients in a typical photochemical smog. The most noxious are the very strong oxidising agents, ozone and peroxyacylnitrates (PAN). Ozone is a desirable component of the stratosphere but a very undesirable product in the troposphere. Life processes depend on controlled oxidation, but very strong oxidizers such as ozone and peroxides lead to uncontrolled oxidation of all organic material within reach. Small quantities of peroxides and superoxides are produced by living cells as byproducts of normal respiration, and very effective enzymes, such as catalase and superoxide dismutase, have evolved to dispose of them efficiently. The human body cannot cope with very strong oxidants in the respiratory tract. Other combustion products such as lead and carbon monoxide are also poisonous, but do not pose the immediate threat of ozone and PAN.

Table 5.2: Components of Photochemical Smog

Gas	Major Source	Concentration
Carbon Monoxide CO	Automobiles	200-2000
Hydrocarbons	Autos, incomplete comb.	20-50
NO_x gases	Automobiles, coal burning	5-35
Sulfur dioxide SO_2	Coal burning	*
Ozone O_3	Photochemical reactions	2-20
Peroxyacylnitrates	Photochemical reactions	1-4

Concentrations in parts per 10^{-8}
* A component of smog but not always of photochemical smog.

Nitrogen oxides are the principal photochemical culprits. Under the high temperature conditions of internal combustion engines, some nitrogen oxides are formed by combination of N_2 and O_2. The two important nitrogen oxides under these condition, are nitric oxide, NO, and nitrogen dioxide, NO_2, which is initially present mainly in its dimerized form N_2O_4, but which is readily dissociated to the monomer. The latter is a brown gas, responsible for the color of photochemical smog. It is photolyzed by visible light of wavelength shorter than 430nm.

$$NO_2 + light \rightarrow NO + O \qquad wavelength < 430nm$$

The oxygen atoms produced in this way can combine with oxygen molecules to give ozone, exactly as they do in the stratosphere. However, we have already seen that nitric oxide <u>destroys</u> ozone. There is therefore no problem, providing the ratio of nitrogen dioxide, which makes ozone, to nitric oxide, which destroys ozone, is small. Normally nitric oxide is converted to nitrogen dioxide by a slow oxidation process.

$$2NO + O_2 \rightarrow 2NO_2 \qquad \text{slow}$$

So long as this remains a slow reaction there is enough nitric oxide around to balance out the undesirable effects of the nitrogen dioxide. Unfortunately the other components of photochemical smog, carbon monoxide and hydrocarbon gases from the incomplete combustion of gasoline, catalyze the conversion of nitric oxide to nitrogen dioxide. These processes depend on the existence of a small number of hydroxyl radicals which can be formed photochemically from nitrous acid, another reaction product, or from the oxygen atoms obtained by NO_2 photolysis.

$$H_2O + O \rightarrow 2OH$$
$$CO + OH \rightarrow H + CO_2$$
$$H + O_2 + M \rightarrow HO_2 + M$$
$$HO_2 + NO \rightarrow OH + NO_2$$

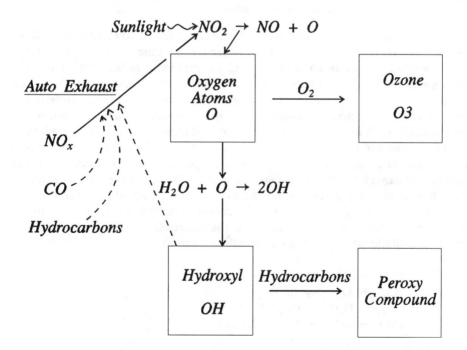

Fig. 5.5: Photochemistry in the Troposphere. How the products of auto exhausts produce toxic ozone and peroxides.

■ *The conversion of NO to NO$_2$ is catalyzed by peroxides and hydrocarbons...*

It should be noted that the formation of HO$_2$, the hydroperoxide radical, requires a third body M as does the formation of ozone. Overall the reactions lead to the catalytic conversion of NO to NO$_2$, since the OH radical used in the first reaction is regained in the third reaction. Hydrocarbon molecules provide similar possibilities for the conversion of NO to NO$_2$ as illustrated by the example of methane.

$$CH_4 + OH \rightarrow CH_3 + H_2O$$
$$CH_3 + O_2 + M \rightarrow CH_3O_2 + M$$
$$CH_3O_2 + NO \rightarrow NO_2 + CH_3O$$
$$CH_3O + CH_4 \rightarrow CH_3 + CH_3OH$$

CH$_3$O$_2$ is methyl peroxide and is formation is typical of the reactions which lead to peroxy compounds such as PAN. Overall then, it is the combination of nitrogen oxides, carbon monoxide, unburnt hydrocarbons and sunlight which leads to the production of photochemical smog.

Demonstration 5.2
Photochemical Smog. If a mixture of carbon monoxide, nitrogen dioxide, methane (natural gas) and air is exposed to uV radiation the formation of smog may be observed. The oxidizing properties of the resulting product can be demonstrated by the bleaching of colored cloth and the decolorization of a dye solution.

The remedies lie principally in the improved design of automobiles. Poisons such as lead can be removed by the use of unleaded gasoline. Tetraethyl lead, the source of the lead, serves as an antiknock agent, providing radicals to ensure the smooth combustion of the gasoline. Compensation for its absence can be obtained by using more aromatic compounds at some increase in price. The other undesirable components can be removed by installing catalytic converters; such converters use expensive metals, such as platinum, as a catalyst and these catalysts are not effective if lead is used. The use of lead compounds in gasoline therefore not only introduces poisonous lead into the atmosphere, but also prevents the removal of other undesirable substances from automobile exhausts. The objective of the catalytic converter, is that the only gases leaving the exhaust system should be water vapor, carbon dioxide and nitrogen gas. It should ensure that hydrocarbons unburnt on leaving the engine, are completely oxidized in the converter. Carbon monoxide and nitric oxide are eliminated by a series of reactions such as:

$$2CO + 2NO \rightarrow 2CO_2 + N_2$$
$$2CO + O_2 \rightarrow 2CO_2$$
$$CO_2 + H_2O \rightarrow CO_2 + H_2$$
$$2NO + 2H_2 \rightarrow N_2 + 2H_2O$$

All these reactions require a catalyst if they are to occur effectively, and modern catalytic converters are remarkably efficient; they will operate for five years without attention, undergoing during this time wide variations in flow rate, flow composition and temperature.

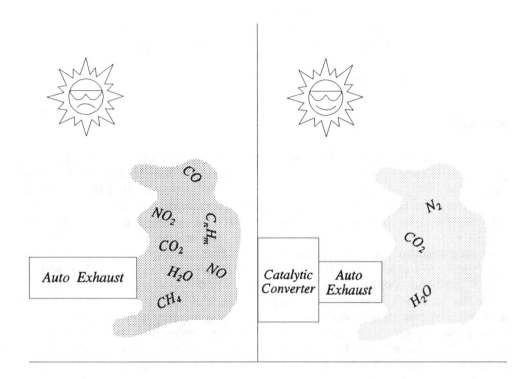

Fig. 5.6: The Chemistry of Catalytic Converters.

Further Reading

Two books discussing urban air pollution problems:

J.D.Butler, *Air Pollution Chemistry*, Academic Press (1979).
Thad Godish, *Air Quality*, Lewis Publishers Inc., (1985).

John Gribbin, *The Hole In the Sky*, Bantam Books (1988). An up to date account of ozone depletion, chlorofluorocarbons and the greenhouse effect. Lovelock's investigations of CFC concentrations in the atmosphere are also described.

INTERLUDE

Dating Gaia

A memorable history of England, comprising all the parts you can remember, including one hundred and three good things, five bad kings and two genuine dates.
(W. C. Sellar and R. J. Yeatman, 1066 and All That)

Introduction

A person's fortieth birthday represents a watershed in his or her life, a vantage point from which to look forward and to look back. With today's extended life expectancy, there is an excellent chance, especially for a woman, that she will live to converse with her great-grandchildren. Looking backwards, for many people at age forty, their parents are most probably still alive and the grandparents certainly clearly remembered. It is quite likely that a person will have childhood memories of at least one great-grandparent. Seven generations, from great-grandparents to great-grandchildren, will have contributed to her experience over the course of her lifetime. In the days before the printed word, the wisdom of the great-grandparents might be passed by direct oral transmission to the great-grandchildren. As Daniel Boorstein put it in his book ***The Discoverers***, "By memory and in memory the fruits of education were garnered, preserved and stored". Today the memory is more likely to be measured in megabytes, but the uniqueness of communication between the generations remains. The great-grandparent was probably born some seventy or eighty years before the birth of our protagonist. Her great-grandchild may well live seventy years after her own death. The total span of their combined experience will be somewhere in the range of 200-250 years given present-day life expectancies. This is the real time unit of human experience, since it relates to the lifetimes of people who know each other as individuals, rather than as dusty records. It is the unit with which to put history in perspective.

The first of Sellars and Yeatman's genuine dates was 1066, the Battle of Hastings. A judicious choice of four or five people, chosen for longevity, could provide a group, some member of which would have personally known someone living in every year since the occurrence of this famous battle. The second memorable date was 55 BC, the arrival of Julius Caesar in England; five or six more well chosen representatives could link us to the Roman legions. After this, genuine dates get relatively rare, but half a dozen additional ancestors would place us with Helen and Achilles at the seige of Troy. Fifteen or eighteen people, a comfortable dinner party, to reminisce on the complete span of our Western civilization. Viewed in this manner, history is short, but the story of Gaia is long. Beyond history lie the days of pre-history, before record-making began, and beyond that lies deep time.

Pre-history is the domain of archeology and deep time that of geology and paleontology. Archeology was long classified as an art, and the dating of the artifacts discovered in long lost cities, was a matter for educated guessing based on accumulated scholarly wisdom and carefully nurtured expertise. A member of the archeological fraternity, using a combination of intuition and experience, could assign a piece of pottery to its correct period and sub-period by visual inspection. The use of scientific methodology to date ancient material is a comparatively recent innovation. It was not uniformly welcomed by the practitioners of the art, one of whom is quoted as complaining "We stand before the threat of the atom in the form of radiocarbon dating. This may be the last chance for old-fashioned, uncontrolled guessing". Nevertheless, scientific dating methods are obviously here to stay, and provide an interesting case history of the interface between the Arts and the Sciences.

The Ages of Artifacts

The most useful dating methods are based on radioactivity. The study of radioactivity was a twentieth century development, and the consequences were unanticipated by late nineteenth century physicists who, as we have seen, considered their subject almost complete. Two relatively common elements, uranium and radium, are naturally radioactive and the discovery that they emitted radiation which fogged photographic plates and heated their surroundings, was of major significance. At first it seemed a challenge to the principle of the conservation of energy, since the origin of the heating effects was not clear, but eventually it was realized that the source lies in the energy contained in the atomic nucleus. The first step on the path to Hiroshima had been taken.

An obvious question to ask concerns the rate at which radioactive nuclei break down to give the observed radiation. The rule was found to be very simple and universal: for a given type of nucleus the rate, in nuclei destroyed per second, depends only on the number of nuclei present. After a given period of time, half the nuclei present will have disintegrated, leaving 50% of those originally present unchanged. After a further period, equal to that taken by the first half to disintegrate, half of the remaining nuclei will have decomposed, leaving 25% of the initial number. The time taken for half of the nuclei to disappear is known as the **half-life** of the isotope. Clearly after three half-lives 12.5% of the original sample will remain, after four half-lives 6.25%, and ever-diminishing amounts thereafter. It is part of the mystery of quantum theory that we can never predict when a given nucleus will decompose, but we can predict with great accuracy the statistical proportion of a large number of nuclei which will decompose in a given period of time. The use of various radioactive materials as clocks, is based on this property.

It has been noted previously that the chemical properties of different isotopes of the same element are identical. The radioactive properties of different isotopes are however not the same, as might have been anticipated, since radioactivity is a nuclear property. Nuclei are made up of protons and neutrons and only certain combinations are stable; instability is manifested in radioactive behavior. Generally, if a nucleus has either too many or too few neutrons for the number of protons it possesses, it will be radioactive and seek a more stable configuration by expelling one or more particles.

The number of naturally occurring radioisotopes is small. The possibility of forming artificial radioactive isotopes occurred to physicists almost as soon as radioactivity was discovered. An obvious method is to bombard stable nuclei with high-energy particles to achieve nuclear changes. Prior to the Second World War, the machinery for accelerating particles to high energies was not available, so physicists had to rely on natural processes. High-energy nuclear particles are not produced anywhere on earth, but they do arrive at our planet from outer space in the form of cosmic rays; cosmic ray research therefore became a subject of some popularity in the 1930's. In the outer reaches of the atmosphere, high energy cosmic rays fragment any atom they encounter to give showers of neutrons, which in turn can react with atoms rather lower in the atmosphere. The most likely atom for a neutron to meet is a nitrogen atom of atomic weight 14, since this is the stable isotope of nitrogen. The resulting nuclear reaction produces a carbon atom of mass 14 and a proton. In effect the ^{14}N nucleus has gained a neutron and lost a proton which reduces its atomic number by one, making it a carbon atom, ^{14}C. ^{14}C is not a stable isotope and will, in due course, emit an electron and change back to ^{14}N. The half-life for this process is 5730 years, which allows time for chemical and biological processes to occur. The likely first event is that it meets an oxygen molecule make carbon dioxide, CO_2. There is therefore always some radioactive carbon incorporated in atmospheric carbon dioxide, since it is being continually formed by cosmic ray bombardment. It is also being continually lost by radioactive decay and in a stable situation the rate of loss will be exactly balanced by the rate of formation. The situation is exactly analogous to that holding for ozone, which is also present in an steady state concentration, except that in this case there is no way that we can deplete the $^{14}CO_2$, since the half-life of a radioactive isotope cannot be changed.

Chemically, $^{14}CO_2$ is identical with normal CO_2 and will be photosynthesized by plants, which in turn can be eaten by animals. Carbon dioxide is inhaled when we breathe in and exhaled when we breathe out, without regard to its isotopic composition. All living things therefore contain a steady state quantity of ^{14}C, since there is constant exchange with atmospheric CO_2. When life stops, renewal of the radiocarbon ceases but radioactive decay continues. The living cells of a tree will contain the same amount of ^{14}C as the atmosphere; dead wood will contain less, since some of its ^{14}C will have been lost by radioactive decay. The extent of the loss measures the length of time since death and this is the basis of the ^{14}C clock.

The idea of using radioactive carbon as a clock was due to Willard F. Libby, who carried out extensive research to make it a practical technique and was awarded the Nobel prize for this work in 1961. The major difficulty is the very low level of radioactivity due to ^{14}C. Approximately 2 atoms of ^{14}C are produced every second for each square centimeter of the earth's surface. It is necessary to obtain the ratio of the number of ^{14}C atoms to normal carbon atoms in a sample of the material under study, which means measuring the number of "counts" on a Geiger counter, which records each radioactive disintegration. In a typical experiment the number of such counts is around 75 per minute but the "background" count, arising from cosmic rays reaching the surface of the earth and from natural radioactivity, is around 500 counts per minute. Elaborate measures must be taken to shield the apparatus from stray radioactivity. Unless this is done, most of the counts recorded on the Geiger counter will not indicate the decay of a ^{14}C atom. Libby first attempted to detect ^{14}C radioactivity using methane gas enriched in the heavier carbon isotopes. In a subsequent experiment he took methane of recent biological origin, obtained from a local sewage plant, and showed that the ^{14}C could be detected at natural levels. It would not have been feasible to use methane from natural gas since all the ^{14}C would have long ago decayed away. This experiment was successful and established that the technique was viable.

The usual procedure for carbon dating in a modern analytical laboratory is to burn carbonaceous material in oxygen, collect and purify the CO_2, and count the radioactivity in a sample of known weight; the lower the radioactive count, the older the material. Charcoal from cooking fires, cloth from garments or any material which would have been derived from a living source at the time of use, provides a suitable material for the analysis. Libby collected contemporary samples from all over the world and showed that the ^{14}C content did not depend on the geographical source of the material. The rate of ^{14}C production from cosmic rays is the same everywhere. He then obtained a number of samples from known historical sources and demonstrated that the ^{14}C dates agreed reasonably well with the actual dates. The technique was now ready for use.

The real value of ^{14}C dating is to obtain dates not available from the historical record, particularly those pertaining to the prehistory of man. There are however some more recent problems of interest. An example is the Shroud of Turin which was shown by radiocarbon dating to be of medieval, rather than of ancient provenance. Various Mycenean and Cretan remains have been dated, but since Troy was excavated well before the advent of the technique it was not studied by this method. There were a number of cities built on the same site, but the accepted date for the Troy of Priam is around 1200 BC.

It would be reassuring to find that where it was possible to check with historical records, radiochemical dating agreed with the accepted chronology. By far the earliest authenticated historic dates come from ancient Egypt, where the records refer to astronomical observations, such as the positions of the star Sirius, which lead to dates which can be calculated with considerable precision. The initial results in this area were encouraging, but more precise measurements revealed discrepancies in dates for material earlier than around the birth of Christ, which rose to a maximum of 500 - 800 years for the earliest Egyptian samples. The radiocarbon dates were always younger than the historical dates. This encouraged archeologists accepting the radiocarbon technique and considerable effort was expended to correct the discrepancy. A possible explanation is that the intensity of cosmic rays reaching the earth was greater in ancient times, leading to the formation of more ^{14}C. The living material therefore started off with more ^{14}C and still has more ^{14}C. Dates from this era would therefore appear younger than they actually are, and need to be corrected for the higher cosmic ray intensity in early times. The solution to the problem came from an unlikely source, the study of tree rings in bristlecone pines which grow in the Southwestern USA. It has been known for many years that the age of trees can be found by counting the number of "rings" on a tree stump, since one such ring is produced every year. In the spring the tree grows rapidly, producing large cells and light colored wood; in the summer the rate of growth diminishes and falls to zero in the fall. The resulting small cells are darker, leading to a succession of lighter and darker bands in a cross-section of the trunk, one for each year of growth. The rings for different years differ in appearance, since climatic conditions are sometimes more favorable for growth than at other times.

The first use of tree ring measurements was therefore to study the history of the weather. In some parts of the world, such as in England, the weather is very variable and can be quite different in two places separated by only a mile or two. In other places, particularly the SW USA, it is quite uniform over a large area. In the latter type of environment the pattern of tree rings, representing the different years of growth, is virtually the same in all trees, particularly those belonging to the same species, over a wide area. Such a pattern therefore provides a method of dating, which is known as dendrochronology. Dendrochronology has the disadvantages that it is only applicable to trees growing in a restricted area and that it is limited in the time span covered. The bristlecone pine does not suffer so seriously from the latter disadvantage. It grows to great ages - trees as old as 4900 years have been discovered - and this age span can be extended by comparing the ring patterns of dead trees and matching the ring patterns with those of younger trees. A characteristic sequence of tree rings back to 5500 BC has been established by overlapping the patterns of different trees, and has been used to date the timbers used in the construction of old Indian pueblos. The real value though, lies in the ability to cross reference this tree ring sequence with radiocarbon dates by analyzing the ^{14}C radioactivity of wood from the different rings.

Only the outer layer of cells in a tree trunk is alive; once a cell has become lignified, exchange with atmospheric CO_2 ceases. Tree ring patterns vary from place to place, but once a single set of rings have been used to calibrate ^{14}C dates, this calibration can be used anywhere in the world. It is then known that a certain number of ^{14}C counts corresponds to an age of 1000 years and another number corresponds to an age of 2000 years. When recalibrated in this manner the radiocarbon dates agree very well with those obtained by archeologists specializing in Egyptian artifacts, and this led to the widespread acceptance of the radiocarbon method of dating. This recalibration raises the question: why was the intensity of cosmic rays greater in ancient times? There is even an answer to this question - variations in the earth's magnetic field affect cosmic-ray intensity. Such variations are well established by measurements of the magnetism of rocks. From time to time the earth's magnetic field reverses its direction, and at times close to the reversal, the field has a very small value. This means that charged cosmic ray particles, which normally would be diverted by the earth's magnetic field, flow in towards the Earth unimpeded and increase the concentration of ^{14}C. Such a reversal is thought to have happened around the time of the Pharaohs, leading to higher levels of ^{14}C. There are indications that at an even earlier time, around 10,000 BC, ^{14}C production was similar to that of today, and so these earlier ^{14}C dates do not have to be substantially corrected.

Radiocarbon dating does not solve all the problems of archeological time measurement, since not all artifacts contain carbon of biological origin. It would be particularly valuable to have a technique which could be applied to pottery samples, since broken shards of pottery are among the most common remains found in sites of ancient habitation. There is one candidate for this task, thermoluminescence. Many minerals luminesce (give off light) when heated and in the case of pottery, the intensity of this luminescence increases with the age of the sample. The luminescence originates in the freeing of electrons trapped in the mineral and released on heating. When the pot was originally fired all such electrons were lost, but with the passage of time more electron defects accumulate, mainly because of exposure to background radiation of the type which complicates ^{14}C dating methodology. There are a number of uncertainties involved in the use of this method, but it promises to complement radiochemical dating. An accuracy of up to 5% in dating has been claimed.

In North America carbon dating has placed the retreat of the glaciers at around 11,400 years ago, and it is reassuring to find that in the areas covered by glaciers, all the dates for sites occupied by humans are later than this. A key period in pre-history is that of the Neolithic cultures, since this corresponds to the adoption of agricultural methods, a necessary prerequisite for the development of civilization. Prior to radiocarbon dating, there were two competing views: a short chronology placing the Neolithic "revolution" in Europe in the time period 3000 BC to 1300 BC, and a long chronology arguing for earlier dates. Various Neolithic sites in Europe have been dated between 2500 and 6000 BC, conclusively favoring the long chronology. The earlier sites are in Greece and the Balkans. To go back to Neolithic times, our dinner party to cover all people up to the present must be expanded to perhaps 35 people, still a manageable group. In other parts of the world, Neolithic settlements cover a rather wider time period. In SW Asia they range from 500 to 7000 BC and in China from 2000 to 4000 BC. In North America, some of the aboriginal sites previously thought to go back to 500 to 1300 AD have been shown by radiocarbon dating to be some 700 to 800 years earlier. Civilization seems to be generally rather older than we thought. Before Neolithic man, the farmer, came Paleolithic man, a hunter and gatherer using stone implements. Many of these sites have been dated in the range 30,000 to 50,000 BC and the view is that the culture arose after the peak of the last ice age at 108,000 BC. Our dinner party now jumps to around 250 guests, some perhaps a little uncouth, and signs of nervousness on the part of the hostess might be expected.

50,000 to 70,000 years is about the limit of ^{14}C dating since by this time less that 0.1% of the original radioactive isotope remains. Further back than this, other techniques to be discussed below are required. To add perspective, it might be noted that an African site where Leakey has uncovered evidence for some of man's predecessors, or at least close relatives, has been dated by the Potassium/Argon method (see below) as 1.75 million years old. Our dinner party has now expanded to some 8000 people and would require the rental of a fairly large arena.

The Ages of Rocks

The occupation of this planet by man, or his relatives, has only occurred in the recent past. History stretches far beyond this era into what Gould has called "deep time". The full appreciation of the true depths of time only developed in the nineteenth century. Prior to this, since the age of the earth had been determined by theological means to be just over 5000 years, all history and prehistory was accommodated within this span. Geological studies established that all rocks were not of equal age, and suggested that lower-lying strata were formed before higher-lying strata. The question: how much before? The importance of this question was emphasized by the discovery of fossils embedded in the different rock strata. Some of these fossils resembled species presently alive on earth, but some did not. Charles Lyell, considered to be the father of modern geology, suggested that the rocks containing fossils clearly related to present day species, were of recent origin and those containing fossils of species now extinct, were more ancient. He was able to construct a relative ordering of the strata based on their fossil content. The question of the age of fossils became crucial when Charles Darwin used the fossil record to argue for the theory of evolution, which clearly demanded very long time spans to accommodate the changes in life observed.

One of the earliest suggestions for estimating the age of the earth - which obviously places a limit on the ages of rocks - was to measure the rate at which salts are eroded from the land and deposited in the sea. This method gives the age of the oceans as some 90 million years, but we now know that this estimate is incorrect because there are processes removing salt from the sea as well as adding it. Similar types of calculation based on the rate of deposition of sediments are also inherently uncertain. Lyell estimated that hundreds of millions of years were necessary to account for the evolutionary changes observed in only a part of the fossil record. It was disturbing to scientists therefore, when Lord Kelvin, who was the most prestigious physicist of his time, by considering the rate of cooling of the earth from its original molten state, calculated in 1862 that the age of the earth, allowing for a fair amount of uncertainty, was around 100 million years or less. This figure did not seem to allow sufficient time for evolution to occur. In retrospect we appreciate that he was unaware of radioactivity and therefore did not allow for the additional heating from this source. With the discovery of radioactivity, not only was this source of error realized, but more exact methods for dating rocks became available.

The use of radioactive decay for this purpose differs from the ^{14}C method described above. The supply of ^{14}C is continuously renewed by cosmic rays. Other radioactive isotopes are not so renewed, and we must rely on the quantities which have remained since the synthesis of the elements. This means that they must be very long-lived, and in fact only 21 naturally radioactive nuclides remain on earth. Four of these are useful for dating purposes. Merely measuring the amount of radioactivity is not sufficient to establish a date; we must at the same time measure the concentration of one of the products of radioactive decay, known as a daughter isotope. Knowing that one atom of radioactive isotope gives one atom of daughter isotope, we can calculate how much radioactive isotope was present when the rock was formed (the sum of the present concentration plus the daughter isotope concentration) and compare it with the amount now present. If we know the half-life of the isotope, this gives us the age of the rock. Errors will clearly arise either if there is daughter isotope present which was not formed by radioactive decay, or if some of the daughter isotope has been lost by erosion of the rock.

The most useful combination of mother and daughter isotopes for radioactive dating is ^{40}K and ^{40}Ar. Potassium is a widely distributed element and the radioactive isotope ^{40}K comprises some 0.0119% of natural potassium. This isotope has a very long life-time of 1300 million years and is therefore capable of dating extremely old rocks. The daughter isotope, ^{40}Ar, is a chemically inert gas and it is considered certain that any Ar found in potassium-containing rocks has arisen from radioactive decay. There is however some tendency for the gaseous argon to escape from the rock, particularly if, during the course of its history, it has been heated to temperatures greater than 200 °C. Dates obtained by this method are therefore considered minimum dates - if some argon has been lost, the rock will be older than calculated. Not all kinds of rocks are suitable for use in this dating technique, since permeable rocks will lose their argon. Igneous rocks, originating in volcanic activity, are considered the most reliable and where the strata are sedimentary in nature, igneous intrusions are used. This technique gives a date of around 570 million years for the Cambrian rocks, the lowest strata containing well defined fossils. This dating is consistent with present evolutionary theory. Among more recent events, the extinction of the dinosaurs at the Cretaceous/Tertiary interface is placed at 65 million years ago. Not all geological events occurred in such distant times. The ages of the Hawaiian islands, for example, decrease steadily from around 5 million years to less than 1 million years on passing down the chain from Kauai, with extinct volcanoes, to Hawaii with still active volcanoes.

The three other isotopes useful for radioactive dating are Rubidium 87 which decays to Strontium 87 with a half-life of 47,000 million years; Uranium 238 which decays to Lead 206 with a half-life of 4510 million years; and Uranium 235 which decays to Lead 207 with a half-life of 713 million years. The major problem with Rubidium is that it is a rare element and often is just not present in the rocks to be dated. In spite of this it has been used to a surprisingly large extent. The use of the Uranium isotopes has the advantage that the two isotopic decay processes give the possibility of cross-checking the dates. It will be noticed that in this case the daughter isotopes are not the direct product of the decay but are formed in a sequence of nuclear reactions involving short-lived radioactive isotopes. The oldest rocks on earth dated by this method are in the range 3,500 to 4,000 million years old. Fossils attributed to microbes have been found as far back as 3,000 million years. Prior to about 2,000 million years there was no large amount of oxygen in the atmosphere, and the microbes had an anaerobic metabolism. Plant life and the most primitive animals appeared about 800 million years ago. All of these dates have been reasonably well established by radioactive dating techniques.

The Ages of the Earth and of the Universe

The age of the oldest rocks does not necessarily correspond to the age of the earth. Estimates of the age of the earth are based on the distribution of Lead and Uranium isotopes. There are three isotopes of lead, ^{204}Pb, ^{206}Pb and ^{207}Pb. The latter two are derived from the decay of uranium, as we have seen above. ^{204}Pb does not result from radioactive decay and must be considered primordial. The essential information is contained in the ratios of the abundances of these three isotopes. Let us consider the fact that all of the ^{206}Pb presently in existence has resulted from the decay of ^{238}U. Knowing the half-life of ^{238}U, it can be calculated that 5,600 million years would be required to form this amount of ^{206}Pb. This represents the maximum possible age of the earth, since if the earth were older there would be a higher proportion of ^{206}Pb than is observed, as ^{238}U is still present to decay. A similar calculation based on ^{207}Pb gives a maximum age of 6,800 million years. The earth must therefore be younger than 5,600 million years but older than 4,000 million years, the age of the oldest rocks. The usually accepted value is 4,600 million years. This is based on the ages of meteorites which are also determined by measuring the ratios of lead isotopes. It is believed that the earth was formed by the accumulation of material resulting from a supernova star exploding, and that meteorites represent residual material which avoided incorporation into one of the major planets. If this model is correct, the age of the meteorites should be approximately equal to that of the earth. Interestingly, the rocks collected from the moon are also dated at 4,600 million years, indicating that the moon was created, more or less in its present form, at the same time as the earth was born.

It only remains to give a date for the beginning of the universe itself. The modern "big bang" theory of the origin of the universe implies a definite date of creation. This is estimated from the rate of recession of the galaxies. Galaxies are getting further and further apart at a rate which is proportional to their present separations. This is a consequence of the model of an expanding universe predicted by the general theory of relativity. If we can extrapolate back to a point in time when all the galaxies were in the same place, we will have a date for the beginning of the universe. The rate of expansion can be measured with considerable accuracy, based on the red shift of light from the different galaxies, but the distances of the galaxies are more difficult to determine. As a result, the initial estimate of the age of the universe was 2,000 million years, which is embarrassingly less than the age of the earth. However, more recent measurements of the distances have increased this to the range 10,000 to 20,000 million years and the favored figure at present seems to be around 16,000 million years.

The Age of Consciousness

In the introduction to this topic of dating, it was suggested that it is a subject which bridges the realms of the Arts and the Sciences. The discussion of the age of the universe has moved us firmly into the domain of science, so it is perhaps appropriate to finish with a question which cannot be answered using any form of radioactive dating. Julian Jaynes, a distinguished psychologist, has posed the question: "How old is consciousness?". More surprisingly he even has an answer - about 3000 years. Clearly this answer depends very much on the definition of consciousness adopted.

In its simplest form, consciousness has certainly been around for a long time. Anyone who has shared a home with a cat can have little doubt that such animals, although of limited intelligence, have a well developed sense of self-interest which must require some form of consciousness. Jaynes suggests the following definition.

> "Consciousness refers to what the average person
> would answer to the question "what are you thinking
> about" ..... a stream of worries, regrets, hopes,
> reminiscences, interior dialogues, plans, imaginations
> - all of which is the stuff of consciousness."

This certainly seems a fair description of what passes through the mind of the "average person". One might have thought though, that this is the way things have been since the beginning of man. Jaynes argues that this is not so. He bases his argument on the study of the earliest literature, Homer's *Iliad* and the Old Testament of the Bible. He considers that consciousness arose as a result of the development of language as a means of communication. This is thought to have occurred some 50,000 years ago, accompanied by, or as a result of, the making of tools in the age of Paleolithic and Neanderthal men.

Language leads to the use of metaphors and this is an essential feature of consciousness. It did not however immediately lead to consciousness as we know it today; the immediate result was the "bicameral" mind, consisting of a decision-making part and a separate, follower part. These were the days when men heard the voices of gods in a very immediate and real way. When summoned, they would deliver commands and provide the instructions by which man lived his life. Nowadays, we tend to dismiss such phenomena as auditory hallucinations, experienced in times of stress by only a few people, such as Joan of Arc and sufferers from schizophrenia. But the societies of the early civilizations were organized as hierarchical theocracies, and modern individual consciousness was not present. Bicameral man had no inner world of the type we experience; there is no analogue "I" narratizing in a mind-space. The earliest literature, such as the most ancient parts of the *Iliad* and the early books of the Old Testament, reflect this lack of introspection and emphasize reliance on outside authority for decisions. The development of present-day consciousness is recorded by the change of literary style. It corresponded to a time when the old gods were failing, perhaps from a combination of population pressures and natural catastrophes, and man was left on his own to make decisions. Different civilizations experienced this change at different times, but for the Western world it took place sometime between 1400 BC and 600 BC. Perhaps the representative from Troy at our exclusive dinner party, being a bicameral man, would not contribute much to the intellectual ferment.

Clearly the above is an intriguing, but probably unprovable, hypothesis which should keep scholars arguing for an extended period of time. Literary analysis is definitely on the Arts side of the great divide. There is though a sleeper in Jaynes' theory. He suggests that the bicameral mind is linked to the hemispheric structure of the brain. It is accepted that the functions of the left and right hemispheres of the brain are different. Perhaps the right hemisphere, previously reserved for communication with the gods, achieved a new role with the development of full consciousness. This could possibly be a topic for future neurobiological research.

Further reading

David Wilson, *Atoms from Time Past*, Allen Lane (1975). An excellent account of the discovery and development of radiocarbon dating.

Two books on the ages of rocks:
Don L. Eicher, *Geologic Time*, Prentice-Hall, 2nd Ed. (1976).
D. York and R. M. Farquhar, *The Earth's Age and Geochronology*, Pergamon Press (1972).

Stephan Jay Gould, *Time's Arrow Time's Cycle*, Harvard Univ. Press (1987). The discovery of "deep time".

Donald E. Osterbrock and Peter H. Raven, editors, *Origins and Extinctions*, Yale Univ. Press (1988). Contains chapters on the ages of the earth and of the universe.
Grahame Clark, *World Prehistory*, Cambridge Univ. Press, 3rd Ed. (1977). The dating of prehistoric man.

Stephen W. Hawking, *A Brief History of Time*, Bantam Books, (1988). Physics and the Big Bang.

Julian Jaynes, *How Old is Consciousness?*, in *Exploring the Concept of Mind*, ed. R. M. Caplan, Univ. of Iowa Press (1986).

Julian Jaynes, *The Origin of Consciousness in the Breakdown of the Bicameral Mind*, Houghton Mifflin (1976, 1990). Jaynes theory of the origin of consciousness. (The former reference is a summary and the latter a more complete discussion.)

CHAPTER SIX

The Chemical Industry

Introduction

The number of chemical substances which occur naturally in our biosphere in significant quantities is really quite small, and most of them have been encountered in previous chapters of this book. There are traces of many more substances in the sea and in the earth, and animals and plants produce a myriad of organic compounds in small amounts.

Chemists working in laboratories have synthesized hundreds of thousands of compounds which do not occur in nature. The vast majority of these substances never emerge from the laboratory, perhaps fortunately. A significant number though - certainly in the thousands - are manufactured by the chemical industry and are present in sufficient quantities to constitute an appreciable component of the contemporary biosphere. All of these chemicals are produced for good reasons, and together they make a large positive contribution to the quality of our lives. This is the upside of the chemical industry and its importance should not be underestimated. In some instances there is also a downside, as we saw in the case of chlorofluorocarbons, and the overall balance may be judged negative. In the present chapter, the chemistry used in the manufacture of a few of the major products of the chemical industry will be examined, and some of their useful properties noted. Discussion of the negative impacts of the chemical and related industries will be deferred to the next chapter.

The chemical industry has its origins in antiquity but the modern version dates back only to the last century. The state of the industry in the nineteenth century is summarized in Figure 6.1.

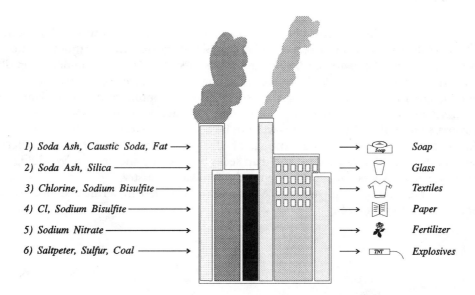

1) Soda Ash, Caustic Soda, Fat →	→ Soap
2) Soda Ash, Silica →	→ Glass
3) Chlorine, Sodium Bisulfite →	→ Textiles
4) Cl, Sodium Bisulfite →	→ Paper
5) Sodium Nitrate →	→ Fertilizer
6) Saltpeter, Sulfur, Coal →	→ Explosives

■ *Six traditional industries...*

In 1850 there were six major chemical-using industries - soap, glass, textiles, paper, fertilizers and explosives; all of these required the manufacture of only simple inorganic materials. The soap industry needed soda ash (Na_2CO_3) and caustic soda (NaOH) to react with naturally-occurring animal fats. Glass required soda ash to combine with silica (sand), and various metal oxides to add color to the product. The textile and paper industries needed bleaches, a demand met with chlorine and sodium bisulfite ($NaHSO_3$).   Textiles at this time were dyed with naturally- occurring compounds extracted from various plants and sea animals. Chile saltpeter, sodium nitrate ($NaNO_3$) was used as a fertilizer, and gunpowder, made from saltpeter (KNO_3), sulfur and charcoal was the mainstay of the explosives industry. The organic chemicals industry developed in the second half of the nineteenth century. It was mostly an outgrowth of the distillation of coal to make coal gas, increasingly used for heating and lighting. Perkin, an English chemist, made the first coal tar dye in 1856, and German chemists rapidly exploited the manufacture of superior dyes from the aromatic (benzene-containing) byproducts of the coal gas industry. About the same time, more effective explosives were made by nitrating aromatic compounds with the then-available nitric and sulfuric acids. The Haber-Bosch process for the fixing of nitrogen was developed in Germany during the First World War when the importation of Chile saltpeter from South America became difficult. At the same time the British organic chemicals industry was developed to counterbalance the absence of imports from Germany.   Thereafter the development of the industry was rapid, but the real expansion came after the Second World War and was associated with the very large-scale production of petrochemicals.

Fertilizers

The benefits of fertilizers are perhaps more obvious than those of any other product. It was discovered very early in man's history that crops cannot be grown continuously on the same land, since the yields in successive years diminish rapidly. The first solution was no doubt to move the community to fresh pastures, but by the middle ages the principles of crop rotation to make the optimum use of the land, had been established. Plants need certain essential elements to grow, and unless these materials are replenished, the crop will not be a success. Nature returns the essential material to the soil by the rotting of dead vegetation and by its bacterial decomposition. This takes time and man seeks to speed up the process by adding the necessary ingredients for growth; hence the fertilizer industry.

Three essential elements are commonly included in fertilizers; potassium, phosphorus and nitrogen.

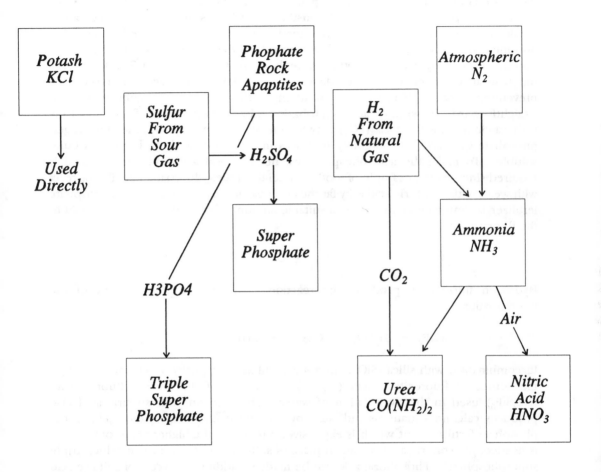

Fig. 6.2: Fertilizers. Potassium, phosphorus and nitrogen are the three elements which must be provided to obtain good yields of food crops.

■ Potash...
■ Phosphorous...

The chemical problems involved in their production are quite different. Potassium is very easy. It occurs in places such as Saskatchewan, Canada as potassium chloride, KCl, and is commonly, but erroneously, known as potash (which is really KOH) and can be incorporated into commercial fertilizers without further chemical transformation. Phosphorus is a little bit more difficult. It occurs as minerals known as fluoro- and chloro-apatites; the former has the composition $CaF_2.3[Ca_3(PO_4)_2]$ and the latter is similar with the fluorine replaced by chlorine. Fluoroapatite is simply a mixed salt of calcium fluoride and calcium phosphate. The apatites are completely insoluble in water and hence cannot be used as fertilizers - they could be spread on the ground but would never reach the plants. This insolubility is not surprising - since calcium phosphate is the principal constituent of bones and water-soluble bones would obviously be ineffective. Hydroxyapatite, the compound obtained by replacing fluorine with hydroxyl, OH, in the above formula, is the enamel on teeth. The use of fluoride in drinking water or toothpaste replaces the OH group with F and increases the resistance of the enamel to dissolution by the organic acids in food, thus preventing cavities. The chemical solution to the problem of solubility is quite straightforward. Phosphoric acid is a tribasic acid and therefore will form three salts with calcium phosphate $Ca_3(PO_4)_2$, hydrogen phosphate $CaHPO_4$, and dihydrogen phosphate $CaH_4(PO_4)_2$. Solubility increases in this series and the last salt is quite soluble. To make the acid phosphate we need to add acid and a strong acid is required since, as the example of tooth enamel illustrates, fluoroapatite will not react with weak acids. Sulfuric acid is by far the cheapest acid available and superphosphate fertilizer is simply made by adding a suitable amount of concentrated sulfuric acid to the fluoroapatite.

$$Ca_3(PO_4)^2 + 2H_2SO_4 \rightarrow CaH_4(PO_4)_2 + 2CaSO_4$$

Hydrogen fluoride is produced by reaction with the CaF_2 component of the fluoroapatite.

$$CaF_2 + H_2SO_4 \rightarrow CaSO_4 + 2HF$$

Its combination with silica (SiO_2), always present as an impurity in phosphate rock, is the source of fluorosilicic acid (H_2SiF_6) and hence of the sodium fluorosilicate (Na_2SiF_6) used in the fluoridation of water. The reaction with sulfuric acid also produces calcium sulfate, as indicated by the above equations, which dilutes the phosphate fertilizer, but which is expensive to remove. If a higher grade of fertilizer is needed, phosphoric acid is used in place of sulfuric acid to give the product "triple superphosphate". Phosphoric acid can be made by adding an excess of sulfuric acid to the phosphate rock and removing the calcium sulfate by filtration, or, in a purer form, by heating phosphate rock and carbon in an electric furnace.

$$Ca_3(PO_4)_2 + 3H_2SO_4 \rightarrow 2H_3PO_4 + 3CaSO_4$$
$$2Ca_3(PO_4)_2 + 28C \rightarrow 6CaC_2 + 16CO + P_4$$

Elemental phosphorus made according to the last equation can be burnt to give phosphorus pentoxide, which dissolves in water to give pure phosphoric acid.

$$P_4 + 5O_2 \rightarrow 2P_2O_5$$
$$P_2O_5 + 3H_2O \rightarrow 2H_3PO_4$$

Phosphoric acid can be reacted with sodium carbonate to give a compound sodium tripolyphosphate. This compound has the formula $Na_5P_3O_{10}$ and its structure is shown in Figure 6.3.

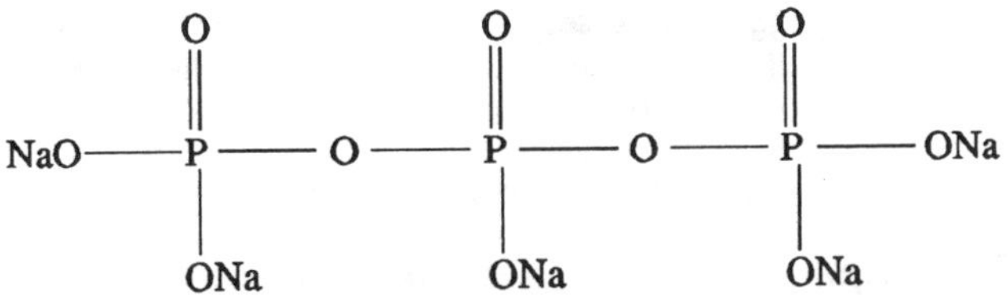

$$Na_5P_3O_{10}$$

Fig. 6.3: Sodium Tripolyphosphate.

This material is widely used in detergents as a "builder". It is not the active component of the detergent but it performs a number of useful functions such as controlling the pH, "sequestering" ions such as Ca^{2+} and Mg^{2+} which make the water hard, and keeping dirt in suspension. The original "Tide" detergent contained up to 50% of this builder. The structure of this compound, with three phosphate groups linked together, closely resembles that of the biologically important molecules which are essential components in living things. It is not surprising therefore, that detergent phosphates serve as an excellent nutrient for algae and other unwanted biomass in water, and have been a major contributor to water pollution problems. Phosphates in powdered soap have now been largely replaced by less environmentally damaging materials.

■ *Sulfuric acid...*

Making phosphate fertilizers requires sulfuric acid, so we should perhaps pursue the subject one step further and ask how sulfuric acid is made. Sulfuric acid is the largest-volume chemical produced, some 40 or 50 million tons being made per year in the USA alone. About 60 or 70% is used in the production of phosphate fertilizer and the remainder has a great variety of uses. It is made from elemental sulfur by the contact process, which involves three chemical steps.

$$S + O_2 \rightarrow SO_2$$
$$SO_2 + \tfrac{1}{2}O_2 \rightleftharpoons SO_3$$
$$SO_3 + H_2O \rightarrow H_2SO_4$$

The first and third steps take place readily but the second is more difficult. It requires a catalyst to increase the rate of a reaction. Finding the best catalyst is often the secret of a successful industrial chemical process; in this case the secret is vanadium pentoxide, the SO_2 and O_2 being passed over this catalyst at 600 °C and the resulting SO_3 being absorbed in sulfuric acid, since absorption directly into water produces acid mists which cause engineering difficulties.

化學

Demonstration 6.1
The Contact Process. To produce sulfur trioxide, dry sulfur dioxide and oxygen are passed over heated vanadium pentoxide. In this experiment the sulfur dioxide and oxygen are dried by passing them through sulfuric acid. Sulfur trioxide is a solid at room temperature and can be condensed in a flask to give needle-shaped crystals. It fumes on contact with moist air due to the reaction with water to give sulfuric acid.

Most of the sulfur used to make sulfuric acid is obtained from the hydrogen sulfide extracted from "sour" natural gas by the Claus process:

$$2H_2S + O_2 \rightarrow 2S + 2H_2O$$

Thus sulfuric acid and phosphate fertilizers, in the modern chemical industrial scheme of things, are ultimately products of the petrochemical industry.

Nitrogen is a little more difficult to obtain in a form suitable for agricultural purposes. It is present in the biosphere in great abundance as nitrogen gas, N_2, but is useless to plant life in this form. To make a fertilizer the nitrogen must be "fixed" into some more accessible form. The great chemical stability of N_2 makes this a difficult problem. Perhaps the most obvious answer would be to oxidize it to nitrogen oxides, as happens to a small extent in automobile combustion, but it turns out that the most economical route is to reduce it to ammonia:

$$2N_2 + 3H_2 \leftrightarrow 2NH_3 \qquad \Delta H = -46kJ/mole$$

■ *Nitrogen...*

This is the basis of the Haber-Bosch process, developed in Germany at the time of the First World War, to replace Chile saltpeter as a fertilizer. It is manufactured on a very large scale, in 1984 some 3.5 million tons were made in Canada and about 14 million tons in the USA. As is indicated by the double arrow in the equation above, the reaction does not spontaneously go to completion, but leads to an equilibrium mixture of the product and starting materials. Economics demand that the process be made as efficient as possible, so the problem is one of adjusting the conditions to produce as much ammonia in as short a time as is practical; this is typical of the problems involved in industrial chemistry. The way a process such as this is run is to pass the heated gases at high pressure over a catalyst. Three parameters can be varied: the temperature, the pressure and the catalyst. The latter makes the reaction go faster but does not affect the position of the equilibrium. (With a poor catalyst we obtain exactly the same amount of product as with a good catalyst, but it takes longer.) At the end of Chapter 3 we saw that equilibrium constants are determined by the changes in free energy during a reaction. Mathematical development of this idea allows the calculation of the equilibrium constant, and hence of the concentrations of the reactants, under different conditions of temperature and pressure. There is however an easier way to find out the qualitative answers to this kind of question. This involves the use of **LeChatelier's principle** which states:

> When any of the conditions which affect the position of a dynamic equilibrium are changed, the position of the equilibrium shifts so as to minimize the effect of the change.

This is a very convenient principle, in many cases it allows us to obtain the information we require without doing any mathematical calculations. In the present case, one molecule of nitrogen plus three molecules of hydrogen give two molecules of ammonia. Four molecules have been transformed to two molecules and therefore, by Avogadro's principle, four volumes of gas become two. What happens then if we increase the pressure under which the reaction is run? The system will try to minimize the effect of the increase in pressure. This can be accomplished by shifting the equilibrium to the right since for the same amount of material, the two volumes of product will exert less pressure than the four volumes of reactants. On the contrary, if the temperature is increased, since the reaction is **exothermic** the equilibrium shifts to the <u>left.</u> If a reaction is exothermic going from left to right, it will be endothermic going from right to left, and the heat absorbed by going in this direction will minimize the effect of the heat provided by the rise in temperature. It is deduced therefore that the Haber-Bosch process should be run at as high a pressure and as low a temperature as possible.

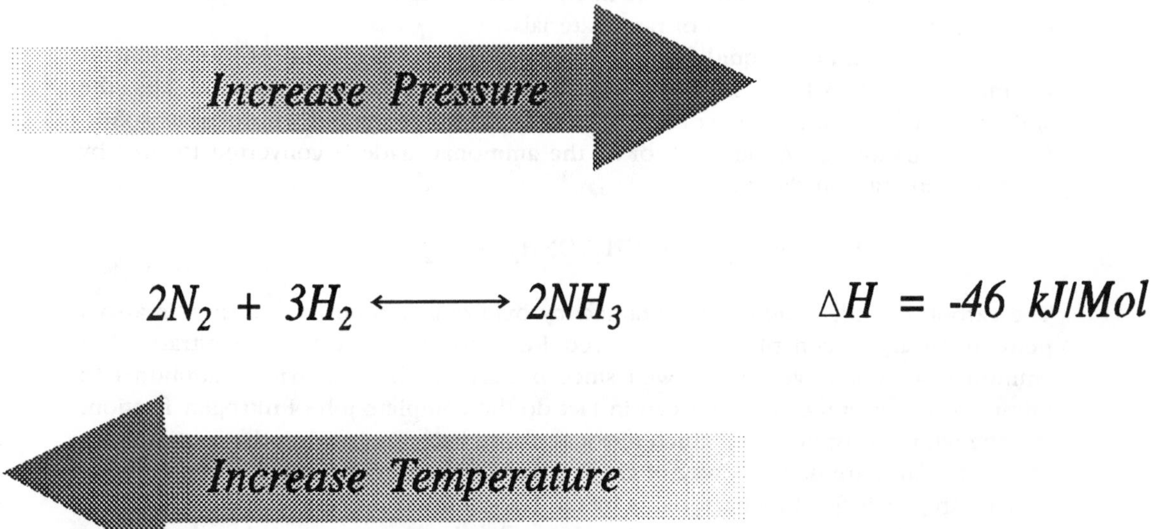

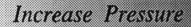

$$2N_2 + 3H_2 \longleftrightarrow 2NH_3 \qquad \Delta H = -46 \ kJ/Mol$$

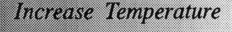

Fig. 6.4: LeChatelier's Principle. The yield of ammonia in the Haber Process is maximized by running the reaction at high pressure and at low temperature.

There are some limitations to the application of LeChatelier's principle to industrial processes. If the temperature is too low, even with a good catalyst, the reaction will be very slow. (If you have to wait a year before obtaining any ammonia, it is not likely to be an economical process.) Similarly there are engineering limits on how high a pressure is used. If the cost quadruples to build a strong enough vessel to contain the higher pressure, it probably isn't worth it. In practice, a temperature of 400-500 °C, an iron catalyst and a pressure of 150-300 atmospheres give about a 30% conversion to ammonia. The unreacted hydrogen and nitrogen can then be recycled to produce more ammonia.

It is obvious that the nitrogen used in this process is most economically obtained from the air. It is less obvious how the hydrogen is best produced. At the present time the most economical source is natural gas which can be reacted with steam:

$$CH_4 + H_2O \rightarrow CO + 3H_2$$

■ *Synthesis gas...*

The mixture of carbon monoxide and hydrogen is known as synthesis gas. Depending on the use its composition can be varied by mixing the steam with air, which decreases the H_2 by oxidation to H_2O, thus increasing the proportion of carbon monoxide. To make ammonia the maximum amount of hydrogen is desirable. Thus in the last analysis all of the fertilizer industry (except potash) is dependent on the petrochemical industry, and specifically on the production of natural gas. When the gas runs out we may be hungry as well as cold; a more likely scenario will be that we are going to have to look for alternative sources of raw materials.

Ammonia, in its liquid form, can be used directly as a fertilizer but is difficult to transport and to handle. Much of it is transformed into ammonium salts, the sulfate, the nitrate or the phosphate, or to urea, which are all fairly innocuous solids, for ease of handling. About 20% of all the ammonia made is converted to urea by reaction with carbon dioxide:

$$2NH_3 + CO_2 \rightarrow NH_2CONH_2 + H_2O$$

The carbon dioxide required is obtained by oxidizing natural gas, so urea is also a petrochemical. Green plants actually require nitrogen in the form of nitrates, but ammonia or urea serve equally well since bacteria in the soil oxidize ammonia to nitrate very efficiently. Bacteria can in fact do the complete job of nitrogen fixation, starting with atmospheric N_2. Such nitrogen-fixing bacteria grow on the root nodules of legumes and are nature's way of closing the nitrogen cycle. About three times as much nitrogen is fixed by bacteria as by the Haber-Bosch process and the reaction is carried out at room temperature and under atmospheric pressure, rather than under the extreme conditions of temperature and pressure characteristic of a modern petrochemical plant. Chemists have been trying to duplicate this feat in a convenient laboratory synthesis for many years, but have so far not succeeded.

Biological enzymes are very much more efficient and effective than man-made catalysts. The major thrust at present is to follow the precept that "if you can't beat them, join them". The objective is to use biotechnological techniques to produce strains of nitrogen-fixing bacteria, which will grow on the roots of crops such as wheat. The crops will then, in effect, produce their own nitrogen fertilizer, an elegant solution to the problem.

Even if the direct use of ammonia as a fertilizer were to vanish because of developments in biotechnology, the chemical would still be in large demand as a feed-stock since it is the source of all synthetic nitrogen containing compounds. This includes everything from explosives to nylon to pharmaceuticals. The major secondary product is nitric acid, which is made by oxidizing ammonia with air over a platinum/rhodium (Pt/Rh) catalyst.

$$4NH_3 + 5O_2 \rightarrow 4NO + 6H_2O$$

The nitric oxide (NO) made in this way is then further reacted with air and water.

■ *Nitric acid...*

$$2NO + O_2 \rightarrow 2NO_2 \quad \text{(exists partly as the dimer } N_2O_4)$$
$$3NO_2 + H_2O(l) \rightarrow 2HNO_3 \quad \text{(nitric acid)} + NO$$

The NO can then be recycled to give more nitric acid. The first step in this process illustrates some common types of problems faced in the chemical industry. The reaction as written is the desirable reaction, but there are a number of undesirable reactions which can occur between the molecules present.

$$4NH_3 + 3O_2 \rightarrow 2N_2 + 6H_2O \qquad (1)$$
$$4NH_3 + 6NO \rightarrow 5N_2 + 6H_2O \qquad (2)$$
$$2NO \rightarrow N_2 + O_2 \qquad (3)$$

Demonstration 6.2
The Catalytic oxidation of ammonia. The commercial catalyst for oxidizing ammonia is made from platinum and rhodium. Copper is also effective and is used in this demonstration. A coil of copper wire is pre-heated in a flame and then suspended over a concentrated solution of ammonia. The gaseous ammonia is oxidized on the hot copper to nitric oxide. This reaction is exothermic and the copper coil glows brightly and eventually melts. The blue color of the solution which develops when the molten copper falls into it is due to a complex of Cu^{2+} with ammonia.

Reactions (1), (2) and (3) all lead to the formation of nitrogen gas, which effectively means that a very cheap material is being made from a relatively expensive material. This is not the way to make money and steps must be taken to discourage these pathways. Reaction (1) is not catalyzed by Pt/Rh but occurs on hot surfaces. It is important to keep the walls of the reaction vessel well cooled. Reaction (2) can be avoided by removing the NO rapidly from the reaction vessel so as not to give it an opportunity to react with incoming NH_3. Reaction (3) requires a high temperature and can be avoided by rapid cooling of the NO product. These are the types of problems which designers of chemical plants must consider and resolve.

Pesticides and Herbicides

Fertilizers represent one side of the chemical industry - the very large-scale production of rather simple inorganic compounds. Pesticides and herbicides show another face of the industry - the relatively smaller-scale manufacture of more complicated organic compounds. In some products the two are combined, as for example the garden product "Weed and Feed", containing both fetilizer and weed-killer. The trend towards the small-scale production of complicated molecules reaches its peak in the pharmaceutical industry, which also represents the maximum in price per kilogram of product.

■ *DDT...*

Pesticides are still large-scale products, with outputs being measured in the millions of pounds, and prices in the area of dollars per pound, rather than the cents per pound of fertilizers. (It is estimated that food prices would be 50-75% higher without the use of pesticides.) The insecticide DDT is said to have saved the lives of 25 million people by reducing malaria and other insect-borne diseases, and to have increased the lifespan of the average inhabitant of India by 15 years. These materials have not had a good press in recent years and some of the positive contributions tend to be overlooked. The usual division is into insecticides, herbicides and fungicides which take about 35%, 58% and 7% of the market respectively. 68% of the products are used in agriculture as opposed to 8% in homes and gardens.

The earliest pesticides were inorganic compounds of copper, lead and arsenic which were not very specific in what they killed. These were supplemented by a number of naturally-occurring organics derived from plant materials. The first synthetic organic insecticide was DDT, the insecticidal properties of which were discovered by Dr. Paul Mueller in 1939. The timing was right for extensive use during the Second World War. Dr. Mueller was awarded the Nobel prize in medicine and physiology for his discovery in 1948. DDT, which is the acronym for Dichloro Diphenyl Trichloroethane, is a relatively simple organic compound and its structure and the equation for its synthesis are shown in Figure 6.5.

Its use has been discontinued in many countries, for two reasons. Firstly, it is persistent and may have long-term effects on the ecology, a subject which will be discussed more extensively in the next chapter. Secondly, the natural selection process of evolution has lead to the appearance of insects which have considerable resistance to the chemical. Since many generations of insects can live their lives in a comparatively short period of time, evolutionary changes occur much more rapidly in insects than in mammals. All insecticides are therefore likely to have a limited useful life-time.

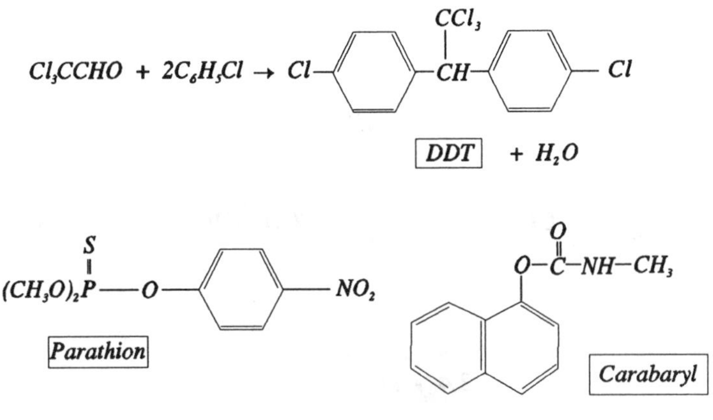

Fig. 6.5: Structures of Insecticides. DDT is made from chlorobenzene and chloral. Newer insecticides are either organophosphorus compounds (Parathion) or carbamates (Carbaryl).

■ Organophosphorus insecticides and carbamates...

Insecticides are generally thought to work by interfering with the operation of a specific enzyme. The problem is that the enzymes in different species are often similar and what is poisonous to the insects may well also be poisonous to other living forms, including man. This is equally true of other toxic substances. For example, polychlorinated biphenyls, PCB's, which are chemically closely related to DDT, were not developed as insecticides but for quite different uses as flame retardants and insulating fluids in electrical transformers. PCB's pose a similar threat to DDT.

Two other classes of insecticides have been developed and examples are shown in Figure 6.2. Organophosphorus insecticides are much more poisonous to humans, being chemically closely related to nerve gases, but may be safer overall since they decompose rapidly in the environment. Carbamates have many desirable properties as insecticides, but again are not without their drawbacks; methyl isocyanate, the essential ingredient in their manufacture, was the cause of the tragedy of the chemical spill in Bhopal, India. The most recent trend in this area is to resort to biological agents rather than chemical insecticides. Pheromones, the insect sex attractants, can be used to draw insects to a site suitable for their safe disposal. These are compounds which are very specific to a single species and therefore present a minimal danger to other species. An alternative is the use of juvenile hormones which prevent the maturation of insects, and hence limit the infestation to one generation.

■ Herbicides...

Herbicides are equally important economically, and have proved just as contentious in their usage as insecticides. The best known are the phenoxy herbicides, 2,4 D and 2,4,5 T, the structures of which are shown in Figure 6.6.

2,4 - D   *2, 4, 5 - T*

Triazine

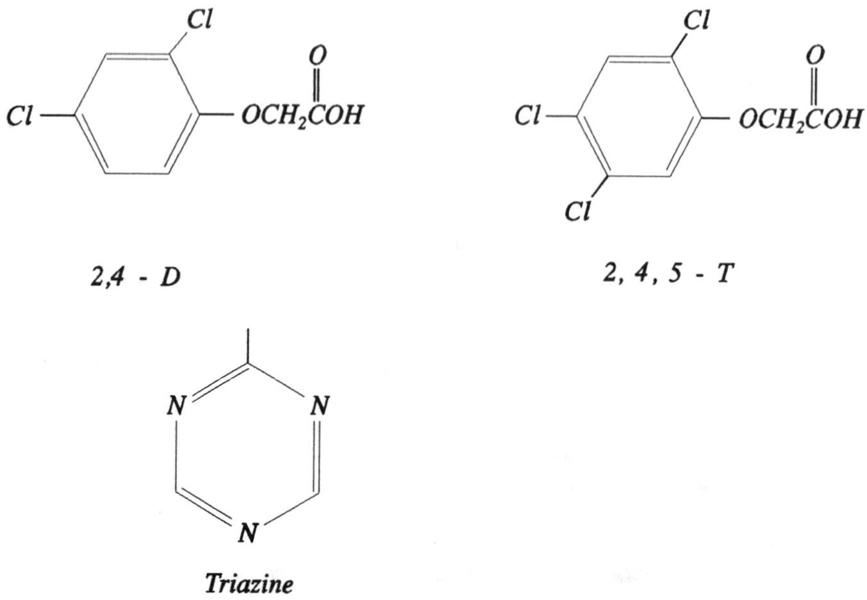

Fig. 6.6: Structures of Herbicides.   The first modern herbicides were the chlorine compounds 2,4-D and 2,4,5-T. The most widely used are now compounds based on the triazine ring.   The triazines used have chlorine- and nitrogen-containing substituents.

This type of herbicide was the basis for the infamous Agent Orange used as a defoliant in the Vietnam war. These particular compounds are <u>not</u> particularly poisonous, they are about comparable to aspirin in this respect, but the earlier products contained dioxin as an impurity which is <u>very</u> poisonous and the reputation of these herbicides has never recovered. There are a number of alternatives on the market these days, a couple of which are shown in Figure 6.6. They are all organic molecules of intermediate complexity, the synthesis of which presents no difficulty to the modern chemical industry.

The Petrochemical Industry

The petrochemical industry has already been introduced as the ultimate source of fertilizers. This is only a small part of its contribution and the present section will describe some of the intermediates produced from oil, which are then used to make a wide variety of consumer products.

Oil and natural gas are mixtures of **hydrocarbons**. The simplest hydrocarbon is methane, CH_4, in which carbon combines with hydrogen with a valency of four, consistent with its position in the periodic table. Methane is the main constituent of natural gas; other hydrocarbons are formed by replacing one of the hydrogens in methane with a carbon-carbon bond, and continuing this process to build up chains of carbons. Thus the two carbon compound, C_2H_6, is ethane, the three carbon compound, C_3H_8, propane and the four carbon compound butane. The structures of some of the simple hydrocarbons are shown in Figure 6.7.

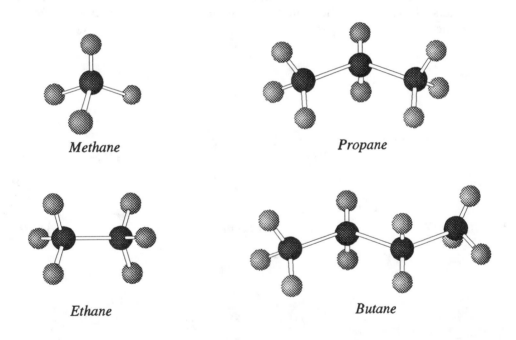

| *Methane* | *Propane* |
| *Ethane* | *Butane* |

Fig. 6.7: Hydrocarbons. Structures of the simplest hydrocarbons are shown. Methane contains one carbon, ethane two carbons, propane three and butane four.

Crude oil is a complex mixture of such hydrocarbons, ranging from low molecular weight to high molecular weight, and the primary function of an oil refinery is to separate the oil into various fractions. Since the high molecular weight compounds have a higher boiling point than the low molecular weight compounds, the separation is accomplished by distillation.

Demonstration 6.3

Distillation. Distillation is the most common method for purifying liquids. When combined with a fractionating column it will efficiently separate liquids with different boiling points. Several different kinds of columns will be demonstrated. Some mixtures cannot be completely separated by distillation. An example is provided by alcohol and water.

Gasoline is mainly composed of hydrocarbons containing 7, 8 or 9 carbon atoms and this is the most valuable fraction. Most of the smaller molecules are used to produce petrochemicals and the heavier fractions go to make heating oil, diesel oil and lubricants. The very heavy residue provides the asphalt used in road-making. Since crude oil rarely provides the optimum mixture of the various hydrocarbons, a number of processes are used to adjust the composition. Catalytic cracking breaks up some of the heavier molecules to give more product in the desirable gasoline range. Catalytic reforming is a process which changes some of the lighter hydrocarbons into the aromatic compounds required by the chemical industry. Thermal cracking changes saturated hydrocarbons into unsaturated olefins which are the source of many polymers. In Figure 6.8 the structures of some of the most important olefinic and aromatic compounds are given.

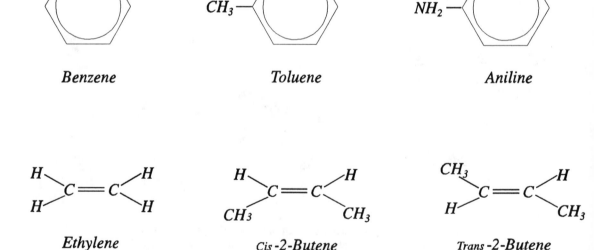

Fig. 6.8: Some aromatic and unsaturated hydrocarbons produced in the petrochemical industry.

An overall view of the petrochemical industry is provided in Figure 6.9.

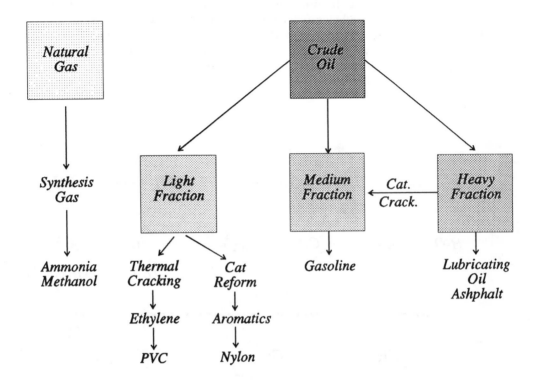

Fig. 6.9: The Petrochemical Industry. Natural gas and crude oil are the source of intermediates such as synthesis gas and ethylene, which are used to make consumer products.

The manufacture of only a small number of products will be considered in the present chapter in a little more detail, to provide some specific examples of the output from the petrochemical industry. Ethylene glycol is used as anti-freeze and provides an example of a chemically simple product. The remaining chemicals we will discuss are monomers which will be used to make the polymeric products discussed in the next section. The simplest is ethylene, leading to polyethylene; vinyl chloride is the monomer for PVC plastics and represents a slight increase in complexity; nylon is a very familiar polymeric product. Its synthesis requires a number of intermediates - butadiene, hydrogen cyanide, adiponitrile, adipic acid and hexamethylene diamine, all derived from the petrochemical industry. The manufacture of nylon provides an example of the more complicated sequence of intermediates typical of modern chemical products.

Ethylene - more correctly called ethene - is made by the thermal cracking of ethane. Low molecular weight hydrocarbons are simply heated to 815-870 °C at which temperature they decompose to olefins and hydrogen.

$$H_3C\text{-}CH_3 \rightarrow H_2C\text{=}CH_2 + H_2$$

There are also some higher molecular weight products and the mixture is separated by distillation. Ethylene will be used directly to make polyethylene. Ethylene glycol is made in two steps from ethylene. First an oxygen atom is added across the double bond, giving a three membered ring, and a molecule known as ethylene oxide. This reaction requires a catalyst and metallic silver fills this role. Heating ethylene oxide with 1% sulfuric acid at 50-70 °C for 30 min converts it into ethylene glycol.

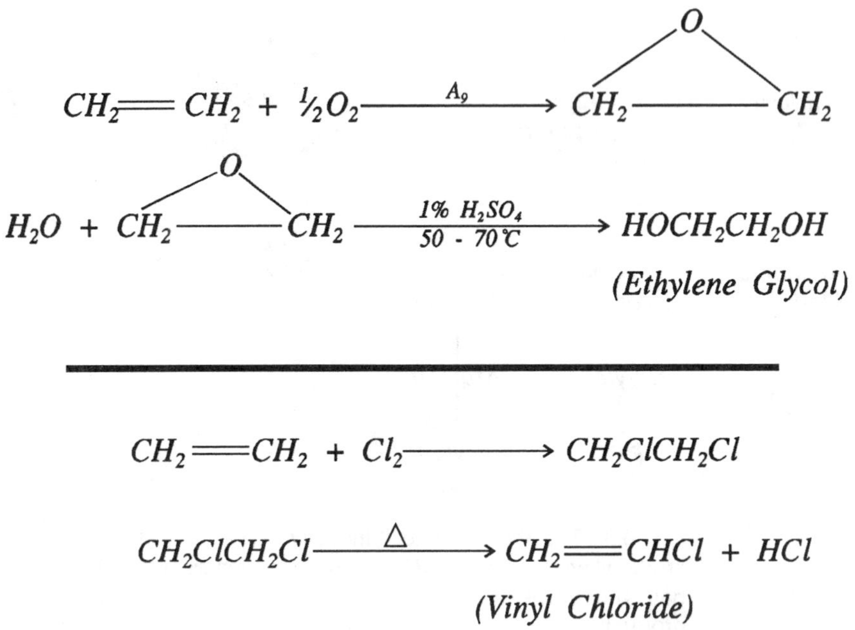

$$CH_2\!=\!CH_2 + \tfrac{1}{2}O_2 \xrightarrow{\ A_9\ } CH_2 \underset{\diagup O \diagdown}{\quad\quad} CH_2$$

$$H_2O + CH_2 \underset{\diagup O \diagdown}{\quad\quad} CH_2 \xrightarrow[50\text{ - }70°C]{1\%\ H_2SO_4} HOCH_2CH_2OH$$

(Ethylene Glycol)

$$CH_2\!=\!CH_2 + Cl_2 \longrightarrow CH_2ClCH_2Cl$$

$$CH_2ClCH_2Cl \xrightarrow{\ \triangle\ } CH_2\!=\!CHCl + HCl$$

(Vinyl Chloride)

Fig. 6.10: The production of ethylene glycol and vinyl chloride from ethylene.

The process for making vinyl chloride is similar. There are again two steps - the first is the addition of chlorine to give ethylene dichloride. This compound is then heated under pressure and loses HCl to give vinyl chloride.

■ *Vinyl chloride...*

$$H_2C=CH_2 + Cl_2 \rightarrow CH_2ClCH_2Cl$$
$$CH_2ClCH_2Cl \rightarrow H_2C=CHCl \text{ (vinyl chloride)} + HCl$$

To make nylon two monomers are needed, adipic acid and hexamethylene diamine (HMDA). The routes to these monomers are a little more complex but in each case the starting materials are the products of oil refining. Benzene is a primary product made by the catalytic reforming of the middle fractions in the distillation of oil; it can be reacted with hydrogen to give cyclohexane, a hydrocarbon containing six CH_2

groups in a ring. This in turn can be oxidized in two steps to give firstly cyclohexanone and then adipic acid. The first oxidation step uses air as the oxidising agent combined, with a cobalt catalyst; the second requires nitric acid. The resulting adipic acid has a chain of four CH_2 groups with a carboxylic acid group, COOH, on each end. The six carbons of cyclohexane have been preserved but two have been oxidized to COOH groups. The chemistry of the production of nylon intermediates is summarized in Figure 6.11.

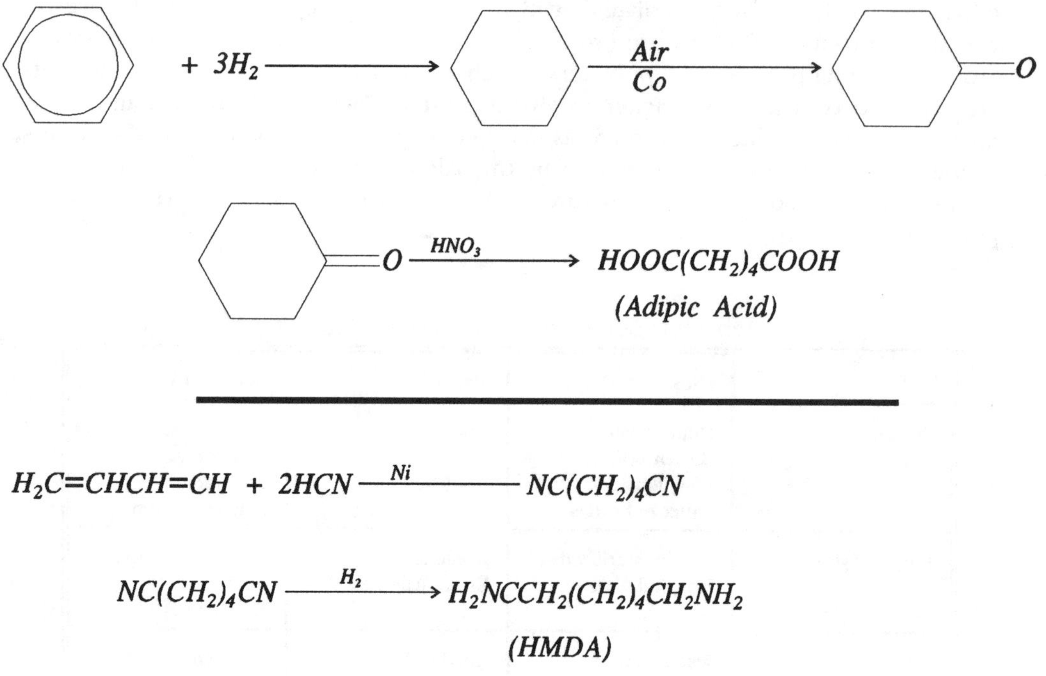
+ 3H2
Air
Co
O
O
HNO3
HOOC(CH2)4COOH
(Adipic Acid)
H2C=CHCH=CH + 2HCN
Ni
NC(CH2)4CN
NC(CH2)4CN
H2
H2NCCH2(CH2)4CH2NH2
(HMDA)

Fig. 6.11: The production of nylon intermediates.

Synthesis of the second nylon monomer, HMDA, starts with butadiene, which in turn is made by the dehydrogenation of butane. This is essentially the same reaction as that leading to the formation of ethylene from ethane, but in this case the product has two double bonds, $H_2C{=}CH\text{-}CH{=}CH_2$ (butadiene). This must then be reacted with hydrogen cyanide (HCN), which is made by the Andrussov process, involving the reaction of methane with ammonia and oxygen.

■ *Nylon intermediates...*

$$CH_3CH_2CH_2CH_3 \rightarrow H_2C{=}CH\text{-}CH{=}CH_2 + 2H_2$$
$$CH_4 + NH_3 + 3/2O_2 \rightarrow HCN + 3H_2O$$

Butadiene and hydrogen cyanide can now be combined to give adiponitrile, a molecule containing four CH_2 groups with a cyanide, CN, on each end. The secret of this reaction is to persuade the cyanide groups to add to the end carbons of butadiene, rather than to the central carbons, and a special nickel catalyst is needed to ensure the correct mode of addition. Finally HMDA can be made by reducing each of the CN groups of adiponitrile to CH_2NH_2 with hydrogen.

Polymers

All of the chemicals discussed in the last section, with the exception of ethylene glycol, are "intermediates", which means that they are not in themselves consumer products, but are used to make materials which can be bought in stores. Most of the final products are polymers, which are molecules in which the same units are repeated over and over again to give a product with a high molecular weight. Such molecules are often referred to as macromolecules; about half the total business of the chemical industry is generated by the sale of polymeric products. Table 6.1 provides information on the structures and uses of some of the more important polymers.

Table 6.1: Some Common Polymeric Products

Name	Uses	Structure	Comments
Polyethylene	High density - Bleach bottles Low density - Squeeze bottles	Unbranched Branched	Metal oxide initiator. Free radical polymerization
Polypropylene	Can be sterilized - Hospital ware	Isotactic Unbranched	Transition metal catalyst as initiator.
PVC	Water gutters Credit cards	Head to Tail High M.W.	Free radical initiator.
Nylon	Clothing. Carpets.	Polyamide. Linkages as in proteins.	Condensation polymer.
Dacron	Clothing - blended with cotton.	Polyester. -R-CO-O-R'-	Condensation polymer.
ABS	Synthetic rubber	Copolymer of Acrylonitrile Butadiene Styrene.	Copolymer better than individual polymers.
Teflon	Lubricant Non-stick frying pans	Linear polymer $-CF_2-CF_2-CF_2-$ High MW	Free radical polymerization

The simplest commercial polymer is polyethylene, in which the $-CH_2-$ group is repeated a large number of times.

There are a number of variations on the theme of the simple repetition of monomer units. If a monomer is designed to have two or more functional groups, chain branching and crosslinking become possible. This can lead to two- and three-dimensional polymer structures rather than simple chains, and the physical properties of the polymeric material can be considerably modified. If the monomer units are not symmetrical, either "head to tail" or "head to head" polymerization becomes possible and so a mixture of products may result. If there are substituents on the atoms comprising the main chain these substituents may be arranged to be all on the same side of the chain or to be on different sides. Neither is there any rule which states that all the monomer molecules must be identical. If two or more different monomers are mixed together in a polymer it is described as a copolymer. It may be either a random copolymer, in which there is no pattern to the order of the units, a block copolymer with similar monomers occurring in blocks, or an alternating copolymer involving alternation of monomer units. By taking suitable combinations of monomers the number of polymeric materials can be greatly increased. Some of these possibilities are illustrated in Figure 6.12.

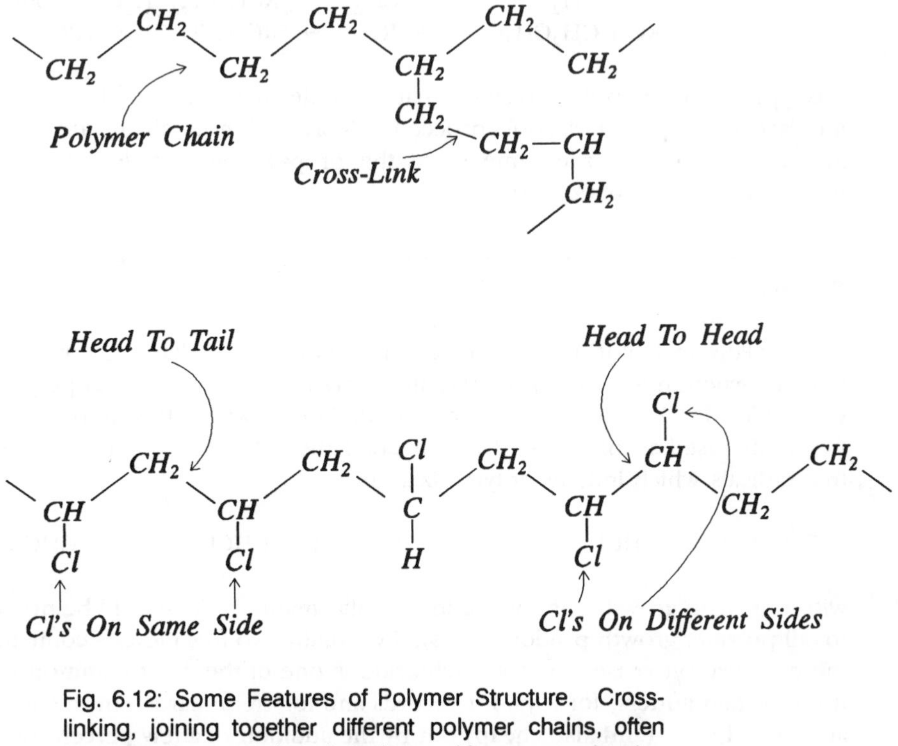

Fig. 6.12: Some Features of Polymer Structure. Cross-linking, joining together different polymer chains, often improves the properties of a polymer. Monomer molecules can be joined either "head-to-tail" or "head-to head". Isomers formed with all the substituents on the same side of the chain are isotactic, those with alternate substituents on opposite sides syndiotactic, and a random distribution of substituents gives an atactic polymer.

■ *Types of polymerization...*

There are two general ways in which polymerization can occur - chain growth and step growth. Chain growth is typically a free radical process, of the type previously encountered in the discussion of the free radical reactions in atmospheric chemistry. Three distinct steps are involved:

> i) **Initiation**, leading to the formation of a free radical, is usually a slow process.
> ii) **Propagation**, in which the initial free radical reacts with a monomer molecule to give another free radical, which in turn reacts to give yet another free radical, is rapid.
> iii) Finally there must be some **termination** process, which removes free radicals and terminates the chain.

These three steps are illustrated by the formation of polyethylene.

$$R \cdot \text{ (initiator) } + \ CH_2=CH_2 \ \rightarrow \ RCH_2CH_2 \cdot \qquad \text{Initiation}$$
$$RCH_2CH_2 \cdot \ + \ CH_2=CH_2 \ \rightarrow \ RCH_2CH_2CH_2CH_2 \cdot \quad \text{Propagation}$$
$$RCH_2CH_2CH_2CH_2 \cdot \ + \ R \cdot \ \rightarrow \ RCH_2CH_2CH_2CH_2R \quad \text{Termination}$$

It is typical of chain polymerization that the molecular weight of the polymer does not increase as the polymerization proceeds. More and more chains are formed but the average length stays the same since the propagation step is rapid compared to initiation and termination.

■ *PVC...*

Polyvinylchloride is a typical chain polymer. It has the composition $(CH_2\text{-}CHCl)_n$, where n is a large number, and is made by the free radical polymerization of vinyl chloride. Peroxides, with the formula ROOR, where R is an organic group, are frequently used as initiators. Upon heating the O-O bond is broken to give two RO free radicals which initiate polymerization, i.e.

$$RO \ + \ CH_2=CHCl \ \rightarrow \ ROCH_2CHCl \ + \ CH_2=CHCl \ \rightarrow \ ROCH_2CHClCH2CHCl$$

with the chain growth continuing in a similar manner. (It should be noted that head to tail polymer growth predominates). Eventually two free radicals come together and the propagation ceases. Polyvinylchloride is one of the most common plastics; it is used for rain gutters, for toys, for records and for credit cards. In this form it is hard and quite brittle (and also cheap) but by the addition of a few percent of "plasticizer" it can be made softer and more flexible. Plasticized PVC is used for wire insulation, for floor tiles and for the inexpensive covering of auto seats.

Polyethylene is also a chain growth polymer. It comes in two forms, high density and low density, made by different processes. The high density form is made by polymerization using a metal oxide catalyst, consists of very long chains with no branching, and is quite hard and tough. It is used for containers such as bleach bottles and can be fabricated into a film for packaging. Low density polyethylene is made using a free radical initiator, but the process requires high pressure to bring about the polymerization, as might have been predicted by applying LeChatelier's rule. There is quite a lot of branching of the chains and this leads to a much less crystalline polymer; it is tough, but quite soft, and finds uses in garbage bags, squeeze bottles and wire and cable insulation.

■ *Nylon...*

The other type of polymerization involves step growth rather than chain growth; nylon is our example of this type of polymer. It is made by heating adipic acid and HMDA (hexamethylenediamine), the two intermediates which were synthesized in the previous section. Adipic acid has COOH groups on both ends of its chain, while HMDA has NH_2 groups on both ends of its chain. A carboxylic acid can combine with an amine to form an amide link, i.e.

$$-COOH \; + \; -NH_2 \; \rightarrow \; -CONH- \; + \; H_2O$$

By removing water from the components this type of reaction a polymer can be formed with alternating adipic acid and HMDA residues, and this is a polyamide. It is known as nylon 66, since both of the components have chains of six carbon atoms. It is used to make shirts, fabrics, carpets and many other items. (The condensation reaction involved is just the opposite of the hydrolysis reactions of water discussed in Chapter 3.) Generally, as this type of polymerization progresses the molecular weight of the product increases, since addition of new molecules to the growing polymer chain is the slow step. It differs in this respect from chain polymerization. The final molecular weight is usually quite low— 10,000 to 25,000 would be normal, which is much less than the hundreds of thousands or even millions usual in chain polymerization. Chemically, proteins belong to this class of polymers and the initial synthesis of nylon was indeed an attempt to reproduce the properties of the protein silk. Proteins are however much more complex because they are copolymers, involving some twenty different amino acids and the various side chains on these amino acids impose very specific geometries on the macromolecules. It is this feature which governs the use of proteins as enzymes and other biological molecules with very specific chemical properties.

Demonstration 6.4

Synthesis of Nylon and properties of lightly cross-linked polyacrylic acid. Commercially nylons are made by reacting carboxylic acids with amines. Their preparation can be demonstrated more conveniently by using an acid chloride rather than an acid.

$$RCOOH \; + \; H_2NR \; \rightarrow \; RCONHR \; + \; H_2O$$
$$RCOCl \; + \; H_2NR \; \rightarrow \; RCONHR \; + \; HCl$$

For this demonstration the amine used is hexamethylene diamine, the same compound used to make the common nylon 66, and the acid chloride is decanedioyl chloride, with eight CH_2 groups between two COCl groups. The product is described as nylon 610 because it alternates chains of six carbons with chains of ten carbons between each amide linkage. This material can be formed very easily at room temperature by pouring a solution of the amine in aqueous caustic soda into the acid chloride. The fibrous nature of the product is readily apparent. Polyacrylic acid, $(CH_2CH(COOH))_n$, is a water soluble polymer. If it is heavily cross-linked it becomes insoluble in water. With just a few cross links it will not dissolve but absorbs large quantities of water. Thus adding a small quantity of this polymer to a large beaker of water leads to the immediate formation of a gel. The beaker can be inverted without losing water. This property of absorbing large quantities of water has obvious commercial applications. The material is used in the manufacture of disposable diapers.

Conclusion

Only a handful of the products of the chemical industry have been described in the present chapter. Many of the items you are wearing or have in your purses or pockets have their origin in some distant petrochemical plant. We would indeed be lost without them and the great benefits derived from the development of this industry over the last forty or fifty years should not be downgraded. However, progress has its price, and some of the less desirable characteristics of synthetic chemicals will be considered in the next chapter.

Further reading

Philip J. Chenier, *Survey of Industrial Chemistry*, John Wiley and Sons, (1986). Covers most of the contemporary chemical industry.

CHAPTER SEVEN

The Hazards of Progress

There are three kinds of lies - lies, damn lies and statistics.
Benjamin Disraeli

Introduction

It is a fact of journalism that bad news always rates larger headlines than good news. Consistent with this generalization, the emphasis in the press and on TV is on the hazards of technology rather than on the benefits of new discoveries. This may be as it should be; the bad news could well require some action on the part of the public at large, whereas the good news does not. If action is required though, it should be based on an intelligent appreciation of the true hazard-to-benefit ratio, rather than a purely emotional response to yet another "environmental atrocity" or the like. A well-educated person should be capable of making intelligent assessments in this area. The need for a certain minimal background in science in order to perform this function is one of the strongest arguments for teaching some science to non-scientists.

■ *Atom bombs and* **Silent Spring**...

The initial concerns for the effects of technological change on human welfare arose from the development of atomic weapons. Even nuclear tests carried out many miles away can lead to fallout with disastrous consequences to human health. Japanese fishermen aboard the Lucky Dragon No.5 on March 1st, 1954 discovered this the hard way when their ship happened to be down wind from an atomic test at Bikini atoll. Many of the scientists involved in the development of atomic weapons felt that military secrecy had been used to hide the relevant facts from the general public, and that they themselves had an obligation to warn people of the unprecedented hazards involved in this technology. For a number of years the "Bulletin of the Federation of Atomic Scientists" printed its doomsday clock, set at a few minutes to midnight, and waged a futile war against the arms race and the development of more and more horrific weapons. A new front was opened with the publication of Rachel Carson's book *Silent Spring* in 1962. Her warning was against the much less obvious dangers of the indiscriminate use of insecticides. This struck a much more responsive chord than the nuclear weapons protests, and insecticides such as DDT were restricted in their use or banned outright within a relatively short period of time. There was soon a flood of protests against a wide variety of "pollution". Everything from waste disposal methods to powdered soap was loudly denounced. Since every action generates its reaction, it is not surprising that books attacking the environmentalists soon appeared, with the counter-argument that the problems invoked had been vastly overstated. An example is *The Doomsday Syndrome* by John Maddox published in 1972. This book represents a well-balanced response by a very reputable scientist, but other articles on the subject were less well considered.

■ *How much should we be worrying about the environment?*

The present chapter will attempt to give as factual account as is possible of some of the main environmental concerns. Problems of a chemical nature will be emphasized, but some spillover into biology, medicine, geography and sociology is inevitable. Three types of hazards will be distinguished.

a) Fatal accidents: in this area there is no disagreement regarding the undesirability of such occurrences. What can be done to prevent them is a much more difficult problem.

b) Threats to human health: the representative problem in this area concerns the dispersion of cancer-causing chemicals. The central questions fall in the area of toxicology and the correct statistical interpretation of data. There are some cases where the reality of the threat seems to have been unambiguously established: cigarette smoking, major concentrations of mercury in fish, and smog are in this category. There is a large class of examples where the jury is still out; it really comes down to the question: how high does a risk have to be to be unacceptable? Most of the better publicized chemical pollutants are in this class. Finally, there are some cases where an earlier scare can be dismissed fairly confidently as a false alarm.

c) Threats to the quality of life: people are not going to die if the fish disappear from our lakes, the whales are no more, or if the trees are killed. Something important will have been lost though, and problems such as acid rain and the eutrophication of lakes are rightfully seen as important. We will all be poorer if we ever do awake to Rachel Carson's silent spring, when the sounds of the birds and insects are no longer heard.

Some Horror Stories

■ *Explosions...*

Many chemicals are explosive or flammable and there have been some spectacular accidents arising from these hazards. For instance, in 1947 in Texas City, Texas a ship loaded with fertilizer caught fire. Unfortunately the fertilizer involved was ammonium nitrate, which as well as being an excellent fertilizer is also a pretty powerful explosive. The ship blew up with an explosion heard 160 miles away. Two aircraft flying overhead were destroyed and oil storage tanks and a chemical plant were set ablaze. Other ships were unable to get away from the scene, and so there were further explosions. A total of 561 people were killed and 3,000 injured in N.America's worst industrial accident. Another example: in 1969 Texas City was the site of another explosion, this time on land. The culprit in this case was a plant manufacturing butadiene by the process described in the previous chapter. The results were spectacular, though there was no loss of life. The explosion was attributed to the failure of a valve, coupled with a second failure in plant design which failed to show the first fault and an operator error in interpreting the information available about the condition of the plant. This is typical: it usually requires three consecutive errors to cause a major accident. (The absence of loss of life reflects the generally high standards of safety precautions in the USA petrochemical industry.) A third example is provided by an explosion in 1974 at Flixborough in England in a plant oxidizing cyclohexane, which is an intermediate step in the manufacture of nylon. The chemistry involved is a little different from that described in the last chapter, since this plant produced nylon 6 rather than nylon 66, but at this stage of the process the intermediates are the same. In this case the history of the accident was protracted, beginning with a crack appearing in a reactor vessel on March 27th and involving a number of modifications, temporary repairs and mishaps leading up to the explosion on June 1st. Twenty-eight people were killed and 88 injured. The enquiry into the accident revealed a complex series of mishaps with human error being the principle contributing factor. It was suggested that English management did not take safety considerations sufficiently seriously but this criticism cannot be applied to most of the North American chemical industry, where safety is taken very seriously.

■ *Leaks of toxic materials...*

A further major source of hazard in the chemical industry comes from toxic materials. In the large majority of cases the problems arise not with the final products, which are distributed to the outside world, but with intermediates used in the manufacturing process. The people at risk are usually the plant workers but occasionally chemicals escape and create hazards for unsuspecting neighbors of a chemical factory. The most notorious case happened at Bhopal, India on Dec. 3rd, 1984. The culprit chemical was methyl isocyanate (CH_3NCO), used in the manufacture of the carbamate family of insecticides. Some 45 tons of this volatile material escaped from a storage tank into the atmosphere and drifted over a heavily populated part of the city. The death toll was 3,329, an additional 20,000 people suffered adverse effects from the gas and 500,000 filed damage claims against Union Carbide, the owner of the plant. The claims were settled in February 1989 for a total of $470 million, far below the amounts claimed. The causes of the accident have not been officially determined, but it seems fairly clear that a combination of engineering malfunctions, inoperative safety valves etc, and human errors lead to the accident. The laws relating to chemical safety are now very stringent at least in North America. For example, in a 1985 case in Chicago, three managers of a small company involved in the recovery of silver form old X-ray films, were convicted of murder. Metal cyanides are used in this process and inadequate safety precautions had lead to the death of an employee from cyanide poisoning. In Ontario, new legislation became effective in 1989: WHMIS - Workplace Hazardous Materials Information System, which requires, among many other things, safety training for all people who are involved in the supervision of laboratories or the handling of chemicals. This includes university professors.

■ *Mercury...*

Two more horror stories illustrate a rather different type of problem. In all of the above cases the hazards involved were well recognized, but the protection against these hazards was inadequate. The situation is more difficult when the hazard is not recognized until after the event. In 1965 some 46 Japanese living in the area of Minamata bay, died from a disease of the nervous system. Many others became sick, and abnormally high numbers of birth defects were reported. There had been indications of the problem since 1953 but the real explanation was not discovered until 1969. The culprit was mercury. This substance was used as a catalyst in a local plant making acetaldehyde and small amounts of it escaped into the sea. This in itself was not particularly serious, since the concentration was very small. What was not understood at the time was the subsequent chemical and biological fate of the mercury. In the mud at the bottom of the bay, bacteria convert the mercury to dimethyl-mercury ($Hg(CH_3)_2$) and similar compounds. This is absorbed into aquatic plants which are eaten by small fish. The small fish are eaten by larger fish, which are in turn eaten by people. The problem is that at each stage in the food chain the mercury concentration increases; there is no efficient metabolic mechanism for eliminating mercury in most living things, so it accumulates. At the top of the food chain —in this case the fish-eating Japanese— the original unimportant concentration had become sufficiently magnified to be lethal. The solution was clear: eliminate the leakage of mercury into the sea. However since this can't be accomplished retroactively, it still leaves many contaminated fish in circulation.

The discovery of this problem had some immediate repercussions in North America. Paper mills use chlorine as a bleach and caustic soda in the pulping process. The most common method of producing these chemicals involves electrolysis of brine (NaCl) in cells containing mercury; some of the mercury inevitably ends up in the local water system. Investigation did indeed reveal unacceptably high concentrations of mercury compounds in fish caught close to paper mills in Northern Ontario, and the local Indians were no longer able to use fish as a food source. There is no short-term solution, but once the problem is recognized the replacement of the mercury process for chlor-alkali production by more modern membrane electrolytic cells, provides an obvious way to prevent further contamination.

■ *Thalidomide...*

A final case is the thalidomide tragedy. Thalidomide was a drug, first sold commercially in 1957, which was intended to replace barbiturates as a tranquilizer and flu treatment for pregnant women. Barbiturates are habit-forming and lead to some 2,000 to 3,000 deaths per year from overdoses. Thalidomide was introduced as a safer alternative. The testing was inadequate and the drug proved to give rise to birth defects, mostly associated with the incomplete development of limbs, both arms and legs. The testing was correctly perceived to be incomplete by US Government scientists, and the drug was not allowed to be sold in that country. The drug companies were allowed to sell it in other countries, and it was the cause of about 8,000 to 10,000 deformities in children, mostly in Germany, with about 100 in Canada. Its sale was allowed in Canada from November 1960 to March 1962 in spite of an earlier ban in Germany and elsewhere. The legal consequences of the tragedy are still unfolding, and in February 1989 a fresh attempt was started to obtain compensation from the Canadian government, based on its tardiness in banning the drug.

In some respects the horror stories described above are the least contentious part of the chemical problem. They all lead to deaths or serious injuries and the causes of these serious effects are not in dispute. Everybody can agree that the strict enforcement of safety regulations in chemical plants, the restriction of the discharge of clearly toxic materials into the biosphere, and the adequate testing of new drugs are all necessary. The more difficult cases arise either when the cause of the problem, the effects it gives rise to, or the real existence of a problem are in dispute. Threats to human health are the most difficult area to judge and the validity, or otherwise, of arguments put forward cannot usually be judged without some appreciation of the methods of toxicology.

Toxicology

■ How poisonous is a poison?

A chemical does not have to kill people to be considered toxic; it only has to produce some "observable detriment to a living entity". The noxious chemical produced by poison ivy is toxic, since it gives rise to an unpleasant skin condition, but it is doubtful whether anybody has ever died from contact with poison ivy. The meaningful discussion of toxicity therefore demands two pieces of information: the nature of the toxic effect must be described and the dose required to produce this effect must be specified. The latter condition is particularly important, and indeed crucial to any sensible consideration of chemical health hazards. It is this information which is most frequently omitted, or given as a number without context, in journalistic reports.

Two absolutely general statements can be made: <u>everything</u> is a poison at high enough concentrations: <u>nothing</u> is a poison at low enough concentrations. A person can die of overeating, so food is a poison. Oxygen reacts biochemically to give radicals and peroxides, which are very detrimental to health. The effects produced are closely related to those resulting from exposure to radiation from nuclear reactions. The body has efficient defenses against these interlopers, but even the most efficient defense mechanism is not perfect, and in the long run damage is done. This is probably one of the causes of aging, so eventually the oxygen we breath contributes to our death! As is the case with all these problems, we must balance the advantages of breathing against the disadvantages. Most people who have considered the problem elect to keep on breathing and suffer the consequences of toxic free radicals.

This is an extreme example, but a very large number of substances present at least small toxic threats. If the risk is sufficiently small, low concentrations of the toxin may well be acceptable but high concentrations will be unacceptable. The only real questions to be answered are, therefore: how high is high enough?, and how low is low enough?, in discussions of toxic materials and the permissible levels of them.

■ The importance of statistics...

Toxicologists define parameters such as LD_{50} and LE_{50}, which are the dosages of a toxin sufficient to cause death in 50% of the recipients, or to cause the toxic effect (e.g. a skin rash) in 50% of the cases. It is not easy to measure these parameters in an unambiguous manner. We usually want to know the toxicity to man, and experiments leading to the deaths of 50% of experimental human subjects are clearly not acceptable. Even experiments leading to the 50% occurrence of poison ivy type skin rashes are not going to be popular. Experiments are therefore usually carried out on animals and, for primarily economic reasons, on small animals such as mice or rats. It is assumed that the important quantity is the dose per unit weight, so that if a man is 100 times heavier than a rat, the LD_{50} obtained is multiplied by 100. This seems a reasonable procedure, but there is no way of checking its validity. It is also necessary to specify how the toxin is administered; it can be taken orally, injected, or absorbed through the skin. There is reason to believe that the toxicity will depend on the method of entry to the body, and indeed there are a large number of experimental results showing such a dependence. Few people will intentionally inject themselves with a toxin, so data obtained by introducing the material into an animal in this way must be suspect. The responses of individual animals or individual people are not all identical; one rat may roll over dead with a very small dose of toxin while another may lap it up for quite a while. This variability must be accommodated by performing many experiments, and then statistically analyzing the results. The reliability of the analysis depends on the number of rats available to the investigator. Typically the number of rats dying at a given dosage level is graphed on a logarithmic scale to obtain LD_{50}. The lethal dose of a toxin is not decisive in predicting its effects at lower concentrations. There are many examples of materials which are beneficial, or even essential, to organisms at low concentrations, but poisonous at higher concentrations. Some vitamins fall in this class.

There are also many cases where low doses of a substance do not give any visible effect, but cause invisible changes to the internal biochemistry of the organism. A variety of measurements other than those leading to LD_{50} are often made. "Whole animal monitoring" records the effect of substances on the respiration rate, heart rate and other vital functions of the animal. "Chronic toxicity" studies involve repeated treatments with non-lethal doses. Other experiments measure carcinogenicity, mutagenicity (the effect on heredity) and teratogenicity (the effect on the fetus of a pregnant animal). All of these considerations go to show that it is rarely possible to state flatly that one substance is a poison and another is harmless. The best we can do is to weigh evidence, for and against, at a known level of dosage using all the data available.

Having made these reservations known, some data can now be examined; it is provided in Table 7.1. The classification scheme is that suggested by Crone in the book *Chemicals and Society*. Many highly effective poisons are of biological origin. *Botulinum* toxin has a lethal dose of less than 10 micrograms per kilogram of body weight. Expressed another way, this is a concentration of 10 parts per billion of body weight, which is not the same as saying you will die by drinking a solution of concentration 10ppb. At this concentration you would have to drink your own body weight of water to approach the lethal concentration— and this is the most toxic substance known. Water pollution concentrations in the ppb range should therefore, with the exception of chemicals which accumulate in the body, be viewed in perspective. The most toxic man-made compounds are typified by the nerve gases developed as chemical weapons and have lethal doses in the range 10 micrograms to 1 milligram per kilogram of body weight, or 10 to 1000 ppb of body weight.

Table 7.1: The Toxicity of Various Materials

Toxicity Class	Lethal Dose	Examples
Biotoxins	< 10 μg/kg	*Botulinium* toxin
Supertoxic	10 μg/kg-1mg/kg	Nerve gases
		Poison of deadly
		Nightshade.
		Dioxin.
Highly toxic	1-50 mg/kg	Sodium Cyanide.
		Organophos. Insect.
Moderately toxic	50-500 mg/kg	DDT, Barbiturates.
		2,4,5 T (maximum)
Slightly toxic	0.5-5 g/kg	2,4,5 T (minimum)
		Aspirin.
		Benzene.
Hardly toxic	> 5g/kg	Natural components
		of the biosphere.

Data from Hugh D. Crone, **Chemicals and Society**.

(1000ppb is equivalent to 1ppm). The most toxic organophosphorus insecticides come in the next class at 1 to 50 mg/kg body weight as do such well-known poisons as sodium cyanide (NaCN). This is of course still highly toxic. Moderately toxic substances are organochlorine insecticides and barbiturate drugs at 50 -500 mg/kg. Aspirin and many commercial solvents are only slightly toxic at 0.5 to 5g/kg. Anything greater than 5g/kg of body weight is hardly toxic. Calcium, for example, is a required dietary element, and is certainly not toxic at the 5g/kg level, but the calcium ingested by drinking a gallon of milk a day may lead to pains in the joints due to the accumulation of excess calcium. On an extreme definition even milk is a toxic substance.

■ *The sensitivity of analytical methods has increased steadily in recent years...*

The measurement of toxicity requires not only information on the effects of the substance on animals, but also a knowledge of the concentration of the material. This is a problem in analytical chemistry and interest has focussed more and more in the low concentration region, leading to the development of the techniques of "trace analysis". The most versatile technique involves the combination of gas chromatography - which allows the separation of complex mixtures containing organic compounds at low concentrations - with mass spectrometry. The latter technique breaks molecules down into fragments of different masses and produces a characteristic "mass spectrum" for each different organic compound. The history of the allowable limits for dioxin has been almost entirely determined by the increasing sensitivity of the analytical methods. Prior to 1957 dioxin was not recognized as a threat, so nobody bothered to measure its concentration. At that time its presence as an impurity in the herbicide 2,4,5-T was established, and it was shown to be responsible for the skin disease chloracne. Since then the allowable concentrations in water have dropped from 10ppm to 1ppm to 0.01ppm (= 10ppb) exactly paralleling the increase in analytical sensitivity.

■ *Epidemiology...*

There is a complementary approach to the study of toxic materials, known as occupational epidemiology. This approach can be more easily applied to human health problems, since it does not involve purposely exposing people to toxins. The incidence of death or lesser effects from a specific disease in a large population is examined, and incidence of the disease is compared to the hazards to which the sufferers had been exposed. This depends entirely on a statistical analysis of the data, and therefore is subject to all the uncertainties of statistical methods. Ideally, a comparison should be made between two groups of people who differ only in a single variable. Sometimes this is possible, and epidemiological studies have established a firm cause and effect relationship between asbestos and lung cancer, and between aromatic amines and bladder cancer - because groups of people who had been, or had not been, exposed to these hazards but were otherwise very similar in background could be defined. In other cases, similar studies have been inconclusive. It has not proved possible, for example, to establish any definitive correlation between the health problems of Vietnam veterans and the use of the herbicide Agent Orange. There are just too many other hazards to which Vietnam veterans were exposed, but which the control group remaining in the USA avoided for the most part. These include for example, antimalarial drugs, insecticides, excessive alcohol consumption, illicit drugs, increased stress, polluted water and contaminated food. It is just not possible to isolate one of these factors, or a combination of them, and associate it with a specific health problem.

Even when the statistics seem impregnable, there is still an argument regarding the real cause of an observed effect. Thus in the case of cigarette smoking and lung cancer, where the amount of data is very large and the correlation almost beyond doubt, it can still be argued that the type of person who smokes cigarettes is a type who has an hereditary disposition to lung cancer, and would have died from this cause in any case. There is no logical rebuttal to this argument except to note that it is contrary to Occam's razor, which requires that we prefer the simplest possible explanation of a set of facts. The simple explanation is that cigarette smoking causes lung cancer. The case is certainly stronger than for the toxic effects of Agent Orange.

Chemical Threats to Health

Having explored all the difficulties of the subject, let us review the present status of health-threatening chemicals. The gravity of the threat is not always obvious. Some chemicals in some circumstances are quite definitely a serious threat, others should be a cause for concern but not for panic, and still others do not pose any significant threat.

Asbestos is a fibrous silicate mineral made up of chains of silicate groups with metal ions such as calcium and magnesium interspersed. The structures of asbestos and of a number of other molecules discussed in this chapter are given in Figure 7.1.

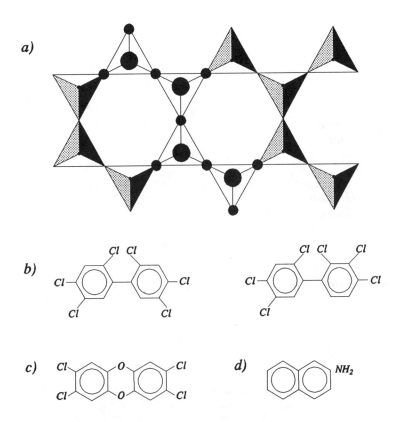

Fig. 7.1: Some Toxic substances: a) Asbestos. The large circles are Si atoms and the small circles are O atoms. SiO_4 tetrahedra (the fourth oxygen is above the plane) are joined together in double chains, giving a fibrous substance which accumulates in the lungs. b) Polychlorinated biphenyls (PCB's) are moderately toxic. c) Dioxin is very toxic. d) Beta naphthylamine, an intermediate in the dye industry, causes cancer of the bladder.

It is heat resistant and chemically inert, and these properties have encouraged its use in various ways. Epidemiological studies have linked it quite conclusively with forms of lung cancer (asbestosis) and workers in asbestos mines suffer very real hazards from asbestos dust. It is probably the sizes and shapes of the fibers, rather than their chemical composition, which causes the problems. Similar diseases are endemic among many kinds of miners who are exposed to fine dust particles, but asbestos happens to be worse than most. It does not seem likely that the danger to the general public from asbestos products used as insulation is very great, but replacement by other materials is certainly a desirable objective. This raises the further point that the means by which the toxin is released into the environment plays a substantial role in determining the extent of the threat. Figure 7.2 illustrates some of the routes by which dangerous chemicals enter the biosphere.

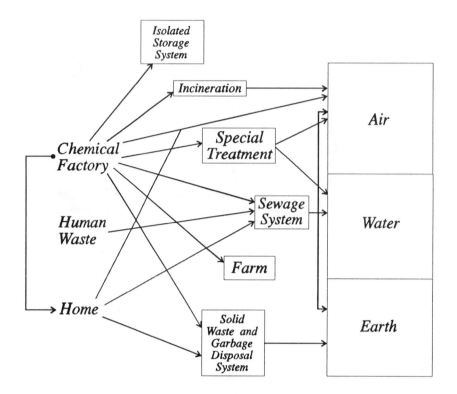

Fig. 7.2: Release of Toxic Materials to the Environment. Toxic materials, produced either industrially or domestically, take various routes to produce air, water or soil pollution.

■ *Sewage...*

Mercury poisoning has been discussed previously and is a genuine threat in cases where the concentrations in fish, or other food, eaten on a regular basis are high.   High-level radioactivity from the fallout from bomb testing is also an unambiguous threat.   The most widespread major health problem though is the inadequate treatment of sewage, which has been an age-old cause of death and disease. It might have been thought that this problem would be concentrated in the underdeveloped countries, but major cities such as Montreal and Toronto lack fully effective sewage systems.   Only restrictions on swimming and the availability of modern medical care prevents the inhabitants of these cities from contracting Third World diseases. The fish and animals living in lakes and rivers are less fortunate. This subject does not have the high tech glamor of more exotic forms of pollution, and tends to be neglected by the environmental movement. The technology for solving the problem is available but, on the scale required for a large city, is expensive. High cost and lack of glamor are a recipe for neglect.

■ *Carcinogens...*

All of the above hazards have unquestionably been the cause of deaths. We now move to some cases where the hazards are clearly real, but probably not life-threatening. There are some chemicals which are well-established as carcinogens. An example of one of the worst is beta napthylamine (structure given in Figure.7.1) which has been used as an intermediate in the dye industry for over a century. In nineteenth century factories no precautions were taken against chemical hazards, and workers exposed to this material for a lifetime stood a good chance of suffering from cancer of the bladder. Statistics were not well kept in that period, so the number of deaths is uncertain, but it was probably in the tens and possibly in the hundreds. With reasonable safety precautions regarding the handling of the chemical, this hazard can be largely eliminated and for this reason this type of cancer-causing agent should not be regarded as a major problem at present. This is true of the large majority of dangerous chemicals which are not dispersed in the biosphere or sold to the public. Only human error and carelessness (both of which are by no means unknown) make them real threats to life.

This brings us to pesticides and herbicides. There are no authenticated cases of human deaths arising from the use of these materials. This does not mean that they are not toxic and not a threat. Paradoxically, it may well be true that the less toxic the material, the greater the threat. There are two factors involved, which are often offsetting: the first is the toxicity of the compound, and the second the ease with which it is broken down in the environment. The newer pesticides, the carbamates and phosphorus compounds, are more poisonous than DDT but break down more easily and therefore do not persist in the biosphere and are less likely to reach toxic concentrations. Figure 7.3 shows typical concentrations of DDT found in water and in living entities.

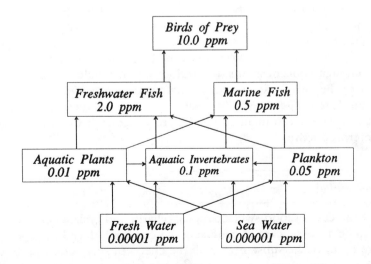

Fig. 7.3: Concentration of DDT in the food chain.

■ *DDT, PCB's and similar compounds...*

The concentration effect on moving up the food chain is very apparent and typical human tissue at present contains 5-10ppm of the material. There is no evidence that it is doing great harm at this level, but as was stated at the beginning of this chapter, everything becomes poisonous at some level of concentration and it would be foolish to allow the accumulation to proceed unabated. If DDT is not particularly poisonous to man, it does nonetheless have very adverse effects on birds and fish, as was pointed out by Rachel Carson, and its restriction on the grounds of adverse effect on the quality of life would be justified. Other chlorinated compounds such as the PCB's (structure given in Figure 7.1) also tend to accumulate in the biosphere rather than being destroyed. Continued exposure to these latter compounds leads to damage to the liver, the usual garbage disposal organ of the body.

It is very unlikely that anyone would develop a serious problem from exposure to a single spillage of PCB's, but if the substances were slopped around indiscriminately deleterious effects would certainly arise in time. For this reason the strict controls on the disposal of chlorinated compounds are probably justified, although the danger has been exaggerated in the press. Dioxin is a rather more serious problem because, although it is far from being the most toxic substance known as has been claimed in popular accounts, it is highly poisonous and it does accumulate in body tissue. The parts per billion concentrations in ground water do not pose an immediate threat and do not justify the scare headlines which have been used. At the same time, we cannot afford to keep on turning it loose into the environment, because sooner or later it will become a real threat. Dioxin was originally made inadvertently as an impurity in 2,4,5-T herbicide. It is no longer present in 2,4,5-T made by modern methods, and the main source is now in chemical dumps such as the infamous Love Canal dump in Buffalo. It is clearly not acceptable to allow this dump to drain into the Niagara River and Lake Ontario, and the public outcry on this issue seems well justified.

The attacks on the herbicides 2,4-D and 2,4,5-T (structures Figure 6.6) are much more weakly based. The former has about the same toxicity as aspirin, and none of the epidemiological studies has produced any definite correlation of the latter with birth defects, an accusation which has been made. Again, there is no doubt that at high enough concentrations, deleterious effects would be observed but this is not relevant to the issue. At the same time, as argued by Donald MacKay in his book *Heritage Lost - The Crisis in Canada's Forests*, these herbicides can play an important role in forest management and to forego their use without adequate reason is counterproductive.

■ *False alarms...*

The case of food sweeteners - saccharin and cyclamates - and food colorings seems to be a classic case of confusing the cancers induced in experimental animals by large doses of the substances with the effects of small doses on humans. In large enough quantities there is no doubt that all of these compounds, together with many thousands of others, will cause cancer. In the concentrations used the risk is very small indeed. At the same time we should ask: do we really need them? If the gain is minute, why take even a minute risk? Looked at from this perspective, their use may not be attractive.

Nuclear Power

Logically this topic should have been included in the last chapter on the chemical industry. Realistically, nuclear power is now regarded by most people as a liability rather than an asset, and it is clearly placed by the majority of the population in the hazard category. Although nuclear affairs fall within the province of physics, in practical terms both the industry and its problems are largely chemical in nature. Purifying radioactive ores is chemistry, the separation of isotopes is largely done by chemical means, the explosion at Chernobyl was chemical in origin, and the treatment and disposal of radioactive spent fuel is a chemical problem.

■ *Constructing a nuclear reactor...*

The essential physics of nuclear power generation can be summarized quite briefly. The first requirement is a fissile material, one that on bombardment with neutrons will undergo nuclear fission with the liberation of more neutrons and a great deal of energy. The source of the energy lies in the fact that the sum of the masses of the fragments is slightly less than that of the original nucleus, and Einstein's equivalence of mass and energy predicts that this excess mass will be converted into a large amount of energy. This appears as heat. The only naturally occurring fissile nucleus is ^{235}U and this is the fuel for the majority of reactors. The main alternative is the man-made isotope ^{239}Pu, obtained by bombarding ^{238}U with neutrons. The large majority of commercial reactors make use of uranium fuel. The neutrons ejected from a disintegrating nucleus usually have high energy. Such neutrons are not suitable for initiating the fission of further ^{235}U nuclei since most of them escape from the reactor before encountering another uranium nucleus, but must be slowed down by giving their excess energy to other atoms. This leads to the second requirement: a moderator to retain the neutrons in the reactor and slow them down for further use.

The best moderator is heavy water, D_2O, but "light" water, H_2O, and graphite are also commonly used. In an operating reactor, each disintegrating U atom must produce just one neutron capable of continuing the reaction. Some neutrons are inevitably lost by other processes, so the actual number of neutrons produced by each fission reaction must be more than one. If the number of useful neutrons produced is less than one per disintegrating nucleus, the nuclear reaction will cease. If it is more than one, more neutrons will lead to more fission which leads to more neutrons, and the reaction will accelerate and become uncontrolled. The third requirement is therefore for some controllable means of adjusting the number of available neutrons. Control rods are constructed from materials which readily absorb neutrons; steel containing boron is commonly used in the construction of such rods. The rods are inserted into the reactor between the fuel elements to absorb more or fewer neutrons and are raised or lowered as required. The fourth requirement is for something to contain the nuclear fuel. The requirements for this material are quite stringent: it must be stable under conditions of high temperature and radioactivity levels, and must absorb as few neutrons as possible. Zirconium is the material best suited for this purpose. Finally, the whole reactor must be contained in concrete, or something similar, of sufficient thickness to prevent the escape of an unacceptable amount of radioactivity. These requirements, as illustrated in Figure 7.4, suffice to build an operating reactor.

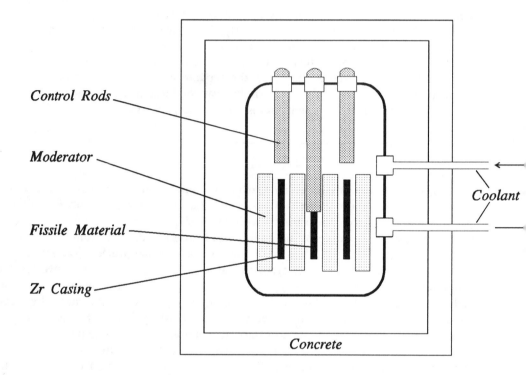

Fig. 7.4: Design of a Nuclear Reactor.

To obtain power from the reactor we must add some means of converting the heat of the nuclear reaction into electricity. This is usually done by producing steam to drive turbines, just as in the case of other generating stations. Some fluid must be used to transfer heat from the reactor to the steam boiler. In most reactors this function is performed by water or heavy water (if the latter is used as a moderator), but a variety of other arrangements is possible.

■ *Enriched uranium or enriched water?*

This in a nutshell is how a reactor works, but the description omits the chemistry which comprises the difficult part of the process. Natural uranium contains only 0.71% of the fissile isotope ^{235}U. If natural uranium is to be used in a reactor very efficient use must be made of the few neutrons available, which means using the most efficient known moderator, heavy water. It is interesting to note that in eons past, when less ^{235}U had been lost by spontaneous decay, ordinary water could have served as a moderator for a natural uranium reactor. (Signs that such reactors occurred spontaneously in the past have been found in Africa.) Natural water contains around 150ppm, or 0.015%, of the heavy isotope deuterium. The choice at present, therefore is either enrich the uranium or to enrich the water. In the USA, since the uranium enrichment process had already been developed for the manufacture of atomic bombs, the choice was to use natural water, or sometimes graphite, and enriched uranium. In Canada the opposite choice was made. The overall sequences, using either natural uranium or enriched uranium, are illustrated in Figure 7.5.

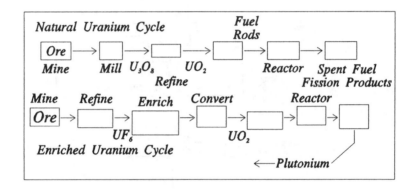

Fig. 7.5: The Uranium Industry.

■ *Purifying uranium...*

Uranium occurs in various places as the ore pitchblende, impure UO_2. It is purified by dissolving in nitric acid to give uranyl nitrate, $UO_2(NO_3)_2$, extracting with an organic solvent, and finally converting back to pure UO_2 in which form it is used in a natural uranium reactors.

If the uranium is to be enriched it must be converted to the volatile compound uranium hexafluoride, UF_6, and the isotopes separated by gaseous diffusion or by centrifugation procedures. Either of these processes require very large and very expensive plants. The chemistry involved can be summarized as follows:

$$UO_2 + 4HF \rightarrow UF_4 + 2H_2O$$
$$UF_4 + F_2 \rightarrow UF_6$$
$$UF_6 + H_2 + 2H_2O \rightarrow UO_2 + 6HF \text{ (enriched } UO_2)$$

Enriching deuterium is also a complicated and expensive process. Very large volumes of water, and therefore very large reaction vessels, must be used. The process used is based on the reaction between hydrogen sulfide and water:

$$H_2O(l) + HDS(g) \rightleftharpoons HDO(l) + H_2S(g)$$

The important feature is that the equilibrium for this reaction lies to the right at low temperature (32 deg C) and to the left at high temperatures (135 deg C). At low temperature, therefore, the deuterium is concentrated in the liquid phase, and at high temperature in the gaseous phase. A suitable arrangement of hot and cold towers in which the gas and liquid are equilibrated, leads to the production of water containing 20% deuterium. Further enrichment to 99.75% D_2O is accomplished by distillation, since the deuterium compound boils at a slightly higher temperature than ordinary water. The process is illustrated in Figure 7.6.

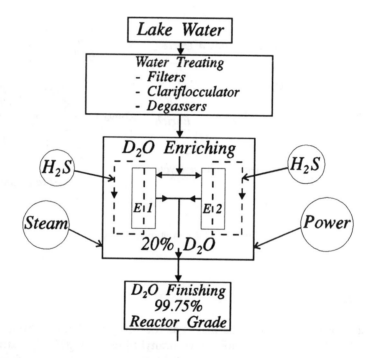

Fig. 7.6: The Manufacture of Heavy Water.

■ *Nuclear waste disposal...*

The other important chemistry in the nuclear industry involves the treatment of spent fuel. This is of course highly radioactive and contains a large number of elements, some of which are useful and need to be recovered, and some of which are waste and need to be disposed of. The original reactors built in the late 1940's and early 1950's were designed to make plutonium for atomic bombs. Even the first large scale power reactor at Calder Hall in England was, although the fact was not widely known, intended primarily for plutonium production. Facilities for treating the spent fuel to extract plutonium by a chemical process were therefore included in the design. The remaining radioactive waste must be disposed of in a safe manner. Immobilization by sheathing in glass, followed by burial in a geologically stable site, is the preferred method, but this is still quite controversial. In the meantime, in many places wastes are being accumulated and stored under water until an agreement on a more permanent method is reached. This is clearly not a satisfactory long-term solution.

■ *Chernobyl...*

With this background we can now consider the question of the safety of the nuclear power industry. In spite of protestations that safety precautions in the industry are such that accidents are very unlikely, there have been a succession of such occurrences, culminating in the accident at the Chernobyl reactor in the USSR in April 1986. All of these accidents have been extensively investigated, and without exception human errors of one kind or another were the major culprit. Regarding Chernobyl it has been stated that if any one of six such errors had been avoided the accident would not have occurred. Hopefully a little is learnt form each succeeding accident but, given Murphy's law[1], future accidents will in all likelihood happen. This is equally true though of any method of producing power, and the real question is whether the benefits outweigh the risks. The answer to this question requires that the results of previous accidents should be carefully examined and the costs compared with the negative consequences of other methods of power generation. Chernobyl was by far the worst accident. How bad was it? Newspaper reports at the time placed the immediate casualties in the thousands. This was a considerable exaggeration. According to information released later, probably correct, 2 people were killed at the site and 203 people were hospitalized for radiation sickness, of whom 29 died within a month. Some additional deaths within this group of people probably occurred. An evacuation of the area was carried out and it seems unlikely that any people other than the 200 or so directly exposed at the site, received a lethal dose of radiation. Many people though must have been exposed to a significant amount of radiation and the long term effects of this exposure are still in question. The Three Mile Island nuclear accident in 1979 caused no deaths and it is very questionable whether anyone suffered any radiation health problem. It is interesting that at the same time as the Three Mile island incident, a dam burst in India killing 1500 people but this received a very minimum of newspaper coverage.

Clearly the nuclear industry does not get a good press. The reasons for this seem to be as much sociological as scientific. All nuclear accidents prior to Chernobyl were shrouded in a veil of secrecy, supposedly for military reasons. Inevitably, rumor made the consequences more dire than they actually were. Nuclear power is always associated in the public mind with nuclear bombs, which are correctly recognized as dangerous. In part this connection is quite real. Power reactors can be, and are, used to make plutonium for bombs; and tritium, used in hydrogen bombs, is a by-product of reactors using heavy water as a moderator. A uranium reactor however cannot

---

[1] "Anything which can go wrong, will."

cause a nuclear explosion. Very highly enriched, bomb grade, ^{235}U is required for bombs and the unenriched or 2-3% enriched material used in reactors is just not sufficient.

The explosions at Chernobyl and elsewhere were chemical in origin. If the reactor gets out of control, temperature rises and steam reacts with metals such as zirconium to give hydrogen. This is very capable of causing an explosion powerful enough to rupture the containment and release large amounts of radioactivity, as happened at Chernobyl. Furthermore, the graphite moderator will burn and maintain a high temperature for a long time; this also happened at Chernobyl. The real fear is associated with low-level radioactivity following an accident. The effects of the large levels of radioactivity present at the site of a nuclear accident are well recognized, but how about the chances of someone 500 kms downwind from a nuclear accident?

■ *The biological effects of radiation...*

The health hazard from low levels of radioactivity is a subject which has perhaps been more extensively researched than any other. In spite of this, the answers are still uncertain. A good review is provided by the article by Arthur C. Upton in *Scientific American*. The problems are essentially the same as those discussed above in the section on toxicology, with the added problem that there is always a natural level of radiation to contend with. A major issue is whether there is, or is not, a threshold level of radiation below which biological effects are not observed. It seems likely that there is no threshold level, but that at low radiation levels the biological effects become negligible. An associated problem is whether the effects of long- term exposure to low-level radiation are cumulative. At the time of the Chernobyl accident newspapers predicted tens of thousands of long-term deaths as a result. It seems probable that these figures, like those for the immediate casualties, were exaggerated. Whether a person in the Ukraine who received a modest dose of radiation from the Chernobyl explosion will have a reduced life expectancy, and if so by how much, is by no means clear. Neither is it clear how extensive the contamination problem actually is in the vicinity of Chernobyl. What is clear is that the radiation levels arising from the accident were moderate in Russia, except close to the reactor site, and minute in North America.

The inherent uncertainties introduced by the use of statistics are made explicit in the epigraph to this chapter, but nevertheless a few numbers will be quoted to give the problem perspective. The unit for measuring radiation exposure is the rem. The LD_{50} for radiation is 400 rems. Any exposure above 100 rem will probably lead to some radiation sickness. The average background radiation from natural sources is about 100 millirem per year, where a millirem is 1/1000 of a rem. It would take a 1000 years to accumulate 100 rems of radiation, but of course there is also the possibility of more subtle long term effects. People in the area evacuated around Chernobyl would probably have received 6 to 10 times the total lifetime background radiation if they had remained where they were, which would have presented a clear risk.

There is also the problem of what to do with the large amount of radioactive contaminated soil left in the environs of the Chernobyl reactor. In Poland there were 25 additional millirem in 4 days, or about 3 months worth of background radiation. In Rome the background level was up 50% for a similar period. In England the additional exposure amounted to 4% of the annual background level. In N. America, comparable readings do not seem to be available, but it was clearly even less. The additional dosage any where other than close to the site, is less than that from an Xray for a broken leg. How many additional cancer cases will it cause over the next 50 years? Nobody knows but the <u>percentage</u> increase, except for those close to the explosion, will certainly be very small. The conclusion of Upton in the article referred to above perhaps summarizes the situation best:

> "According to the view that no amount of radiation is entirely without
> effect, some risk must be presumed to be associated with any activity
> involving low-level radiation, no matter how small the dose may be.
> Some such risks, compared with the other hazards of daily life, seem
> negligible. Still, no risk can be regarded as acceptable if it is readily
> avoidable or if it is not accompanied by a commensurate benefit."

Which brings us to the inevitable question: how do the risks of nuclear power compare with those from alternative power sources?

Alternatives to Nuclear Power

There are three major alternatives to nuclear reactors for the generation of power, plus a number of presently uneconomical methods which may, or may not, become important in the future.

Hydroelectric generation at present offers the cheapest form of electric power. It is not without its environmental hazards and many more people have lost their lives in dam accidents than in nuclear accidents. The flooding of large areas to make reservoirs also has negative ecological consequences. Hydro power plants have to be built where geography demands, and the major limitation at present lies in the expense of transmitting power over large distances. (The development of high temperature superconductors may change this situation.)

Coal-fired generating stations are also economical. Their major drawback is their role in producing acid rain, which is the major topic of the next section, but the cost of life in mining accidents should not be forgotten. Oil-fired stations are less economic, and given the uncertainties in future, world oil prices may not be the best direction for expansion. Solar power is at present prohibitively expensive - about 100 times more than coal - but is attractive in the long term because it is an endless source of energy with no major environmental hazards. The use of solar heating plays a role at present by reducing power demands, but the generation of electricity using photovoltaic cells does not look as though it will become economic in the immediate future unless there is a large advance in the technology. Solar power can be used indirectly by cultivating plants suitable for use as "biomass". In Brazil sugar from sugar cane has been fermented to give alcohol for use as a fuel. This was competitive while oil prices were high, but has fallen on hard times with the fall in oil prices. The cultivation of fast-growing poplar trees has been advocated. These again could be used as a source of alcohol but fermentation to give methane might be more viable on a large scale. Again, at present, the economics do not look promising but it seems inevitable that these ideas will be revived when the oil starts to run out. Windmills will probably play a part in the generation of small amounts of power at remote sites, but are unlikely to be developed on a large scale. Power from nuclear fusion, which it is claimed will present only low radiation hazards, also appears to be far in the future. (However a very recent report that fusion has been accomplished in a very simple chemical experiment, electrolysing D_2O and absorbing the deuterium atoms in palladium metal, may radically change this forecast. Most scientists, at least until now, have been sceptical about the correctness of the reports.)

Acid Rain

At present most electricity is generated by burning coal and we must live with the consequence, acid rain. Coal-burning power stations are not the only source of acid rain, but they are clearly the most important. Since burning any fossil fuel produces carbon dioxide, it also contributes to the greenhouse effect, which is discussed in the next section. The topic of acid rain is not without its controversial aspects. There is no argument that rain falling in certain parts of the world —the N.Eastern parts of the USA, Eastern Canada and Scandinavia are the best documented examples— is more acidic than natural rain. Figure 7.7 shows the average acidity of rainfall in North America for the year 1980. (J. Gibson and C. Baker, National Atmospheric Deposition Program, March 1982, see *Acid Rain* by A. M. Kahan)

Fig. 7.7: The Acidity of Rain in N. America. Rainfall with the lowest pH's occurs in the Appalachian region and in Ontario, Canada.

■ *How acid is our rain?*

Natural rain has a pH of 5.6, the slight acidity resulting from the absorption of atmospheric carbon dioxide. In parts of North Eastern America, particularly the Appalachian regions of the USA and the Muskoka region of Ontario, the average pH is around 4.2, representing an increase in acidity by a factor of 25. Individual rainfalls with a pH of as low as 2.1 have been recorded. Demonstration 7.1 shows the pH of water from some local sources.

Demonstration 7.1
The pH of water and household substances. Tap water, rain water and water from other local sources is tested for pH using a pH meter. The pH of several household substances, e.g. ammonia cleaner, bleach and Drano can also be measured.

It is clear that the chemicals causing this increased acidity are sulfuric and nitric acids, with the former predominating by a factor of about two. The major source of sulfuric acid comes from the burning of sulfur-containing coal. Nitric acid comes partly from coal and oil-fired electricity-generating stations and partly from automobile emissions.

The detrimental effects of acid rain are threefold: the acidification of lakes and rivers, with the subsequent loss of fish and other aquatic life, the destruction of trees and the corrosion of stonework and glass in old buildings. The latter effect is of particular concern in Europe but, for obvious reasons, has been less publicized in N. America. It has been claimed that the ancient buildings in Athens have deteriorated more in the last 25 years than in the previous 2,400 years. There appears to be a clear correlation between the presence of acid rain and the appearance of the deleterious effects described above, but the exact chemical mechanisms involved are still uncertain. To start with, sulfur is released as sulfur dioxide, SO_2, and must be oxidized by air to the trioxide, SO_3, before it can dissolve in rain to make sulfuric acid. It used to be thought that this oxidation took place on the surface of smoke particles, but the idea was disproved in England: the amount of airborne sulfuric acid increased when the smoke decreased with anti-smoke legislation. It is now thought that the main oxidation mechanisms involve ozone and other photochemically generated oxidants.

$$SO_2 + O_3 \rightarrow SO_3 + O_2$$
$$SO_3 + H_2O \rightarrow H_2SO_4$$

Support for this idea comes from the observation that sulfuric acid levels are higher in the summer, when photochemistry is more active, than in the winter. Nitric acid also comes from the photochemical oxidation of NO and NO_2, the primary nitrogen contaminants. The various reactions involving nitrogen oxides in photochemical smog generation were considered in Chapter 5. It is becoming clear that acid rain and photochemical smog are closely linked problems.

■ *Killing fish...*

The role of acid rain in killing fish first came to the fore in Norway in the 1970's. It was immediately a political issue, since the pollutants were traced to power stations in Britain, built with tall chimneys to disperse the pollutants, which were then carried to southern Norway on the prevailing SW winds. It proved very difficult to establish a firm correlation between the killing of fish and the acid rain. Changes in acidity due to a build-up of humic acids in the soil when farmland was abandoned[2] were suggested as an alternative source.

There is also wide variation in the effects of the rain depending on the type of rock involved (limestone will neutralize the acid, granite will not). Part of the effect on fish is probably indirect. Increased acidity dissolves more aluminum, and aluminum salts interfere with the operation of a fish's gills. In Ontario this aspect of the problem is well documented. The amount of acid deposition is about 20-40 times greater than in British Columbia and is greater than in any part of the USA except New Hampshire. A large number of lakes have a pH less than 5.0, which is considered the critical value. This has lead to considerable biological change in addition to killing fish. One result is an increased growth of certain types of algae at the expense of more desirable biota. The solubility of many heavy metals, such as mercury, increases and this leads to dangers in eating the fish even in lakes where they are still present.

■ *Killing trees...*

The role of acid rain in damaging trees is a more recent concern. In parts of Southern Germany, 30-50% of the trees in the forests are dead or dying and the link to acid rain seems very likely although it has not been conclusively proved. This problem only appeared in the 1980's and particularly affects evergreen trees. In Canada there have been similar, but rather less drastic, effects on Maple trees, particularly in Quebec. (The link between the death of the maple trees and acid rain has been questioned recently - drought may be the cause.) Current theories tend to put the blame on changes in metal ion concentrations. Nitric acid, when neutralized by the metals in the soil, is an excellent fertilizer and sulfur is also an essential element. Up until recently acid rain appeared to be accelerating the growth of trees, but the long-term effect is negative. Eventually the soil becomes acid, and required metals such as calcium and magnesium are removed, leaving poisonous metals such as aluminum. It has also been suggested that magnesium, an essential component in chlorophyll the photosynthesizing compound, is removed from pine needles by the combined effects of ozone and acids. Whatever the mechanism, the death of the trees seems certain and the role of air pollution almost certain.

There are a number of corrective measures to the acid rain problem. Lakes can be neutralized by adding limestone, a technique which has been shown to be at least partly effective and not prohibitively expensive. Methods have been suggested for removing sulfur from coal before it is burnt, but they seem to be excessively

---

[2] Decomposition of plant material leads to acidic humic materials which accumulate if the land is not planted again.

expensive. A more realistic method is to remove sulfur dioxide form the flue gases before they are released into the atmosphere. Several methods can accomplish this. Limestone scrubbing involves the following chemistry.

$$CaCO_3 \rightarrow CaO + CO_2$$
$$2CaO + 2SO_2 + O_2 \rightarrow 2CaSO_4$$

Limestone is cheap but the product, calcium sulfate, cannot be recycled and is practically worthless. An alternative is sodium sulfite scrubbing.

$$Na_2SO_3 + SO_2 + H_2O \rightarrow 2NaHSO_3 \text{ (sodium bisulfite)}$$

■ *Solutions to the problem...*

The sodium bisulfite solution can be removed and heated to reverse this reaction, giving off SO_2 and regenerating sodium sulfite. The SO_2 can be used to manufacture sulfuric acid. A somewhat similar process involves sodium citrate which forms a complex with sulfur dioxide, which can be decomposed on heating. The use of magnesium oxide in the cycle:

$$MgO + SO_2 \rightarrow MgSO_3$$

and the reverse reaction to recover SO_2 for use in the manufacture of sulfuric acid is possible. Thus a number of methods are available but all are quite expensive on the very large scale which would be necessary for a coal-fired generating plant. The reluctance of the power companies to install such equipment is therefore hardly surprising.

On a more optimistic note, the following specific example is worth citing. Twenty years or so ago the problem of the eutrophication of lakes such as Lake Erie was a large concern. The problem in this case was the accumulation of phosphates from detergents and fertilizers in the lake, which lead to the excessive growth of algae, removing oxygen from the water, and killing other aquatic life. This problem seems to have been solved, mainly by the removal of phosphate builders from detergents, and Lake Erie is now considered relatively healthy. If such a large problem as lake eutrophication can be solved, then perhaps acid rain will also be neutralized.

The Greenhouse Effect

■ *Temperature control in the biosphere...*

The burning of any fossil fuel, whether it is coal, oil, natural gas or gasoline, results in the production of carbon dioxide, CO_2. This gas has no direct deleterious effect and is an important component in the natural biosphere. One of its functions is to play a part in the control of Gaia's temperature. The temperature at the surface of the earth is determined by the balance between the energy absorbed from the incident sunlight, and that lost by re-radiation. Most of the radiation reaching the surface is visible light, which is reflected by white materials but absorbed by black or colored materials. The energy represented by this radiation is transformed to heat, and a dark colored object sitting in the sunlight becomes hot. A hot body will re-radiate energy, but this radiation is primarily in the infra-red part of the spectrum. The glass covering a greenhouse lets in the visible light from the sun, but absorbs and in its turn re-radiates the infra-red emitted by the warm plants and soil it contains. The well known result is that the temperature inside a greenhouse is higher than that outside. (A further large contribution to the heating results from the inability of the air trapped in the greenhouse to escape and mix with the outside air. This is not the greenhouse effect under discussion.) Carbon dioxide and certain other gases play a role, analogous to that of greenhouse glass, in the atmosphere. They are transparent to visible light and do not impede the passage of the sun's light through the atmosphere, but absorb and re-radiate infra-red radiation. The major components of the atmosphere (nitrogen, oxygen and argon) are transparent to both visible and infra-red radiation. The more carbon dioxide in the atmosphere, the more the sun's energy is retained by the earth, and the hotter the surface becomes.

Demonstration 7.2
The greenhouse effect. Greenhouse gases absorb infrared radiation but not visible light. The light received from the sun is mostly in the visible part of the spectrum but that reradiated from hot objects on the earth's surface is mostly infrared. Greenhouse gases therefore help the biosphere retain the sun's energy and eventually lead to a rise in temperature at the earth's surface. In this experiment infrared radiation from a hot source is passed through several gases. The cells containing these gases have windows made from salt, sodium chloride, since this material does not absorb in the infrared. Glass does absorb in the infrared, hence its use in greenhouses. If the cell is filled with nitrogen or oxygen the infrared passes straight through and leads to an increased reading on a thermocouple situated at the other side of the cell. If the cell is filled with carbon dioxide or methane the infrared is absorbed, leading to no increased reading on the thermocouple. A second thermocouple, attached to the side of the cell does show an increased reading, showing that the energy absorbed has heated the gas and the surrounding cell.

Carbon dioxide is not the only gas with greenhouse properties. Water vapor, methane and CFC's are all similar in this respect. Carbon dioxide, though, is the one that is most affected by man's activities. Not only are we adding CO_2 by burning fossil fuels, but we are also increasing the CO_2 concentration by destroying vegetation, particularly in the form of natural tropical jungle. Plant growth involves photosynthesis, in which process CO_2 is absorbed from the atmosphere and converted to organic material. In the absence of industrial activity, the amount of carbon dioxide removed by photosynthesis is just balanced by the amount added by the respiration of animals and plants, and by natural forest fires. Over the last 150 years, man's activities have tipped the balance, so that the amount of carbon dioxide in the atmosphere is steadily increasing. The concentration of CO_2 in earlier times can be estimated from measurements on air samples trapped at various depths in glaciers. Up until about 1850 it had been constant at 270-280ppm for many thousands of years. In 1958 it had risen to 316ppm and in 1985 had reached 345ppm. It is estimated that it will be double its pre-industrial value by late in the next century. About half of the CO_2 released is retained in the atmosphere and about half is dissolved in the sea, primarily due to the reaction:

$$CO_2 + CO_3^{2-} + H_2O \rightarrow 2HCO_3^-$$

The effect of doubling the amount of CO_2 in the atmosphere on the surface temperature of the earth has been calculated by a number of investigators. There are a number of difficulties with these calculations, such as estimating the changes in cloud cover, but an increase in average temperature of 2-3 °C with doubling of the CO_2 concentration seems to be a well accepted figure. There are, as we all know, considerable fluctuations in the temperature which exceed this calculated increase, but a careful analysis of temperature data for the period 1880-1980 seems to indicate an increase of 0.5 °C, which is consistent with the calculations. This sounds a small increase but changes at individual locations will be much larger and the effect on weather patterns is largely unpredictable. Paradoxically the greenhouse effect could lead to colder winters in some parts of the world, but this would be accompanied by warmer, drier summers. Perhaps the best-known prediction is that melting of the Polar Ice Cap will cause flooding in low-lying coastal regions such as Florida.

■ How hot will it get?

Carbon dioxide is not the only greenhouse gas. Water vapor is very effective in this respect and may be expected to increase in concentration with warmer temperatures, by evaporation from the sea. Methane is another significant contributor. Its concentration in the atmosphere has also increased dramatically in the last century. This has been attributed to increases in cows and in rice paddies, both of which produce methane by anaerobic fermentation. It has also been pointed out that CFC's, as well as destroying ozone, are very effective greenhouse gases. These additional sources are calculated to increase the greenhouse effect of CO_2 by another 50%. As a result, some recent articles predict an increase in the average temperature of 5 °C by the year 2050. Since, geologically speaking, we are now in the middle of an interglacial period, this would take us into an uncharted temperature region. Suggestions have been made that the greenhouse effect could be countered by seeding the upper atmosphere with sulfur dioxide to encourage the formation of sunlight-reflecting sulfuric acid droplets. This does not sound a very attractive alternative and probably the only real remedy would be to stop, or curtail, the use of fossil fuels.

Conclusion

■ Which hazards pose the greatest threat?

Each type of technology presents its own risks, and comparisons are difficult. In many cases we are comparing apples and oranges. How should the small additional risk of suffering from cancer 20 or 30 years in the future, due to radiation from nuclear power, be ranked in comparison to the effects of acid rain and greenhouse temperatures resulting from burning coal? There is clearly no easy answer. A recent book by Peter Sprent on *Taking Risks* can only recommend that we obtain more information before taking decisions. This conclusion can be emphasized by looking at some of the data presented in the *Scientific American* article by Arthur C. Upton quoted earlier. Some 30 hazards were ranked according to actual actuarial contribution to the number of deaths in the USA. It should, of course, be remembered that not all undesirable or toxic effects lead to death. The top five hazards, accounting for well over 90% of the deaths, were smoking, alcoholic beverages, motor vehicles, handguns and electric power, in that order. Three groups of people, chosen from the league of women voters, college students and business and professional club members were asked to rank the hazards. The women voters gave the top five as nuclear power, motor vehicles, handguns, smoking and motorcycles in that order. The students opted for nuclear power, handguns, smoking, pesticides and motor vehicles, and the business community for handguns, motorcycles, motor vehicles, smoking and alcoholic beverages. Nuclear power actually ranked 20th, behind X-rays, bicycles, hunting and contraceptives. Pesticides were 28th in the list although they were ranked 9th by the women voters, 4th by the students and 15th by the business persons. None of this means that either nuclear power or pesticides are desirable features of our present society, but it does indicate that many people's assessment of the relative risks of different hazards is inaccurate.

Further reading

Hugh D.Crone, ***Chemicals and Society***, University of Cambridge Press (1986). A well balanced discussion of chemical hazards.

Luciano Cagliotti, ***The Two Faces of Chemistry***, English Ed. MIT Press (1983). An excellent source book for information on many chemical processes and hazards, but now a little out of date.

Charles Perrow, ***Normal Accidents***, Basic Books (1984). The risks that we accept by living with high risk technologies.

John Maddox, ***The Doomsday Syndrome***, McGraw Hill (1972). Written to counter some of the more extreme positions taken by the early environmental groups.

Donald MacKay, ***Heritage Lost - The Crisis in Canada's Forests***, MacMillan (1985). Arguing for better forest management in Canada and the controlled use of herbicides.

Two books on nuclear power. The first is a little out of date, but has good technical background. The second concentrates on the Chernobyl disaster:

i) Walter C. Patterson, ***Nuclear Power***, Penguin Books (1976).
ii) L. Ray Silver, ***Fallout From Chernobyl***, Deneau (1987).

Jeannie Peterson, Ed., ***The Aftermath, Consequences of Nuclear War***, Pantheon Books (1983). The nuclear winter theory.

Fred Pierce, ***Acid Rain***, Penguin Books (1987). An up to date account of this topic.

Peter Sprent, *Taking Risks*, Penguin Books (1988). An attempt to quantify the question of risks.

Arthur C. Upton, "The Biological Effects of Low-Level Ionizing Radiation", *Scientific American*, Vol 246 No 2 p41 (1982). Includes an excellent analysis of public perceptions of various hazards.

William B. Innes, "It's Raining Nitrates and Sulfates", *Chemtech*, p440, July (1984).

Henry I. Bolker, "Scaring Ourselves to Death", *Canadian Chemical News*, p18, Feb (1986).

R. F. Addison, "PCB's in Perspective", *Canadian Chemical News*, p15, Feb. (1986). Short articles on acid rain and chemical hazards.

Richard A. Houghton and George M. Woodwell, "Global Climatic Change (The Greenhouse Effect)", *Scientific American*, April (1989).

Stephen H.Schneider, *Global Warming*, Sierra Club Books, (1989). A detailed analysis of the greenhouse effect.

Scientific American, Special Issue September 1989, "Managing Planet Earth". A series of articles on environmental and related issues.

John Gribbin, *Hothouse Earth*, Grove Wedenfeld (1990). The Greenhouse Effect and Gaia. Discussion of geological and biological factors affecting climate.

Archie M. Kahan, *Acid Rain*, Fulcrum (1986). Science and politics of acid rain, from a US perspective.

Big Science, Big Business and Big Government

*A billion here and a billion there and it starts to add
up to real money.
(Senator Everett Dirksen, discussing the US Defense Budget.)*

Introduction

The starting point for modern science is often taken to be 1662, the founding of the Royal Society of London. During the seventeenth and eighteenth centuries, science was essentially an amateur sport. From time to time, gentlemen got together at the Royal Society, or at one of the similar institutions which had come into being, to present their latest results and to exchange current gossip. At a slightly later date, the papers read at society meetings were published, so that the members could digest them at their leisure. Much of the discourse was philosophical in nature, but the more serious scientists had private laboratories in which they performed the experiments reported at the society's meetings. To be a serious scientist in those days required at least a modest amount of independent wealth. In the nineteenth century, the focus shifted from the private laboratory to the university, but the ambience remained much the same. The amount of money available to support research was small or zero. This situation continued well into the twentieth century; up until 1918, the total equipment budget for the Cavendish laboratory in Cambridge, by that time the most prestigious physics laboratory in the world, never exceeded £550 (about $2500 at the prevailing rate of exchange) per year. Even allowing for inflation, this sum would hardly satisfy a single researcher at a small university in the 1990's.

Science and Technology

Science is often paired with technology. Up until the present century this pairing was not emphasized. There is a story, perhaps apocryphal, that Michael Faraday, the discoverer of electricity, on the occasion of a demonstration at the Royal Institute in London, was asked by the then prime minister of England, Mr Gladstone, what was the use of electricity. Faraday replied that he didn't know but that he was sure that a future prime minister would find a way of taxing it. This may be compared with the reception of a recent major discovery, that of high temperature superconductors. Shortly after this discovery in 1987, it was announced by the president of the United States, Mr. Reagan, that a conference would be held in Washington to exchange information on the topic, but that attendance would be restricted to Americans, on the grounds that it had been organized primarily for the benefit of US industry, and the research would be sponsored by the Department of Defense. (This in spite of the fact that the discovery originated in Europe.) In this case the possible technological implications completely overshadowed the scientific aspects, which traditionally demand free exchange of information. This change in attitude has not come about instantaneously, but can be traced back to the end of the nineteenth century. At that time the synthetic dye industry had developed in Germany and the usefulness of liaison with academic chemists had become apparent. They could be consulted on the finer points of organic chemistry and they could be persuaded to send their students to work in the dye industry; these motivations have remained dominant. The custom was taken a step further when Haber, from the University of Berlin, and Bosch from the industrial company BASF, collaborated during the 1914-1918 war to invent the Haber-Bosch process for fixing nitrogen described in chapter six. This idea of mutual collaboration between universities and industry gradually spread to the English-speaking countries between the wars, but involved only a minority of scientists and did not greatly influence the way they worked. The big change came in a dramatic way with the Manhattan Project in the 1940's. The key new feature was the involvement of government and in retrospect this set a precedent which made post-war science completely different from the pre-war version.

We now have three types of activity: fundamental science, applied science and technology; and three foci for research: universities, industry and government. At present research in all three areas and at all three types of location are intermingled and interconnected. It would be simple to say that fundamental research was the province of the universities, applied research that of government and the development of new technology the responsibility of industry. Some people, particularly older university faculty, would like it to be this way but it is very unlikely that the clock could be turned back to such a simpler time, and far from obvious that such a result would be desirable. The input of fundamental science in providing a base for new technologies is obvious. There is also a very real feedback by which applied research has enriched the universities, both intellectually and financially. Nevertheless, it is proper to pose the question whether the expansion of applied science in universities has changed the nature of these institutions to the extent that the liberal arts concept is seriously challenged.

Government, Industry and the Universities

First though, the ways in which government and industry interact with university science will be considered. It is rightfully held that a major function of a university scientist is to undertake research. This reflects the belief that the objective of a university is not only to pass on the learning it receives from a previous generation, but to add to the store of knowledge. (This is what distinguishes a university from an advanced version of a high school.) Unfortunately, modern scientific research is expensive and all scientists depend on outside support to finance their research: for instance, a new high energy particle machine for the physicists, such as that to be built in Texas, costs several billions of dollars. Chemistry is relatively inexpensive, but the cost of various kinds of spectrometers, considered by most chemists to be essential to their research, is fast approaching a million dollars. Government is the prime provider of such support. A scientist would like this support to come with no strings attached, so that the money can be used to follow wherever curiosity leads. It is argued that only in this way will really original research result. There are many historical examples to show how pure research has lead to unanticipated technological advances: Faraday's electrical discoveries were only an early example of this possibility. Scientists have not hesitated to use these examples to plead for increased funding for curiosity motivated research. However there are even more examples of pure research which have not lead to practical results. An honest scientist will also admit that much of this research does not even lead to results of fundamental importance. There is some justification for the often-heard plea that university scientists should occasionally come down to earth and do something useful. The politicians have always held this view and the contemporary version is expressed in a recent (April 1989) speech by the Canadian Minister for Science and Technology -

> "Our standard of living is threatened ---- Canada must become more self-sufficient by investing in science and technology needed to keep the nation competitive. Knowledge is the prime commodity in the world today - our educational system is the primary provider of that commodity ".

Science, according to this view, is an investment which leads directly to economic benefits which will keep the nation competitive. Evaluated on this basis, curiosity-driven research may be found wanting and governments try other approaches. In Canada so called strategic grants have been introduced to persuade scientists to work in areas where commercial development seems promising. There are many schemes to persuade industry to collaborate with universities in the development of promising technology. A scientific tax credit scheme in Canada in the early 1980's cost the government 2-3 billion dollars, far more than the amount ever provided to the universities, and produced very little in the way of tangible benefits. Research also costs the university in administration money, the so-called overhead to provide buildings and services. They have to try and recover this money from the government or other sources. There are thus obvious sources of financial tension between the government and the universities, since they rarely admit that their objectives in the research area are vastly different.

As an alternative, a researcher can obtain money from industry. The strings in this case are usually more obvious and more direct. The support usually, but not always, involves a contract rather than a grant, which means that the exact research to be performed is specified in advance rather than left to the imagination and discretion of the investigator. The topic is likely to be one of direct interest to the industrial sponsor and there will be some agreement regarding the development of any useful results. This usually will involve the applications for patents. A patent is concerned with the ownership of a discovery. It prohibits persons other than the patent-holder from making use of the discovery for a certain length of time, usually eighteen years. Other people wishing to make use of the discovery must negotiate a license from the patent holder, which he may or may not be willing to grant. It thus provides a large commercial advantage to the holder of a patent on an economically profitable topic. Universities nowadays often take steps to ensure that they obtain a share in the patent rights of any discovery made in their laboratories. When the patent laws are changed - as they have been recently in Canada for the benefit of the international drug companies - very large amounts of money are at stake. Patents can become the driving force even in university research, as is illustrated by the recent case of the announcement of a possible "cold" nuclear fusion reaction, when the publication of the result was preceded by a press conference including an announcement of patent applications. Thus, whether they like it or not, universities are heavily involved in applied research and technology. The only real question is whether this is incompatible with the liberal arts concept of university scholarship.

As indicated earlier, the present situation has evolved in the last 50 years. In the 1920's and 1930's there was very little outside financial support for university science. This was an exciting time in physics, with the development of quantum theory and sub-atomic physics. Philanthropic organizations, such as the Rockefeller Foundation, were the only outside supplement to the very meager funds of the leading research centers such as Gottingen University in Germany. In spite of this, a tremendous number of new results and ideas were generated in Europe. In the 1930's many of the leading physicists, being Jewish, were forced to leave Germany and found refuge at the relatively wealthy USA universities. They brought with them their scientific knowledge and also first hand insight regarding the politics of Nazi Germany. They were the nucleus of the group who persuaded the American government that the German scientists could produce an atomic bomb, and then designed and built the bomb for the Allies. This was the first large scale involvement of government in a science based venture. Its success lead to two decades of government support for fundamental science, much of it militarily motivated, but with a general trust in the ultimate worth of curiosity-motivated research. In the 1960's and early 1970's the belief that the scientists always know best was challenged and replaced by a demand for social relevance and environmental responsibility. The cry was for democracy rather than technocracy in making decisions in science and technology. In the 1980's there was a reaction, particularly in the USA, against government regulation of the environment (or anything else) and a move towards deregulation, privatization, changes in the patent law favorable to industry, relaxation of anti-trust laws and a general emphasis on market determined scientific objectives. Thus much of the change brought about in the early 1970's was reversed, and decision-making on scientific issues again became less open. As detailed in the book *The New Politics of Science* by David Dickson, this has lead to increased government support of science, accompanied by increased private sector control of scientific objectives. This is claimed to be the prescription for competing with the Japanese technological success. Canada's science policy has followed a respectful step or two behind the American leadership.

Three Case Histories of Applied Research

The most interesting questions are probably not in the higher realms of government science policy, but in the nature of applied research as it is practised in the laboratory. This topic can be approached by looking at three well-documented examples of scientists at work. They all deal with applied research but there the similarity ends. One example involves research carried out in government laboratories, one in a university environment and one in industry. The first group considered were top level scientists, many with Nobel prizes. The second group were mostly undergraduates. The third group were modern professionals. The first example, the development of the atomic bombs between 1942 and 1954, represents the start of the modern era of applied research. The second group, christened the "true hackers" by

Steven Levy in his book *Hackers*, were active in the period 1959-1969. In retrospect their attitude towards the programming and use of computers has had a profound effect on life in the 1980's. Our third example deals with the development of a new computer in the period 1978-1980 as described by Tracy Kidder in *The Soul of a New Machine*. This is applied research in contemporary society.

The Atom Bomb Scientists

The story of atomic scientists has been told many times, but perhaps the most sympathetic rendition was the almost contemporary account (1956) given by Robert Jungk in *Brighter Than a Thousand Suns*. He describes the gradual encroachment of politics on the academic seclusion of physicists in universities such as Gottingen. Many of the most brilliant scientists left Germany for the USA, bringing with them first-hand opinions on the undesirability of a German victory in the coming war, and a realistic fear that this could be achieved if Hitler were to possess the atomic bomb. A group of expatriate scientists, lead by Szilard with the backing of Einstein, brought this possibility to the attention of the American government and recommended that the Allies should, as a purely defensive measure, build the bomb themselves. This recommendation was accepted and the largest-ever project in applied science was launched. It was christened the Manhattan Project, General Groves of the US army was put in charge, and money was lavished to make it a success. Under the leadership of Robert Oppenheimer a group of scientists was brought together at Los Alamos, New Mexico, to design and build the bomb. None of these scientists had ever worked on an applied project before, and they found the problems they faced to be very different from those they encountered in academic science. Perhaps to their own surprise, they enjoyed it. As the future Nobel prize winner, Richard Feynman, said "...we started it for a good reason, then you're working very hard to accomplish something and it's pleasure, it's excitement". The reaction set in when the first bomb had been successfully tested and its potential for destruction fully realized. At this time the Allies were invading Germany and the real extent of German progress in atomic weapons became apparent. They had made very little progress and there had been no real threat that they would develop a bomb. Sam Goudsmit, the scientist charged with evaluating the German effort, remarked: "Isn't it wonderful that the Germans have no atomic bomb? Now we won't have to use ours". His military liaison officer quickly disillusioned him by saying "Of course you understand, Sam, that if we have such a weapon we are going to use it". This, of course proved to be correct. It rapidly became apparent that scientists might have designed and built the bomb, but the politicians and military were in complete control.

It is interesting to compare the account of the development of the atomic bomb in *Brighter Than a Thousand Suns* with the "official" account given by General Groves in his autobiography *Now It Can Be Told*. In the latter version of events the physicists play a much smaller role. Scientists tend to think that they are the central characters in a research project but the bureaucrats see them as only a small, but unfortunately necessary, part of the overall scheme. In present North American society the latter view is probably the more realistic. Scientific protests against the further development of atomic weapons were ineffective in the years immediately following the war. General Groves later remarked, "What happened is what I expected, that after they had this extreme freedom for about six months their feet began to itch, and as you know, almost every one of them has come back into government research, because it was just too exciting". Somewhat unwillingly, scientists accepted the secrecy imposed by the military, and their absolute dominance was made clear when the scientific leader of the Los Alamos laboratories, Robert Oppenheimer, was denied a security clearance - in spite of the fact that his loyalty was unquestioned - in 1954. Oppenheimer was supported by the large majority of scientist in the USA but this support carried no weight with the politicians and generals.

The Hackers

Los Alamos, the site of the nuclear bomb research, also has another first. The first use of a computer on a real problem occurred there. The trouble was that it was difficult to keep the experts concentrating on the problem at hand, since they preferred to devise new programmes with their latest toy. Richard Feynman records the initial difficulties. "If you have ever worked with computers you understand the disease - the delight in being able to see how much you can do".

Fifteen years later, in 1959, computers had reached the universities. At MIT in Boston, Mass. the mystique and ritual associated with the early IBM mainframe monsters (large in size because they used vacuum tubes rather than transistors) was already well developed. They were for officially-sanctioned users only and were run in a batch mode: computer cards were handed in and output was handed back without the researcher actually touching the machine. This separation of the operators from the users severely restricted the chances for originality in the development of programming methods. The chances for a mere undergraduate to get close to such a machine were remote to zero. Several serendipitous events changed this situation. A group of students belonging to a model railroad student club realized that computers were the logical outlet for their fascination with complex control systems. At the same time, one of the first transistorised computers was moved into the building and, in contrast to the IBM philosophy, it was built for interactive use. A person could sit at a keyboard and try various programs almost instantaneously. Furthermore, the people in charge were sufficiently generous to allow students access to the machine, if they were willing to take a time slot at 3:00 a.m. or thereabouts. This was all that was needed for the birth of the "hackers". They were devoted to writing computer programs for its own sake, and entered into this project with such gusto that the art of programming was for ever changed. The first computer they worked on had only 4K of memory so the code had to be very efficient. Competition amongst the hackers brought this efficiency to a fine art. They believed in starting at the beginning, and first wrote an assembler in machine language and then all of the services, such as converting binary numbers to decimal, which we now take for granted.   In 1961 a PDP-1 computer, manufactured by DEC not IBM, appeared followed by a PDP-6 in 1963 and the hackers were able to branch forth in many directions. The first computer game, Spacewars, occupied much of their time, but the first music programming (Bach fugues), the first chess program, the beginnings of "artificial intelligence" using the LISP language, and the initial computer control of robots all received some attention. Diversions such as telephone hacking for free calls, and practical jokes, and illegal midnight modifications to the hardware were not unknown. Out of all this activity an ethic of sorts grew: access to computers should be unlimited and information should be distributed freely; people should be judged by their ability at programming computers, not by their degrees; authority should be mistrusted and decentralization promoted. Above all there had to be an alternative to the IBM way of doing things by building bigger and bigger machines and insisting on timesharing. This way of thinking, and technological improvements, lead inevitably to the personal microcomputer, and the road from MIT to California and the Apple is chronicled by Steven Levy in *The Hackers*. The microcomputer revolution would not have occurred, or at minimum would have occurred differently, if some undergraduates had not been able to gain access to computers in the middle of the night. The contrast between the anarchism of the hackers and the rigid organization and secrecy of General Groves' Manhattan Project is absolute. The onslaught of the microcomputer in the last five years suggests that the contribution of hackers may be the more lasting and worth-while, even if their legacy includes computer viruses. The similarities between the atomic scientists and the hackers are perhaps more fascinating than the differences. Both groups were willing to work very long hours on a project in applied science. Both were dedicated to achieving their objectives but both were as much dedicated to the research itself as to the objectives.

The Professionals

Our final example revisits some of the same territory ten years later. By this time the computer field had sub-divided. IBM and the mainframe still reigned supreme but microcomputers were looming on the horizon. In between were the minicomputers, which had carved out a profitable niche in the more scientifically oriented industries. The dominant company here was DEC, the makers of the original PDP computers, and now selling a very successful line of VAX computers. A newer company, Data General, sought to compete in this area, by building a so-called 32-bit super mini. Tracy Kidder tells the story in *The Soul of a New Machine*. The practical problems of designing hardware and software are not dissimilar in type to those encountered fifteen years earlier by the Hackers, but are vastly more complex. The particular challenge in this case was to make the software compatible with earlier Data General computers. Teams of highly trained PhD's were now required rather than a talented undergraduate willing to stay up late. Commercial considerations dictated that security should be tight, with admission to the working areas being restricted to project members. Great dedication and long hours - 7 a.m. to 7 p.m. - were expected from the team members. The enthusiasm for the project was such that these conditions were accepted more or less without complaint. It is clear that a well-defined applied scientific project generates its own momentum and will be supported by the participants almost regardless of the physical and mental discomforts. The project was a qualified success, as the final computer, announced in April 1980, was competitive, but not clearly superior to those of other companies.

Conclusion

In *The New Politics of Science* David Dickson decries the impact of big business and big government on science in the 1980's. He is particularly concerned with the adverse effects on the universities. The case studies given trace the divergence of academic research and industrial research. University research was developed using government funds as a public resource and is now in danger of being auctioned off to the highest private bidder. More and more, the fruits of university research appear as patents rather than publications. In new areas, such as biotechnology, the line between industry and university is becoming blurred, with faculty participating in the private companies and carrying out commercial research in university laboratories. His chapter on the universities and industry is sub-titled "knowledge as a commodity". (This is exactly the phrase used by the Canadian Minister of Science and Technology, in the speech quoted earlier.) Knowledge, in his estimation, is not only a commodity, but the prime commodity, and the universities are exhorted to produce more of it. As a commodity, it can be priced and traded on the free market in the same manner as pigs bellies and grain futures; this is where the real clash with the liberal arts ethos occurs.

Applied research itself is not inimicable to liberal arts values. What counts most is a group activity, rather than an individual activity, and this mode of doing research is becoming more and more widely accepted at universities. This is where much of the action and challenge in science is found at present, and it seems quite appropriate that the universities should share in the excitement if they have the expertise to do it. It is what happens after the research has been successfully concluded that counts. In the three examples considered, the military tried to keep the technology of the atom bomb secret. This was not a successful strategy. (The Russians rapidly developed their own atomic weapons - the atom spies probably contributed little - and in fact appear to have developed a workable H bomb before the Americans.) The "Hackers" showed that applied research does not have to be commercially orientated. In the final example concerning the commercial development of computers, the push was to develop a new machine even though a perfectly adequate computer for the job was already on the market. Clearly, re-inventing the wheel should not be a university activity. Both absolute secrecy, and restricted publication, are completely abhorrent to traditional university attitudes. The knowledge developed by the hackers was freely shared, an idea which seemed subversive to the authorities at the time, but which paid enormous dividends by preparing the way for the individualism of the microcomputer era. The antithesis of liberal arts is knowledge which is bought and sold as a commodity, rather than freely disseminated in open discussion.

Further reading

Robert Jungk, *Brighter Than a Thousand Suns*, Penguin Books (1956). The story of the atomic scientists from a scientist's perception.

Leslie R. Groves, *Now It Can Be Told*, Harper and Brothers (1962). The other side of the atomic scientists story.

Stephen Levy, *Hackers*, Dell Publishing (1984). Contains an account of the development of microcomputers and computer games as well as the story of the MIT students.

Richard P. Feynman, *Surely You're Joking, Mr. Feynman*, Bantam Books (1986). Contains some interesting anecdotes of life at Los Alamos.

Tracy Kidder, *The Soul of a New Machine*, Avon Books (1982). Industrial research in computers.

David Dickson, *The New Politics of Science*, University of Chicago Press (1984, 1988 with new preface). A liberal view of the present situation.

Part III: Far From Equilibrium

CHAPTER EIGHT

Entropy, Equilibrium and Life

Introduction

■ *The entropy crisis...*

At the beginning of Chapter 2 we suggested a simple experiment to introduce the idea of chemical equilibrium. Chemical reactions, in the example used the reaction of sodium carbonate with hydrochloric acid, do not continue indefinitely but eventually reach "equilibrium". Some of the factors which determine how far a reaction will proceed before equilibrium is attained were introduced at the end of Chapter 3. The terms enthalpy, entropy and free energy were used. It is now time to return to this topic and ask how chemical equilibrium is related to the chemistry of life.

Another very simple experiment serves to introduce the topic. Consider two plastic cups, one containing hot coffee and the other (inverted) a mouse. Let us measure the temperature of both, and also the temperature of the room. (The blood temperature of mice is close to that of humans, and markedly higher than normal room temperature.) By the time you have finished reading this chapter, the temperature of the coffee will be very close to that of the room. The temperature of the mouse, assuming that it is still alive, will not have changed. The coffee has attained thermal equilibrium, a process which is essentially the same as the establishment of chemical equilibrium. The mouse, being alive, is able to maintain a "steady state" temperature which is markedly different from the temperature of its surroundings. Living things also maintain chemical compositions which are far from equilibrium and, from the narrow point of view of a chemist, this is what distinguishes the living from the non-living.

Consider first energy and chemical equilibrium in non-living systems. In 1973, and again in the late 1970's, the flow of oil from the Middle East to Europe and North America was interrupted due to an embargo imposed by the OPEC producers. The resulting economic dislocation was described as an "energy crisis". This is a misnomer; since the First Law of thermodynamics states that energy can only be interconverted among its different forms, but never destroyed, it follows that we can never "run out" of energy. The real problem is that not all energy is available to provide electricity and to power our automobiles. Some forms of energy are better than others for these purposes, and what distinguishes useful energy from useless energy is entropy. This is the subject of the Second Law of thermodynamics. The amount of useful energy available is continually diminishing so what we face, sooner or later, is an "entropy crisis". The term **entropy** was introduced in Chapter Three and an indication given that it was important in determining the position of chemical equilibrium. Since the present section of the book is entitled *Far from Equilibrium*, it is appropriate that the idea of entropy be examined in more detail.

The ideas associated with thermodynamics and entropy were formed at the beginning of the nineteenth century. At that time the steam engine was becoming widely used, and the question of designing such an engine to be as efficient as possible naturally arose. (An engineer would like to get the maximum mileage from a ton of coal fed into the boiler of a steam locomotive.) The Second Law of thermodynamics states the limit of the maximum efficiency attainable. It also tells us that perpetual motion machines will not work. In a device such as a steam engine, a certain amount of heat is supplied by burning coal or some other fuel. The First Law of thermodynamics tells us that this amount of heat is equivalent to a certain amount of mechanical work. It would obviously be desirable to convert all of the heat to mechanical work. Yet the Second Law of thermodynamics states that it cannot be done.

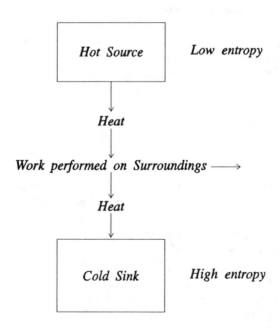

Fig. 8.1: The Thermodynamics of a Steam Engine. The essential feature of a steam engine is that hot steam expands, pushing a cylinder down, and cold steam contracts returning the cylinder to its original position. The net effect is to convert heat energy to mechanical energy.

■ *Converting heat to work...*
■ *Entropy measures the quality of energy...*

In order to perform mechanical work by moving a piston in a cylinder, energy must be provided from a hot source to make the working gas expand, and removed to a cold source when the cylinder is returned to its original position. If the temperature of the hot source is T_H and that of the cold source T_C, the fraction of the heat that can be converted to work under the absolute optimum conditions, is $1 - T_C/T_H$. If the hot source is at the temperature of boiling water, 100 °C (= 373K), and the cold source at room temperature, 25 °C (= 298K), the maximum efficiency is $1 - 298/373$ (= 0.201) or about 20%. Even this efficiency could only be achieved under perfect conditions (ie. no loss through friction), and the real efficiency is always less. Clearly, the higher the temperature of the hot source and the lower the temperature of the cold source, the greater the fraction of heat transformed to work, but we can never transform it all.

Heat energy from different sources does not always deliver equivalent amounts of work. The hotter the source of the energy, the more of it can be converted to mechanical energy by coupling it with a cold source of constant temperature. Heat in a high temperature source is therefore of "higher quality", in the sense that it is more readily converted to work, than heat in a low temperature source. Sunlight corresponds to energy at the temperature of the surface of the sun, several thousand °C, and is therefore high quality energy suitable for powering Gaia[1]. The quality of the heat supplied by a source is measured by its entropy, defined in units of heat/temperature. A kJ of energy at 1000 K has a lower entropy, and is more easily converted to work, than a kJ of energy at 100 K. Enthalpy measures the quantity of heat, entropy measures the quality of heat according to the prescription that the lower the entropy, the better the quality. When heat is transferred from a high temperature source to a low temperature source (and this is the only way that heat can be transferred) there is an increase in entropy.[2] If the hot and cold sources are linked to an engine, some of the heat is transformed to work en route, so that less heat arrives at the cold source than leaves the hot source. The increase in entropy will be smaller, but there is a limit to how much smaller. In the limit of optimum efficiency the entropy change will be zero and this, according to the Second Law, is the best we can possibly do. In all real engines there is an overall increase in entropy. In an isolated system the entropy always increases with time. This is an alternative way of phrasing the Second Law of thermodynamics. It is, mathematically, exactly equivalent to the statement that heat always passes from a hot body to a cold body and never in the opposite direction.

It is fair to ask at this stage: why should this be of any interest to anybody but an engineer designing steam engines? This question, and others similar to it, deserve through exploration. In the 1950's, the English writer and scientist C. P. Snow spoke

---

[1] Heat arrives from the sun as radiation, mostly visible light as discussed in Chapter 5. The distribution of energies is determined by the temperature of the radiating source, the sun.

[2] The quantity of heat transferred divided by the lower temperature must be greater than heat transferred divided by the higher temperature.

of *The Two Cultures* and deplored the inability of the literary community to appreciate the wonders of science.   He specifically used the example that understanding the Second Law of thermodynamics is the scientific equivalent to being familiar with Shakespeare. Clearly, scientists consider that there is something more fundamental than steam engines involved. It is indeed true that thermodynamics can be applied to many scientific problems, ranging from chemical reactions to black holes, but the generality lies in understanding the nature of entropy and what it tells us about the way the universe operates.

Entropy and Probability

■ *Sharing energy...*

The model of gases known as the kinetic theory provides a model for understanding the properties of gases such as pressure and temperature. In this model, a gas contained in a closed vessel consists of a very large number of very small molecules, all in rapid motion, colliding frequently with each other and with the walls of the vessel. The latter collisions are responsible for the pressure exerted. If energy is added to the system, the molecules move more rapidly and this is equivalent to a rise in temperature. If the volume of the gas is kept constant, the faster moving molecules at the higher temperature will exert an increased pressure. If one wall of the vessel is a moveable piston, increased temperature leads to expansion of the gas and movement of the piston. How does entropy fit into this picture? The following analogy may be helpful.

Imagine a pool game played with completely elastic balls[3] on a table with perfectly elastic cushions and a completely friction-free surface. Balls would continue to bounce around on such a table indefinitely, since no energy would be lost as heat. The game is started by imparting some energy to the cue ball, which thus, in effect, has a high temperature, while the motionless balls in their starting positions have a low temperature. As soon as the cue ball hits another ball it loses some of its energy, and an equivalent amount of energy is gained by the other ball. In due course all of the balls get involved and are moving around the table in a very complex pattern. The energy originally imparted to the cue ball will be equally shared by all the balls on the table. The system will have reached a uniform temperature. This does not mean that at any given instant all the balls will be moving with exactly the same velocity; on the contrary, some will be moving fast and some slow, but averaged over a period of time no individual ball will have a higher kinetic energy than any other.

Strictly speaking, the concept of temperature can only be applied to a collection of objects, so that it is not true to say that the original cue ball in the example above had a high temperature, but the principle that eventually it will share its energy equally with all the rest of the balls is valid. The situation is exactly the same if we mix some hot gas with a volume of cold gas. The molecules of hot gas, corresponding to the cue ball, collide with molecules from the cold gas and share their energy with these cooler molecules which correspond to the stationary billiard balls.

---

[3] A perfectly elastic object rebounds without any loss of energy.

Within a short period of time the average energy of all the molecules is the same and the system has a constant temperature. Heat has flowed from the hot source to the cold source to bring about thermal equilibrium. It is very unlikely that on the pool table, all the energy at any given time will have accumulated again in the cue ball, such that the cue ball will be in motion while the other balls are at rest. Very unlikely, but not impossible. If instead of 10 or 12 billiard balls we are dealing with the 10^{23} molecules in a mole of gas, "very unlikely" becomes exceedingly improbable. Such a situation, in which all of the available energy has accumulated in one ball, corresponds to heat flowing from a cold source to a hot source, which is contrary to the Second Law of thermodynamics. Entropy is closely associated with probability and the Second Law states that nature always favors the most probable arrangement. There is only one way in which all the energy can be accumulated in the cue ball, but there are many ways in which it can be spread around amongst all of the billiard balls. It is assumed that each of the ways of distributing energy has an equal chance of occurring, so that the probability of a certain energy distribution among the billiard balls is proportional to the number of ways of attaining this energy distribution. Intuitively this is a very reasonable assumption, and it does indeed seem to correspond to the way that nature operates.

The ideas associated with probability, as outlined above, can be phrased in mathematical terms. In other words, the chances that a random fluctuation will place all of the energy, or even a large part of the energy, of a collection of molecules in a single molecule can be calculated.

Demonstration 8.1
Computer simulations of the statistical basis of entropy. A number of computer programs are available to demonstrate the statistical distribution of energies among a population of molecules. The simplest demonstrate that if a collection of molecules with high energy is allowed to exchange energy with a collection of molecules with low energy, after a short period of time the distribution of energies in the two populations is very similar. Another program can be used to calculate the entropy of such a system as it changes with time.

■ *The natural tendency of energy is to disperse...*

Another formulation of the Second Law is to say that the natural tendency of energy is to disperse. It is not very probable that all of the energy available to a system will congregate in one small group of molecules. It is much more likely that energy will be spread evenly among all the possible energy carriers. (This is equivalent to saying that the distribution is disordered or chaotic.) If energy is accumulated in one specific place, which is thereby made different from other places, a degree of order has been imposed on the system. There is an exact mathematical relationship between disorder, as measured by the number of ways in which a given state of a system can be attained, and entropy.

Demonstration 8.2.

Le Chatelier's Principle. It is convenient to demonstrate Le Chatelier's principle by using a reaction involving a color change to detect the change in the position of the equilibrium. A suitable reaction is that between pale yellow ferric ions (Fe^{3+}) and colorless thiocyanate ions (SCN^-) to give red-brown $Fe(SCN)^{2+}$ ions.

$$Fe^{3+}(aq) + SCN^-(aq) \leftrightharpoons FeSCN^{2+}(aq)$$

The position of this equilibrium can be changed by adding excess ferric ions, by adding more thiocyanate, by removing thiocyanate or by changing the temperature. Adding Fe^{3+} according to LeChatelier's principle will move the equilibrium to the right. The experiment shows that the color becomes much darker corresponding to the formation of more $FeSCN^{2+}$. Adding SCN^- produces the same result. Thiocyanate ions can be removed by adding silver nitrate since this leads to the precipitation of insoluble silver thiocyanide. This produces an almost colorless solution, showing that the equilibrium has moved to the left. The reaction is exothermic. Cooling the solution, accomplished by placing a tube containing the reaction mixture in ice, leads to an increase in color showing that the equilibrium has moved to the right. Placing the tube in a beaker of hot water results in the opposite effect. Another reaction which works equally as well, is provided by the equilibrium between blue $CoCl_4^{2-}$ and pink $Co(H_2O)_6^{2+}$.

$$CoCl_4^{2-} + 6H_2O \leftrightharpoons Co(H_2O)_6^{2+} + 4Cl^-$$

Adding water shifts the equilibrium to the right and the solution becomes pink. Adding chloride ion shifts it to the left and the solution becomes blue. When the solution is cooled the equilibrium shifts to the right and the solution becomes pink. When the solution is heated the opposite effect is observed.

Entropy is not solely concerned with the distribution of energy, but the concept can be applied whenever a large number of entities can be distributed in different ways. Thus, just as there is flow of heat to attain thermal equilibrium when a hot body and a cold body are placed in contact, there is a flow of molecules to achieve pressure equilibrium if a gas at high pressure is allowed to expand into a region of lower pressure. In both cases the overall system increases its entropy. The total entropy change is the sum of the entropy changes from all sources and, as we shall see below, is the important quantity.

Entropy and Chemical Equilibrium

■ *Different kinds of molecules have different enthalpies...*

The discussion above has been concerned with the idea of physical equilibrium. In such a process all parts of a system reach the same temperature and pressure, and the entropy of the system has been maximized. The system has changed to achieve its "most probable" state (this corresponds to a uniform distribution) with an equal sharing of kinetic energy among all parts of the system. Having reached this state it will remain there; it is at equilibrium. Very similar considerations apply to chemical equilibria. The only difference is that, as far as kinetic energy is concerned, all molecules are equivalent, but this is not true for chemical energy. Different kinds of molecules correspond to different levels of chemical energy, or in other words, some molecules are more stable than other molecules. Chemical equilibrium is the result of two, often competing, influences. On the one hand, there is a tendency to favor the most stable type of molecules, minimizing enthalpy. Another way of looking at this is to note that an exothermic reaction converts high grade chemical energy to low grade heat energy, increasing the entropy. A decrease in enthalpy is equivalent to an increase in entropy. There are also other sources of entropy increase, such as the tendency to maximize the entropy (probability) of the system by having a random collection of all the possible types of molecules. The more molecules there are, the more ways they can be arranged. Thus if one molecule dissociates to give two molecules, there is an increase in entropy. If four molecules react to give three molecules there is a decrease in entropy. The change in entropy from molecular rearrangement of this kind can be combined with the change in enthalpy of the chemical reaction, to give a change in **free energy**, a term introduced in Chapter 3. It is the change in free energy which determines the position of a chemical equilibrium.

■ *Energy and entropy factors often work in opposite directions...*

The simplest examples involve changes of state rather than chemical changes. Many substances can exist as either gases or liquids. As gases, the molecules are spread around in a large volume of space, but as liquids they are clumped together in a much smaller volume. If we think of space as divided into a discrete number of very small cells, there are many more such cells in the volume occupied by the gas than in that occupied by the liquid. There are therefore many more ways of distributing the molecules in the gaseous state than in the liquid state, which is equivalent to saying that the entropy of the gas is much greater than that of the liquid. On the other hand, the clumped-together molecules in a liquid attract each other, effectively forming weak chemical bonds. Thus the enthalpy effect favors the liquid, and the entropy effect favors the gas. When a liquid is heated the kinetic energy of the molecules increases, and eventually is sufficient to overcome the chemical forces holding the liquid together. The entropy effect becomes dominant at high temperatures so that eventually the liquid boils.

Similar considerations apply to the phase transitions between liquids and solids. In a solid, the atoms or molecules are arranged in a manner which leads to the strongest bonding between neighbors and the lowest energy for the overall collection of atoms or particles. Such an arrangement is, of necessity, an orderly rather than a random pattern and thus it is a low-entropy configuration. At low temperatures the energy gained more than compensates for the unfavorable entropy. At high temperatures this is no longer so and the solid melts.

The application of these ideas to chemical reactions is straightforward. The simplest situation is a chemical reaction in which a single molecule dissociates to two molecules. An example is the colorless dinitrogen tetroxide which dissociates to the brown nitrogen dioxide on heating, a reaction of environmental importance which was discussed in Chapter 5.

$$N_2O_4 \leftrightarrows 2NO_2$$

In N_2O_4, the NO_2 fragments are required to associate only in pairs, which is a much more ordered arrangement than allowing them to roam freely. Dissociation of N_2O_4 therefore corresponds to an <u>increase</u> in entropy which favors the reaction. The process of dissociation though, breaks the N-N bond in N_2O_4 which results in an unfavorable energy or enthalpy factor. The reaction is **endothermic**.

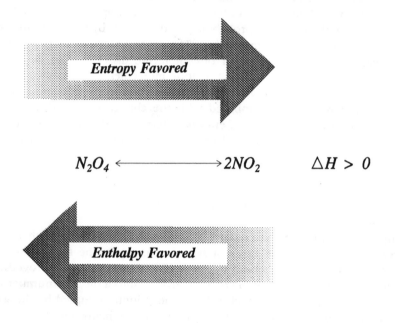

$$N_2O_4 \longleftrightarrow 2NO_2 \qquad \Delta H > 0$$

Fig. 8.2: The Thermodynamics of the Dissociation of N_2O_4.

■ *Entropy and chemical reactions...*

The position of the dissociative equilibrium is determined by the combination of these two factors. More dissociation occurs at higher temperatures since, as in the case of condensation to a liquid, the entropy term becomes more important at higher temperatures. We might ask: what is the effect of an increase in pressure on the position of equilibrium? Increase in pressure will tend to decrease the volume of the system and hence inhibit the ability of the molecules to roam freely. The entropy term is therefore less influential and the equilibrium will be moved to the left, i.e. more association. The reader will recognize that these considerations are the basis of LeChatelier's principle, introduced in Chapter 6.

A second example, based on chemistry encountered previously, is provided by the Haber-Bosch process for producing ammonia from hydrogen and nitrogen.

$$N_2 + 3H_2 \leftrightarrow 2NH_3$$

The conditions favoring the production of ammonia had been deduced from LeChatelier's principle. The reaction is exothermic, indicating that the gain in chemical energy resulting from the formation of 6 N-H bonds is greater than the loss of an N-N bond and 3 H-H bonds. In this case though, the entropy factor is unfavorable since four particles are reduced to two, resulting in a more orderly arrangement of lower entropy. As deduced previously, ammonia formation is favored by lower temperatures and higher pressures. The idea that entropy favors reactions leading to an increase in the number of molecules applies equally to reactions in solution. In such cases concentration plays a role analogous to that of pressure in the gas phase. If the reaction involves a color change, it is easy to demonstrate how changing concentrations of the reactants shifts the position of equilibrium.

■ *Solvation and entropy...*

Thermodynamics is of course equally applicable to non-living and to living systems. Nearly all biochemical reactions occur in aqueous solution. It is of great importance to apply these simple thermodynamic ideas to reactions of biochemical importance to determine whether they are likely to occur or not. The reader should be warned though that simple arguments of the type developed above, often lead to incorrect predictions in biological situations. The fault is not with the thermodynamics, but with the neglect of complicating factors. One such factor is the great importance of the solvation of biological molecules in aqueous solutions. This contributes to both the energy and the entropy terms; hydrogen bonds, the major solvating interaction, are quite strong and cannot be neglected in the decision of whether a reaction will be exothermic or endothermic; solvation introduces greater order and hence lower entropy. Water is itself a highly ordered liquid, giving it a low entropy, and the effect of solute molecules in breaking this ordered structure is also often important. It turns out, for example, that a combination of solvation effects is the deciding factor in determining the position of equilibrium in many reactions leading to the formation of biopolymers, such as proteins. The position of these equilibria is in fact unfavorable for the formation of proteins, and at thermodynamic equilibrium there would be no proteins and no life. Fortunately living things at not at thermodynamic equilibrium; to discuss living processes it is not sufficient to consider only equilibrium thermodynamics. We must think about systems which are far from equilibrium and are participating in a wide variety of chemical reactions. The fact that living systems are never at equilibrium is due to their constant intake of food (energy).

The study of the rates at which chemical systems approach equilibrium constitutes the subject of chemical kinetics, and a brief description of this area is necessary before proceeding to consideration of systems far from equilibrium.

Reaching Equilibrium - Chemical Kinetics

■ *Rates of reaction depend on the concentrations of reactants...*

In Chapter 3 we introduced the idea that at equilibrium a reaction was proceeding at equal rates in the forward and backwards directions. The equilibrium constant was shown to be equal to the ratio of the forward and the backward rate constants. The study of the rates of reactions is known as **chemical kinetics,** and it is usually a part of studies to determine the **mechanism** of a reaction. Probing the mechanism of reactions is the heart of chemistry and a major objective in biochemistry. The rate of the reaction is the change in concentration of a reactant per unit time. The simplest case is one where a reactant A gives a product B, i.e.

$$A \rightarrow B$$

It is clear that the more A is present, the faster B will be formed, so that we can write:

$$Rate = k[A] \text{ where [A] is the concentration of A}$$

k is called the rate constant. This reaction is known as a unimolecular, or first order, reaction. The next simplest case occurs when two molecules A and B collide to give a third molecule C. The frequency of collisions depends on the concentrations of both A and B.

$$A + B \rightarrow C$$

The rate equation for this reaction, by a simple extension of the previous ideas, is

$$Rate = k[A][B]$$

This represents a bimolecular, or second order, reaction. The extension to higher order reactions is obvious.

Most chemical reactions occur in two or more steps. To understand how they work we must write down several equations to show the different steps. This information comprises the mechanism, or reaction path, for the reaction. A simple example is provided by a reaction in which a bromide ion, Br^-, is replaced by a hydroxide ion, OH^-:

$$RBr + OH^- \rightarrow ROH + Br^-$$

In this equation R could be an organic group such as CH_3, or it could be a metal ion such as Co^{3+}. There are two simple mechanisms for such a reaction, plus several more complicated ones. The first simple mechanism is to initially add the OH^- ion to the R group, so that we have an intermediate with both OH and Br attached to the R group. The reaction is completed by the Br^- ion falling off this intermediate, i.e., the mechanism is:

$$RBr + OH^- \rightarrow RBr(OH)^-$$
$$RBr(OH)^- \rightarrow ROH + Br^-$$

A simple alternative is for the reaction steps to occur the other way round, first lose the Br^- then add the OH^-, i.e.

$$RBr \rightarrow R^+ + Br^-$$
$$R^+ + OH^- \rightarrow ROH$$

These mechanisms are illustrated in Figure 8.3. As shown there are two possible reaction sequences leading to the same final product.

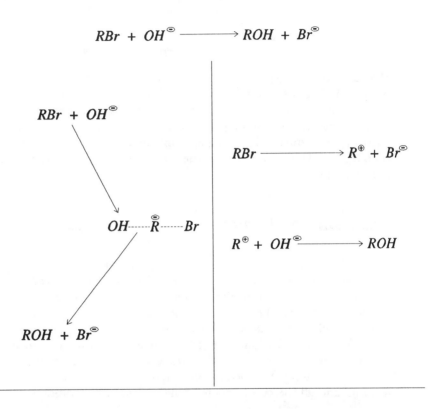

Fig. 8.3: The Mechanism of a Hydrolysis Reaction. The reaction can proceed either by way of a higher coordinate intermediate or by way of a lower coordinate intermediate.

■ *Multistep reactions...*

Each of these reaction steps has its own individual rate. The rate of the overall reaction is determined by the rate of the slowest step. In both of the above mechanisms the rate of the first step is slow, since an unstable intermediate is formed, and that of the second step is fast. For the first mechanism the rate will therefore be given by $k[RBr][OH^-]$, and for the second mechanism by $k[RBr]$. Thus different mechanisms give different rate equations. Many mechanisms are much more complicated than this, with a large number of reaction steps. An example of such a complex mechanism is provided by the so-called iodine clock.

Demonstration 8.3
The Iodine Clock experiment. This reaction involves the reduction of potassium iodate (KIO_3) by sodium bisulfite ($NaHSO_3$). It is a multistep reaction, but not an oscillating reaction. The solutions of potassium iodate and sodium bisulfite are mixed and stirred. The starch which is added to the mixture gives a dark blue color as soon as iodine is present. There is a delay of around 30s before this color appears. During this delay time the slower steps of the reaction are taking place. Since iodine is a final product its concentration cannot oscillate. The overall reaction is:

$$5I^- + 6H^+ + IO_3^- \rightarrow 3I_2 + 3H_2O$$

This reaction involves a number of slow steps culminating in a rapid reaction to produce iodine, detected by the blue color it produces with starch. As a result of this complex mechanism there is no apparent reaction for some period of time, and then a sudden production of iodine. In complex mechanisms it is quite usual for several steps to have similar rates, leading to mathematically complicated expressions for the overall rates. This is particularly true for the type of oscillating reaction discussed later in this chapter.

Catalysts and Enzymes

Reactions of biochemical interest are usually complex and also involve chemical catalysts known as enzymes. The subject of catalysis will therefore be examined in a little more detail to see just what such an enzyme must be able to accomplish. Most of the industrial processes described in Chapter Six require catalysts. Normally industrial catalysts are heterogeneous, which means that the catalyst is a solid and the chemical reactants are gases which flow, usually at high temperatures and pressures, over the catalyst. The reaction takes place at the surface of the solid catalyst. Enzymes are homogeneous catalysts; their reactions take place in an aqueous medium and all the components of the system are in solution.

■ *Reaction mechanisms...*

The nature of catalysis can be appreciated by considering in a little more detail the reaction mechanisms described previously for the replacement of Br^- by OH^- in an organic bromide. Of the two mechanisms described, one required an intermediate of higher coordination number, and the other an intermediate of lower coordination number. In each case, if we are considering the substitution of a simple organic compound such as CH_3Br, the intermediate violates the octet rule and must therefore be expected to be unstable and of high energy. The situation is illustrated in Figure 8.4.

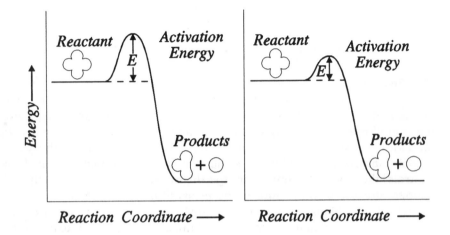

Fig. 8.4: Activation Energy. Energy must be provided to push the reactant molecule over the hill to give products. In a catalyzed reaction, shown on the right, the hill is lower.

■ *Catalysts provide a more effective mechanism...*

Even if the reaction has a favorable equilibrium constant, represented in the diagram by a lower energy for the products than for the reactants, it is still necessary to provide at least enough energy to surmount the barrier represented by the unstable intermediate, as is illustrated in Figure 8.4. (The energy plotted in this diagram is technically the "free energy" which includes both the enthalpy and the entropy contributions to the equilibrium constant, as discussed above.) An "activation energy" is required to make the reaction go. This can be large compared to the energy change during the reaction. The function of a catalyst is to provide a mechanism which requires less activation energy. The right-hand diagram of Figure 8.4 shows such a pathway.

■ *Catalyzing the hydrogenation of ethylene...*

A number of simple, homogeneously catalyzed reactions have been studied in detail and their mechanisms are quite well understood. An example will illustrate how they work. A simple reaction is that between ethylene and hydrogen to give ethane.

$$H_2C=CH_2 \ + \ H_2 \ \rightarrow \ H_3CCH_3$$

Without a catalyst this reaction proceeds only very slowly at room temperature. It is not difficult to see why. To form ethane from ethylene and hydrogen without a catalyst it is necessary to first break the H-H bond, then add one of the hydrogen atoms to the first carbon atom, and to complete the reaction by adding the second hydrogen to the other carbon, i.e.

$$H_2 \rightarrow H + H$$
$$H_2C=CH_2 + H \rightarrow H_3CCH_2$$
$$H_3CCH_2 + H \rightarrow H_3CCH_3$$

The first step in this sequence involves breaking an H-H bond which requires 435kJ/mole of energy. Only at high temperature does the hydrogen molecule possess enough energy for this bond to be broken. The second and third steps are rapid, but the overall rate of the reaction is determined by the rate of the slowest step, and is therefore very slow at room temperature. (For comparison: if a thruway is reduced to one lane by construction, it is the rate of flow through this single lane which controls the speed of traffic on the highway.) Without a catalyst, both high temperature and high pressure are necessary to make the reaction go. It is observed, though, that bubbling hydrogen and ethylene, at room temperature and pressure, through solutions containing certain rhodium compounds leads to the rapid formation of ethane. The rhodium compounds are homogeneous catalysts for this reaction. In their presence a quite different mechanism becomes possible. The nature of this mechanism is illustrated in Figure 8.5.

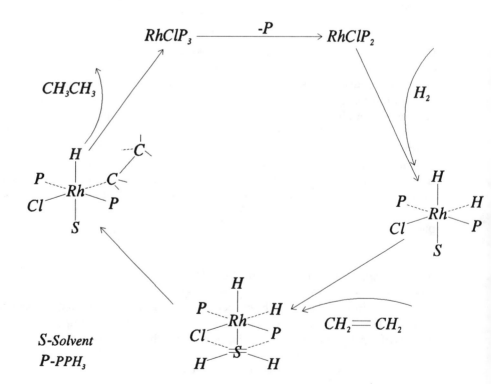

Fig. 8.5: Mechanism of the Hydrogenation of Ethylene using a Rhodium Catalyst.

The circular diagram for this mechanism is of a type commonly used to illustrate catalytic processes and emphasizes the cyclic nature of the reaction. The compounds within the circle are intermediates in the reaction, and the reactants and products are shown outside the circle with arrows pointing in or out. Thus in this case we start with a compound labelled Rh(I), which can react with hydrogen. The important feature is that this molecule can react with a <u>molecule</u> of hydrogen (not an <u>atom</u>) to form two Rh-H bonds. This is not very expensive in energy, since the breaking of the H-H bond occurs at the same time as the formation of two (fairly weak) Rh-H bonds and the net energy requirement is quite small. In the next step an ethylene molecule attaches itself to the Rh atom. This places the carbon close to one of the hydrogens bonded to Rh, and this hydrogen can be easily transferred to the carbon. The reaction is completed by transferring the second hydrogen to the other carbon. The resulting ethane molecule is detached from the metal, which is then ready to start another catalytic cycle. None of the individual steps requires a great deal of activation energy, and the overall process is therefore rapid. This mechanism illustrates another feature of homogeneous catalysis. - all of the reactant molecules are collected together by attaching them to the catalyst in just the right geometric arrangement to form the product. This feature is especially important in enzymatic catalysis.

The particular catalytic reaction just cited is not of a type found in biological systems. A second simple example takes us rather closer to the typical enzymatic reaction.

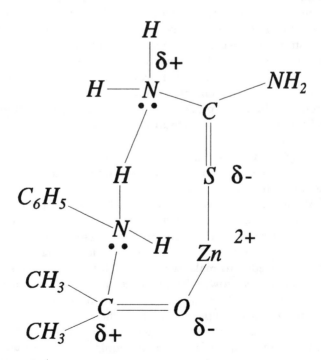

Fig. 8.6: The Catalysis of Anil Formation using a Zinc Catalyst.

The reaction is between acetone and aniline, two very common organic reagents, to eliminate a molecule of water and form an anil.

$$(CH_3)_2CO \;+\; C_6H_5NH_2 \;\rightarrow\; C_6H_5N=C(CH_3)_2 \;+\; H_2O$$

■ *Catalysts activate substrate molecules...*
■ *Catalysts position substrate molecules in the right arrangement to react...*

This reaction can be catalyzed in many different ways but the mechanism shown in the figure illustrates several important features. The essential steps are that a bond must be formed between the carbonyl carbon and the nitrogen of the aniline, a proton must then be transferred from the amine group to the carbonyl oxygen, and finally a molecule of water must be lost to give the anil. The first, and critical, step can be facilitated in two ways. The nitrogen of the aniline has a lone pair of electrons and it is this lone pair which attacks the carbon to form the C-N bond. The carbonyl bond is polar, with the more electronegative oxygen getting a larger share of the bonding electrons, leaving some positive charge on the carbon. The greater the positive charge on the carbon, the more readily it will accept electrons from the nitrogen to form a C-N bond. As well, the greater the polarity of the C=O bond, the faster it will be attacked by the nitrogen. Notice that in the reaction mechanism as shown, both of these occur by bonding the oxygen of the carbonyl to a positively charged metal ion such as Zn^{2+}, using one of the oxygen's lone pairs, i.e. $-C=O \rightarrow Zn^{2+}$. Since the oxygen has donated electrons to the zinc ion, it will in turn withdraw more electrons from the neighboring carbon. The carbonyl group has been "activated" for attack by the aniline. The next step is to ensure that an aniline molecule is present at the right place and in the right orientation, with its nitrogen atom pointed to the carbonyl carbon, ready to react. This can be done by designing the catalyst so that the aniline NH_2 can hydrogen bond to some suitable correctly positioned atoms. Activating the carbonyl group reduces the enthalpy of activation. Correctly positioning the aniline provides a more favorable entropy of activation. Together they combine to make an effective catalyst.

Enzymes use the same strategies for catalysis, but use them much more effectively and are much more specific for a single reaction, than are the non-biological catalysts illustrated in Figure 8.6.

We make one final point in this discussion of catalysis. In Figure 8.4, the products of the reaction are at a lower free energy than the reactants, so that at equilibrium the reaction will have proceeded largely to the right. This diagram also shows that much more energy must be provided to make the reaction go from right to left than is needed to make it go from left to right, for the following reason. The forward reaction has a lower energy of activation than the backward reaction, and the forward reaction therefore has a larger rate constant then the backward reaction. In the catalyzed reaction, depicted on the right hand side of this diagram, the same is true; the required activation energies, measured by the height of the hill to be surmounted, are reduced by equal amounts and the forward and backward rate constants are therefore both increased proportionately. The difference in free energy, which determines the equilibrium constant, is the same for both the uncatalyzed and the catalyzed reactions. Catalysis therefore does not affect the position of equilibrium, as was stated in our original definition in Chapter 3.

Non-equilibrium Systems

■ *Isolated, closed and open thermodynamic systems...*
■ *Entropy can decrease if energy is provided...*

The previous sections have discussed some of the features of reactions taking place in a chemical system not at equilibrium, but approaching equilibrium. We will now consider non-equilibrium chemical systems in a little more detail. It is usual to distinguish three kinds of thermodynamic systems - isolated, closed and open. Isolated systems do not exchange either energy or matter with the outside world; the entropy of an isolated system can only increase with time. Closed systems may exchange energy, but not matter, with their surroundings; open systems can exchange both energy and matter. An isolated system must eventually reach equilibrium and this maximizes its entropy. Closed and open systems need not reach equilibrium while there is a continuing input of energy or matter. Gaia is a closed system, since the amount of matter is constant, but energy is continually reaching us from the sun. An individual living animal is an open system in this thermodynamic sense, since it can exchange both energy and matter with its surroundings. The important feature in both cases is that entropy can decrease within the system. As is implicit in the Second Law, we cannot get something for nothing, and if entropy is to decrease (which in our analogy requires pushing the system uphill towards a less probable state) energy must be provided. The situation is not fundamentally different from that in a steam engine; in this case some of the disordered motion of a hot gas is converted to the ordered motion of a piston moving in a cylinder. Energy must flow through the engine if work, in the form of orderly motion, is to be obtained. Energy must flow through a living cell if it is to grow orderly structures of membranes and nuclei, and build up high quality chemical and electrical energy. The further a system is maintained from chemical equilibrium, the greater the complexity of the structures it is able to support. A living entity is much further from equilibrium than a steam engine and is able to maintain a much richer and more complicated system. All living things import high quality (low entropy) energy and export entropy. Plants can take in their energy as sunlight, but animals require chemical energy in the form of food. If both the living cell and its surroundings are considered, there is indeed an increase in total entropy as demanded by the Second Law, but <u>within</u> the living entity entropy can decrease. The same is true of Gaia as a whole. She can increase her overall complexity, thereby decreasing entropy, by exporting entropy to space. The entropy of the Earth has decreased but that of space has increased by a greater amount. High quality energy in the form of sunlight is taken in, low quality energy in the form of heat is re-radiated.

Thermodynamics tells us what is possible and what is not possible, but never provides any information on how to accomplish a possible project. Life is thermodynamically possible; to understand the chemistry of a living system though, we must look beyond thermodynamics. What is needed is the means for creating the order of living things out of the chaos of the non-living environment. Scientists have only recently begun to understand the detailed means for accomplishing this transformation. In addition to needing a continuous source of energy, several other conditions must be satisfied.

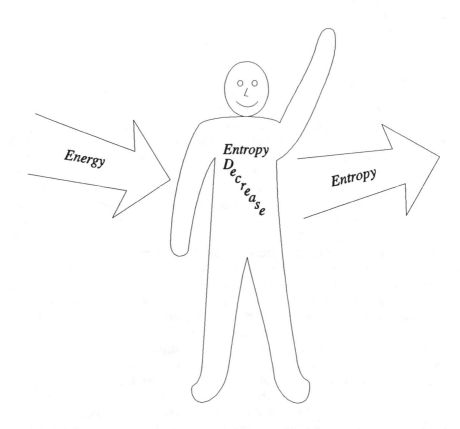

Fig. 8.7: The Thermodynamics of Life.

Feedback

■ *Positive and negative feedback...*

If order is to be produced from chaos, a system must satisfy a number of criteria. It must be maintained far from equilibrium by a flow of energy. It must also be complex; a simple chemical reaction will not do, instead there must be a whole series of connected reactions. The reactions must be connected by "feedback".

The idea of feedback is a familiar one in everyday life. A house thermostat works by sensing the temperature of a room, and when it is hot enough, sending a signal to shut off the furnace. After a while, the temperature has fallen, and a signal is sent to turn the furnace on again. This is an example of negative feedback, since a change in temperature produces a response in the opposite direction. Positive feedback is also possible. It occurs in electronic oscillators, where some of the radio frequency signal is fed back to produce an oscillation of increasing amplitude. It is often an unwanted effect as when, for example, a loudspeaker is positioned too close to a microphone in a public address system, and a howl of amplified noise results. In this case the feedback is positive, and a very small fluctuation in the noise gives rise to a very loud squeal which, unless corrected, will build up to the limit of the amplifier. The effect of feedback on complex systems is investigated using a modern branch of mathematics named "chaos".

■ *Why somebody doesn't do something about the weather...*

Appropriately enough the initial discoveries in this field occurred in the area of weather forecasting. The weather is certainly a complex system, being influenced and determined by a host of factors such as atmospheric pressure, temperature fluctuations and humidity. It seemed reasonable to suppose that if the weather conditions were measured at a large number of widely scattered sites, and the results fed into a large enough computer, the future weather could be predicted with as much accuracy as was desired. Various computer models of the weather were devised to test this possibility. Surprisingly, even with comparatively simple models, the computer did not give consistent results. The equations used involved a great deal of positive feedback, and as a result a minute change in input parameters could give rise to a massive change in the final weather pattern. The example often quoted is that a butterfly flapping its wings can lead to a hurricane elsewhere in the world. Since the input data for a weather forecast can never be 100% complete and accurate down to the activities of all butterflies, beyond two or three days weather forecasts are always going to be speculative. Since the results of such models are unpredictable they can be described as "chaotic". There is however order in this chaos and the order can be described in mathematical terms. This is in accord with our experience - the weather is unpredictable but stays within certain limits.

■ *Homeostasis...*

Studies of negative feedback have a longer history. Mammals can to a large extent control their temperatures and other factors subject to external influence, by a process known as homeostasis. Perspiration in hot weather leads to cooling, and shivering in cold weather to warming. Lovelock has pointed out that Gaia has similar control mechanisms, many associated with the presence of life on earth. Over the last 3.8 billion years the luminosity of the sun has increased by 30% but the temperature of the earth has remained within the narrow range suitable for carbon-based life. He has modelled this situation by devising "Daisyworld". This world is covered to a greater or lesser extent by a blanket of daisies. There are white daisies which reflect the light which falls on them and black daisies which absorb the light which falls on them. Daisies do not grow below 5 °C or above 40 °C, and prefer a temperature of 20° C. No daisies will grow until the luminosity of the sun produces a temperature of 5 °C. Black daisies will be preferred and by absorbing more light, raise the temperature of the planet towards the optimum value of 20 °C. If the temperature gets too high, white daisies will grow preferentially and cool the planet by increasing the proportion of light reflected. The daisies therefore act as an effective thermostat to control the temperature of the planet. Figure 8.7 shows some of the results of Lovelock's modelling.

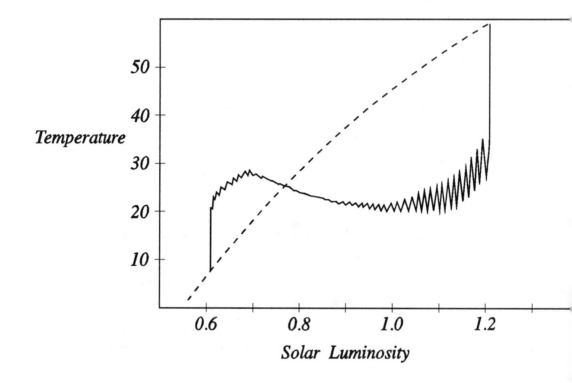

Fig. 8.8: Daisyworld. Feedback on Daisyworld maintains a temperature suitable for growing daisies over a range of solar luminosities.

Chemical Control and Oscillating Reactions

■ *Autocatalysis = self-catalysis = positive feedback...*
■ *Inhibition = negative feedback...*

Chemical feedback is based on catalysis. As discussed above, a substance which increases the rate of a chemical reaction by providing an easier path is known as a catalyst. Something which decreases the rate by blocking the path is an **inhibitor**. It sometimes happens that a product of a reaction will also behave as a catalyst for the reaction, in which case the reaction is said to be **autocatalytic**. This leads immediately to a positive feedback situation, since the more product is formed, the faster the reaction proceeds. There are also more complex situations involving **cross-**

catalysis, in which the product of one reaction catalyses a second reaction, which in turn catalyses a third reaction, eventually leading to a catalyst for the first reaction. It is also very common in biochemical situations for a product molecule to act as an inhibitor, so that the reaction is turned off while the reaction is still incomplete; this corresponds to negative feedback and prevents the uncontrolled production of any biochemical product. Biological systems use positive feedback for growth, and negative feedback to exercise control. A typical biochemical process comprises a very complex network of inter-related chemical reactions. The details of any individual system are dauntingly complicated but the principles can be illustrated with simpler examples.

There are a number of relatively simple inorganic reactions which illustrate feedback. The emphasis here though is on the word "relatively". The system has to be fairly complex with a number of intermediates, to show the properties associated with autocatalysis. We will first examine a pseudo-chemical system to get a feel for what can happen.

The classical example is the predator-prey ecological model of rabbits and foxes. The input for this problem can be represented by a series of "chemical" equations. Thermodynamically it is an open system - both energy and matter can be added and taken away. Rabbits eat grass and produce more rabbits. The supply of grass is assumed to be inexhaustible and represents a continuous energy input. If rabbits are represented by R and grass by G the chemical equation is:

$$R + G \rightarrow 2R$$

This reaction is autocatalytic - it shows the well-known property of rabbits that the more you have, the faster they increase in number. Foxes, F, eat the rabbits, corresponding to negative feedback, and also reproduce, i.e.,

$$F + R \rightarrow 2F$$

The foxes themselves though, either die or are hunted and become pelts.

$$F \rightarrow P$$

Given rates for these three processes (analogous to chemical reactions), we can calculate how the populations of foxes and rabbits vary with time. Several variations are possible, depending on the relative rate constants selected for the different reactions. Some results obtained for one of the more interesting combinations of rate constants are shown in Figure 8.8.

Demonstration 8.4
Rabbits and foxes simulation. The mathematics involved in the equations for the rabbits and foxes problem have been programmed into a computer which will calculate how the populations of rabbits and foxes will vary with time. The rate constants for the three different reactions can be varied.

The results are qualitatively quite reasonable. Initially the population of rabbits increases rapidly, providing food for the foxes. Foxes then increase and rabbits decrease. A shortage of rabbits starves the foxes, which then decrease and allow the rabbits to increase again. Both populations oscillate, with the fox population maximum always occurring after the rabbit population maximum. It should be noted that in this "chemical" scheme the grass is the reactant and the fox pelts the product, and neither of these oscillate. It is only the rabbit and fox "intermediates" which oscillate with time.

Population

Rabbits   Foxes

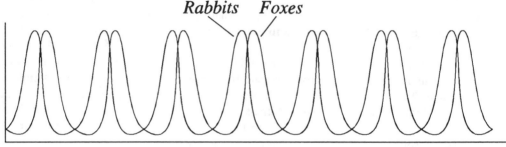

Time

Fig. 8.9: Rabbits and Foxes. Feedback leads to oscillations in the populations of both the rabbits and the foxes.

Real chemical reactions can also oscillate in this manner. An example is the Briggs-Rauscher reaction.

Demonstration 8.5
The Briggs-Rauscher Reaction. This is a true oscillating reaction. It again involves the reduction of potassium iodate. The other reactants are hydrogen peroxide and malonic acid. When these reactants are mixed and then stirred, there are a sequence of color changes from blue to yellow to colorless to blue to yellow etc. The blue again arises from iodine (made visible with starch) but in this case the iodine is an intermediate. The oscillations cease when the reactants have been exhausted. To obtain continuous oscillations the reactants would have to be supplied continuously.

■ *Oscillating reactions...*

This reaction involves the oxidation of malonic acid ($CH_2(COOH)_2$) with hydrogen peroxide (H_2O_2) and potassium iodate (KIO_3) and has a complicated mechanism. Iodine is one of the intermediates and its presence is made apparent by adding a little starch to the mixture, which gives a blue color with iodine. The appearance and disappearance of the blue color shows the oscillating nature of the reaction. The results of this demonstration should be compared with those obtained for the "Iodine Clock". The iodine clock experiment, in spite of being a complicated multistep reaction, proceeds smoothly to equilibrium; there is only one color change. The Briggs-Rauscher reaction does not proceed directly to equilibrium; the oscillations only gradually die away, leading to the suspicion that under some circumstances the attainment of equilibrium might be postponed indefinitely. The family of oscillating reactions involving the oxidation of malonic acid with bromates or iodates, often in the presence of metal ions such as cerium(IV), was discovered by the Russian chemists Belousov and Zhabotinski, and is the most extensively investigated family of such reactions. In spite of this the mechanism is still not entirely certain, and as many as 21 different chemical intermediates participate in the reaction. The simplest model for this reaction which will reproduce the oscillating behavior involves five different reaction steps, and the resulting kinetics equations are exceedingly complex. A complete analysis of the kinetics of these reactions is very similar to that encountered in the studies of weather forecasting.

There is another way of carrying out oscillating reactions of the Belousov-Zhabotinski type. Instead of mixing the solutions and observing the periodic fluctuations of the various species as time progresses, one can start the reaction at one specific place, and then observe the diffusion of the reaction products from this point. As the reactive intermediates spread out from the starting point, the autocatalytic nature of the reaction results in the formation of bands of colored material in very characteristic patterns. An example of such a pattern is shown in Figure 8.9.

Fig. 8.10: Pattern from B-Z reaction.

Demonstration 8.6

The Belousov-Zhabotinski Reaction. The oscillating reaction of Demonstration 8.6 produced patterns in time. If the products of such a reaction are allowed to diffuse from the point of reaction at a constant rate, patterns in space can also be obtained. This is an example of a dissipative structure, since it is formed by the dissipation of (chemical) energy. The reaction demonstrated involves the reduction of sodium bromate (rather than the iodate) with malonic acid using a substance called feroin as a catalyst. The reaction commences as a single point and the colored products are separated into bands as they diffuse away from the point of initiation.

■ *Dissipative structures...*

In this example, simply carrying out a chemical reaction has resulted in the formation of structure on a macroscopic scale. Such structures are called "dissipative structures" since their formation results from the dissipation of energy. They can only be formed and maintained in circumstances in which energy is continuously supplied to the system to keep it far from chemical equilibrium.

Catalysis in Thermodynamically Open Systems

■ *Enzymes and catalysis...*

The chemistry of thermodynamically open living systems differs from the more familiar reactions studied in test tubes in one further important respect. In the examples of catalysis considered above, such as the hydrogenation of ethylene, the catalysts show a very important limitation. They can speed up the reaction but they cannot alter the composition of the final product mixture. The reaction of hydrogen with ethylene without a catalyst may take weeks or years to reach equilibrium. With a catalyst it may reach equilibrium in a matter of minutes but the proportion of ethane to ethylene will be the same no matter how long it took to get there. In a typical living system equilibrium is never attained (at least prior to death) but there are usually steady state concentrations of a large number of biochemical substances. These steady state concentrations are largely determined by the catalytic enzymes present.

For instance, consider a simple example of a protein formed by the polymerization of amino acids. The equilibrium constant for polymerization is small, and at equilibrium the amount of polymerized protein would be negligible. However if we provide energy in the form of ATP, and also add an enzymatic catalyst, the reactions of the activated amino acids to form protein can be quite rapid, since the added energy effectively makes it a "downhill" reaction; the backwards hydrolysis reaction remains slow. A steady state is reached in which the majority of the amino acids present have been polymerized to form protein. If the supply of energy were to be cut off, the protein molecules would fall apart, but as long as energy is continuously supplied the chemical contents of the living cell remain stable, although not at equilibrium. The steady state concentrations of all the key biochemicals are largely determined by the catalytic enzymes present.

Conclusion

The Second Law of thermodynamics states that entropy always increases with time. Entropy is associated with disorder and chaos, and the more disordered the arrangement, the higher its probability of taking place. Living organisms are highly ordered systems, and at first sight it seems that their formation is contrary to the Second Law of thermodynamics. There is no real contradiction, since living organisms are thermodynamically open systems and exist far from chemical equilibrium. The energy which the system obtains from outside is used to create ordered structures, and the greater order within the system is balanced by greater disorder in the outside world. Living organisms export entropy. Thermodynamics tells us that this is possible, but it does not tell us how it happens. Chemists are beginning to understand the mechanisms responsible for the formation of structure and order in complex systems. Order can be created from chaos by the dissipation of energy. The more feedback loops and the higher the degree of chemical complexity, the better the chance of building living systems. The chemistry of life has more than enough complexity for this to occur. The next chapter will consider the chemical nature of some of the components of living organisms.

Further reading

P. W. Atkins, *The Second Law*, Scientific American Library (1984). An easy-to-read, elementary but complete account of the Second Law of thermodynamics.

James Lovelock, *The Ages of Gaia*, W. W. Norton (1988). Source of the discussion of Daisyworld.

James Gleick, *Chaos*, Viking (1987).

I. Prigogine and I. Stengers, *Order Out of Chaos*, Bantam Books (1984). Two non-mathematic introductions to complex systems.

Irving R. Epstein, "Patterns in Time and Space Generated by Chemistry", *Chemical and Engineering News*, p24, March 30 (1987). A short article on oscillating reactions.

The Chemistry of Time

*"What, then, is time? If no one asks me, I know what
it is. If I wish to explain it to him who asks me, I do
not know."*

St. Augustine

Introduction

The idea of time has always been elusive, as is demonstrated by the well-known quotation from St. Augustine. Time is a factor in many fields of study. G. J. Whitrow has written a rather grand survey entitled *The Natural Philosophy of Time*; it includes chapters on Human Time, Biological Time, Mathematical Time and Relativistic Time. The physics and cosmology of time are also discussed at length. References to the chemistry of time though are few, and mostly implicit rather than explicit. Nevertheless chemistry plays an important role in determining our ideas concerning time. Chemistry is the study of change, and change involves time. Chemistry is also the link between time in simple systems, as measured by a stopwatch, and time in complex systems, as measured by the clock which, say, tells a bear that the time for hibernation has arrived.

Time has three essential features: duration, direction and the unique properties of the present. Physical science has no particular problems with duration. The direction, or the so-called arrow of time, has proved difficult to explain in terms of simple physical models. The uniqueness of the present has no scientific explanation, but some intriguing medical observations in this area will be described later in this interlude.

The duration of time can be measured by a variety of physical methods, from sundials to pendulum clocks to quartz oscillators. Consideration of time as one of the fundamental dimensions of nature is a relatively recent development. In the middle ages the basic unit of time was a day, subdivided into smaller periods by the regular daily religious observations of monks, and no account was taken of the fact that the length of a day varied with the season. An hour or a minute was not therefore a constant quantity suitable for formulating a theory of motion. Galileo first described motion by using time as the independent variable, and this development set the stage for Newton's laws of motion. Prior to this, the distance covered was always taken to be the important quantity when studying motion. Galileo's description represented a major change in the way of thinking of medieval philosophers.

It has been suggested that people of that time were prepared for this change by the invention of polyphonic music. Such music, in which two or more different melodic lines are played together, requires the concept of dividing time into discreet, identical intervals so that the correct temporal relationships between the different melodic lines can be maintained. It also became necessary to develop a written notation for specifying different time intervals; music of this type was familiar to all educated people in the time of Galileo. Prior to the development of counterpoint in music, there had been no clear, quantitative concept of intervals of time. This is an interesting historical finding, in that a fundamental scientific idea originated in the arts rather than the sciences, demonstrating again that the two cultures are closely connected. The concept of time as a dimension was strengthened when Einstein combined time with the spatial dimensions to make "spacetime".

Time is also measured by a variety of biological clocks. There are clocks which determine our sleeping and waking hours, clocks which control the timing of the migration of birds, and clocks which vary the composition of our urine at different times of day. These clocks are biological in purpose, but chemical in mechanism. Their essential features are contained in the chemical oscillation experiments described earlier; a chemical oscillation, like a pendulum, can be the basis for a timing device. The actual chemical cycles involved are largely unknown and must be of considerable complexity. This complexity brings with it an additional feature: the swing of a pendulum can be reversed, but the cycle of a chemical clock can only be traversed in one direction.

The direction of time is much more difficult to come to grips with. No one doubts that there is a difference between the past, the present and the future, and we all have an intuitive grasp of this difference. However, Newton's whole system of mechanics is based on equations which are reversible in time - time can run backward just as easily as it can run forward. Quantum theory has the same property. The only classical physical law which deals with this aspect of time is the Second Law of thermodynamics, stated in the form that the entropy of an isolated system always increases with time. Modern cosmology postulates an expanding universe, which gives a direction to time, but the mathematics would equally allow for a contracting universe, so a definitive direction again eludes us. Much effort has been devoted to the task of deriving a preferred direction in time in model systems of particles obeying Newton's laws. Some very distinguished scientists, most notably Einstein, believed that this is not possible, and that the arrow of time is a subjective, or psychological, phenomenon. The above comments regarding biological clocks suggest that the arrow of time may be a physical reality associated with complex systems such as those found in living organisms. If this is so it raises the question: how much complexity is needed to define an arrow of time? We discuss some aspects of this question below.

Entropy and The Arrow of Time

If we were to make a video showing the trajectories and collisions of a collection of molecules in a gas, and were to then show the video on a VCR, there would be no means of telling whether we were playing the video forwards or backwards. In either case we would simply see a succession of collisions and rebounds. Similarly if we were to film the motions of the planets around the sun, if the film were played forwards the planets would rotate clockwise, and if it were played backwards the planets would rotate anti-clockwise. There is no means of telling, *a priori*, whether the planets should rotate clockwise or anti-clockwise, and it is impossible to tell just from viewing the film whether it is being played forwards or backwards. The same is true of a pendulum, or any other physical timekeeping device.

The only law of physics which imparts a directionality to time is the Second Law of thermodynamics, which can be stated in the form that the entropy of a closed system always increases with time. A great deal of time and effort has been spent in trying to prove this law from the "simpler" postulates of kinetic theory.

Boltzmann, one of the great physicists of the nineteenth century, devoted a large part of his career to attempts to deduce the Second Law of thermodynamics from Newtonian dynamics. He identified entropy with probability and then attempted to show that a system would always evolve towards the most probable state. Unfortunately, closer analysis of the arguments have shown that, although they sound plausible, they are logically flawed. Boltzmann conceded the validity of the criticisms and was so discouraged as to commit suicide.

It is worth-while looking at a simple example of the type of argument used. In this example, known as Ehrenfest's Urn experiment, balls are transferred between two urns in a random manner and the attempt is made to show that the probability of the system evolving in one direction is greater than the probability of it evolving in the other direction, and therefore that there is a preferred direction to time. A simplified version considers just four balls and two urns. There is just one way of obtaining an arrangement in which all four balls are in Urn 1. Similarly there is only one way of arranging the four balls in Urn 2. There are however six ways of specifying that there be two balls in each Urn - the first Urn could contain balls 1,2 or balls 1,3 or balls 1,4 or balls 2,3 or balls 2,4 or balls 3,4. The second Urn must contain the balls not in the first Urn. The arrangement of two balls in each Urn is therefore the most probable, and corresponds to the largest entropy. In the experiment, we start with all the balls in one Urn and then randomly move a ball from one Urn to another. If we start with all the balls in Urn 1, the first move must be to transfer a ball from Urn 1 to Urn 2. In the second move there is a 3:1 probability of transferring a ball from Urn 1 to Urn 2, since there are three balls in Urn 1 and only 1 in Urn 2. Table IN5.1 collects together the probabilities of the different situations. After a sufficient number of transfers the populations of the two Urns will occur in the ratios of 1:4:6:4:1 as reflected by their probabilities. If a large number of balls, rather than just four, are used it becomes very unlikely that any distribution much different from the most probable will occur after the system has been in motion for some time. Boltzmann considered the energy distribution of a large number of colliding molecules and, using more complex mathematics, reached the same conclusion - entropy, defined in terms of the most probable distribution of energy, attains a maximum.

Demonstration IN5.1
Simulation of Ehrenfest Urn Experiment. This is a simulation of a simplified version of an experiment suggested by Ehrenfest in the nineteenth century. There are four balls, numbered 1-4, and two urns, A and B. We start with all four balls in one urn A and proceed by transferring one ball at a time between the urns. The first transfer must be from urn A to urn B. There is a 3:1 probability that the second transfer will also be from A→B since there are 3 balls in A and only one in B. Transfers proceed on a random basis. The computer will keep track of the populations of each urn as the experiment proceeds and of the numbers of transitions between the different arrangements of the balls. Over a sufficiently long period of time the number of times the states with all four balls in one urn, with three in one and one in the second, and with two in each urn, occur in the ratios of 1:4:6. The transition probabilities are likewise found to agree with the theoretical calculations given in Table IN5.1. If the experiment was performed with more balls the agreement with theory would be closer. If there were 10^{23} balls, corresponding to a gram molecule of gas, the deviation from the theoretical distributions would be very small indeed.

Table IN5.1: States and Transition Probabilities for Urn Experiment

State	No of balls in 1st Urn	No of balls in 2nd Urn	Weighting	Transition Probability
A	4	0	1	
				A→B 1.00
				B→A .25
B	3	1	4	
				B→C .75
				C→B .50
C	2	2	6	
				C→D .50
				D→C .75
D	1	3	4	
				D→E .25
				E→D 1.00
E	0	4	1	

The problem of proving that a large number of isolated, chemically reacting molecules, exchanging energy by collisions, will attain a distribution corresponding to chemical equilibrium is essentially identical to the problem of showing that a system of colliding particles will attain thermal equilibrium. This latter is the problem considered by Boltzmann; if the thermal equilibrium problem is solved, the chemical equilibrium problem is solved. Unfortunately, as indicated above, Boltzmann's proof did not survive critical review. One of a number of faults found is contained in the argument that if a large number of collisions is needed to reach equilibrium, and since each individual collision can occur with equal probability, then if the velocities of the particles are reversed all of the collisions can also be reversed and the system will move from equilibrium to its initial non-equilibrium position. This argument shows that a decrease in entropy is just as probable as an increase in entropy. The fundamental problem is that it is logically impossible to derive a preferred direction for time, starting with conditions under which there is no such direction. Boltzmann was forced to the unsatisfactory conclusion that entropy could either increase or decrease in different parts of the universe, and that we just happened to live in a segment where entropy increases. It is now believed that there is no general derivation of irreversibility (the arrow of time) from Newtonian dynamics.

In spite of this conclusion, there is no doubt that the Second Law of thermodynamics holds in our world of experience. Heat flows from hot sources to cold sources, chemical reactions proceed towards equilibrium, and we live our lives from birth to death and not vice versa. The approach of science is that if we ask a question and obtain an answer which is clearly wrong or ridiculous, we are probably asking the wrong question. Current thinking looks upon the arrow of time as a "selection rule" which determines what will happen and what will not happen. The choices are only presented in systems of sufficient complexity. The Second Law of thermodynamics, as illustrated by thermal and chemical equilibria, involves a selection of allowable initial conditions. Boltzmann "proved" the Second Law by starting with a system in which all the molecules have random motion and behave independently of each other. This is a permissible initial condition. To reverse the process and arrive back at the starting point, the initial condition is that the positions and velocities of all the molecules involved are known. This is an inadmissible initial condition. The greater the complexity of a system, the more opportunities there are to invoke time-directing selection rules. A simple pendulum does not define an arrow of time; a chemical oscillator of the type described previously does. The key feature in this case is the presence of feedback which determines that the reaction must proceed in one direction.

Prigogine and Stengers have considered the origin of the arrow of time in much greater depth in their book ***Order Out of Chaos***. The essential conclusion is that the arrow of time is most strongly evidenced in complex systems, far from equilibrium. Such systems, to which energy is continuously supplied, will evolve in a manner which defines the direction of an arrow of time. Living entities are, almost by definition, complex systems existing far from chemical equilibrium. It is perhaps not surprising then, that the directional properties of time are so closely connected with life that Einstein considered it to be subjective.

Biological Clocks

Even the simplest biological organisms seem to possess mechanisms which control their life processes and determine the order and timing of their actions; this kind of control clearly had a high evolutionary priority. It is speculated that the earliest life forms existed before the atmosphere had developed its ozone layer, and that in the daytime ultraviolet radiation would be lethal to an unprotected living cell. The organism therefore needed some timing mechanism to allow it to carry out functions which were ultraviolet sensitive at nighttime. Contemporary biology provides examples of a wide range of timing devices. The simplest type operate at high frequencies, and determine the rate of heart beats, of breathing and of regular electrical pulses characteristic of the nervous system. Since the chemical mechanisms causing muscle contraction are known, ATP must be supplied to the right sites on the muscle protein at the right time intervals. It is not difficult to envisage oscillating chemical reactions which will perform this function; the timing of heart beats is also quite similar to the periodicities of known oscillating reactions. Chemical oscillations have been demonstrated in many biochemical processes. One of the best - studied examples is the oxidation of glucose in yeast cells, for which oscillations in the chemical intermediates are readily observed. The possibility of supplying ATP for muscle contractions at timed intervals is immediately apparent.

Most biological clocks operate with much longer time cycles. The most common have periods of around 24 hours and are therefore labelled circadian ("around a day"). A typical example, which can be easily studied, is the process by which some plants fold their leaves at night to preserve moisture and open them in the day to receive sunlight for photosynthetic purposes. The obvious question to ask is whether this is determined by some kind of internal clock, in which case there is said to be endogenous control, or whether it is a simple response to an external factor such as sunrise. (This can be investigated by, for instance, varying the periodicity of artificial lighting.) The evidence is strongly in favor of the presence of an internal clock which is brought into phase, or entrained, at regular intervals by a separate process involving the reception of a short pulse of light. Many other biological processes show a circadian rhythm. A series of experiments was carried out at the South Pole to conclusively demonstrate the endogenous nature of such rhythms. The experiments, which included leaf movements in beans, the daily activities of hamsters, and fungal growth, were mounted on a platform which was rotated counter-clockwise at one revolution every 24 hours. This motion, combined with the location at the South Pole, ensured a constant geometric relationship to the sun and hence eliminated the possibility of the reception of external information from this source as the controlling factor in periodic behavior. The experiments confirmed that there are "free-running" circadian rhythms which are independent of external influences. If they are not entrained at regular intervals, such rhythms tend to get out of phase with solar time. The typical periods vary from 23.5 to 26.5 hours and tend to the longer limit in the absence of entrainment. For this reason, experiments in which human subjects have spent long periods in caves without any objective method of measuring the time elapsed, show that the subjects usually tend to underestimate the number of days they have spent underground.

It appears that a vast amount of animal biochemistry fluctuates on a circadian basis. An example is the concentration of sodium and potassium ions in the urine, which is larger at night. These effects are attributed to circadian variations in hormonal levels. It has been shown that certain drugs - for instance the anti-cancer drug cis-platin - are more effective and produce less serious side effects when administered at the optimum time in the circadian cycle.

Jet lag is a result of the body's hormonal cycle getting out of phase with local time. It has been shown that certain drugs can alter the circadian rhythm, raising the possibility that they may be used to counteract the effects of jet lag. Different drugs would be required for travel from east to west than from west to east. It has also been suggested that psychological depression arises from abnormalities in biological rhythms, and therefore may also be susceptible to treatment by drugs. It was originally thought that some master clock in the body had overall control of this time dependence of hormonal levels. Current theory is that there are several interconnected clocks rather than one that controls all the others.

The navigational abilities of birds depend on their ability to sense the time of day. They use celestial objects, primarily the sun, to navigate. The position of the sun in the sky varies with the time of day and with the season, but the birds are able to sense the correct time and date, make the appropriate corrections, and reach their destinations with amazing accuracy. Animals also have long-term clocks which control their periods of hibernation and dormancy. The number and periodicities of the known biological clocks has steadily increased as more aspects of the behavior of animals and plants have been investigated.

Several theories have been suggested to account for circadian and longer rhythms. They are all chemical in nature. As pointed out above, most of the known chemical oscillators have periods in the seconds or minutes range. There does not seem to be any good reason why more complex systems should not be associated with longer periods. It is also possible that two or more chemical oscillators could be coupled in a manner which would produce a longer period. Other suggestions involve DNA, of a type described as a chronon, coding for the enzymes necessary to control the day's activities, and transcribing at an appropriate rate. Yet another suggestion is that there are slow cyclic changes in the ion concentrations on different sides of membranes and that these changes would suffice to produce a clock operating on the right time scale. It may be that none of the above theories is correct, but all alternatives will almost certainly involve chemical reactions with the necessary autocatalytic or cross-catalytic properties to oscillate. The basis of biological time must be chemical in nature.

When is "Now"?

The third feature of time is even more difficult to explain than time's directional property. The present is definitely different in its properties to the past and the future. The past we can remember, the future we can only guess, but the present is experienced. Again, physics does not suggest any objective difference between different instants of time which would correspond to the existence of a unique "present". It has been strongly suggested that the present is a purely subjective phenomenon. Conversely, it has also been argued that since we all experience the same "now" it must be objective. (When the pass is dropped in the endzone, 50,000 people seem to observe the play concurrently.)

Some experiments by a medical researcher, Benjamin Libet, and his collaborators throw at least a little light on the nature of "the present". Libet was able to perform experiments on patients who had electrodes inserted in their brains for medical diagnostic purposes. The patients were conscious during the process (it sounds rather gruesome), but apparently the procedure is not painful. The skin on a patient's hand could be stimulated with a mild electric shock and the reception of a signal at a specific point on the brain recorded by a movable electrode. There was about a 15 ms delay between the stimulation at the hand and the reception of the signal at the brain. This result was consistent with many previous experiments. Libet also showed that the experiment could be run backwards - stimulation at the correct site on the brain lead to a tingling sensation at the hand - similar but not identical to that experienced during direct stimulation at the hand. The really interesting results occurred when stimulation was applied to both the hand and the corresponding brain site. The tingling sensation corresponding to brain stimulation was felt <u>after</u> that from hand stimulation. The extent of this time lag was investigated by delaying the hand stimulation for varying periods of time. It was shown that the delay of the brain impulse was about 1/2 s or 500 ms. The interpretation of these results is that it takes about 500 ms for the brain to process the impulse it receives from the hand and to present it to the mind as a conscious experience. However, to become conscious of a stimulation only 1/2 a second after the stimulating process occurred is clearly undesirable. Libet therefore makes the following two postulates:

a) " ... the primary evoked response of sensory cortex to the specific projection input is associated with a process which can serve as a time marker."
b) " ... after delayed neuronal adequacy is achieved, there is a subjective referral of the sensory experience backwards in time so as to coincide with the initial time marker."

What he is saying here is that when we perceive something, the immediate signal received acts as a time marker. When the brain has processed the data, which takes about half a second, it is able to persuade our consciousness that the event occurred at the time of the original marker. Libet was further able to demonstrate the site at which process b) occurs. It is the last relay of the circuit in the thalamus, i.e. the brain is responsible for keeping our conscious feelings synchronous with happenings in the outside world. Other investigators, most notably the psychologist Dennet in the book *Consciousness Explained*, have criticized Libet's experiments. This is very much an area at the frontiers of our present knowledge.

There is now some understanding of the neurochemistry which occurs in the transmission of a nerve impulse from one circuit to another. How a "referral backwards in time" can be achieved is certainly beyond our present chemical understanding. It has been suggested that this is the boundary between the physical brain and the spiritual mind. If that is the case, we may never have a chemical explanation of all the intricacies of time. The chemistry of time, though, is likely to remain an intriguing field of investigation.

Further Reading

G. J. Whitrow, *The Natural Philosophy of Time*, 2nd Ed., Oxford University Press (1980). A wide-ranging discussion of all aspects of time.

Jeremy Campbell, *Winston Churchill's Afternoon Nap*, Simon and Schuster (1986). The human nature of time, the clocks and rhythms which control our life.

John Brady, *Biological Clocks*, Edward Arnold (1979). An introduction to biological clocks in plants and animals.

Geza Szamosi, *The Twin Dimensions*, McGraw-Hill (1986). How the human mind invented time and space. Includes a discussion of time and polyphonic music.

Tony Rothman, *Science a la Carte*, Princeton University Press (1989). Includes a more complete description of the "Ehrenfest urn model" and its implications for entropy and the arrow of time.

Benjamin Libet, Elwood W. Wright, Jr., Bertram Feinstein and Dennis K.Pearl, *Brain*, 102, 193-224 (1979). A shorter account of Libet's results can be found in: Jonathan Winson, *Brain and Psyche*, Anchor Press, (1985).

Ilya Prigogine and Isabelle Stengers, *Order Out of Chaos*, Bantam Books (1984). A relatively simple account of recent developments in non-equilibrium thermodynamics and their implications for biology and philosophy.

Ian Stewart, *Does God Play Dice?*, Basil Blackwell (1989). A general discussion of chaotic phenomena including oscillating reactions.

CHAPTER NINE

The Chemistry of Life

Introduction

The first chapter of this book outlined the chemical composition of the biosphere. The major chemical components are few in number and simple in structure: diatomic and triatomic gases in the atmosphere, water and simple salts in the oceans, metal silicates and oxides on land, make up by far the largest portion of our environment. The components are more numerous when we examine the chemical composition of a living organism; a multitude of substances are involved, and most are very complex in composition and structure. As we have seen, a living organism is a thermodynamically open system, so all its components are interconnected by a complex web of chemical reactions, giving rise to continuous chemical change and unrest. Life is chemical complexity. In the present chapter the structures and functions of some of the major molecules of biological importance will be outlined. Of necessity the list is incomplete, and the description of some of the chemistry simplified.

■ *Basic requirements...*
■ *Biochemical objectives...*

It is useful to start by listing some of the functions of living organisms which are necessary for their continued survival. All of these functions require chemical manipulations.

1. The raw materials necessary for the construction of the organism must be either extracted from the environment, or synthesized from still simpler molecules. The chemical raw materials are mostly organic substances such as amino acids.

2. These raw materials must then be assembled to form muscles and membranes and nerve cells and a host of other complex structures. To accomplish this the simple molecules - amino acids for example - must be used to form complex molecules such as proteins.

3. The necessary chemical reactions must proceed rapidly and efficiently under the mild conditions of temperature and pressure in the body. Many of these reactions are not thermodynamically favored. Energy must therefore be provided to drive the reactions and very efficient catalysts, known as enzymes, must be present to maintain high steady state concentrations of the desired products.

4. There must be a mechanism for providing the required energy; this energy must be available where it is needed, and in a form suitable for immediate use. We shall see that the universal currency of energy

in living organisms is the molecule adenosine triphosphate, ATP.

5. The production of ATP requires energy which is generated by chemical means. The raw materials for this process must be obtained from the environment and transported to the sites where ATP is required. In animals, respiration provides the energy; food must be digested and transformed to suitable fuel molecules; oxygen must be collected from the atmosphere, transported to the energy production site, and when necessary stored until needed.

6. There must be effective means for regulating and controlling all of the above functions. Some regulation is local, at the site of the chemical reactivity, and is performed by the enzymes. There must also be overall control of the body's chemistry by the brain. This is accomplished by special substances known as hormones and neurotransmitters.

7. There must be some means for storing the instructions for performing the above functions, and for passing the information to the next generation. This is accomplished using nucleic acids.

8. The organism must protect itself against attack from outside by poisonous substances, semi-living entities known as viruses, and small forms of life (bacteria). This is accomplished by the body's immune system, again composed largely of protein-like molecules known as antibodies.

The above objectives, and others which could be added to the list, clearly call for some sophisticated chemistry. Such varied functions cannot be carried out using the simple molecules encountered in the early parts of this book. The chemical complexity of biochemistry is inevitable.

Proteins

■ *Amino acids...*

Proteins are polymers made by the condensation of amino acids. They are the most widespread biological compounds, and they have numerous applications; structurally they are used in skin, bones, cartilage, ligaments and hair; the major constituent of muscle is protein; they are found in association with lipids (fats) and related molecules in cell membranes, and in the packaging for other components of the body; most significantly, they control virtually all the chemistry of life due to their presence as enzymes, hormones and antibodies.

The building blocks for proteins are the nineteen amino acids, plus proline, shown in Table 9.1.

Table 9.1: Structures of Amino Acids

General Structure:	R - CH - COOH $\begin{vmatrix} \\ NH_2 \end{vmatrix}$	

Name	Abbrev	R=
Glycine	Gly	H—
Alanine	Ala	CH_3—
Valine	Val	$(CH_3)_2CH$—
Leucine	Leu	$CH_3CH(CH_3)CH_2$—
Isoleucine	Ile	$CH_3CH_2CH(CH_3)$—
Phenylalanine	Phe	$C_6H_5CH_2$—
Methionine	Met	$CH_3SCH_2CH_2$—
Serine	Ser	$HOCH_2$—
Threonine	Thr	$CH_3CH(OH)$—
Cysteine	Cys	$HSCH_2$—
Tyrosine	Tyr	$p(OH)C_6H_4CH_2$—
Trytophan	Trp	(see below)
Asparagine	Asn	H_2NCOCH_2—
Glutamine	Gln	$H_2NCOCH_2CH_2$—
Glutamic Acid	Glu	$HOOCCH_2CH_2$—
Aspartic Acid	Asp	$HOOCCH_2$—
Lysine	Lys	$H_2NCH_2CH_2CH_2CH_2$—
Arginine	Arg	$H_2NC(NH)NH(CH_2)_3$—
Histidine	His	(see below)

Tryptophan **Trp**

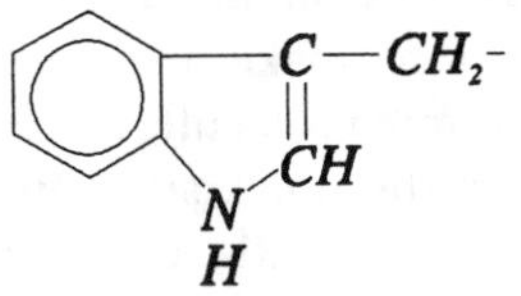

Histidine **His**

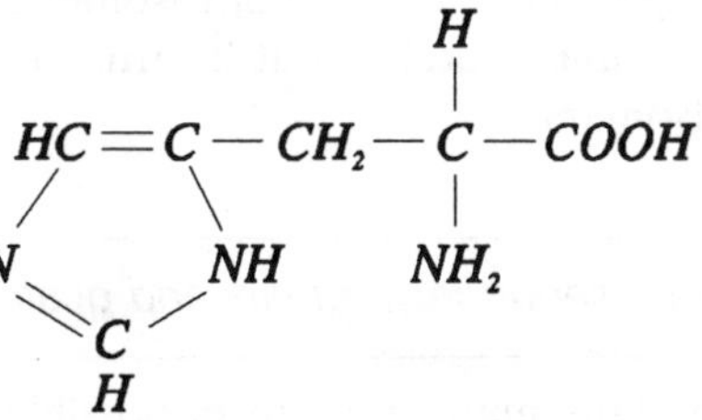

Proline **Pro**

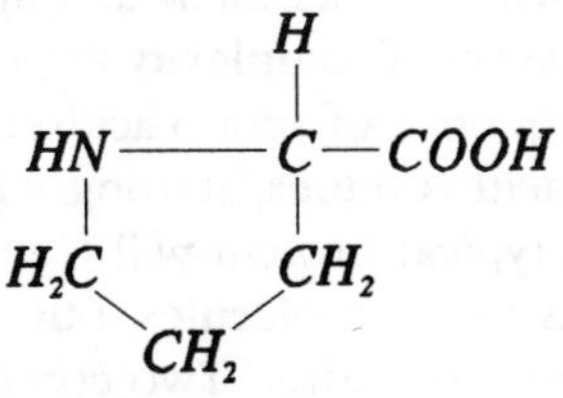

These compounds are all alpha amino acids, with a carboxyl group (COOH) and an amino group (NH_2) both attached to the same carbon atom. (There is one exception, proline has an NH group rather than an NH_2 amino group.) Polymerization occurs by the elimination of a molecule of water, the carboxyl group provides an OH and an amino group on a second amino acid the remaining H. As a result, an amide group, -CONH-, is formed to link the two amino acids:

$$-COOH \ + \ -NH_2 \ \rightarrow \ -CO\text{-}NH\text{-} \ + \ H_2O$$

Chemically this linkage is identical to that found in nylon. Proteins are therefore polymers containing the repeating group

$$(-CH(R)\text{-}CO\text{-}NH\text{-})_n$$

■ *Essential amino acids...*
■ *The number of possible proteins is vast...*

The side chain R is generally different for each sub-unit, being chosen from the nineteen different R groups (plus proline) shown in the table of amino acids, #9.1. Of these amino acids, about half can be synthesized by the human body, but the remainder cannot and are therefore known as "essential" amino acids. They are essential in the sense that they must be included in a balanced diet. In the digestive process, proteins are broken down to their component amino acids. If therefore a protein contains all the essential amino acids it fulfills the dietary necessities; this is true of the proteins in milk and also in most forms of meat, eggs and fish.

An enormous number of different proteins is possible. If the first amino acid can be chosen from a pool of 20 different items and the second from the same 20, there are 20 x 20 = 400 ways of combining two amino acids to form a **dipeptide**, and 20 x 20 x 20 = 8,000 ways to make a tripeptide. With 60 amino acid residues, corresponding to a small enzyme molecule, there are 10^{78} combinations, far more than the total number of atoms in the universe. This does not exhaust the possible forms of proteins. Most amino acids can exist in two isomeric forms, related to each other as mirror images. The use of both isomeric forms would considerably increase the number of possible proteins, but it turns out that nature has chosen to use only one form, the L isomers.

■ *The primary, secondary, tertiary and quaternary structure of proteins...*

Each of the many millions of possible proteins has a unique overall structure. It is this characteristic which make them ubiquitous in biochemistry. Conventionally we distinguish several layers of complexity in protein structure. The primary structure is determined by the sequence of amino acids; this sequence can be written as a long, linear string of amino acid residues, starting with the NH_2 terminal and ending with the COOH terminal. A typical protein will contain between 50 and 150 amino acids. Proteins do not exist as linear molecules, but are twisted into various shapes which represent their secondary structure. Two common arrangements are the alpha helix (spiral) and sheet structures shown in Figure 9.1. Less ordered regions are often referred to as random coil. It is the combination of these elements which determines whether the protein will be suitable to make muscle or to act as an enzyme.

The secondary structure is largely held together by hydrogen bonding involving the -CO- and -NH- groups on the protein backbone, as is shown in the diagram. The whole protein often has a very specific shape because different regions, classified above as alpha helix, sheet or random coil, are grouped together in a specific way. This is known as the tertiary structure and is determined by interactions involving the side chains of the amino acids. The most common such interactions are again hydrogen bonding in nature, but -S-S- bridges between cysteine residues in different parts of the chain (see Table 9.1 for the structure of cysteine) are also very important contributors to the tertiary structure. Finally, some proteins contain two or more distinct amino acid chains, which are held together by weak bonds to give an overall quaternary structure.

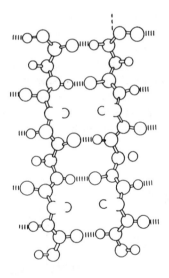

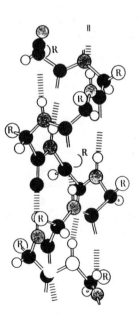

Fig. 9.1: Protein Structure. Protein polymers assume different types of structure as determined by hydrogen bonding and by the steric effect of substituents. Two common types of structure are shown - the ß pleated sheet and the α helix.

Enzymes

The heart of biochemistry lies in understanding the operations of the chemical catalysts known as enzymes. The subject of catalysis was discussed in Chapter 8, and the basic requirements of enzymes were specified. Almost without exception all of the fundamental chemical reactions which take place in a living cell involve proteins functioning as enzymatic catalysts.

■ *The hydrolysis of ATP drives biochemical reactions...*

A characteristic of enzymatically catalyzed biochemical reactions is that they do not occur in isolation, but are joined together to form series of linked reactions. A single reaction will only proceed spontaneously if it is thermodynamically favored; in the metaphor employed previously the reaction must be "downhill" if it is to proceed spontaneously. Most of the reactions necessary to accomplish the biological functions listed above are not spontaneous; they are "uphill" reactions which will only occur in special circumstances. (To make them go is analogous to raising a weight to a higher level; this can be accomplished by using a pulley with a large weight attached to the other side, as is illustrated in Figure 9.2.) Biochemical energy is stored in certain "energy rich" molecules, most notable adenosine triphosphate, ATP. By linking the hydrolysis of ATP, which is spontaneous, with, for example, a reaction leading to muscle contraction, "uphill" chemical reactions are made possible.

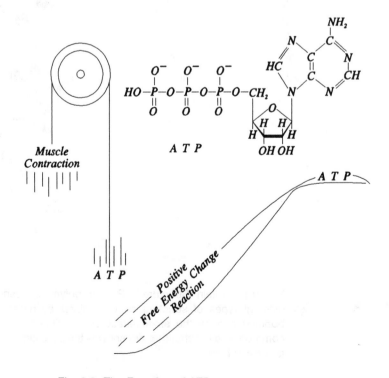

Fig. 9.2: The Function of ATP.

■ *Enzymes are: a) effective b) specific ...*

It is the very specific shape of an enzymatic protein which gives it its catalytic properties. This shape is expressed by the tertiary and quaternary structures of the protein molecule. Tertiary and quaternary structures are in turn determined by the secondary structure adopted by the different regions of the protein, and this is ultimately dependent on the primary amino acid sequence. Once a molecule with the right sequence of amino acids has been synthesized, it will automatically arrange itself in the lowest-energy geometric configuration, which will be the catalytically active form. Not all proteins have this property, in fact most do not. Such proteins do not have a well-defined preferred geometry, and they will not act as enzymes. There is always a region of the enzyme known as the active site. Molecules whose reactions are catalyzed by the enzyme are called substrates; the substrate molecules are bound at the active site, and this is where the chemical action takes place. The lock-and-key model provides a simple explanation of enzymatic activity. The substrate is the key and the active site of the enzyme is the lock, shaped so that a specific substrate will fit exactly. This idea is illustrated in Figure 9.3.

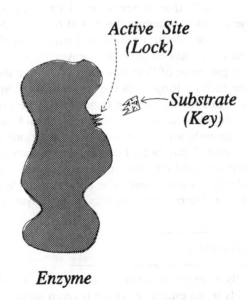

Fig. 9.3: The Lock-and-Key Mechanism for Enzyme Activity.

Since only one type of substrate molecule will fit, the enzyme is specific for one reaction. The substrates are usually bound to the enzyme by relatively weak forces, such as hydrogen bonding. The example of anil formation given in the previous chapter, suggests that as well as fitting in the lock the substrate molecules should also be "activated" to facilitate the reaction. There is also an "induced fit" model which suggests that the active site changes its shape to fit the substrate when a suitable reactant molecule approaches. Whatever the details of the mechanism, enzymes are <u>extremely</u> effective catalysts, exceeding the efficiencies of synthetic catalysts by many orders of magnitude.

No more than five or six amino acid residues - often located at different points in the primary chain - are involved in the actual active site of the enzyme. One might ask, what function do the other hundred or so amino acid residues serve? Their primary function is to determine the geometry of the molecule so as to give exactly the right shape for the active site. A side group at a position distant from the active site can impart a particular twist to the protein molecule, resulting in just the right configuration at the critical point. Other sites on the enzyme are involved with **inhibition**. As noted above, most enzymatically catalyzed reactions are part of a sequence of chemical reactions leading to some biological objective:

$$A \rightarrow B \rightarrow C \rightarrow D$$

■ *Different parts of an enzyme molecule perform different functions...*

If the end product is molecule D, then, when a sufficient amount of D has been synthesized, it is necessary to turn off the tap, otherwise the organism will be flooded with much more of it than is necessary. To accomplish this, D will act as an inhibitor for the enzyme which catalyzes the A → B reaction. Sometimes D will compete with A for the active site on the enzyme and prevent further synthesis. More often than not, D will lack the right shape to fit the A active site but will fit at another site on the enzyme. The presence of D at this site can change the shape of the molecule so that the active site lock no longer fits the substrate key. Synthesis of B is therefore turned off and if B is not made, neither C nor D will be produced. This type of feedback provides biochemical control. Positive feedback is also possible, leading to the possibility of growth, and of the oscillating reactions involved in biological clocks. It may be that once D has been made it is necessary to "turn on" another enzyme to make the next essential compound, E. Sometimes the turning on is accomplished by a compound called a coenzyme. The necessity for these control processes adds to the requirements, and hence the complexity, of enzymes.

■ *Sickle-cell anemia...*

Finally it might be asked: how critical is it to have <u>exactly</u> the right sequence of amino acids in an enzyme? There is often some flexibility. All animals possess a number of enzymes involved in the digestion of food; in different species the structures of these enzymes are often very similar, but not identical. They all work more or less equally well, indicating that evolutionary processes have led to slightly different solutions to the same problem. Evolution would be very difficult if any small change in the amino acid sequence completely destroyed enzymatic activity. Only by experimenting with such minor mutations can nature exercise natural selection and achieve evolutionary progress. On the other hand, there are cases where a single amino acid substitution produces devastating consequences. An example is in the protein hemoglobin, part of red blood cells, where substitution of valine for glutamic acid at a specific position, leads to the disease of sickle cell anemia. In this case a single change, in a chain of 146 amino acids, can cause death.

Respiration

In the previous chapter the point was made that a continuous flow of energy is necessary to maintain life. Animals obtain this energy flow by respiration, and plants by photosynthesis, which uses sunlight as an energy source. Respiration also occurs in plants, using some of the carbohydrates produced by photosynthesis. The ultimate energy source is the sun in either case, since animals must obtain food either directly by consuming photosynthetic plants, or indirectly by eating plant-consuming animals. The organic fuel obtained in this way is oxidized, using atmospheric oxygen, to provide energy; this overall process is known as respiration. In the present section the outline of the biochemical pathways involved in this process will be traced. Figure 9.4 shows these pathways in diagrammatic form.

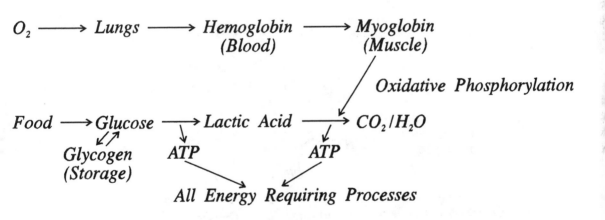

Fig. 9.4: Respiration Pathways.   The reactants for respiration are oxygen and food. The immediately useful product is ATP.

■ *Food is our fuel...*

Respiration is combustion, and requires both oxygen and fuel. Oxygen comes from the air, and fuel from the food we eat. There must be storage facilities for both of these components to allow for times of urgent need. The oxygen and fuel must be brought together at the reaction site - small bodies found in living cells called mitochondria - and combined efficiently to provide energy in a form which can be readily utilized by the body. There must be a control system to turn the various steps on and off as required. Waste products, some of them poisonous, must be treated using a suitable disposal process. The problems, in short, are basically those encountered in running an ecologically sound nuclear reactor or internal combustion engine, but the chemical problems are much more formidable.

Oxygen enters the body at the lungs and the first requirement is to transport it to the muscles, or to other sites where energy is required. The transportation medium is the blood, or specifically the red blood cells, and the substance involved in oxygen transportation is hemoglobin, the red pigment of the blood. Oxygen is stored in the muscles using a second compound called myoglobin; hemoglobin and myoglobin are chemically closely related; both are proteins of a rather special type. In addition to the usual polypeptide chain they have a so-called prosthetic group, in this case called a heme molecule, which is the actual site of chemical reactivity. The structure of the heme group is shown in Figure 9.5.

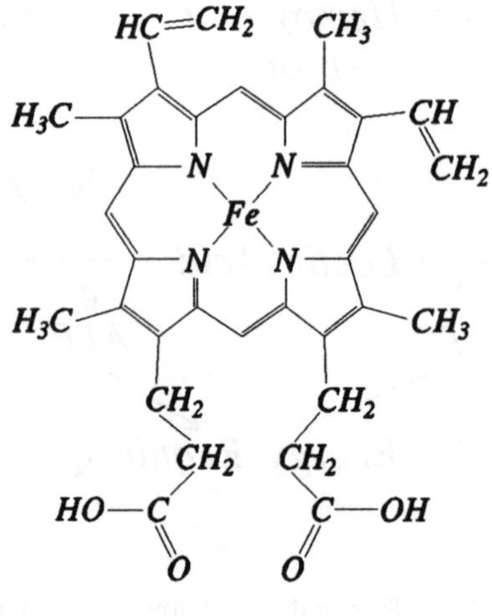

Fig. 9.5: The Structure of Heme.

■ *Hemoglobin is a unique iron compound...*

The characteristic structural feature of heme is an iron atom surrounded by, and bonded to, four nitrogens contained in a **porphyrin** molecule. The molecular oxygen, O_2, must be bound in a reversible way so that it can be made available when needed.

This cannot be accomplished using a purely carbon-based molecule and inclusion of a metal such as iron is necessary; for this reason iron is an essential element for all mammals. Even using iron, it still requires some special chemistry. In hemoglobin and myoglobin the iron is present in the +2 oxidation state and the normal reaction of oxygen leads to iron in the +3 oxidation state. (This is what happens in the process of rusting.) This form of oxidation is fatal to the respiratory process. The oxygen must instead be attached to the iron without changing its diatomic structure, to give oxyhemoglobin or oxymyoglobin. The bright red color of arterial blood, in contrast to the dark color of blood being returned to the lungs in veins, indicates the presence of oxyhemoglobin. The iron is also directly attached to the protein through a side chain imidazole group, and it is the special environment provided by the polypeptide group wrapping itself round the heme group, which gives the iron its ability to bind oxygen. Oxygen binding has been duplicated in synthetic molecules, but not as efficiently as in these proteins.

■ *The cooperative effect in oxygen transport...*

Hemoglobin differs from myoglobin in that it contains four heme groups rather than one, each with its associated polypeptide chain. There is a good reason for this difference. Hemoglobin not only has to acquire oxygen readily in the lungs but also has to relinquish it readily in the muscles. If it is to perform its function efficiently it should always leave the lungs with the maximum amount of oxygen, and return to the lungs with no oxygen. To accomplish this the four sub-groups in hemoglobin act in a cooperative manner. Attachment of an oxygen molecule to the first heme group makes it easier for the second group to bind oxygen, and a similar effect is observed for the third and fourth groups. When it reaches the muscles, the oxygen is relinquished to the stronger-binding myoglobin. Again there is a cooperative effect, with each succeeding oxygen being more readily released than its predecessor, so that deoxygenation goes to completion. Hemoglobin also carries carbon dioxide, a waste product of respiration, back to the lungs. (Carbon dioxide does not bind to the iron but to another part of the protein.) Carbon dioxide also plays a role in controlling the blood pH, which affects oxygen binding to hemoglobin. Carbon dioxide is acidic and when it is exhaled from the lungs, the pH increases slightly to 7.6 which is the optimum pH for binding oxygen to hemoglobin. Extracting carbon dioxide in the muscle lowers the pH to 6.8 which helps hemoglobin release its oxygen to myoglobin.

The chemistry at this point gets fairly complicated, but can be summarized by the two equations:

$$O_2 + 4e + 4H^+ \rightarrow 2H_2O + \text{energy} \quad (e = \text{electron})$$
$$ADP + P + \text{energy} \rightarrow ATP$$

The energy liberated by respiration is used to make ATP. ATP, as pointed out earlier, is the immediate source of energy for nearly all biological processes. ADP is the closely related molecule adenosine diphosphate, and P is not in this case a phosphorus atom, but a phosphate group. The structures of these molecules are shown in Figure 9.6.

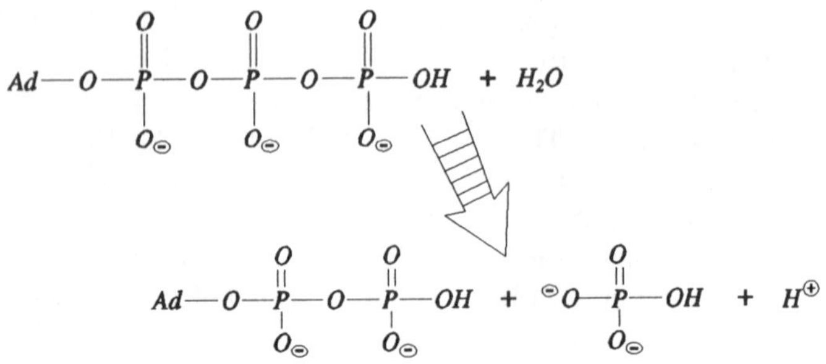

$$Ad-O-\overset{\overset{O}{\parallel}}{\underset{\underset{O_{\ominus}}{\mid}}{P}}-O-\overset{\overset{O}{\parallel}}{\underset{\underset{O_{\ominus}}{\mid}}{P}}-O-\overset{\overset{O}{\parallel}}{\underset{\underset{O_{\ominus}}{\mid}}{P}}-OH \; + \; H_2O$$

$$Ad-O-\overset{\overset{O}{\parallel}}{\underset{\underset{O_{\ominus}}{\mid}}{P}}-O-\overset{\overset{O}{\parallel}}{\underset{\underset{O_{\ominus}}{\mid}}{P}}-OH \; + \; \overset{\overset{O}{\parallel}}{\underset{\underset{O_{\ominus}}{\mid}}{{}^{\ominus}O-P}}-OH \; + \; H^{\oplus}$$

Fig. 9.6: The Hydrolysis of ATP.

■ *ATP - the source of biochemical energy...*

The hydrolysis of ATP to ADP is a spontaneous reaction which can be easily linked to other chemical reactions. It is this reaction which serves as the weight which can be made to raise other weights if suitably linked by a pulley. The e in the above equation represents an electron. Oxymyoglobin provides the oxygen and water the $4H^+$, but what provides the 4e? The electrons are obtained from our fuel, the food we eat. The above equation is more easily seen as oxidation if we remember that $4e + 4H^+$ is equivalent to 4 hydrogen atoms or two hydrogen molecules. The equation then becomes the more familiar:

$$O_2 \; + \; 2H_2 \; \rightarrow \; 2H_2O$$

Our fuel though, does not provide hydrogen molecules, but is instead an indirect source of an equivalent number of electrons. Many molecules can provide fuel for respiration, but the most generally used is glucose, which has the formula $C_6H_{12}O_6$. If the carbon in glucose is oxidized to carbon dioxide, electrons are made available according to the equation:

$$C_6H_{12}O_6 \; + \; 6H_2O \; \rightarrow \; 6CO_2 \; + \; 24H^+ \; + \; 24e$$

■ *Glucose - the most common fuel...*

Sugars and other carbohydrates are broken down (digested) to give glucose, which is maintained at a constant concentration in the blood. Failure to maintain a correct glucose level in the blood results in diabetes. Glucose can be stored in a polymeric form as glycogen, from which glucose can be recovered in time of need. The oxidation of glucose takes place in many steps but they may be divided into two main stages. The first of these is anaerobic (requires no air) and leads to the production of lactic acid; the second is aerobic (requires oxygen) and completes the oxidation to carbon dioxide and water. These two stages are represented by the equations:

$$C_6H_{12}O_6 + 2ADP + 2H_3PO_4 \rightarrow 2C_3H_6O_3 + 2ATP + 2H_2O$$
$$C_3H_6O_3 + 18ADP + 18H_3PO_4 + 3O_2 \rightarrow 3CO_2 + 21H_2O + 18ATP$$

■ *Sprinting and marathon running...*

These equations do not give any information on the mechanism, which involves a large number of steps (each catalyzed by a specific enzyme), leading ultimately to the controlled, stepwise transfer of the electrons to the final O_2 electron acceptor. The overall process is known as oxidative phosphorylation, since ADP is phosphorylated to ATP, and takes place at specialized bodies located within cells known as mitochondria. Lactic acid, $C_3H_6O_3$, has the structure $CH_3CH(OH)COOH$ and is the end product of the anaerobic oxidation. It builds up in the muscle during short periods of vigorous exercise. During longer periods of less vigorous exercise the full aerobic process can be brought into play, but is limited by the rate of transfer of oxygen to the muscles. A sprinter produces a large amount of energy for a short time using the anaerobic mechanism; a marathon runner uses energy at a lower rate, determined by the availability of oxygen, but can maintain muscle activity for a much longer time.

The mechanism by which ATP causes a muscle to contract is quite well understood. ATP binds to one of the proteins which make up muscle tissues and thereby releases the bonding to another protein, allowing the two layers of muscle to slide relative to each other. Hydrolysis of the ATP allows the proteins to bind again and contract. This process is shown diagrammatically in Figure 9.7.

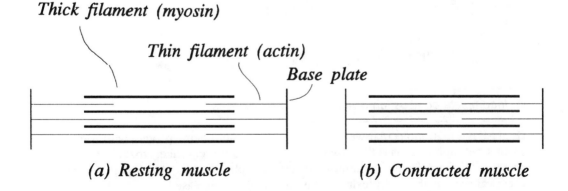

Fig. 9.7: The Mechanism of Muscle Contraction. Muscles contract due to the sliding of two layers of protein (myosin and actin). This is controlled by the association of ATP with the muscle and its subsequent removal by hydrolysis to ADP.

■ *The body is more energy efficient than your car...*

A little arithmetic shows that for each molecule of glucose completely oxidized, 38 molecules of ATP are synthesized. 41% of the energy obtained from the glucose oxidation has been stored in the ATP, a thermodynamic efficiency which is superior to the typical 20% figure for an automobile engine. Almost all of the body's chemical, electrical and mechanical activities are driven by the energy resulting from the hydrolysis of ATP to ADP.

Several of the enzymes in the latter part of the oxidative phosphorylation chain are heme proteins with structures closely related to those of hemoglobin and myoglobin. They are known as cytochromes. Their operation is blocked if cyanide groups become complexed to the iron atom, which occurs very readily - and this accounts for the poisonous nature of cyanide - CN^-. Carbon monoxide binds very strongly to the same site as O_2 in hemoglobin, and therefore kills by preventing oxygen from reaching essential muscles, such as those in the heart. The final enzyme in the oxidative phosphorylation chain is known as cytochrome oxidase. As well as two iron atoms it also contains two copper atoms, and these four metal centers combine to transfer four electrons in one step to a dioxygen molecule. It is most important that this four-electron transfer be completed cleanly, since the intermediate oxidation states, superoxides, peroxides and hydroxyl radicals, resulting from the transfer of one, two, and three electrons respectively, are all extremely reactive and poisonous. They are in fact just the types of substances produced photochemically by air pollution.

Although cytochrome oxidase is very effective, it is inevitable that small quantities of reactive intermediates will be produced over long periods of time. They are efficiently decomposed by enzymes present for this purpose. An example is catalase which decomposes hydrogen peroxide. It is one of the most effective catalysts known: one molecule of catalase can decompose six million molecules of hydrogen peroxide per second. This rate of increase is much larger than any achieved with a synthetic catalyst. Its properties can be illustrated by adding a drop of blood to a hydrogen peroxide solution and observing the immediate decomposition to oxygen and water.

$$2H_2O_2 \rightarrow 2H_2O + O_2$$

■ *Incomplete combustion give poisonous substances...*

Catalase is a high molecular weight (220,000 - 250,000) heme protein with four heme groups per molecule, as is the case for hemoglobin. It seems likely that all these heme proteins evolved from a common ancestral molecule and developed specialized chemical uses as the complexity of the biochemistry increased.

Photosynthesis

In the overall economy of Gaia, respiration and photosynthesis are complementary processes. Photosynthesis uses solar energy to synthesize carbohydrates, of which glucose is the most important, from water and carbon dioxide. Oxygen is the byproduct of this reaction. Respiration completes the cycle by reacting oxygen and carbohydrates to give carbon dioxide and water. Plants provide oxygen for animals and animals produce carbon dioxide for plants. The overall photosynthetic process can be represented by the equation:

$$6CO_2 \; + \; 12H_2O \; \rightarrow \; C_6H_{12}O_6 \; + \; 6O_2 \qquad \Delta H \; = \; +2879kJ$$

This simple equation hides a very complex sequence of chemical steps. The overall reaction is very highly endothermic, 2879kJ/mole, and energy is provided by the sun. The first step is therefore to absorb the solar radiation and the molecule used for this purpose is chlorophyll, the structure of which is given in Figure 9.8.

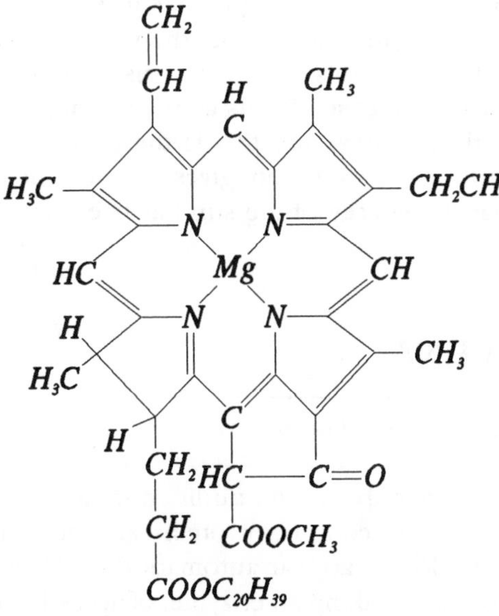

Chlorophyll A

Fig. 9.8: The Structure of Chlorophyll.

■ *Energy from the sun...*

Chlorophyll is the pigment which imparts the green color to leaves. The similarity of its structure to that of hemoglobin and the other heme proteins is readily apparent. There are some differences in the organic part of the molecule, but the major difference is that instead of an iron atom it has a magnesium atom. The disentangling of the photochemistry of chlorophyll proved very difficult, and the details have only recently become known. Chlorophyll can be extracted from leaves, but the extract does not have all the properties of the material in living plants. In its natural state, chlorophyll is closely associated with protein molecules in membranes, and this type of environment is essential for its full reactivity. There are a series of light reactions, providing the energy, followed by a series of dark reactions to synthesize the carbohydrates. In the light reactions, red light is absorbed and drives the reaction:

$$2H_2O \rightarrow O_2 + 4H^+ + 4e$$

The electrons produced in this way are used to reduce carbon dioxide to glucose in the dark reactions.

$$6CO_2 + 24H^+ + 24e \rightarrow C_6H_{12}O_6 + 6H_2O$$

Comparison with the equations given in the previous section, shows that the reactions of photosynthesis are just the reverse of those of respiration. Much of the glucose produced in this manner is used to make cellulose, which is simply a polymeric form of glucose. Plants contain as much as 75% of their weight as cellulose and other carbohydrates, and this is the primary feedstuff for animals. Combining photosynthesis and respiration gives no net chemical reaction. The only lasting change is that the energy of the sun has been used to construct and maintain living organisms.

DNA and RNA

■ *Biochemical information handling...*

The sections above have outlined some of the chemical mechanics of operating a living system. The complex proteins and other molecules necessary to make the system operate do not appear automatically. There must be some means of storing the instructions for making an enzyme, of accessing this information at the right time, and of passing these skills to the next generation. All of these functions are performed by nucleic acids which are therefore the central molecules in the story of life. The revolution in molecular biology of the last 30 years has largely resulted from the discovery of the structures and functions of nucleic acids. They come in two brands: RNA's, ribonucleic acids, and DNA's, deoxyribonucleic acids. Each nucleic acid molecule consists of three parts; the first is a sugar, ribose in RNA and deoxyribose in

DNA. Figure 9.9 shows the structures of these sugars and also, for comparison, that of glucose, the energy storing sugar.

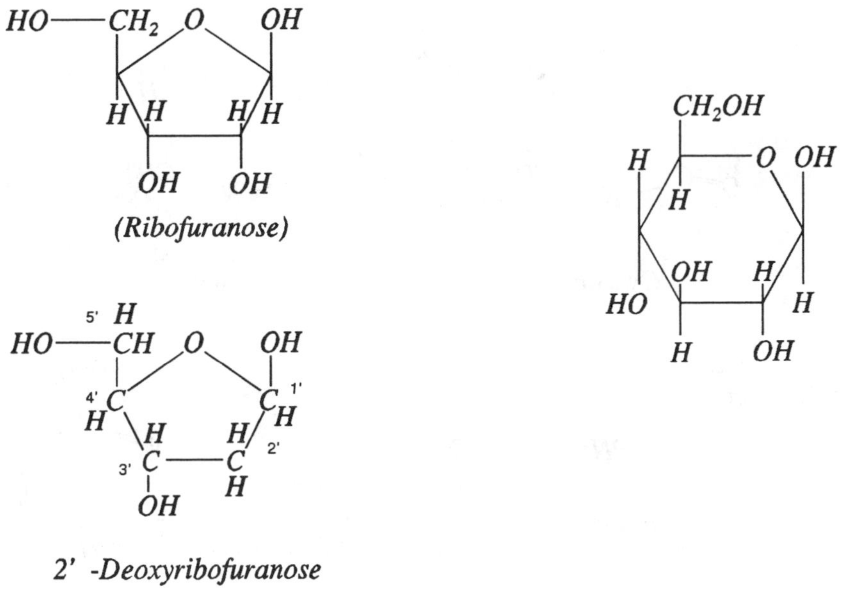

HO——CH_2 O OH

H H H H

OH OH

(*Riboofuranose*)

CH_2OH

H ——O OH

H

OH H

HO H

H OH

5' H

HO——CH O OH

4' C C 1'

H H H H 2'

3' C——C

OH H

2' -*Deoxyribofuranose*

Fig. 9.9: The Structures of Sugars. Ribose and Deoxyribose are the sugars associated with Nucleic acids. Glucose is the most important fuel sugar.

RNA and DNA differ only in the presence or absence of an oxygen atom at the 2 position of the sugar. The second component of the nucleic acid is a phosphate group, which is attached to the sugar. DNA's and RNA's are polymers and the individual molecules are linked through the phosphate groups. The third component is a nitrogenous base. The similarity to the structure of ATP probably indicates a common evolutionary origin, but in DNA and RNA the base end of the molecule, rather than the phosphate, plays the key role. Four different kinds of bases are found in RNA, and four in DNA. Three out of four are common to both molecules, and the fourth differs only in the presence or absence of a methyl group. Figure 9.10 shows the structures of the bases and Figure 9.11 illustrates how the various components are assembled to give a complete nucleic acid molecule.

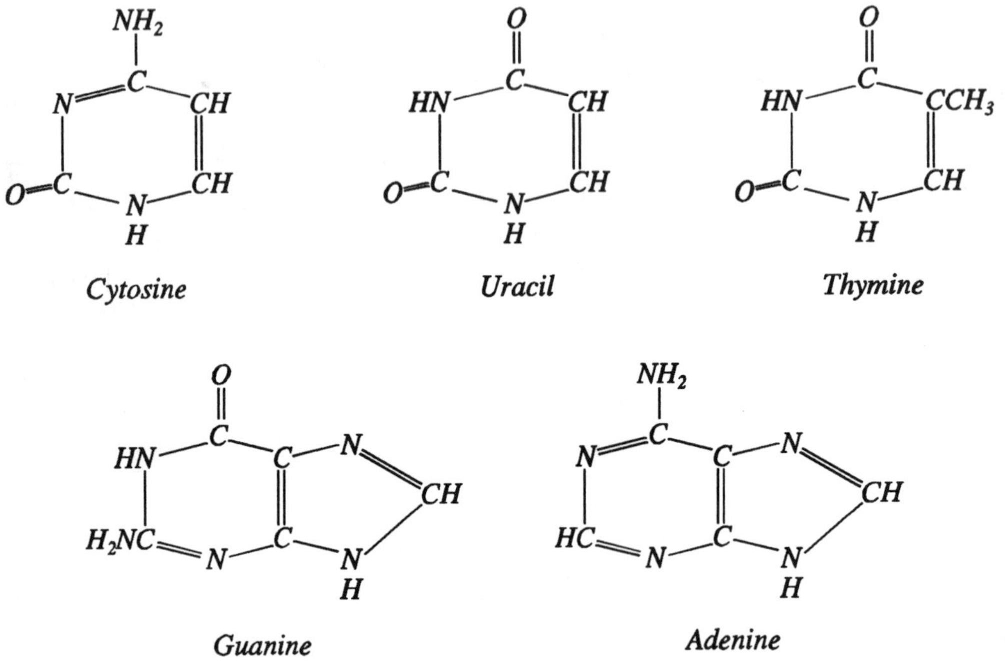

Fig. 9.10: The Nitrogen Bases used to make Nucleic Acids.

■ *Structures of nucleic acids...*

The key to nucleic acid function lies in the facts that a) they are polymers and b) there is in each case a choice of four different bases for each unit in the polymer chain. There are usually several thousand bases in a DNA molecule. Beginning at one end, the first base can be chosen in four ways and the second in four ways. There are therefore $4 \times 4 = 16$ ways of choosing the first two bases and $4 \times 4 \times 4 = 64$ ways of choosing the first three bases. There are clearly an enormous number of ways of constructing a polynucleotide with a thousand or more bases. The sequence of bases in a DNA molecule comprises the information which provides the instructions for synthesizing the multitude of different protein molecules needed for structural and enzymatic purposes in a living organism. DNA molecules are the chemical manifestation of the genes, which biologists from the time of Mendel have postulated as the agents for transmitting heritable characteristics. The explanation of how they do this was first proposed by James Watson and Francis Crick in 1953. They, together with a third chemist Maurice Wilkins, were awarded the Nobel prize for this work in 1962.

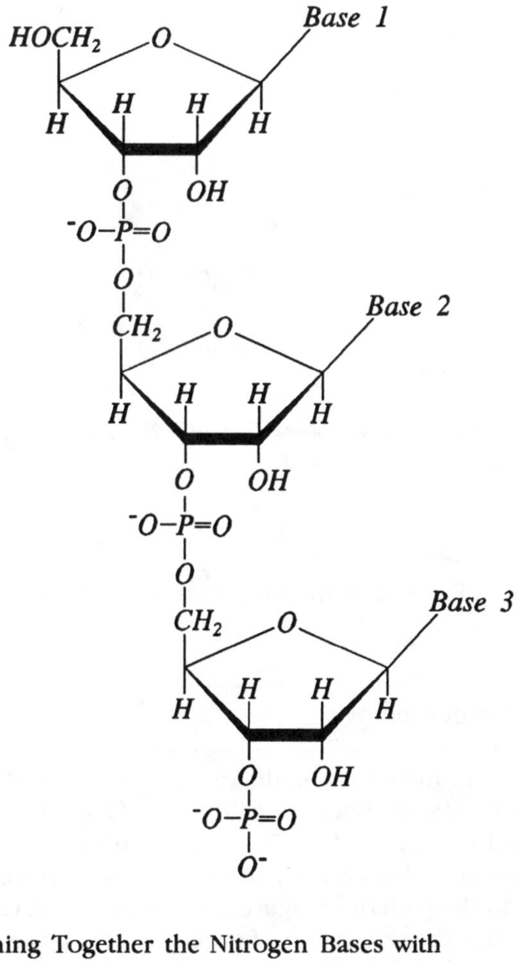

Fig. 9.11: Joining Together the Nitrogen Bases with Sugars and Phosphate Groups.

Like all really great ideas, Watson and Crick's mechanism for DNA replication, and for protein synthesis, is basically simple. They noticed that the four bases in DNA can be divided into two pairs such that the members of each pair fit together like the pieces of a jigsaw puzzle. The glue holding the pair together is made from hydrogen bonds. Adenine and thymine have a comfortable fit with two hydrogen bonds, and cytosine and guanine can be snugly engaged with three hydrogen bonds; the resulting structures are shown in Figure 9.12.

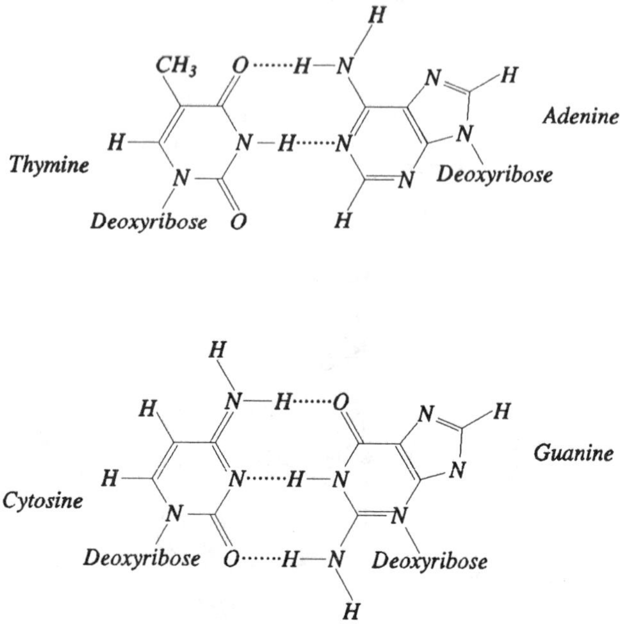

Fig. 9.12: The Pairing of Bases in DNA by Hydrogen Bonding.

■ *DNA - the genetic material...*

The second feature of the structure is that a DNA molecule consists of not one chain of nucleic acids, but two chains twisted together in a double helix or spiral. This is illustrated in Figure 9.13. The bases in the two chains are exactly matched, so that each base in one chain has a partner in the second chain which can hydrogen bond according to the pattern of Figure 9.12. Watson and Crick realized that this structure explained how the replication of genes can take place, to conserve the characteristics of an individual and to pass on a parent's share of these characteristics to the next generation. If an enzyme were to start to unwind the double helix of DNA, there would be space for another base to move in and pair with each of the uncoupled bases in the first position of the chain. The base moving in must be the complementary molecule demanded by the pairing scheme of Figure 9.12. On further unwinding the next base is exposed and the correct unit added to the new growing chain. By continuing this process, two double helices each with <u>exactly</u> the same base sequence as the original double helix are synthesized. This process is illustrated in Figure 9.13.

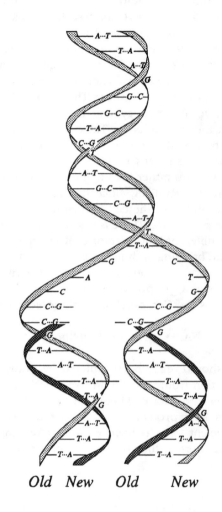

Old   New   Old   New

Fig. 9.13: Putting DNA together as a Double Helix. This
diagram also shows how the two chains can be separated
and each used to form a new DNA molecule. This is the
mechanism of replication.

■ *RNA - the link to proteins...*

This process explains how genetic information is preserved. If some of the
genes are obtained from two different parents, it also explains how characteristics are
passed to the next generation. It remains to describe how this information is used to
synthesize proteins with a specific sequence of amino acids. DNA contains all of its
information in the form of a code - the so-called genetic code. The sequence of four
different kinds of bases in the nucleic acid must be translated into a sequence of
twenty different kinds of amino acids in a protein. Clearly one base cannot code for

one amino acid since this would allow for only four different amino acids. A two-base code would allow for $4 \times 4 = 16$ amino acids, still an insufficient number. If the bases are taken three at a time there are $4 \times 4 \times 4 = 64$ possibilities, and this is more than enough. It also allows for some degeneracy - a given amino acid can correspond to several triplet "codons" - and for some combinations which provide "punctuation" during the transcription process - i.e., they mark where on the gene a sequence for a protein starts, and where it finishes. The elucidation of the genetic code was a major triumph for molecular biology and the results of much painstaking research are summarized in the code given in Table 9.2.

The actual synthesis of protein involves the second kind of nucleic acid, RNA. The first step is very similar to that of replication. The DNA message is copied onto a single strand of RNA, rather than a double strand of DNA. This single strand version is known as messenger RNA, since it takes the information to the site of protein synthesis, small bodies in the cell known as ribosomes. Here it encounters another form of RNA, transfer RNA. There is one form of transfer RNA for each different amino acid, with each different kind of transfer RNA carrying the appropriate codon, as listed in Table 9.2, and bringing with it a molecule of the corresponding amino acid. In this way the amino acids are brought together at the ribosome in the right sequence and joined by means of appropriate enzymes. The whole process is symbolized by what became known as the Central Dogma of molecular biology:

$$DNA \rightarrow RNA \rightarrow Protein.$$

This diagram should really be completed by drawing dotted arrows or some other form of connection from the protein to the DNA and RNA, since protein, in the form of enzymes, is essential for making the nucleic acids, as well as the nucleic acids being essential for making protein. It is these enzymes which make the whole process remarkably efficient. It has been demonstrated that if radioactive amino acids are injected into an animal, they become incorporated into proteins within a matter of minutes.

Nutrition

■ *Components of a healthy diet...*

The list of biochemical functions given at the beginning of this chapter clearly indicates that chemical raw materials must be provided if life is to exist on a continuous basis. Oxygen from the air is one such raw material, but all the rest must come from the food we eat. The study of what we need to eat to obtain the necessary raw materials (and what we are better off not eating) is known as nutrition. Food must provide the fuel to maintain our body temperature and to drive the chemical reactions described above; it must also provide the components needed to construct our various body parts. Some of the substances required for the construction process can be synthesized in the body from simple compounds; some cannot, and must be included in a healthy diet. Five classes of chemicals are usually identified as being the necessary components of such a diet, namely:

a) Carbohydrates.
b) Fats.
c) Proteins.
d) Minerals.
e) Vitamins.

Table 9.2: The Genetic Code

UUU	Phe	UCU	Ser	UAU	Tyr	UGU	Cys
UUC	Phe	UCC	Ser	UAC	Tyr	UGC	Cys
UUA	Leu	UCA	Ser	UAA	END	UGA	END
UUG	Leu	UCG	Ser	UAG	END	UGG	Trp
CUU	Leu	CCU	Pro	CAU	His	CGU	Arg
CUC	Leu	CCC	Pro	CAC	His	CGC	Arg
CUA	Leu	CCA	Pro	CAA	Glu	CGA	Arg
CUG	Leu	CCG	Pro	CAG	Glu	CGG	Arg
AUU	Ile	ACU	Thr	AAU	Asn	AGU	Ser
AUC	Ile	ACC	Thr	AAC	Asn	AGU	Ser
AUA	Ile	ACA	Thr	AAA	Lys	AGA	Arg
AUG	Met	ACG	Thr	AAG	Lys	AGG	Arg
GUU	Val	GCU	Ala	GAU	Asp	GGU	Gly
GUC	Val	GCC	Ala	GAC	Asp	GGC	Gly
GUA	Val	GCA	Ala	GAA	Glu	GGA	Gly
GUG	Val	GCG	Ala	GAG	Glu	GGG	Gly

Codons per Amino Acid

Ala	4	Arg	6	Asn	2	Asp	2
Cys	2	Gln	2	Glu	2	Gly	4
His	2	Ile	3	Leu	6	Lys	2
Met	1	Phe	2	Pro	4	Ser	6
Thr	4	Trp	1	Tyr	2	Val	4
End	3						

Carbohydrates are our primary source of fuel, but not all such substances are useable. Sugars and starches are the major fuel source. Typically they constitute about 50% of a N.American diet and 65% in less developed countries. Sugars, such as glucose and sucrose, are used directly, and more complex polysaccharides (polymers of simple sugars) such as starch are easily broken down to give simple sugars. The most widespread polysaccharide, cellulose (the main constituent of plant tissues), cannot be digested or broken down by man, but cattle harbor bacteria in their stomachs which will convert cellulose to sugars. In a human diet cellulose serves a useful purpose in providing the "bulk" necessary for efficient elimination of solid waste.

■ *Calories...*

The effectiveness of a food source as a fuel is usually given in terms of the "Calories" that it provides. Calories are a measurement of energy, simply related to the units of joules which we have used previously in this book; the use of Calories in nutrition is a matter of tradition and not easily changed to achieve consistency with other sciences. A food Calorie is actually 1000 calories (1kcal) where a calorie is the amount of heat needed to raise the temperature of 1g of water 1 °C; a food Calorie is equivalent to 4.2kJ. All organic molecules can be burnt to provide energy. Typically, protein and carbohydrates provide about 4 Calories per gram of food, and fats are better suppliers of energy at around 9 Calories per gram. These numbers are obtained by burning the food in a calorimeter, in just the same way that heats of combustion are measured in other areas of chemistry.

■ *Food, exercise and body weight...*

Depending on the weight and size of a person, about 1500 - 1800 Calories per day are required just to keep the basic operations of the body (heart, brain, temperature maintenance etc) going. Physical activity and exercise increase the energy requirements; typically brisk walking uses up a further 300 Calories per hour and running up to 900 Calories per hour. As a result, a not particularly active man needs to obtain 2500-3000 Calories per day to break even. Evolution has lead to the development of various energy storage mechanisms which come into play when the energy intake is greater than the expenditure of energy. The short-term mechanism is to make glycogen, a polymer of glucose, which is mainly stored in the liver. The longer-term strategy is to make fat, the positions of storage of which are usually obvious. This strategy has clear advantages for an animal faced with an abundance of food in the fall, followed by a severe shortage in the winter. While our supermarkets remain open for 12 months of the year, energy storage as fat in humans is a largely unnecessary feature for urban dwellers, and has a number of undesirable side effects. A normal person has about 80% of his energy storage in the form of fat; this number may be well over 90% for an obese person. As long as the energy intake of a person exceeds the energy usage, the amount of fat will increase. We need to use about 3500 calories, probably 5-10 hours of exercise, to eliminate 1lb of fat. If the exercise makes us hungry, the Calories can be rapidly replaced.

■ *Different types of fat have different functions...*

The most direct source of stored fat is fat which is eaten. Dieticians consider that the intake of fat should be no more than 30% of a healthy diet, but it is often a high as 45% among Western populations. It is however important to distinguish between two different kinds of fat, typical structures for which are given in Figure 9.14.

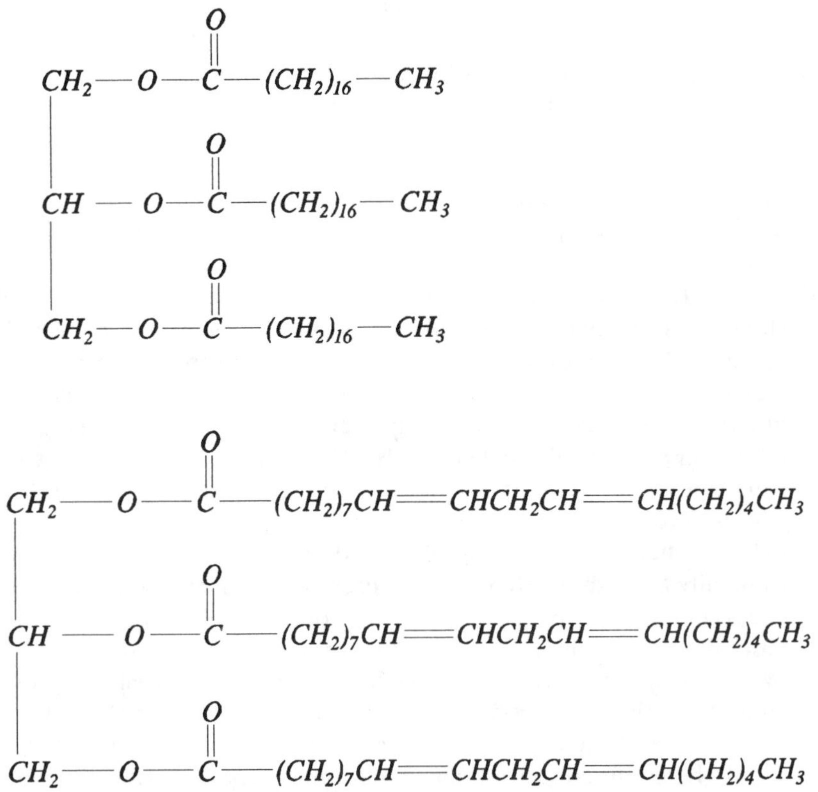

$$CH_2-O-\overset{\overset{\displaystyle O}{\|}}{C}-(CH_2)_{16}-CH_3$$

$$CH-O-\overset{\overset{\displaystyle O}{\|}}{C}-(CH_2)_{16}-CH_3$$

$$CH_2-O-\overset{\overset{\displaystyle O}{\|}}{C}-(CH_2)_{16}-CH_3$$

$$CH_2-O-\overset{\overset{\displaystyle O}{\|}}{C}-(CH_2)_7CH=CHCH_2CH=CH(CH_2)_4CH_3$$

$$CH-O-\overset{\overset{\displaystyle O}{\|}}{C}-(CH_2)_7CH=CHCH_2CH=CH(CH_2)_4CH_3$$

$$CH_2-O-\overset{\overset{\displaystyle O}{\|}}{C}-(CH_2)_7CH=CHCH_2CH=CH(CH_2)_4CH_3$$

Fig. 9.14: The Structures of Saturated and Unsaturated Fats.

All fats are esters made by combining glycerol, a molecule quite similar to the ethylene glycol previously encountered as anti-freeze, with organic acids. The organic acids can be either saturated, in which case there are no double bonds in the structure, or unsaturated with at least one double bond in the fatty acid chain. From the nutritional point of view these two types of fat are very different. The saturated fats are energy storage molecules. They can be burnt to give energy when carbohydrates are in short supply but otherwise accumulate. Unsaturated fats are vital components in various body parts, notably the fatty sheath which surrounds nerves and which lines arteries; they are sometimes referred to as "essential" fatty acids since they cannot be completely synthesized in the body. Brain tissue has a particularly high requirement for unsaturated fats. In general, solid animal fats are saturated, and liquid oily fats derived from plants unsaturated, but the advantage of plant fats is lost if they are hydrogenated to give higher melting margarine. Thus not only the absolute amount of fat ingested is important, but type of fat must also be carefully considered.

Proteins are necessary in a diet to provide a source of amino acids to make the many different molecules necessary to sustain life. The point has been made previously that of the 20 amino acids required, only 10 can be synthesized in the human body so that the remaining 10 are "essential" amino acids. Proteins can also be burnt as fuel, although they are less efficient fuel sources than carbohydrates or fats. This is partly because the combustion is incomplete, with the nitrogen appearing as urea, excreted in the urine. Some protein is always burnt, but the body's own muscle protein is only used for fuel as a last resort when starvation is imminent. It is usually considered that about 15% of the caloric intake in the form of protein is a healthy level.

■ *Essential minerals...*

The final two components of a healthy diet are required to fill specific chemical needs of the body. Inorganic substances, called "minerals" by nutritionists, make up about 4% of our body weight and require constant renewal and replacement. Calcium is needed to make bones and teeth, and iron for the hemoglobin in the blood. Phosphorus is the third important mineral required, being used for bones and as a component of nucleic acids, ATP and various other essential substances. Numerous other elements are needed for specialized purposes: sodium and potassium play an essential role in controlling the passage of molecules through cell membranes: iodine is needed by the thyroid gland: zinc is a constituent of some 90 enzymes. Generally all of these elements are present in a normal diet and no supplements are necessary. Interestingly the one exception, which has been controversial, is fluorine. Fluorine is not really essential, but serves a useful purpose in preventing tooth decay by replacing hydroxy apatite with the more acid resistant fluoroapatite. The controversy has centered on whether it is desirable to introduce fluorine in the drinking water, in which case people have no choice about taking it, or whether it should be confined to toothpaste and other products with optional usage.

In the case of sodium and potassium, the balance between the two metals may not be optimal in modern diets. We tend to take in too much sodium, mostly as salt in prepared foods, and too little potassium. The extra sodium is thought to contribute to high blood pressure, which is in turn associated with susceptibility to heart attacks. Potassium is present in good concentrations in vegetables, which are recommended for this and other reasons.

■ *Vitamins...*

Vitamins are a recent addition to dietary concerns. They are organic chemicals which are usually present in a healthy diet, but cannot be synthesized by the human body. Their lack leads to certain specific diseases. Vitamin C has the longest history; its absence in the diet causes scurvy, a wasting disease historically associated with seamen. Vasca di Gama is said to have lost 100 out of a total of 150 men to this disease during his voyage to round the Cape of Good Hope. In the nineteenth century it caused much of the mortality among British seaman searching for the NW passage in the Arctic. The British Admiralty was aware that scurvy could be prevented by eating citrus fruit (limes or lemons) but did not provide sufficient quantities of the right kind of fruit. Neither did they learn from the Inuit who obtained the vitamin by eating seal meat and similar food. 20-60 mg per day of vitamin C, are all that is required but the Navy rations only provided about 10% of this requirement. It has been claimed that much larger doses, 1-10 <u>grams</u> per day, prevent colds and cancer but the evidence for these claims seems fragile. In the 20th century a handful of other vitamins have been discovered and given alphabetical labels from A through E. If a balanced diet is maintained, taking additional pills to supplement any of these vitamins should be unnecessary. Selling vitamin supplements is nevertheless a profitable business.

Conclusion

The above is a very brief summary of a small part of the very complex chemistry of life. There are many components which have not been mentioned: hormones, the chemical messengers which coordinate the chemistry of different parts of the body: neurotransmitters, the chemicals which provide the link between the electrical impulses in the nerves and brain, and the chemical energy of ATP molecules: antibodies our protection against foreign invaders. These are just a few of the more specialized biological molecules. In some respects though, these molecules are nearly all variations on the chemical themes introduced above; their structures are predominantly based on polypeptide chains; they are often associated with other small molecules, acting as coenzymes, in much the same manner as the heme group contributes to the specialized function of hemoglobin; many interact with, and are controlled by, simple metal ions such as Na^+, K^+ and Mg^{2+}. We now have a broad understanding of the chemistry of life, although many of the fascinating details remain to be discovered. The outstanding question, to which we turn in the final chapter, is: how is this complex chemistry of life derived from and related to the simpler chemistry of our environment to give a unified chemistry of Gaia?

Further Reading

The Molecules of Life, Readings from Scientific American, (1985). A rather detailed description of biochemical molecules.

James D. Watson, *The Double Helix*, Signet Books (1968). A journalistic account of the discovery of the DNA structure.

Horace Freeland Judson, *The Eight Day of Creation*, Simon and Schuster (1979). A much more detailed account of the development of molecular biology.

Ronald F. Fox, *Energy and the Evolution of Life*, W. H. Freeman (1988). Covers much of the material in this chapter but with an emphasis on energy relations rather than structure.

CHAPTER TEN

Chemical Evolution

Introduction

The first section of this book described the chemical composition of our environment; the present section has considered some of the chemistry of living organisms. In both cases there is a lack of equilibrium, evidenced by the high concentrations of substances such as oxygen and proteins, and chemical change is constantly occurring. There is a continuous flux of energy and matter between the different components of the biosphere. Neither the atmosphere nor living organisms are at chemical equilibrium, and balance is maintained only by a constant flow of energy from the sun. Change and chemistry are necessary partners, as suggested by the Chinese phrase describing the subject.

■ *The Big Bang...*

The questions might be asked: how has the biosphere reached its present condition, and will it always be the same in the future? Something is known of the past. Current theories consider that the universe had a well defined beginning at the time of the "Big Bang". The theory of evolution tells us that the forms of life have changed over the history of the earth; since the biosphere is closely coupled to life, parallel changes in its chemistry are to be expected. If there have been changes in the past, changes in the future are clearly possible. As man influences the biosphere more and more by his activities, change - possibly in an unfavorable direction - becomes increasingly likely. In this concluding chapter the evolution of the materials of chemistry, and their incorporation in the biosphere will be described.

The Synthesis of Atoms

■ *Nucleosynthesis in stars...*

Before molecules can be constructed from atoms, the atoms themselves must be formed. It is believed that the process started in a cataclysmic event some 16 billion years ago - the Big Bang. Initially the temperatures were much too high to allow the existence of atoms, let alone molecules, but after a short period of cooling, hydrogen and helium, in a ratio of 3:1, were formed. The chemical possibilities were still very restricted. However, as time passed gravitation resulted in the condensation of this matter into galaxies and stars. It is in the stars that the remaining elements are synthesized. When a star is formed, gravitational potential energy is converted to kinetic energy, and the temperature of the matter rises. The bigger the star, the higher the temperature possible at its center.

At high temperatures, nuclear reactions of the type providing the energy of the hydrogen bomb, can take place. In our own sun the conversion of hydrogen to helium occurs. Four atoms of hydrogen combine in several steps to make one atom of helium. The helium has a little less mass than the four hydrogens, this extra mass is converted to energy, and it is a small part of this energy which powers our biosphere. In larger stars the temperatures are still higher and the synthesis of more massive elements becomes possible. Two helium nuclei can make beryllium, and three can make carbon.

■ Supernovae...

The production of intermediate elements involves hydrogen nuclei. Carbon and oxygen are the next to be produced in quantity, and this occurs when the supply of hydrogen needed to produce helium is depleted. The star shrinks, and if it contains sufficient mass, the temperature rises sufficiently to allow the next stage of nuclear synthesis. As heavier and heavier elements are formed, the yield of energy from each nuclear reaction gets less and less. Iron is the most stable elements and the formation of elements beyond iron requires energy, rather than producing energy. Since at the center of a very massive active star a great deal of energy is available, there is some synthesis of the heavy elements. However, the source of the heavier elements in our biosphere is thought to be a rather special process which occurs with particularly massive stars. There comes a time in the evolution of such stars, when the production of energy from the synthesis of the lighter elements is no longer sufficient to counteract the gravitational force pulling the matter together. At this point there is a catastrophic collapse of the star, producing extremely high temperatures in the small volume of collapsed matter. The energy is available to synthesize all the elements, up to and including the heaviest radioactive elements found at the end of the periodic table. After a very short time a rebound of the collapsing star takes place and the newly synthesized elements are scattered over a considerable region of space. To an outside observer this process appears as a supernova, the sudden appearance of a very bright star, one of nature's most spectacular events. In due course the material formed in a supernova will condense to form another generation of stars and, at least in some cases, the planets which accompany them. Our earth and its biosphere were formed from the debris of a supernova explosion which occurred some 5 billion years ago.

The Formation of Molecules

■ Molecules in space...

Molecules cannot exist in stars - at stellar temperatures any molecule would be immediately decomposed to its constituent nuclei and electrons. Most, but not necessarily all, of the molecules in our biosphere were made here on earth. Recently a selection of molecules, including many necessary for the development of life on earth, have been found in outer space. Heavy atoms, produced by supernova, are present in interstellar space. As they cool they can condense to form molecules; some forty or fifty different molecules have been detected in interstellar space by spectroscopic methods. Table 10.1 lists some of these molecules.

Table 10.1: Some Interstellar Molecules

Number of Atoms	Inorganic Molecules	Organic Molecules
2	H_2, OH, NO, HCl, SiO	CH, CN, CO, CS, CC
3	H_2O, H_2S, SO_2, HNO	HCN, C_2H, HCO, SiCC
4	NH_3	H_2CO, HNCO, C_3N
5		HC_3N, NH_2CN, HCOOH
6		CH_3OH, CH_3CN
7		CH_3NH_2, CH_3CHO

■ *The chemistry of comets...*

There are probably many other kinds of molecules in space —dust clouds for example are thought to contain many metal oxide molecules— but the opaqueness of such clouds hinders their chemical analysis using earth-based spectroscopic instruments. Future space exploration will no doubt add to the list of molecules in space. Collisions between atoms in space are infrequent, but molecules once formed are unlikely to be lost by reaction with other molecules. Most of the simple diatomic inorganic molecules are present; more interestingly, there is a selection of organic molecules of surprising complexity, such as alcohols and amines. There are also a large number of unstable molecular fragments which persist in outer space because of the low density of matter. In a planetary environment these fragments would react very rapidly to produce more complex organic molecules. Such organic molecules have been reported in meteoric material of the type from which the earth was formed. Space probes have also been able to get close enough to comets to investigate their chemistry. The composition of comets is thought to resemble that of the material which formed the outer planets. They contain quantities of water, methane and ammonia plus again a selection of organic molecules. Organic chemistry could have been well started by the time the earth had cooled from its original molten state.

The principal constituents of the sun are hydrogen and helium, but the planets contain mainly other elements. Planetary formation placed most of the heavy metallic elements in the inner planets, leaving a predominance of the lighter, gas forming elements for the outer gas giants, Jupiter, Saturn and Neptune. Hydrogen and helium are gaseous and the low gravity of the earth results in their loss to space. Segregation of the planetary material to form the core, the mantle, the atmosphere and the oceans seems to have been a relatively rapid process. Iron is the most stable element and its high density lead to its accumulation in the earth's core. The mantle is composed of dense rocks consisting of silicon, aluminum and other metal oxides formed from their elements shortly after the earth's formation.

The Chemistry of the Earth's Crust

■ *Silicon chemistry...*

The lithosphere, the earth's crust, is formed mainly from less dense rocks which float on the mantle. The geologists have classified them, and given them names such as feldspars and granites. To a chemist they are nearly all variations on the theme of silicate chemistry, and it is appropriate to introduce this topic in the present chapter. Silicon is in the same group as carbon and comes immediately below it in the Periodic Table. We might therefore expect that the two elements would show similarities in their chemical properties. There are indeed some superficial similarities; they form hydrides, CH_4 and SiH_4, and the most important oxides are CO_2 and SiO_2. The chemical properties of these substances with similar formulae are, however, quite different. SiH_4 is spontaneously flammable and is not a hydrocarbons analogue. SiO_2, silica, was encountered in Chapter 2 and has quite different properties from CO_2; it is a solid, sand or quartz, rather than a gas. Carbon and silicon both play important roles in the biosphere; carbon is the element characteristic of life; silicon determines the properties of the land we live on.

■ *Si-O bonds are very stable...*

The chemistry of silicon differs from that of carbon primarily because of the great strength of Si-O single bonds compared with any other bonds involving the element. The large size of silicon compared to carbon prevents a close enough approach to oxygen to form double bonds. Thus in CO_2 carbon forms two double bonds but in SiO_2 silicon forms four single bonds arranged, as might be expected, in a tetrahedral geometry. As a result silica, in the form of quartz or sand, is an extended molecular structure with each silicon bonded to four oxygens and each oxygen bonded to two silicons. A form of this structure is shown in Figure 10.1.

 Si

○ *O*

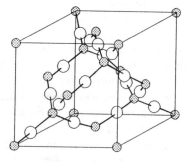

Fig. 10.1: The Structure of Quartz.

■ *Silicates...*

Just as CO_2 is an acidic oxide and forms carbonates, SiO_2 gives rise to silicates. Carbonates are based on the ion CO_3^{2-} which has resonance structures containing two single and one double bond. These structures are very similar to those shown for the nitrate ion in Chapter 4. In silicates no double bonds are involved, so the silicon must be bonded to four oxygens, giving the tetrahedral ion, SiO_4^{4-}. We get to the right charge by considering an ion formed from Si^{4+} and four O^{2-} ions giving a net negative charge of 4 x 2 - 4. Each silicate ion in a simple silicate must therefore be balanced by four positive charges. Four Na^+ ions, or two Ca^{2+} ions, or one Mg^{2+} ion and one Fe^{2+} ion, and many other combinations are all acceptable. There are however other possibilities. Just as phosphates can form chains as in ADP and ATP, two silicates can be bridged by an oxygen to give $\{O_3Si\text{-}O\text{-}SiO_3\}^{6-}$. (Charge = 2 x 4 - 7 x 2). This ion obviously requires six positive charges to make a neutral crystal. Other ions are formed by three silicate tetrahedra sharing corners (Figure 10.2) and continuation of the process leads to an infinite chain of silicate tetrahedra (Figure 10.2). We do not have to restrict ourselves to joining the silicate tetrahedra in a chain - we can also make two-dimensional layers from them.

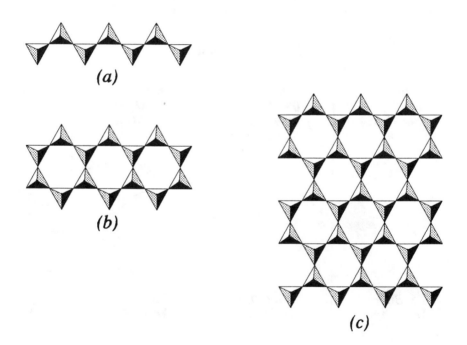

(a)

(b)

(c)

Fig. 10.2: Complex Silicate Structures. SiO_4 tetrahedra can be joined together to make chains and cross-linked to make sheets.

The more numerous the bridging oxygens, the smaller the negative charge per silicon, and the fewer the number of cations required to balance this charge. Eventually we arrive back at the three-dimensional bridged structure of silica, which requires no metal ions for charge neutrality. All silicate structures are made by joining together SiO_4 tetrahedra, but the possible ways of doing this are quite numerous and this is reflected in the multitude of silicates found in nature. There are also some other variations. A silicon can be replaced by aluminum to give an aluminosilicate; clays are aluminosilicates. However aluminum has one less electron than silicon, so the negative charge of the ion is reduced by one unit, leading to the requirement for one less positive ion in the lattice. In its own way, the chemistry of silicon is as extensive as that of carbon, and provides most of the materials encountered in the lithosphere. Silicon compounds were formed by crystallization from the molten mixture of oxides when the earth cooled shortly after its formation.

A Brief History of the Biosphere

There is evidence that life, in the form of simple, single-celled organisms, started some 3.6 billion years ago, only a billion years after the formation of the earth. The nature of the biosphere at this time differed considerably from its present composition. Figure 10.3 summarizes some of the changes which are thought to have occurred in the biosphere since the formation of the earth.

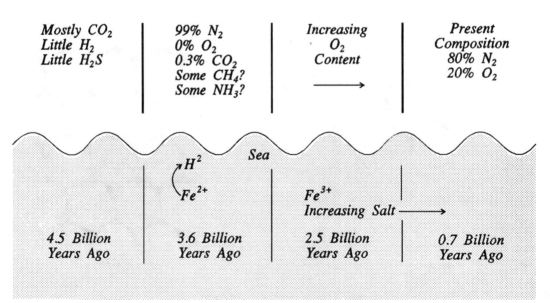

Fig. 10.3: The Evolution of the Biosphere. The compositions of both the atmosphere and the sea have changed considerably since the formation of the Earth 4.5 billion years ago.

The time corresponding to the beginning of life is known as the Archean age. At this time the sun's radiation was some 25% less than at present but the surface temperature of the earth was on the average some 13 °C higher. The composition of the atmosphere was considerably different from that found today. It contained no oxygen and there was some 200-1000 times more carbon dioxide. The major component was nitrogen, but some scientists speculate that methane and ammonia may also have been present. The higher temperature was due to the greenhouse effect, caused by the larger concentration of carbon dioxide. The lack of oxygen had a number of chemical consequences; for example, iron and other metals present at the earth's surface, would be largely in their lower oxidation states, Fe^{2+} in the case of iron.

Demonstration 10.1
Oxidation/reduction properties of iron compounds. Fe^{2+} can be oxidized to Fe^{3+} by an oxidising agent such as potassium permanganate ($KMnO_4$). This may be demonstrated by adding a ferrous sulfate ($FeSO_4$) solution to purple potassium permanganate and observing the loss of color. If caustic soda (NaOH) is added to ferrous sulfate solution a precipitate of ferrous hydroxide is formed which slowly changes color from white to reddish brown as it is oxidized by air to the ferric compound. The oxidation process can be speeded up by adding hydrogen peroxide, a more powerful oxidising agent than air. The reverse process of reducing Fe^{3+} to Fe^{2+} is also quite easy. If potassium iodide (KI) is added to a solution of ferric chloride the iodide is oxidized to iodine and the Fe^{3+} reduced to Fe^{2+}.

$$2Fe^{3+} + 2I^- \rightarrow 2Fe^{2+} + I_2$$

Addition of a little starch produces the characteristic blue color with iodine.

Ferrous compounds are much more soluble than ferric compounds and would have been largely concentrated in the sea. They slowly react with water, particularly in the presence of sunlight, to give ferric compounds and hydrogen.

$$Fe^{2+} + H_2O \rightarrow Fe^{3+} + 1/2H_2 + OH^-$$

■ *The time before oxygen...*

The hydrogen, having a very low density, would be slowly lost from the atmosphere into space. Some could also have been used to reduce carbon dioxide and nitrogen to methane and ammonia, providing a possible source of these gases in the Archean atmosphere.

$$CO_2 + 4H_2 \rightarrow CH_4 + 2H_2O$$
$$N_2 + 3H_2 \rightarrow 2NH_3$$

■ *Amino acids and nucleic acids could have been formed in the primordial biosphere...*

If the loss of hydrogen to outer space had persisted, there would be no oceans left at the present time. Once oxygen appeared, ferrous compounds were rapidly oxidized to the less soluble ferric compounds.

Another consequence of the lack of oxygen was the absence of an ozone layer; most of the ultraviolet radiation therefore reached the surface of the earth and was available for photochemical reactions of the type encountered in the discussions of atmospheric photochemistry. This was an important consideration in the synthesis of the organic compounds needed for life. Some of the simpler molecules may have been synthesized in space, as described above, and were present when the earth was formed. The specific amino acids and nucleic acids required were probably made during the formation of the biosphere. We now understand some of the chemistry involved in this process.

Experiments were first carried out in 1952 in which mixtures of water, ammonia, methane and hydrogen - all of which were thought to be present in the primitive atmosphere - were circulated past an electric discharge, simulating natural lightning. The formation of many organic compounds was demonstrated within the period of a week. Subsequent experiments have given similar results using ultraviolet lamps as a source of energy. Sixteen of the 20 amino acids found in living organisms, plus all five of the nitrogen bases needed for nucleic acids have been produced in this way. The raw materials needed for life can clearly be produced relatively easily, but a further large step is necessary to produce life itself. Discussion of this step will be deferred to the next section.

When life first appeared, it existed in an environment in which the molecules it needed to build and regenerate itself, primarily amino acids and nucleic acid constituents, were available for the taking. It is envisaged that in time this easy source of raw materials was depleted; life was then faced with the prospect of manufacturing its own essential molecules. For this purpose it needed to tap a new source of energy. It is thought that the first source of energy was light or heat which split hydrogen sulfide, which is present in volcanic emissions. (There are still bacteria in existence which use this process. They exist in particular in the deep ocean, adjacent to hot water supplies from volcanic vents, and give rise to ecosystems quite different from those on land or in the ocean shallows.) The splitting of hydrogen sulfide produces electrons, which can be used to reduce carbon dioxide to give glucose and other desirable products.

$$H_2S \rightarrow 2H^+ + S + 2e$$

Demonstration 10.2

The oxidation of hydrogen sulfide. Hydrogen sulfide is much more easily oxidized than water. If H_2S gas, characterized by its rotten egg smell, is bubbled through an aqueous solution of bromine, the red-brown color of the bromine is lost.

$$H_2S(g) + Br_2(aq) \rightarrow 2H^+(aq) + 2Br^-(aq) + S(s)$$

The sulfur formed is precipitated as a fine white powder. A similar reaction occurs with iodine.

$$H_2S(g) + I_2(aq) \rightarrow 2H^+(aq) + 2I^-(aq) + S(s)$$

It is not possible to oxidize water with bromine or iodine.

It will be recognized that this process is very similar to the splitting of water which occurs in the presently dominant version of photosynthesis. Hydrogen sulfide can be oxidized by even mild oxidizing agents, such as bromine or iodine, but the splitting of water is chemically more difficult. The thermal splitting of H_2S offers the possibility of storing only a small amount of energy; the photochemical splitting of water is more difficult, but has the potential to store much more energy. It also makes use of a much more common raw material. It is thought to have been a later development, since it requires the invention of chlorophyll, a very sophisticated catalyst.

$$2H_2O \rightarrow 4H^+ + O_2 + 4e$$

■ *Energy from the photochemical splitting of water...*

Recently, considerable effort has been made to discover an artificial catalyst for the photochemical splitting of water, since this would provide a favorable route for utilizing solar energy. Some success has been reported but a commercial process seems far away.

■ *Energy can be produced much more rapidly by respiration than by photosynthesis...*

When life turned to the photochemical splitting of water for its energy source there were very important consequences, resulting mostly from the byproduct oxygen. Oxygen production is thought to have commenced about 2.5 billion years ago, but the proportion of oxygen in the atmosphere did not reach its present level until about 600 million years ago. Initially, most of the oxygen was used to oxidize ions such as Fe^{2+}, which had the effect of stabilizing the oceans by preventing the reduction of water. The less soluble ferric iron was precipitated to give the ores which are our present source of iron. Only when this process was complete, did atmospheric accumulation of oxygen commence. Before this occurred, an early form of bacterial life lead to the anaerobic (without air) decomposition of organic material to give methane. This process is less efficient than respiration but requires less sophisticated chemistry. Such bacteria still persist, producing methane as marsh gas. Bacteria are still the predominant life form on earth in terms of total biomass, and are responsible for most of the chemistry carried out by Gaia. Oxygen, as well as reacting with inorganic substances such as iron, was also used in the photochemical oxidation of methane, regenerating carbon dioxide. Eventually though, enough oxygen was produced by photosynthesis to allow its accumulation in the atmosphere in sufficient quantities to support respiration in the form we know it at present. Respiration can provide energy much more rapidly than any of the earlier processes, and the stage was therefore set for the evolution of mobile forms of life, and eventually of mammals. At present the ratio of carbon dioxide to oxygen in the atmosphere is determined by the balance between respiratory processes removing oxygen and producing carbon dioxide, photosynthetic processes producing oxygen and removing carbon dioxide, and the "burial" of carbon. This carbon cycle was described in Chapter 1. Carbon is also buried in the forms of oil, coal, peat and less well characterized material known as kerigen. The first two are our present sources of fossil fuels. All these processes lead to a diminution in the amount of carbon dioxide in the atmosphere and a corresponding increase in oxygen content. These processes are included in the more complete carbon cycle illustrated in Figure 10.4, which also gives some data indicating the relative importance of the different processes.

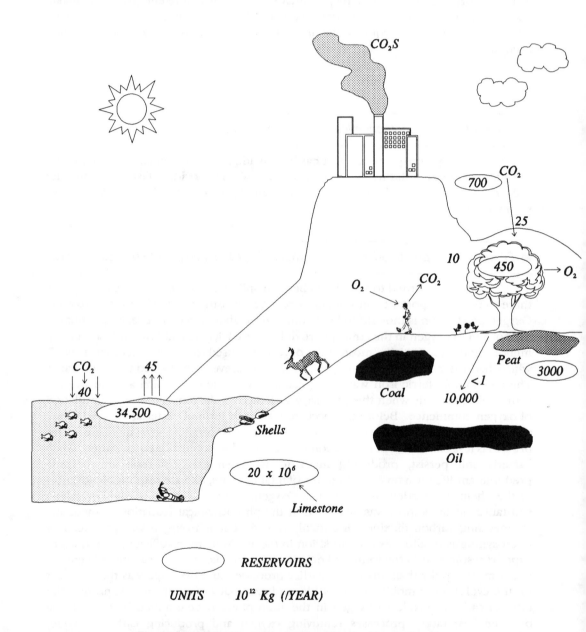

Fig. 10.4: A More Complete Carbon Cycle. Reservoirs of carbon are shown as circled numbers in units of 10^{12} kg. Uncircled numbers represent the flows of carbon between the different reservoirs in units of 10^{12} kg/year.

As a result of the diminution in the amount of carbon dioxide in the atmosphere and the consequent lessening of the greenhouse effect, the average temperature of the earth's surface has fallen from 28 °C in the Archean age to 15 °C today, in spite of the 25% increase in solar radiation which would be expected to lead to higher temperatures. The parallel increase in oxygen also resulted in the formation of the ozone layer, with its consequent modification of surface photochemistry.

What can we predict for the future? It was noted earlier that long-range weather forecasting, since it depends on many non-linear processes, is inherently inaccurate no matter how good our input data or how large our computer. The same is true to an even larger extent for the construction of models of the future biosphere. Since in the past it is fairly certain that more carbon dioxide in the atmosphere was associated with higher temperatures at the earth's surface, it seems a reasonable guess that if we allow the percentage of carbon dioxide to continue increasing, we will probably get warmer weather. Some recent data tending to support this prediction are shown in Figure 10.5.

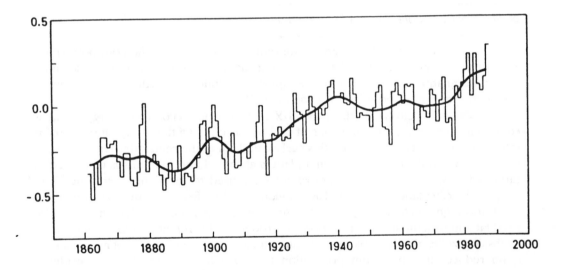

Fig. 10.5: Recent Temperature Trends. There has been a small but significant increase in the average temperature over the last 100 years.

■ *What will be the consequences for living things of current changes in the composition of the atmosphere?*

A rise in temperature is probable, but not certain. There are natural fluctuations in the earth's temperature which, in geologically recent times, have lead to ice ages at approximately 100,000 year intervals. Geologists have been able to trace these fluctuations by measuring the ratio of the isotopes ^{16}O and ^{18}O in sea-shells buried to different depths on the ocean floor. This ratio depends on the relative amount of water in the oceans and in the polar ice caps, which changes during an ice age. Combining this data with astronomical data has demonstrated that the origin of ice ages lies in small variations in the earth's orbit with time, which lead to different exposure of the poles and equatorial regions to solar radiation. These small changes can be amplified by changing ocean currents, for example. At present, we are just about at the mid-point between glaciations, so that normally we would expect a long-term cooling trend as the next ice age started to exert its influence. The uncertainty lies in predicting whether this effect will be greater or smaller than the increased greenhouse warming. As the data of Figure 10.5 shows, the changes during the twentieth century thus far are quite small, but the trend is towards increasing temperatures. The consequences of a rise in temperature in terms of higher sea levels and changing food production are also by no means completely predictable. Similarly, if we lose our ozone layer there will be photochemical consequences but nobody really knows quite what these consequences might be. The concern in this area has risen markedly in recent years, and ozone depletion is now thought to be a major threat to both human health and our food supply.

■ *How many people can the biosphere support?*

One thing seems fairly certain: we cannot continue expanding our population and energy use at the rate we have done over the last century. There is a maximum human population that the earth can support. The following outlines an estimate of the earth's maximum population made in 1967.

The sun delivers to the earth 4×10^{13} kcal per second of energy. This is equivalent to burning 6 million tons of coal per second. Of this energy input, 50% is reflected before it reaches the earth's surface and 3% of the remainder falls on plants or trees. ⅔ of the energy falling on a plant is absorbed and ⅔ of this is converted to carbohydrates. If all of this carbohydrate were used to meet the energy needs of people, the calculation says that 1000 billion could be fed. This number though, is much too high since carbohydrate by itself does not provide an adequate diet. We need fat and protein and the equation for producing this is that 100 lbs of grass gives 10 lbs of gazelle, gives 1 lb of tiger. Taking into account the necessity of having a food chain reduces the maximum population to 150 billion. Even this is considered unrealistic since it neglects other factors such as living space and waste disposal. There were of course many other similar considerations, and the final estimate was a maximum population of 15 billion. In 1967 the quoted population of the world was 3-4 billion. It is now over 5 billion and is projected to reach 8 billion by 2015. Clearly our room for expansion is limited, and if there is deterioration of the biosphere, room for expansion will become even more restricted.

The Chemical Evolution of Life

■ *How did life get started?*

As described above, there is no large problem in accounting for the availability of the molecular building blocks of life. The puzzle is to decide how these building blocks can be assembled to produce a living entity from inanimate material. Most scientists today believe that living things were formed from non-living things without divine intervention. If such intervention is necessary, it surely comes at the point where man is separated from the animals, which is an area certainly beyond the scope of chemistry. The production of a complex chemical system, such as a virus or simple bacterium, from its components is a legitimate chemical concern. The basic problem is that the chemistry of life forms a closed cycle. DNA makes RNA makes proteins, but we need the proteins, in the form of enzymes to make DNA. If we have a supply of enzymes we can make all kinds of DNA. If we have a supply of DNA we can produce protein. If we have neither it is difficult to know where to start. Fox, in his book *Energy and the Evolution of Life*, uses the metaphor of the Uroboros (the serpent which swallows its tail) to present the problem.

■ *How were the first amino acid polymers formed?*

In principle this chemical problem is soluble if there is a continuous supply of energy to drive the necessary reactions. How this happened is still a matter for speculation. One suggestion is that the very first step on the road towards life was a chemical reaction which linked the energy-requiring formation of a pyrophosphate (P-O-P) bond to energy available from the oxidation of iron or sulfur. The raw materials for both of these reactions were readily available. Once there is a supply of pyrophosphate, mechanisms for the polymerization of amino acids can be devised. Figure 10.6 shows how an amino acid can react with a pyrophosphate ion to give an activated monomer, which can in turn reacts with another amino acid to give a dimer.

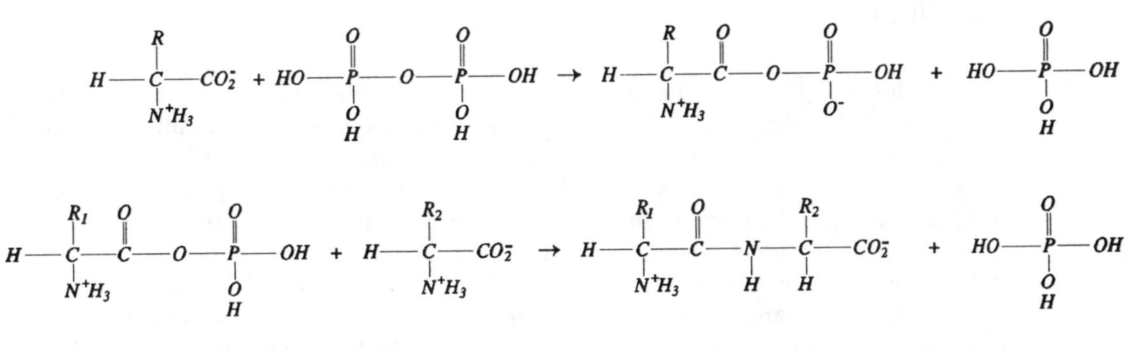

Fig. 10.6: A Possible Mechanism for the Initial Polymerization of Amino Acids.

■ *Was RNA the first biopolymer?*

Continuation of the same process leads to a polymer. This in itself does not suffice, since the amino acid polymers will still be destroyed by hydrolysis faster than they can be made. The various competing reactions are shown in the Figure. Only if the polypeptide can be formed very rapidly in an <u>enzyme-catalyzed</u> reaction is it possible to maintain a significant concentration of the polymers in a non-equilibrium situation. It is the Uroborus problem: if we have catalytic polymers there is a mechanism for making more. There have been at least two suggestions as to how the first polypeptides may have been formed. One is that they could have originated during the evaporation of amino acid solutions, which has been shown to give short-chain polypeptides, named proteinoids, which could then be sufficiently stable in aqueous solution to catalyze more polymerization using the energy from pyrophosphate hydrolysis. Another suggestion is that the regular arrangement of charged ions in clay type materials could have formed a template for making specific, catalytically active polypeptides. Which, if either, of these suggestions is correct remains to be proved. If a source of free energy —supposedly pyrophosphate molecules— is available it can be used in either of two ways. Order can be generated reducing entropy, or enthalpy can be stored for future use. Once we have polypeptides to provide enzymes, the construction of nucleic acids and all of the rest of biochemistry becomes possible. There is another school of thought which maintains that the initial biological polymers were nucleic acids (RNA rather than DNA is preferred) and a detailed system of catalytic reactions, called hypercycles, has been proposed to generate self-propagating nucleic acids. The introduction of proteins to catalyze the nucleic acid polymerization and replication was, according to this theory, a later development. The details are far from being completely understood. This is a very active area of research, and in principle the problem is soluble using only the principles of chemistry.

Conclusion

This brings us to the limit of our present knowledge in describing the evolution of our biosphere. We are on fairly firm ground in describing how the inorganic components of the biosphere came to their present form. All of the major substances present in the lithosphere, the hydrosphere and the atmosphere have been identified, and geochemists, chemical oceanographers and atmospheric chemists can write down very plausible chemical equations describing their formation. The origins of biochemistry are less well understood but there is no lack of theories and suggestions in this area. We started this book by introducing the speculative Gaia hypothesis. It seems appropriate to finish it in an Epilogue by revisiting the Gaia hypothesis.

Further Reading

Ronald F. Fox, *Energy and the Evolution of Life*, W. H. Freeman and Co (1988). Deals with the chemical problems of evolution.

Robert Shapiro, *Origins*, Bantam Books (1987). A discussion of the chemical origins of life.

Two papers dealing with the hypercycle model for molecular evolution. The second paper is quite brief and easy to follow:

i) M. Eigen, W. Gardiner, P. Schuster and R. Winkler-Oswatitich, *Scientific American*, 244, 88-118, April (1981).
ii) John Maynard Smith, *Nature*, 280, 445-446 (1979).

William F. Loomis, *Four Billion Years*, Sinauer Associates Inc (1988). The chemistry associated with evolutionary processes.

Epilogue

Gaia Revisited

Evolution and Thermodynamics

The basis of biological evolution is chemical evolution, as was first clearly enunciated by the physicist Schrodinger, of wave equation fame, in a short book entitled **What is Life?** published in 1944. Heredity is determined by genes and genes are constructed from nucleic acid molecules. Evolution is therefore reduced to chemical change, specifically to changes in the sequence of nucleic acids which constitute genes. Such changes are called mutations and their accidental occurrence and mixing by the mechanism of sexual reproduction forms the basis of the present orthodox interpretation of Darwin's theory of evolution by natural selection.

During evolution, very complex and highly ordered structures are formed from simple starting materials. At first sight this is contrary to the Second Law of thermodynamics, since the highly ordered structures must have low entropy and be formed from starting materials of higher entropy. The discussion in Chapter 8 showed that there is actually no conflict with thermodynamics, providing a constant source of energy is available to maintain the system far from equilibrium. Where the energy comes from in the first place, and whether the expanding universe is approaching or departing from thermodynamic equilibrium, is a matter for the cosmologists to debate. The whole idea of entropy may well be misleading in the context of systems far from equilibrium since there is no clear method for calculating the decrease in entropy which occurs during the construction of a biological organism. What is clear is that high quality energy is needed to drive a living system. The technical name for such high quality energy is "free energy", and the Second Law can be stated in the form that free energy always decreases. Chemical equilibrium corresponds to a minimum free energy as was stated earlier in Chapter 3. The free energy flux densities, i.e., the free energy passing through 1g of material in 1s, have been calculated for a number of situations. Some of this information is given in Table EP.1.

Table EP.1: Free Energy Flux Densities

Location	Flux Density (ergs s^{-1} g^{-1})
Galaxy as a whole	1
Sun	2
Top of Atmosphere	80
Plants	500
Animals	17,000
Human Brain	150,000

In units of ergs s^{-1} g^{-1} the flux is approximately 1 throughout the galaxy and 2 in the sun (1 erg is equivalent to 10^{-10} kJ). Although there is an enormous amount of energy generated in the sun, it is spread over an enormous mass of material. In the earth's atmosphere the sun's radiation provides a flux of 80. In plants the energy is more concentrated and we have a flux of 500. In animals this rises to 17,000 and in the human brain to 150,000. These numbers are calculated from the information that a brain, with average mass 1,300g, needs 40kcal (168kJ) of energy from food to carry out its functions. The other values have been obtained in a similar manner. The more complex the structure, the greater the free energy flux density needed to maintain it.

Given enough free energy flux anything is possible. This leaves the question, is it probable? There have been many calculations to try to assess the probability of life arising spontaneously from the products of the disintegration of a supernova. The orthodox view is that it is very improbable. Another form of this question is to ask: what are the chances of us meeting other life, if and when we travel to the distant stars? Scientists take this possibility seriously enough to have carried out searches of the radiation reaching the earth, looking for signs of intelligent communication. Calculations of the probabilities of life arising are at best little more than guesses, and the general conclusion is that although life is very improbable, the universe is very large and has been around for a long time, so that there is an acceptable probability that life will occur. There is still a suspicion though, that we don't know or don't completely understand all the rules of the game. It has been suggested, for example, that given a large free energy flux, the evolution of complex structures, rather than being unlikely because of their low entropy, is in actual fact inevitable. Increasing complexity may be a necessary consequence of large scale energy production in stars.

The Game of Life and the Anthropic Principle

One of our problems is that we really don't know how to handle the mathematics of situations of a complexity corresponding to the evolution of life, and the best that we can do is to simulate them on a computer using a model which we hope will be appropriate. A mathematician, John Conway, in 1970 devised a computer game called Life. The essence of the game of Life is that it starts with a simple pattern of dots on a computer screen and provides some equally simple rules which decide how the pattern changes from one generation to the next. These rules simply state that the probability of adding a dot or of removing a dot depends only on the number of neighboring positions which are populated. In a very few generations patterns of great complexity can evolve, and self-reproducing structures, representing life, become possible. In 1974 *Time* magazine complained that "millions of dollars in valuable computer time have been wasted by the game's growing horde of fanatics." Whether this computer game has any relevance to the real game of life is anybody's guess, but it certainly illustrates in a dramatic way how complex structures can arise spontaneously from simple postulates.

There is another approach to this question of probabilities. If a poker player is dealt five cards face down, and if he is a good player, he knows the probability of having been dealt a full house. When he picks up the cards and looks at them, the earlier assessment of probability is meaningless. Either he has full house or he doesn't, the probability is either 1 or 0. In our present existence we have looked at the cards, and found life. This knowledge must be incorporated in our model of the universe. The situation is similar, in some limited respects, to that encountered in quantum theory: before the observation we must talk in terms of probabilities, after the observation we have certainty. We are a participant in the game of life rather than merely an outside observer.

The recognition that the existence of life is a necessary component in any model of the universe we may construct is known as the Anthropic principle. This principle originated with the cosmologists and comes in two flavors, weak and strong. It arose from a consideration of a number of unlikely and improbable coincidences. Typical is the nucleosynthesis of carbon which depends on an "accidental" numerical coincidence of two energies. To the best of our knowledge there is absolutely no physical reason why these two energies should be almost the same, but if they were not there would be no carbon in the universe and no life as we know it. One coincidence could be shrugged off, but it turns out that there are a whole series of such unlikely facts. Some of these are chemical in nature. An example concerns the properties of water and the strengths of the hydrogen bonds it forms. This leads to the lower density of ice than water at its freezing point, which is essential for the existence of sea life, and to the details of the structure of enzymes. They are also crucial to reproduction by means of nucleic acids; the hydrogen bonds must be strong enough to hold together the double helix of DNA, but not so strong as to prevent replication. If the hydrogen bonds had been a little bit stronger or a little bit weaker, life as we know it would not exist. The weak Anthropic principle is content to put certain constraints on the possible values of fundamental constants and simply say that there is no point in considering physical models involving different constants, since we would not exist to observe them. The strong Anthropic principle can be phrased in several different ways which all say, in effect, that the universe is the way it is because we are here to observe it. The considerations for chemical and biological evolution are much the same. We can say that it is unlikely, but since we are here to investigate it, it must have happened; this corresponds to the weak Anthropic principle. Alternatively, if this is our philosophical inclination, we can believe that evolution and the existence of mankind is an inevitable consequence of the way the universe is constructed. This corresponds to an extreme form of the strong Anthropic viewpoint. Some people go beyond this, and say that the physical universe is a construct heavily dependent on the human mind, and must therefore require the existence of humanity.

Gaia - A Reprise

The question can be posed: how does the Gaia hypothesis fit into the broader issues of evolution and life raised in the last section? So long as we are content to discuss the chemistry of carbon cycles and the salt concentration of the sea, the Gaia hypothesis is not very controversial. In much the same spirit as in the case of the Anthropic principle, the Gaia hypothesis can be characterized as weak - life has some influence on the composition of the biosphere-; moderate - biota modify the environment; or strong - biota control the environment. At the weak level few scientists disagree with the idea. Geologists are generally not willing to go beyond the moderate version, placing most of the control mechanisms in the hands of slow geological processes with only a relatively minor assist from living things. The biologists' major concern is to make sure that the Gaia hypothesis does not in any way deny that natural selection is the driving force for evolution. W. Ford Doolittle, a well known biologist, has detailed some of the criticisms evoked by Lovelock's ideas in an article entitled "From Selfish DNA to Gaia." The first line of attack is that it is a teleological theory. The teleological viewpoint was originally associated with natural theology, and postulated that everything in the universe had been designed for a purpose and that change represents the unfolding of this purpose. In support of this argument, many examples demonstrating how different types of living species were specifically suited to the particular environment in which they existed, were quoted. The classic argument is that of Paley, who noted that anyone finding a watch would recognize that it was manufactured, rather than an accidental product of nature. Similarly, the intricacies of a living organism proved the existence of a creator. The theory of evolution altered this argument, saying instead that organisms, through the process of natural selection, had adapted to the environment in which they found themselves. It is the difference between the present form of an organism being determined by a push from the past —in the form of changes imposed by reactions to its environment— or being determined by a pull from the future in the form of some overall progress towards a preordained perfection. The biologists, having adopted the theory of evolution, have always used the adjective teleological in a distinctly derogatory manner. There is a certain teleological flavor to the Gaia hypothesis since there is a feeling that everything on earth has been organized for the purpose of producing life. However, evolution is a very flexible theory. If any living thing exists today, it must have been better adapted to its environment than the competition, and is therefore the result natural selection. Lovelock has specifically disavowed any teleological intent to the Gaia hypothesis.

A second area of controversy concerns the conflicting claims of reductionism and holism, introduced in the prologue. The traditional scientific viewpoint is reductionist. Every observation is to be "explained" in terms of more fundamental ideas. Genetics and biology have a biochemical explanation. Biochemistry is derived from chemistry and chemistry from physics. There is a vague feeling that the buck stops at physics, somewhere in the region of quarks. At present the biologists are the biggest supporters of reductionism, perhaps because they are furthest from the final resting place of the buck. Holism adopts the view that the whole may be greater than the parts, and that there are some things that cannot be explained in terms of simpler entities. It is argued, for example, that increasing complexity in a system leads to "emergent" properties which could not have been predicted from the simpler components. Life itself is an emergent property which could not have been predicted from a perfect knowledge of chemistry. The reductionist would take the view that this limitation arises because we don't fully understand the simple components.

The Gaia hypothesis is definitely holistic in outlook. It certainly implies that we can only understand our biosphere by looking at it as a whole. The various components mesh together to produce something Lovelock called Gaia, with a strong implication that Gaia is more than the sum of the components of the biosphere. The reductionist view, as propounded by W. Ford Doolittle, is critical of this attitude. The level at which natural selection operates has been pushed downward from the species, to the individual animal, to the gene and even to DNA. The book *The Selfish Gene* by Richard Dawkins expounds this viewpoint. In his view the course of evolution is determined by natural selection, and a change will not occur unless it benefits a specific individual or leads to the better survival of a particular gene. From this viewpoint, to talk about processes and changes which benefit the whole biosphere rather than individual organisms, is contrary to orthodox evolutionary theory. A recent book entitled ***Biospheres*** by Dorian Sagan takes the Gaian idea to the extreme of suggesting that the biosphere may be a replicating entity and human beings the agents to bring about this replication. In his book ***Godel, Escher, Bach***, Douglas Hofstadter suggests that neither reductionism nor holism possess the complete truth, but that a merger of the two approaches is necessary; this seems to be a sensible approach.

There is another way of looking at the relationship of Gaia to evolutionary theory. Natural selection, as proposed by Darwin, is based on the belief that acquired characteristics are not inherited; the contrary view, the Lamarckian heresy, has been put forward and the demolished a number of times over the last century and a half. The most recent occasion was during the reign of Lysenko as the czar of Russian biology in the time of Stalin. According to orthodox evolutionary theory, changes only occur by accidental mutations which, if they enable the organism to survive more easily in the environment in which it finds itself, will lead to the more favored reproduction of the mutated organism. At the molecular level this principle corresponds to the Central Dogma of Crick; nucleic acids control the formation of proteins, which in turn control the functions of the organism, but proteins cannot feedback information to the nucleic acids. Changes in DNA, the final depositary of inheritable characteristics, can only be brought about by accidental mutations. It would seem, though, that there is still a possibility of feedback if living organisms affect the environment in which they find themselves. Individually, their influence on the overall environment is negligible but, taken as a whole, they can determine the contents of the biosphere, which constitutes their environment and determines their chance of survival. This is the essence of the Gaian hypothesis and Lovelock has pointed out its evolutionary consequence. Establishment of a feedback mechanism for evolution would certainly help to account for the steady upward trend towards more complex species, characteristic of evolution over the last billion or so years. Michael Crawford and David Marsh, in a book entitled ***The Driving Force*** have put forward the thesis that "substrate driven change", in the form of changes in the nutrients available to an organism, complements natural selection in determining evolutionary trends. An obvious major turning point was the availability of oxygen, produced by photosynthetic bacteria as described above, which resulted in life leaving the sea and colonizing the land and the air. The availability of oxygen, and hence the utilization of the more efficient respiratory chemistry, is much greater on land than in the sea since the solubility of oxygen in water is quite limited. Fresh water can dissolve more oxygen than salt water, particularly in well-oxygenated rapids, hence the development of the spawning habits of salmon. On land there tends to be a shortage of calcium and an excess of phosphorus, leading to light bones and the development of birds. Unsaturated fatty acids (essential for the development of the nervous system) became available from plant sources of food and this was a necessary condition for the evolution of mammals. It is suggested that the availability of a new nutrient can suppress the expression of a gene required for the synthesis of that substance, and make available the DNA for mutation to a new gene. The analogy is with computer disks; errors in replication limit the maximum amount of DNA, and the more efficiently the memory storage can be used, the more complex the programme available to the organism. The emphasis is on the availability of nutrients, obtained primarily as a product or byproduct of the metabolism of other organisms, but this is clearly a further example of Gaian control of the biosphere.

All of this is speculative and goes to show that science in general, and chemistry in particular, is living and growing rather than complete and static. Chemistry is incomplete in its solutions to the relatively small problems. How does a specific enzyme work? It is lacking in solutions to larger problems. How does a living Uroborus get started? Science, in partnership with other disciplines, can also contribute to the really big problems? What is the real meaning of time and is the development of the universe determined by a strong Anthropic principle? The answers aren't known, and may never be, but the challenge is there, is being accepted, and should engage the interest of all well-educated people. This is the message that a science course should deliver to liberal arts students.

Further Reading

John M. Robson, editor, ***Origin and Evolution of the Universe - Evidence for Design***, McGill-Queens University Press (1987). Discusses present-day attitudes to teleology and contains the article "From Selfish DNA to Gaia" by W. Ford Doolittle.

Lousie B. Young, ***The Unfinished Universe***, Simon and Schuster (1986). Discusses thermodynamics and evolution and related topics.

Eric Chaisson, ***The Life Era***, Atlantic Monthly Press (1987). Evolution, both physical and biological.

Richard Dawkins, ***The Blind Watchmaker***, W. W. Norton and Co. (1986). The reductionist view of evolution.

P. C. W. Davies, ***The Accidental Universe***, Cambridge University Press (1982). The Anthropic principle, particularly from the point of view of astrophysics.

William Poundstone, ***The Recursive Universe***, William Morrow and Co. (1985). Computer simulation of complex systems, particularly the game of Life.

John D. Barrow and Frank J. Tippler, ***The Anthropic Cosmological Principle***, Oxford University Press (1988). An exhaustive discussion of the Anthropic effect.

Daniel R. Brooks and E. O. Wiley, ***Evolution as Entropy***, University of Chicago Press (1986). A very technical discussion of thermodynamics and biology.

Tony Rothman, ***Science a la Mode***, Princeton University Press (1989). A collection of essays including one criticizing Evolution as Entropy.

Two popular books representing the orthodox view of evolution:

Francis Crick, ***Life Itself, Its Origin and Nature***, Simon and Schuster (1981).
Richard Dawkins, ***The Selfish Gene***, Paladin Books (1978).

George A. Seielstad, *At the Heart of the Web*, Harcourt Brace Jovanovich, (1989). An astronomer argues for "The Inevitable Genesis of Life".

Pierre Teilhard de Chardin, *The Vision of the Past*, Collins (1966). A Jesuit paleontologist presents a heterodox religious view of evolution.

Lawrence E. Joseph, *Gaia - The Growth of an Idea*, St. Martin's Press (1990). Discusses some of the controversial issues relating to the Gaia hypothesis.

Erwin Schrodinger, *What is Life?*, Cambridge Univ Press (1944). An influential essay by a distinguished physicist which makes specific proposals concerning the chemistry by which life got started.

David Layzer, *Cosmogenesis*, Oxford Univ Press (1990). "The growth of order in the universe." Cosmology, evolution and the mind.

Erich Jantsch, *The Self-Organizing Universe*, Pergamon Press (1980). A general discussion of self-organization and evolution.

Michael Crawford and David Marsh, *The Driving Force*, William Heinemann, (1989). Develops the thesis that evolutionary changes have been determined by the availability of different nutrients.

Dorian Sagan, *Biospheres*, McGraw-Hill (1990). Development of the Gaia theme.

GLOSSARY

Amino acid	A substance containing both a carboxyl group (acid COOH) and an amino group (NH_2).
ATP	Adenosine Tri Phosphate. The direct source of the energy needed to drive biochemical reactions.
Autocatalysis	A situation which arises if one of the products of a reaction is a catalyst for the reaction. It leads to positive feedback.
Carbohydrates	Sugars, starch, cellulose.
Catalyst	A substance which speeds up a chemical reaction by providing a different mechanism.
Chemical	The final resting state of a chemical system.
Chemical Kinetics	The study of the rates of chemical reactions.
DNA	Deoxyribo Nucleic Acid. The chemical substance which provides the mechanism for heredity.
Endothermic	A chemical reaction which occurs with the absorption of heat.
Enthalpy,H	The chemical energy associated with a substance. If two substances react with a decrease in enthalpy, this decrease in chemical energy appears as heat.
Entropy, S	A measure of the quality of energy - the ease with which the energy can be converted to useful work. Low entropy = high quality.
Enzyme	A protein with catalytic properties.
Equilibrium	It corresponds to the minimum free energy of the system.
Exothermic	A chemical reaction which occurs with the evolution of heat.
Free Energy	The combination of enthalpy and entropy which determines the position of equilibrium.
Heat Energy	Energy associated with the random motion of molecules in a solid, a liquid or a gas.

Inhibitor	A substance which prevents a reaction from occurring by interfering with its mechanism.
Kinetic Energy	Energy associated with motion.
Lipids	Fats.
Negative Feedback	A situation in which the product of a process decreases the rate of the process. Example: thermostatic control.
Oscillating	A chemical reaction which leads to rhythmic variations in the concentrations of some of the reaction components.
Photosynthesis	The use of sunlight by plants to synthesize carbohydrates.
Positive Feedback	A situation in which the product of a process increases the rate of the process. Example: the reproduction of rabbits.
Protein	A biopolymer made by joining together many amino acids.
Reaction Mechanism	A description of the individual chemical steps by which a reaction takes place.
Respiration	The reaction of carbohydrates with oxygen to provide energy.
RNA	Ribo Nucleic Acid. The chemical substance responsible for the correct synthesis of proteins.
Steady State	A state of a chemical system which is not at equilibrium, but which is maintained without changes in the concentrations of the reactants. To maintain such a state energy must be continuously provided. If it is not, the system reverts to its equilibrium concentrations.
Temperature	A measure of the heat energy in a body. The higher the temperature, the faster the molecules are moving.
Thermal Equilibrium	The result of the free exchange of heat between parts of a system. At thermal equilibrium the temperatures of all parts of the system are equal.
Vitamins	Essential minor components of our diet.